Thunder in the Argonne

BATTLES AND CAMPAIGNS

The Battles and Campaigns series examines the military and strategic results of particular combat techniques, strategies, and methods used by soldiers, sailors, and airmen throughout history. Focusing on different nations and branches of the armed services, this series aims to educate readers by detailed analysis of military engagements.

SERIES EDITOR: Joseph Craig

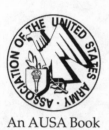

An AUSA Book

THUNDER IN THE
ARGONNE

A NEW HISTORY OF
AMERICA'S GREATEST BATTLE

DOUGLAS V. MASTRIANO

UNIVERSITY PRESS OF KENTUCKY

Scholarly publisher for the Commonwealth,
serving Bellarmine University, Berea College, Centre College of
Kentucky, Eastern Kentucky University, The Filson Historical Society,
Georgetown College, Kentucky Historical Society, Kentucky State
University, Morehead State University, Murray State University,
Northern Kentucky University, Transylvania University, University of
Kentucky, University of Louisville, and Western Kentucky University.
All rights reserved.

Editorial and Sales Offices: The University Press of Kentucky
663 South Limestone Street, Lexington, Kentucky 40508–4008
www.kentuckypress.com

Library of Congress Cataloging-in-Publication Data

Names: Mastriano, Douglas V., author.
Title: Thunder in the Argonne : a new history of America's greatest
battle /
  Douglas V. Mastriano.
Description: Lexington : University Press of Kentucky, 2018. | Series:
  Battles and campaigns | Includes bibliographical references and
index.
Identifiers: LCCN 2018000771| ISBN 9780813175553 (hardcover : alk.
paper) | ISBN 9780813175577 (pdf) | ISBN 9780813175584 (epub)
Subjects: LCSH: Argonne, Battle of the, France, 1918. | World War,
  1914-1918--Campaigns--Meuse River Valley. | World War,
1914-1918--United States.
Classification: LCC D545.A63 M37 2018 | DDC 940.4/36—dc23
LC record available at https://lccn.loc.gov/2018000771

This book is printed on acid-free paper meeting
the requirements of the American National Standard
for Permanence in Paper for Printed Library Materials.

Manufactured in the United States of America.

Member of the Association of University Presses

To my wife, Rebecca, and son, Josiah,
for making this book possible,
and
Corporal Ellis James Stewart
80th Division, September 1917–November 1918
42nd Division, November 1918–May 1919

What you do in life matters . . .
It echoes across the generations . . .
. . . and into eternity

Contents

Preface

It took one hundred years to finally have a national monument dedicated to the brave soldiers, Marines, and sailors who fought in World War One. The attempts to gain momentum for this much overdue tribute to the heroes of this bloody and costly confrontation were continually delayed by bureaucratic inertia, competing political agendas, and lack of interest.

The plight of the national monument in Washington, D.C., reflects the national memory of the war. It is generally relegated to the dustbin of history. Yet, this national amnesia misses the fact that World War One thrust the United States onto the world scene as a dominant economic, political, and military power. To compound matters, many of the trouble spots where the nation currently finds itself entangled are directly linked to World War One. This includes the Baltic nations of Estonia, Latvia, and Lithuania, Ukraine, Iraq, Syria, Jordan, and Israel, to name a few. How can adequate resolutions be made in these areas of the world with a lack of understanding of their linkages to the First World War?

And then there is the Meuse-Argonne campaign, which is the largest ever American offensive. Encompassing 1.2 million Americans and 600,000 French, the Meuse-Argonne forged the modern American army and, through the fire of combat, brought forth the military leaders of the Second World War. These rising leaders included Marshall, Patton, MacArthur, and scores of others. They brought with them their experiences of 1917 and 1918, defeated the Nazis, and made the world a better place.

The Meuse-Argonne campaign was America's first truly modern war. The men of 1918 participated in armored warfare, aerial bombing, massed artillery fires, chemical warfare, and joint military operations with the fledgling Air Service, and fought in multinational operations with the French Army. Indeed, the Meuse-Argonne left an enduring legacy on both the nation and its army. *Thunder in the Argonne* tells the untold story of what happened in the Meuse-Argonne and how it forever changed our world. And with this knowledge, the nation can shape a better and more informed future.

The legacy of the Meuse-Argonne Offensive echoes across the generations to us today.

Thunder in the Argonne endeavors to tell the complete story of the Meuse-Argonne. Doing so requires describing both the Allied and German perspectives. This means that often on the same page German, French, and American units are discussed. To ameliorate confusing the reader, national origin of the units is provided, such as the U.S. 77th Division. Although this is not the division's proper title, it is necessary to ensure clarity. Additionally, the kingdom of most German units is included in their respective titles. Imperial Germany during the First World War included the kingdoms of Saxony, Bavaria, Prussia, and Württemberg. When relevant, the kingdom of origin is included. For instance, the reader will encounter the 1st Prussian Guards Division, 2nd Württemberg Division, etc.

The United States of America was not a formal "ally" of the French or British. As such, America was officially an "associated power." This status had more to do with political mistrust of the Allies' political end state of the war than practical application in the disposition of American military power on the Western Front and elsewhere. However, for all intents and purposes, it behaved as a member of the Alliance, and as such, any discussion of Allies includes the United States without deference to its unique political status.

1

The War That Changed the World

It is a good thing for all Americans, and it is an especially
good thing for all young Americans, to remember the men
who have given their lives in war and peace to the service
of their fellow countrymen, and to keep in mind the feats of
daring and personal prowess done in time past by some of the
many champions of the nation. . . .
                                        —President Theodore Roosevelt

This book tells the complete story of the Meuse-Argonne campaign,
the largest ever American offensive. Not only does it provide the
American and German side of the story (a first), but it also describes
the attack in the strategic context of the Western Front. In addition
to this, the stories of sacrifice by the men in the line are perhaps
the most important facet of the Meuse-Argonne. Their actions in
the face of overwhelming and impossible odds still echo across the
generations. Finally, this book has a message for the readers today
on how decisions made one hundred years ago shaped our world
and how the challenges that we face are not unlike those of the First
World War generation.

The First World War was a clash of empires and incredible innovations. Four dynasties, whose power was once supreme, collapsed
in this war. This included the Romanov (Russian), the Hohenzollern
(Prussian), the Habsburg (Austro-Hungarian), and the Ottoman
(Turkish). Fanatical Bolshevik mobs, led by disciples of a strange
blend of atheistic Darwinian theology and class envy, wrestled
to seize power from old monarchies. Entire societies were trans-
formed, and new nations were created (Yugoslavia and Czechoslovakia), given independence (Estonia, Finland, and Latvia), or
reborn (Lithuania and Poland). With the collapse of the Ottoman

Empire, the map of the Middle East was redrawn by the British and French, who had already planned to partition it in accordance with the secret Sykes-Picot Agreement. The existence of Syria, Jordan, and Iraq goes back but a century, and the troubles there today are rooted in World War One.

Beyond these cataclysmic transformations, the character of war was forever changed. The First World War brought with it not just conflict on the land and sea, but also in the air. The first air campaigns were launched by Germany during this fierce struggle, destroying sections of London and other major European cities. The tank became a dominant innovation, in addition to the introduction of chemical warfare, small unit tactics, flamethrowers, and a plethora of modernizations that still exist today.

Yet, despite leaving an enduring influence on modern society, few understand the Great War, and fewer still know about the battles that brought it to an end. One of the most important players in ending the war was the U.S. Army, which would conduct its largest ever attack late in 1918. Incredible feats of heroism would come forth across blood-stained French fields and forests in bringing the war to a conclusion.

Called the "Meuse-Argonne Offensive," the Franco-American attack began on 26 September 1918 and continued until the armistice of 11 November. The Supreme Allied Commander, France's Marshal Ferdinand Foch, assigned the United States the most difficult sector to attack, where the Americans would face thickly defended German lines and terrain deemed impossible to fight through. Foch's decision to place the fledgling American army here was justified as the United States had the freshest army in Europe. After four years of war, most of the European nations, especially France, the United Kingdom, and Italy, were worn or on the brink of collapse. Marshal Foch's plan was to unleash his eager Americans on the most important part of the German defenses, toward the Sedan rail network. Should the Americans capture this vital rail hub, the preponderance of the German forces deployed along the Western Front would be vulnerable to being cut off or, worse yet, captured. This would pose a major concern for the entire German Imperial Army in 1918 and compel it to deploy some of its best units to blunt the American offensive. This concept of operations was agreed upon by the American commander, General John J. Pershing, who believed that the American army would succeed.

To assist the Americans in accomplishing this mission, Marshal Foch assigned French officers and soldiers to Pershing's command, bringing much needed experience to this otherwise inexperienced force. Additionally, scores of French infantry divisions would serve in the Meuse-Argonne sector to facilitate American success against a determined German foe and impossible terrain. The Fourth French Army, operating west of the Argonne Forest, was given the mission to protect the American flank and to complement Pershing's advance. Finally, since President Wilson's America was not prepared for war, the French provided the United States with aircraft, artillery, tanks, and a vast amount of other equipment. Often the aircraft and artillery were manned by experienced French crews, making the Meuse-Argonne truly a Franco-American operation.

Yet, in the context of the Western Front, the Meuse-Argonne campaign was one of four major pushes that Marshal Foch organized to knock the Germans out of the war in 1918 via an en echelon attack. Perhaps, ironically, the inspiration of this approach was the daring tactics of the Prussian king, Frederick the Great, or of Napoleon Bonaparte. The objective of an en echelon is to launch a series of attacks across a front to not only fix enemy units, but also to draw away reserves, so that by the time that the later attacks occur, the enemy has little to no reserves remaining to defend the newly threatened sectors. A successful en echelon attack forces the enemy to neglect or weaken portions of his front, creating a vulnerability that the attacker can exploit. With this aim, Foch ordered Pershing's American Expeditionary Forces (AEF) to start the offensive on 26 September 1918.

The Franco-American attack would be followed by the First and Third British Armies' offensive near Canal du Nord on 27 September, followed on 28 September by the Belgian Army north of Ypres. The fourth attack would kick off on 29 September with a combined Franco-British attack near St. Quentin. These four Allied hammer blows were to be sustained attacks, designed to maintain so much pressure on the German lines that they fixed enemy units in their sectors and enabled breakthroughs or success elsewhere.[1] The Meuse-Argonne campaign, combined with the effects of the French, British, and Belgian attacks, succeeded in ending the war a year earlier than most had believed possible.

The fighting for the Americans and French in the Meuse-Argonne was particularly fierce. As Foch predicted, the Germans

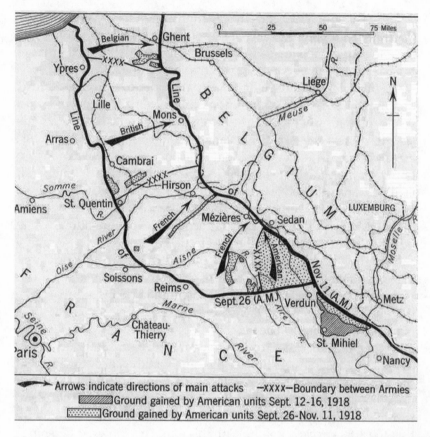

Map 1.1. American and Allied Attacks on the Western Front, 26 September–11 November 1918. (American Battle Monuments Commission)

rushed the preponderance of their strategic reserves to the area, making it difficult for the AEF to advance. Pershing responded by pouring over 1.2 million men into this area of the front (not including French forces), making the Meuse-Argonne Offensive the largest ever American operation in history. The severe terrain, combined with adept German defense, made the fighting in the Meuse-Argonne region intense. This was compounded by the lack of training of many American Doughboys going into the line, resulting in the Meuse-Argonne being one of the bloodiest episodes in America's history. Indeed, the Germans defended every ridge and every hill, making the Americans pay dearly in lives for each foot of ground liberated. As the fighting dragged on, the Germans grew concerned about the repeated audacious American attacks and were forced to pull twenty-one of their divisions from the French and British sectors to obstruct the American steamroller. By the time the war ended, the United States employed some twenty-two divisions in the line, the equivalent to fifty-five French or British divisions.[2] To blunt this, Germany committed forty-seven of its divisions and the last of its reserves to the Meuse-Argonne area.[3] Although the breakthrough at Sedan did not occur until the twilight of the armistice, incredible pressure was placed on the Germans. This forced them to use their strategic reserve divisions to blunt the ferocity of the American attack. Doing so created gaps in the German lines farther north, enabling French and British units to break through. In the end, the German Imperial Army could not stop the Americans, who gradually were able to push the Germans back. General Pershing believed that this was in large part because the Americans were by nature better fighters in addition to being untainted by the malaise of trench warfare, but this is far too simplistic a view.

In the end, Foch's grand strategy worked. The sustained pressure of these four massive attacks across a large portion of the Western Front was too much for the German Army to bear, especially as the numeric superiority that it enjoyed in March 1918 no longer existed. Thanks to the arrival of the Americans, the Allies now had a 37 percent advantage in men over the Germans, giving them the strategic ability and flexibility to launch this new broad front offensive.[4]

Despite the Americans' lack of experience in modern warfare, they made a significant contribution to ending the war. Although facing 25 percent of Germany's entire strength on the Western Front, the AEF broke the German lines on 1 November, penetrated the *Kriemhilde Stellung* (Hindenburg Line), and played a key role in forcing the Germans to sue for peace. Despite being America's biggest ever military campaign, few have heard about the Meuse-Argonne Offensive. Overshadowed by the Second World War, much of the heroism, sacrifice, and horror of the Meuse campaign have been forgotten. Yet, the amazing feats of Sergeant Alvin York, Major Charles Whittlesey of the Lost Battalion, and Lieutenant Sam Woodfill, accomplished in the midst of this maelstrom, echo across the ages. There is something about these acts of heroism that transcends the changing face of war and should inform the citizens of today. Woodfill, York, Whittlesey, and so many other heroes of the

Argonne remind us that despite the passing of time, how people respond in moments of testing and in days of trial do matter and can shape future generations. This makes the restoration of the memory of the Meuse-Argonne campaign during the centennial commemoration of particular consequence and importance.

As to the importance of the Americans in the Great War, during and shortly after the conclusion of the conflict, the Allies were unanimous in the opinion that the entry of the United States and its Meuse-Argonne Offensive made victory in 1918 possible. However, some ten years after the guns fell silent, detractors rose who questioned the importance of the Americans in the Great War militarily, and more specifically, the contribution that the Meuse-Argonne Offensive played in ending the war. Even today, prominent Great War historians differ in their views, with much of the discussion entangled with awkward comparisons of the American Meuse-Argonne Offensive to other campaigns. It remains hotly charged even today with strong feelings that often cloud the issue, preventing a thorough discourse on the veracity of the evidence being presented. Adding to the challenge is that many of the flawed arguments perpetuated in the late 1920s and early 1930s are still being touted as fact today.

To complicate matters, when applying critical thinking to ascertain the importance of the Meuse-Argonne Offensive and its strategic impact in ending the war, one continually is drawn to the larger question beyond this: just how important was the United States in ending the Great War in 1918? The reason why this must be addressed is that it is the question that is continually raised among British writers. Because of this, it is difficult to proceed in a discussion of the Meuse-Argonne within the spectrum of Foch's grand strategy without also attending to aspects of America's economic, financial, and even psychological contributions to the Allies when it entered the war on their side. Although well beyond the spectrum of the Meuse-Argonne Offensive per se, it is important to discuss this matter and provide a more holistic understanding of the Meuse-Argonne.

Although entering the fray late, there is little disagreement that the timing of the American entry saved the Allies from collapse. With the French Army largely stymied from the 1917 mutinies of the failed Chemin des Dames Offensive, the Russians and Romanians quitting the war, and the arrival of an additional 1 million German soldiers from the east, things did not bode well on the Western Front during the first seven months of 1918. Even then, the war still could have been lost.

As the United States belatedly mobilized, the Germans launched a series of massive attacks against the Western Front in an attempt to end the war before sufficient Americans arrived to tip the scales in the Allies' favor. By 1 May 1918, there were just 429,659 Americans in France. At this pace, the Germans might be able to win the race against time.[5]

This sluggish American entry into the war was due to President Wilson's naive approach to the European crisis. Even with war between Germany and the United States obvious in 1915 and 1916, President Wilson did nothing to prepare the nation for it and even used "He kept us out of the war" as a campaign slogan in his contested 1916 bid for reelection. Although more ships were being sunk, killing hundreds of American citizens, Wilson clung to his peace position regarding the Great War. The presidential election was among the closest in America's history, but Woodrow Wilson won as the peace president. In doing this, he tied his nation's hands and gave the Germans one more opportunity to strike a fatal blow in the form of the spring 1918 offensives.

Not surprisingly, when war was finally declared against Germany in April 1917, the United States was woefully ill-prepared.[6] Despite this lack of preparedness, many in the German High Command understood that the American Expeditionary Forces would ultimately give the Allies a quantitative advantage in soldiers and thereby end any chance of a German victory.[7] Regarding this, German general Erich Ludendorff said, "With the American entry into the war, the relative strengths would be more in [German] favor in the spring than in late summer . . . unless we had by then gained a great victory. . . . Only a far reaching military success which would make it appear to the Entente powers that, even with the help of America, the continuation of the war offered no further prospects of success, would provide the possibility of rendering our embittered opponents really ready to make peace. This was the political aim of the Supreme Command in 1918."[8] With that mind-set, Ludendorff launched his massive attacks against the Western Front to knock the Allies out early in 1918, before America arrived with enough troops to make an impact on the outcome of the war.

In the midst of the 1918 crisis, the French and British worked out an ambitious shipping plan to move the Americans to Europe faster than thought possible.[9] In the end, the German spring-summer offensives of 1918 failed, with the Americans playing an important part in pushing them back in June and July at the Marne and Belleau Woods.[10] Thanks to the Allies' help, the AEF would be ready for independent operations by September, much earlier than any had anticipated.

However, 1918 was a tumultuous year for the Allies. For the first seven months it seemed as if the Germans would win. Ludendorff's powerful attacks created panic in Paris and came close to dealing the decisive blow he needed to give Germany the chance to sue for peace from a position of strength. As the last of Ludendorff's attacks faded in July, the tables were turned on the Germans. Foch believed that now the Allies had the opportunity to win the war. By September 1918 the stage was set for the decisive campaign of the war, which, if successful, would end it one year earlier than anyone had planned or even hoped. With the conditions present for a decisive blow, Foch developed his grand plan to engulf the Germans across a vast section of the Western Front. The Allied attacks would stretch from the English Channel to Verdun and overwhelm the German Army.

The Americans would kick off this broad offensive and attack through the Meuse-Argonne region, fighting against some of Germany's best divisions and striking at the very heart of their vital Western Front command and control: the Sedan-Mezieres rail network. According to Hunter Liggett, the commander of the American First Army, without this rail network the German Army in France and Belgium would literally wither on the vine.[11] Mark Ethan Grotelueschen, in his book *The AEF Way of War* (2007), notes that the challenge that this attack encompassed was multiplied by its being fought across the worst terrain along the active Western Front, and that the German defensive belts here were closer than anywhere else in France.[12] Attacks of some sort continued there throughout most of the war, although it was one of the areas along the Western Front that most highly favored the defense. The distances between no-man's-land and the third line of German defenses across the Western Front varied in late 1918. For the British and French forces farther north, distances from the front line of troops to the third belt of German defenses ranged from thirty to sixty kilometers in depth.

In the Argonne, however, the depth was the thinnest, being barely eighteen kilometers.

With this shallow sector, the Germans had little space to give up in the defense, and thus were compelled to defend every line tenaciously.[13] The British Expeditionary Forces (BEF) commander, Field Marshal Sir Douglas Haig, saw this and wrote to Foch, "I therefore do not propose to attack until the American-French attack has gone in [the Meuse-Argonne region]. This latter attack might draw off some of the enemy's reserves from our front. I therefore would like to attack two or three days after the main American-French attack. If we could arrange this; there was a chance of the enemy's reserves being unavailable."[14] The Meuse-Argonne Offensive forced the Germans to commit most of the reserves to guard their vulnerable flank, giving Haig the opportunity that he foresaw.

The Germans used the terrain to their advantage and here the inexperienced American army paid a high price for victory. But in the end they could not stop the Americans, who gradually were able to push the Germans back. General Pershing believed that this was because the Americans were fresh and untainted by the malaise of trench warfare. As the fighting droned on, the Germans pulled twenty-one of their divisions from the French and British sectors to blunt the American attack.

The Meuse-Argonne Offensive lasted forty-seven days, with the Americans fighting a quarter of the German Army. It is estimated that the Germans suffered 100,000 casualties in the Meuse-Argonne region and lost another 26,000 soldiers as prisoners. In addition, they lost 847 pieces of artillery and roughly 3,000 machine guns. More than 1.2 million Americans served and fought there, making it America's largest and bloodiest military operation in the twentieth century.[15]

2

The German Attack of 1914 to the Crisis of 1918

Only on account of the timely assistance rendered by Americans to the Entente nations [Allies] were the latter not only saved from utter defeat, but also enabled eventually to gain military ascendance.

—General Erich Ludendorff

The Austro-Hungarian Archduke Ferdinand and his wife, Sophie, decided to spend the week leading up to their fourteenth wedding anniversary in Bosnia. During an official visit to Sarajevo on 28 June 1914 (just two days before their anniversary), a radical Serbian nationalist named Gavrilo Princip assassinated the couple, sending chills across Europe. Within days evidence was uncovered that pinned the assassination on Serbian-sponsored terrorists. After delivering an ultimatum that the Serbs could never accept, Austria declared war on the fledgling republic. But this would not be another local Balkan war. Other nations, acting within a complex web of alliances, would turn this tragedy into the First World War. The fateful shots fired in Sarajevo would unleash a war that the world never dreamed possible, and forever change the course of human events and redefine nations across the globe. Before marching against Serbia, Austrian emperor Franz Joseph appealed to the German emperor, Wilhelm, to ensure that Germany would stand with him. Franz Joseph had good reason to do this, as he shared a large border with Imperial Russia. Russia had aligned itself with the Serbs, and any Austrian action would trigger a reaction from Czar Nicholas of Russia. Kaiser Wilhelm gave Franz Joseph a blank check: Germany would stand with Austria in any action it took.[1]

Meanwhile, Russia responded to the crisis by ordering a general mobilization of its military. The archaic Russian system lacked sophistication, and it was an all or nothing proposition, meaning that its army mobilized not just along the Austrian border, but also the German border. An ally of Serbia, Russia would not stand by as Austria attacked its Slavic friend. Berlin watched the buildup of Russian forces along its East Prussian border and feared the worst. France and Russia were close allies, surrounding Germany and posing the likelihood of a two-front war. Kaiser Wilhelm ordered his army to mobilize, giving France no option but to order a general mobilization as well.

The prospect of fighting a two-front war was not new to Germany. France and Russia shared a common fear of Germany and had developed extensive financial, economic, and military cooperation over the previous two decades to counter that threat.[2] In 1892 they signed the Franco-Russian Alliance Military Convention, pledging mutual defense should Germany or Austria-Hungary attack either nation. The Franco-Russian treaty was the worst-kept secret on the Continent, and knowing this, Germany prepared to fight a two-front war.[3]

The German answer to the threat of Russia and France in 1905 was a bold operational approach now referred to as the Schlieffen Plan. The Schlieffen Plan was a daring envelopment that would throw the preponderance of the massive German Army through neutral Luxembourg and Belgium behind the French Army and rapidly capture Paris.[4] The key to success was rapidity. The German General Staff assumed that it would take Russia six weeks to mobilize its armed forces; therefore, victory against France had to be achieved in that time frame. Once the French were defeated, the German Army would quickly be moved on trains to East Prussia to then defeat the Russians.[5]

However, the 1905 plan was outdated when it was implemented in 1914. To make matters worse, several of the key planning assumptions, those considerations necessary to ensure victory, also proved wrong. The key ingredient of the Schlieffen Plan was bypassing the French Army by attacking through Belgium. The Germans wrongly planned on meager Belgium defenses that would easily be brushed aside. This German planning assumption was essential, as the Schlieffen Plan could only succeed by rapidly defeating France. However, the Belgian Army proved tougher than the German Army anticipated, throwing off the timing and tempo of the German attack.

To compound matters, the British decided to honor their treaty to defend the neutrality of Belgium (Prussia signed the same treaty in 1839) by deploying part of their army to the Continent. German planners had not expected the British Empire to be an adversary and now had an extra eighty thousand enemy soldiers in their path. This, combined with robust Belgian defense, was enough to doom the Schlieffen Plan to failure, yet there was an even greater problem facing Germany. As part of their alliance, the French had invested heavily in modernizing the Russian rail networks over the past decade. This reduced the time that Russia needed to mobilize its army, allowing Russia to advance into East Prussia well before the German Army could complete its defeat of France even if everything went according to plan, which it did not.

Despite these challenges, the German Army swept into France with incredible speed, driving the French and British armies back. During their advance, a fifty-kilometer-wide gap developed between the First and Second German Armies east of Paris near the Marne River.[6] French marshal Joseph Joffre rushed his Fifth Army and the British Expeditionary Forces (BEF) into this fissure, forcing the Germans to end their offensive and to abandon the Schlieffen Plan.[7] The Western Front transitioned to a defensive war, with elaborate trenches soon extending from the Swiss border to the English Channel. The German chief of General Staff, General Helmuth von Moltke, understood the gravity of this reversal and is reputed to have told the German emperor, Kaiser Wilhelm, "*Majestät, wir haben den Krieg verloren*" (Majesty, we have lost the war).[8]

Drawing on the vast resources of their global empires, France and Britain rushed men and materials from across the world in their effort to deprive the Germans a victory. With growing concerns about the conduct of the war in the east, the Germans maintained a defensive posture in the west in 1915, instead focusing with their Austro-Hungarian partners on the fight in the Balkans and Russia. Being likewise frustrated by their inability to break the stalemate along the Western Front, the British and French sought an alternative strategy. Their plan in 1915 was to defeat Germany's Ottoman (Turkish) ally. The plan was to launch a combined naval and amphibious assault along the Dardanelles, defeat the Ottoman Army, and then march on the Ottoman capital of Constantinople. However, the eight-month Gallipoli campaign gained nothing but nearly a half-million casualties and a defeat for the British and French.[9]

German soldiers from the 120th Württemberg Regiment board trains for the front confident of victory, with "Paris and back again" written on the side of the car. (Mastriano Collection)

In 1916, under the leadership of General Erich Georg Anton von Falkenhayn, the Germans again focused on the Western Front. Falkenhayn's plan was to destroy the French Army in a massive campaign in the Verdun region. This was the war's longest campaign, lasting nine months and producing up to 1 million casualties. Although Falkenhayn came close to achieving his objective of "bleeding the French Army white," he neither destroyed the army nor broke its spirit. Meanwhile, farther north, the British (and French) launched a massive attack of their own on the first of July. Called the Battle of the Somme, the operation cost both sides combined over 1 million casualties, yet the Allies failed to break the German line. Thus ended the second year of the war, with the belligerents suffering incredible casualties and having little to show for it.

However, the armies were adapting, and the foundations of modern warfare were developing. The French created one of the most important innovations: the abandonment of the Napoleonic style of attacking an enemy line with large formations of soldiers. Instead, the French began to adapt smaller formations (small unit tactics) that would bypass strongholds and advance to their objective. The Germans copied this new approach and applied it with Teutonic perfection in the form of storm troop tactics later in the war. Other improvements in combined and joint war fighting encompassed the integration of aircraft in ground combat, coordinated artillery fires, the use of chemicals, and the introduction of tanks. The way of war was radically changing, and many of these innovations remain with modern armies a century later.

The following year was turbulent at the geo-strategic level. Unrestricted German submarine warfare, combined with a botched attempt to convince the Mexicans to invade America, forced the ambivalent President Wilson to declare war. The Americans were not actually part of the French/British-led alliance, but were rather an "associated power." This meant that although willing to work in concert with the Allies, the United States would exercise a separate chain of command, thereby making the command structure on the Western Front a coalition rather than a pure alliance.[10] This was a strategic decision by President Wilson designed to provide the United States greater influence both during and especially after the war.

Meanwhile, Germany and its Austro-Hungarian partners enjoyed incredible success in both the Balkans and Russia. By the end of the year, Czarist Russia collapsed to the Bolshevik Revolution and quit the war, freeing up more than 1 million German soldiers from the Eastern Front. Due to the lack of American military preparedness, the United States would need a year before it could bring sufficient forces to Europe to make a difference on the Western Front. This gave the Germans a window of opportunity to complete a victory in the First World War.

The German plan in 1918, under the watchful eye of Generals Erich Friedrich Wilhelm Ludendorff and Paul von Hindenburg, was to transport the preponderance of the army from Russia early in the year. The Germans planned on initially launching one massive offensive to break the Allies. Having failed to achieve this, the Germans, in the end, launched five major attacks to knock the Allies out of the war before sufficient American forces arrived to tip the scales against them. The German Spring Offensives came close to achieving their objectives, but the British and French worked out an ambitious shipping plan to get the fledgling American army into Europe faster than the Germans believed possible. Yet, it was a desperate time for the British and French. The German Army ruptured the front in the Somme, nearly destroying the British Fifth Army under General Hubert Gough in March. The Germans achieved

Hindenburg, Ludendorff, and Kaiser Wilhelm at the Imperial Headquarters in Spa, Belgium. With the capitulation of Russia late in 1917, nearly 1 million German soldiers were freed up to attack the French and British in 1918. The plan was to win on the Western Front before the American army arrived in sufficient numbers to turn the balance against Germany. (National Archives)

another impressive penetration during their Aisne Offensive in late May, creating some panic that Paris might actually fall. However, by July the German attacks on the Western Front culminated, thereby giving the French-led coalition the initiative. With more than a million American soldiers already in France, and another million on the way, the tide was turning against Germany.

The greatest result of the five German Spring Offensives was that they forced the Western Allies to finally agree on a clear and single chain of command. Prior to this, the nations on the Western Front exercised significant autonomy over their forces. This often resulted in uncoordinated military actions and poor cooperation between the armies. The crisis of 1918 was a desperate time that required

After arriving in Europe, American Doughboys march through Perth, England, on their way to France. The lack of preparedness by the United States gave Germany an opportunity to win the war in early 1918. (National Archives)

the appointment of French general Ferdinand Foch as the supreme commander (generalissimo) who would exercise authority and control of the forces deployed across the Western Front and Italy. Foch would be promoted to Marshal of France on 7 August 1918. He was the first Supreme Allied Commander, a role that would be imitated in the Second World War when American general Dwight D. Eisenhower served in this capacity. This decision to appoint a supreme commander was a revolution in military affairs and marked the first time in four years that the Allies finally achieved unity of command and effort, with Foch having the final say on where units would deploy. Thanks in large part to this decision, the Allies were able to survive the five German offensives of 1918. As the last of the German attacks were repulsed by the Americans and French near the Marne River in mid-July, Foch saw an opportunity to end the war a year earlier than anyone believed possible.

3

Dithering, Dreaming, and Speechmaking

> After World War I broke out . . . we were convinced that the
> plain duty of the United States was to join the Allies . . . and
> that it was cowardly to be neutral . . . I wonder if many of the
> world's future troubles might not have been averted.
> —Eleanor Butler Roosevelt (Mrs. Theodore Roosevelt Jr.)

The unpreparedness of the U.S. Army for war on the Western Front
was due to the national strategy that Woodrow Wilson charted during his presidency, and the high losses of American soldiers in the
Meuse-Argonne, with negligible gains in comparison, were the
result. Presidential leadership matters in the United States, and it
shapes the effectiveness and strength of the nation's armed forces.
Most books on the Meuse-Argonne avoid a serious discussion of
how the U.S. national strategy, and the decisions made by Wilson
between 1914 and 1918, condemned to death thousands of young
American men due to poor training, poor equipment, and lack of
readiness for the realities of modern war.

Wilson entered presidential politics with foreign affairs far from
his agenda. After winning the hotly contested 1912 presidential election, his desire was to transform America domestically. Before being
sworn in, he confided to a friend, "It would be the irony of fate if my
administration had to deal chiefly with foreign affairs."[1] His words
were prophetic, as the fate of nations rested on his shoulders, and
the decisions he made shaped our world.

Few could predict that the assassination of Archduke Ferdinand
in Sarajevo would trigger a global catastrophe. Yet the shots fired on
that idyllic summer day of 28 June 1914 would lead to the collapse
of four dynasties, redraw the borders of vast swaths of Africa, Asia,
and Europe, and set the conditions for a second and bloodier world

17

President Woodrow Wilson throws out the first ball in game two of the 1915 World Series held in Philadelphia, Pennsylvania. The series pitted the Boston Red Sox against the Philadelphia Phillies. Wilson was the first president to attend a game, and this personified his focus on domestic politics. (National Archives)

war. As the European powers stumbled toward all-out war in the summer of 1914, several of its leaders were vacationing, making the calamity of 1914 seem peculiar, if not the predestined will of God. But God's Providence was *not* the reason for this calamity; rather, it was Europe's leaders who created the complex web of alliances that caused this world war.

As armies clashed in Europe, President Wilson delivered a message to Congress on 19 August 1914 in which he outlined the American strategy. Wilson declared, "The United States must be neutral in fact, as well as in name, during these days that are to try men's souls. We must be impartial in thought, as well as action."[2] Neutrality was the guiding principle of American strategy for the duration of the war. Yet Wilson's declaration of neutrality was difficult if not impossible to maintain. The United States was an exporter of manufactured goods and raw materials to both warring factions in Europe. In this, France and the United Kingdom had the advantage with their Atlantic access and geography. How could the United

States maintain pure neutrality when its trade gave the British and French an advantage?

Stalemate dominated the Western Front in 1915. The French failed to retake Alsace-Lorraine, the Germans did not capture Paris, the British faced a powerful German navy, and Russia was stymied in the East. Wilson's secretary of state, William Jennings Bryan, was at a loss as to how the United States could bring peace.[3] Yet, "Bryan said there was no reason to be alarmed, because in case of trouble a million men would spring to arms between sunrise and sunset. That they would be untrained and unarmed didn't seem to matter."[4] With a weak and feckless American strategy in place, the Germans sought an alternate way to knock the British out of the war. The plan was to use submarines (U-boats) to deprive the United Kingdom of what it needed to remain in the war. If successful, this would force London to withdraw its support from France and would lead to victory for Berlin in Europe.

Wilson's strategy of maintaining neutrality evolved to include using diplomacy to end the war through American-led negotiations.[5] The president wanted to "reset" relations with the Germans, French, and British, none of whom was eager to rebuff the credulity of the American proposition. Berlin offered the most hope to Wilson's diplomats for a negotiated peace. This, however, had less to do with wanting peace than with Germany's having the advantage. It had already conquered large sections of France and Belgium. In exasperation, the French ambassador to the United States, Jean Jules Jusserand, rebuffed the Americans' naivety, saying, "we would accept [peace] . . . when the Germans . . . give us back the lives of our dead ones."[6]

Meanwhile, President Wilson was on a collision course with the German Imperial Navy. As the front lines on the Western Front continued in a stalemate, the German leadership decided to give their fleet of U-boats a free hand in sinking merchant vessels on the open seas. Until March 1915, German U-boats as a rule did much to ensure that only vessels in violation of law (carrying goods of war) were attacked. This often required the German U-boats to surface and either inspect a vessel or allow its occupants to abandon ship before it was torpedoed. Merchant ships from the belligerent nations took advantage of this German policy by ramming the U-boats or firing on them. This, combined with the stagnation on the Western Front, compelled Kaiser Wilhelm to issues orders on 3 April 1915 to "torpedo [merchant ships] on sight." The German

Foreign Office alerted the world's neutral nations of this change in policy.[7] Just a few days before this change in policy, however, a German U-boat sank the SS *Falaba* on 28 March 1915, killing American citizen Leon Thrasher.[8] After this, the U.S.-flagged ship *Gulfight* was attacked, killing two more Americans. Things came to a head with the sinking of the *Lusitania* on 7 May 1915. The ship sank so rapidly that 1,195 passengers and crew died, including 128 Americans.[9]

Outrage spread across the United States against Germany. President Wilson was at a crossroads, where the viability of his strategy toward the war was clearly not working. Yet his only action was to send three diplomatic notes to Berlin that (1) affirmed the right of Americans to transit the open seas, (2) repudiated the counterarguments from Germany that the British naval blockade was illegal, and, finally, (3) informed the Kaiser that any further sinking of ships with Americans on board would be viewed as "deliberately unfriendly" toward the United States.[10]

Despite the loss of American lives and the attacks on U.S. vessels, Wilson refused to reconsider his strategy. He took no serious action to prepare the nation for war, or to protect its citizens from further loss of life or material. Peace at all costs was his view, and the platform of his Democratic Party. So incensed was William Jennings Bryan over the harsh tone Wilson used in the second note to the Kaiser that he resigned as the secretary of state.[11] Yet the tone, from any perspective, was not hostile or threatening. This, however, betrays the state of Wilson's party and his administration that kept America weak and unprepared. Just three days after the sinking of the *Lusitania* Wilson gave his "Too proud to fight speech," where with inconceivable detachment from reality he proclaimed, "The example of America must be the example not merely of peace because it will not fight, but of peace because peace is the healing and elevating influence of the world and strife is not. There is such a thing as a man being too proud to fight. There is such a thing as a nation being so right that it does not need to convince others by force that it is right."[12]

This speech declared that Wilson's strategy toward the First World War remained unchanged. Thus, in 1916, as the First World War entered its second and bloodiest year, the credibility and power of the United States was tarnished by inaction and dithering. Indeed Wilson and his political party stood for "peace at almost any price." Newton D. Baker, the new secretary of war, declared in 1916, "I am a pacifist. I am a pacifist in my hope; I am a pacifist in my prayers; I am a pacifist in my belief."[13] History would judge that neither Bryan nor Baker could see beyond their ideology to grasp how dangerous and detached the American strategy had become. Indeed, they refused to believe that not all people were as good intentioned or as well meaning as they believed themselves to be. Meanwhile, as Baker pontificated on his opinions on pacifism and peace, generations of men were perishing along the Western Front.

In the face of German submarine warfare and the inability to secure a mediated peace, the "reset" had failed. Yet the Wilson administration would try to talk the belligerents out of fighting. President Wilson clung to the idea that through high-minded speeches, cleverly crafted diplomatic letters, and appealing to the logic of learned men, he could negotiate an end to the calamitous war. The focus of Wilson's energies for the next year would be to find a way to end the war via American arbitration.

It was a presidential election year in 1916, and with reelection his primary focus, Wilson's approach to the Great War did not change.[14] The Democratic Party invoked the slogan "He Kept Us Out of the War,"[15] and during the 1916 convention Wilson pledged to keep the nation neutral and lambasted his Republican rivals as amateurs when it came to foreign affairs.[16] It was he, an enlightened leader of an enlightened party, who would lead the nation into a "new age."[17]

Despite regurgitating the oft-repeated lines regarding neutrality, it was evident in 1916 that the war would forever change Europe. Because of this realization, Wilson's vision for the postwar world began to modify. In a speech delivered to the League to Enforce Peace, Wilson called for international institutions to prevent such a calamity from occurring again. This idea would become the basis for the League of Nations. Wilson went on to list three fundamentals that would forever change the old international order. His first fundamental attacked colonialism and declared the right for all people "to choose the sovereignty under which they live" (self-determination). Wilson's second fundamental, influenced by the tragic situation in Belgium, asserted that all nations, small or large, have the right to territorial integrity. His third fundamental was that the world should live in freedom and peace.[18] This final idea hinted that only a democratic (republican) form of government could make this possible. The relevance of Wilson's calling for a new international order and his three guiding principles should not be lost to the reader, as these were key concepts for the Clinton and two Bush administrations in 1990–2008.[19]

Relying on lofty speeches and high-minded expression, Wilson spoke of achieving "peace without victory."[20] The hollowness of his rhetoric was background noise to the now exhausted and bloodied participants of the war. He pontificated how a peaceful future would include a new balance of power, with cooperation among the nations to maintain peace, freedom of the seas (and freedom of trade), and a new birth of freedom and justice (democracy) around the world.[21] The lofty rhetoric notwithstanding, the reality of the war would soon crash upon the United States. In an endeavor to break the British, Kaiser Wilhelm ordered unrestricted submarine warfare to resume on 1 February 1917. As more than one hundred German U-boats sank half a million tons of shipping in just twenty-eight days, Wilson was compelled to sever diplomatic ties with Berlin.[22] Yet, beyond this, Wilson dithered on how to respond. Further complicating matters for him, however, the British released an intelligence intercept in which German foreign secretary Arthur Zimmermann pledged support for Mexico if it attacked the United States.[23] This, combined with the effects of the unrestricted submarine warfare, was too much for the United States. Facing overwhelming public pressure, Wilson acquiesced. On 2 April 1917 Wilson asked Congress to declare a state of war against Germany.[24]

Wilson's speech was a dramatic turn when he called for the nation to defeat the German Empire. This would encompass mobilizing the nation for war and rapidly expanding the army and navy. The goals that he laid out in this wartime strategy included upholding his three principles, world peace, liberation of the oppressed peoples, and creating a partnership of democratic nations to ensure peace in the future (which he would later call the League of Nations), so that "The world must be made safe for democracy."[25]

Despite the declaration, the U.S. Army was not ready to fight a modern war. The American army in April 1917 encompassed barely 200,000 men, smaller than the 1914 Belgian army. To compound matters, the army only had experience and doctrine for fighting small counterinsurgency wars. Yet this small force would expand to more than 4 million. Two million of these would serve in Europe by the end of the war. Raising the manpower to create a large army was only part of the challenge. The equipping, training, and readiness of this large army required *time*.

As the Americans belatedly mobilized for war, there was a crisis in Europe. British manpower was weakening, a portion of the French Army mutinied, and Russia fell to a revolution. In the midst of this, the Americans needed a year to get a substantial force to France and it seemed that it would be too late. With the French down and the Russians out, Germany seized the opportunity. During the winter of 1917–1918 a million German soldiers moved from the Eastern Front to knock the British and French out of the war before enough Americans arrived to make a difference. The German gamble nearly succeeded.[26]

Meanwhile, after declaring war, Woodrow Wilson appointed General John J. Pershing to lead the American Expeditionary Forces (AEF). In their only meeting during the war, General Pershing and Secretary of War Newton Baker met with President Wilson on 24 May 1917. President Wilson delegated considerable discretion to Pershing in the organization and operation of the AEF.[27] As the AEF hastily prepared for war, Wilson outlined his wartime grand strategy in January 1918 in a speech dubbed "The Fourteen Points." This was the birth of Wilsonianism.[28] The key concepts in this revolutionary vision for the future encompassed five basic fundamentals, which some have referred to as "Liberal Imperialism."[29]

(1) Democratic states provide peace and stability.
(2) Free trade is key to global prosperity.
(3) International laws and international institutions are essential to maintain order, peace, and security.
(4) Collective security is a must to maintain peace.
(5) The United States is "chosen" to lead this new world order.[30]

These emerged as foundational principles of how the United States would interact with the world during the negotiations at Versailles in 1919 and especially after World War Two. However, there were still eleven months of fighting before Wilson would see his ideas considered.

Of all the requirements to build and deploy this new and massive AEF, the most difficult task was to maintain an independent American army. The Allies pressured (and at times threatened) Pershing to amalgamate his forces into existing British and French military

The commander of the American Expeditionary Forces arrives at St. Nazaire, France, on 26 June 1917. (National Archives)

formations. From a pragmatic perspective, this made sense. With amalgamation, the Americans could enter combat rapidly, serving with experienced units and leaders. Additionally, it seemed that the Allies might actually lose the war when the Germans unleashed their powerful spring 1918 offensives.[31] Pershing allowed a temporary assignment of American units to French and British command, but once the emergency of 1918 ended he demanded a return of his forces to the AEF.

With the Germans culminating on the Western Front in July 1918, Supreme Allied Commander (Generalissimo) Ferdinand Foch summoned Pershing and the British and French Army leaders (Haig and Pétain respectively) to his headquarters on 24 July 1918. Foch intimated that the Allies should take the initiative and launch a series of attacks against the Germans. The assembled leaders at first balked at the idea, but in the end Foch won them over. The Allies would launch a massive counteroffensive in September 1918.[32] This attack began on 26 September 1918 with a large Franco-American attack in the Meuse-Argonne region of France, which was followed by the other armies across the Western Front. The war would end in forty-seven days, with the Americans pouring more than 1.2 million men into the fight and holding more of the front than any nation except France. Although late to the war, the United States earned a prominent seat at the peace talks in 1919.

When the First World War ended on the eleventh hour of the eleventh day of the eleventh month of 1918, the United States emerged as a powerful force in the world. Although Woodrow Wilson entered the peace talks at Versailles with hopes of creating a new world order, it was not to be. The European victors wanted to punish Germany for the war, even as they carved up the Middle East and other areas of the world to dominate. It would take a Second World War before many of Wilson's goals and his strategy would be realized.

Yet the lack of military preparedness under the Wilson administration was his greatest blunder. His desire for peace was noble, but as it became increasingly clear that war would eventually reach America's shores, he did nothing. In the end, the United States generated a large fighting force, but the cost came at a high price when untrained and ill-equipped men died fighting a seasoned and modern German Army.[33]

The strategy and approach of President Wilson are worthy of contemplation, as there are lessons for us to ponder today. Indeed, historians have a laboratory; it is called the past. The efficacy of studying history is to understand the past and hopefully create a better and more informed future. As a writer in a nineteenth-century book wrote, "The vision recurs; the eastern sun has a second rise; history repeats her tale unconsciously, and goes off into a mystic rhyme; ages are prototypes of other ages, and the winding course of time brings us round to the same spot again."[34]

The lessons of Wilson's strategy in the First World War echo across the generations to us today, one hundred years later. Long and articulate speeches are no replacement for preparedness and action. Dithering and indecision are poor excuses for a coherent strategy. America experimented with a reset of relations and leading from behind during World War One, and it proved disastrous. As the world commemorates the centennial of the most catastrophic year of the First World War, it seems that there are eerie similarities to today. The wise would look to the past to avoid the mistakes of the past.

4

The Plan for Victory

The moment has come to abandon the general defensive . . .
and to pass to the offensive.
　　　　　—Ferdinand Foch, memorandum of 24 July 1918

With the German 1918 offensives blunted, the Supreme Allied Commander (Generalissimo), Ferdinand Foch, believed that the time was ripe for the Allies to go on the offensive to end the war.[1] This ability to envision such an opportunity is what the renowned Prussian theorist Carl von Clausewitz called military genius. Military genius is when a leader can make right decisions despite the lack of clarity and information.[2] Such an attribute had been rare among the Western Powers' leaders throughout the war, and it seemed that Foch had developed this ability.[3]

It was during the Second Battle of the Marne; Foch saw what no one did. As the fighting raged on, he determined that the German Army had culminated (lost the momentum to maintain the offensive) and that the opportunity to end the war had arrived.[4] To make his case to the coalition's national army leaders, Foch drafted the memorandum of 24 July 1918 that outlined the condition of the German Army and how the war could be brought to an end. The opening paragraph of the memorandum brilliantly captured the moment: "The Fifth German offensive, halted at its very start, was a failure. The offensive taken by the French Tenth and Sixth Armies has turned it into a defeat. This defeat must first of all be exploited thoroughly on the field of battle itself. That is why we are pursuing our attacks without pause and with all our energy. But the consequences go far beyond the battle itself. The enemy's defeat forms a basis on which should rest the general attitude to be adopted by the Allied armies."[5]

Foch met with the French commander, General Philippe Pétain, the American commander, General John Pershing, and the British

26

With the fall of Russia in 1917, Germany transferred nearly 1 million men to France. Many of these were trained in storm troop tactics to increase their ability to shatter the French and British lines. (National Archives)

commander, Field Marshal Douglas Haig, at his Chateau de Bombon headquarters on 24 July 1918. With all of the Allied commanders assembled, he gave them the memorandum and read its contents to them. Foch announced his intention to have the Allies go over to the offensive. Foch then asked the national army commanders for their opinion of the proposal.[6]

Haig balked at the idea, saying that his army was still reeling from the beating it took in the spring. Pétain also disagreed, saying that after four years the French Army was "bled white, anemic." Pershing refused to support the plan, saying that the Americans still needed time to form an army.[7] Of the three, it seems that Pershing missed Foch's intent in the memorandum of 24 July. Instead of thinking how he could support this grand plan, Pershing was caught up with how to equip the AEF with French and British equipment.

Although disconcerting at first glance, the concerns of the national army commanders were justified. It had been a trying and tumultuous year. The five German offensives of 1918 had devastated parts of the French and British armies and caused panic in Paris. Conventional wisdom was that the remaining months of 1918 would be used to consolidate gains, rearm, refit, and prepare for the final offensive to end the war, which would begin in the spring of

General Philippe Pétain (France), Marshal Douglas Haig (UK), General Ferdinand Foch (Supreme Allied Commander), General John Pershing (USA). The photograph was taken at Foch's headquarters in the Chateau de Bombon. (National Archives)

1919. The concept in Plan 1919, as envisioned by J. F. C. Fuller, its lead planner, was an attack consisting of thousands of tanks and airplanes shattering the German front and wreaking havoc behind the lines. Fuller's concept was a foreshadow of what war would look like in World War Two, as seen in the Blitzkrieg.[8]

The memorandum went on to describe Foch's concept of the operation, which was to maintain pressure on the German Army with a series of smaller attacks, and this was to be "executed with such rapidity as to inflict upon the enemy a succession of blows."[9] The succession of blows was both to keep the Germans off balance and to set the conditions for the final Grand Offensive. August and early September 1918 would be used to shape the environment and secure the ground for a larger offensive. Foch believed that it would be a mistake to allow the German Army the winter months to refit, reorganize, and retrain. He gave each of the commanders a copy of his 24 July memorandum and asked them to study it in greater detail at their respective headquarters. He asked for an answer by the end of the following day. After having had time to review his concept, the three Allied commanders expressed support of the plan, with the French and British taking the lead in offensive operations in August.[10]

Foch's concept seemed to be confirmed after the British and French armies cleared the Germans from key areas on the Western Front. The final confirmation that it was indeed time to take the fight to the Germans occurred on 8 August near Santerre, where thirteen thousand Germans were captured.[11] Foch discussed his concept of operations for a Grand Offensive with Pétain and Pershing on 30 August, and three days later he issued formal instructions for this plan to end the war in 1918.[12] After Foch conferred with the king of Belgium, orders were issued laying out his plan for the Grand Offensive:

> 26 September—A Franco-American attack between the Suippe and the Meuse.
> 27 September—An attack by the British First and Third Armies near Cambrai.
> 28 September—An attack by Army Group Flanders between the sea and the Lys, under the command of the king of Belgium.
> 29 September—An attack by the British Fourth Army, supported by the French First Army, in the direction of Busigny.[13]

Foch's broad front offensive ironically borrowed extensively from the ideas of Frederick the Great, the famed eighteenth-century king of Prussia, as well as France's own Napoleon Bonaparte. The plan would also be echoed in General Dwight D. Eisenhower's approach on the Western Front in late 1944 and early 1945. Foch's plan was to launch an en echelon attack that would stretch from Verdun to the English Channel to pressure the Germans across a large portion of the Western Front. This would force the Germans to commit their reserves early, and by the time the later attacks were launched there (theoretically) would be a lightly defended area that would allow a breakthrough.[14]

Foch's en echelon attack would begin with the Americans and French in the Meuse-Argonne on 26 September, followed by the British First and Third Armies on 27 September, then King Albert's forces north of Ypres on 28 September, and finally the 29 September Franco-British attack near St. Quentin.[15] The force of these four massive assaults would, conceivably, be too much for the Imperial German Army to bear. The main problem for the Allies was

Germany's twenty-some strategic reserve divisions. By this point in the war, there were two German armies, the frontline troops, poised to delay, fix, and slow any Allied attack, and the strategic reserves. The reserves were rushed across the Western Front via railroad as needed to maintain the integrity of the line. The German strategic reserve divisions were the source of strength for the German Army on the Western Front late in 1918, or as Clausewitz would have it, they were the center of gravity.[16] To achieve success, Foch needed either to destroy the German strategic reserve divisions or to force their early commitment to prevent them from being used elsewhere to foil an Allied breakthrough. To accomplish the task of forcing the commitment of the German strategic reserves, Foch pinned his hopes on the American Meuse-Argonne Offensive.[17]

Foch believed that a sustained attack in the Meuse-Argonne region would draw the German strategic reserves because of its proximity to the vital Sedan-Mezieres rail network. It would be a catastrophe for the Germans if this line were cut, as it was a critical transportation node for Germany. If it were lost, a portion of their army would be cut off.[18] Because of this, Marshal Haig predicted that the Germans would be forced to commit their strategic reserves to contend with the Americans in the Meuse-Argonne to protect their lines of communication at Sedan.

An obstacle to Foch's plans was the AEF commander. Although General Pershing had many burdens, one of his chief concerns was ensuring that the AEF would fight as an independent American army. The pressure to amalgamate the American forces into the French and British armies was enormous, especially during the crisis of 1918 triggered by the five German offensives. Amalgamating the Americans would get them into battle quickly. However, Pershing believed in the importance of having an independent army, and the strategic leverage it would have in both ending the war and giving the United States influence in postwar Europe.[19]

With this in mind, Pershing insisted that he command an independent American army. However, Foch was under pressure from his prime minister, Georges Clemenceau, to force the Americans to amalgamate. The prime minister failed to convince Pershing to allow the American forces to be folded into existing French and British units. Out of frustration, Clemenceau called Pershing "stubborn" and then demanded that Foch order Pershing to amalgamate the AEF into French and British formations on the Western Front to get them into the fight more quickly. Foch attempted to convince Pershing of the utility of this. However, Pershing refused to budge and flatly exclaimed that there would be an independent American army.[20] With such a view, Foch simply did not comply with the wishes of Clemenceau to force the issue, fearing that it would damage the alliance.[21] Foch was sympathetic to Pershing's insistence on fielding an independent American army and was willing to adjust his plan to accommodate the American wishes, despite the political pressure placed on him by the intractable Clemenceau.[22] Of this, Foch said, "I was convinced more than anybody else of the necessity of forming with the least delay a great American army under the orders of its commander, since I knew perfectly well that soldiers of a national army never fight as well as under the orders of the officers of their country . . . who speak the same tongue, fight for the same cause, have the same sort of ideas and act in a manner familiar to the men under them."[23]

Another complication posed by General Pershing was the reduction of the St. Mihiel salient in the Woëvre region. This mission had been assigned to Pershing by Foch in July and was to be the first army-level operation conducted by the Americans in France. However, this plan had been adopted before Foch came up with his broad front attack. It would take considerable time to reposition the American units spread across the Western Front. This dispersion had occurred during the crisis of 1918, when American forces were rushed across the Western Front to fortify weak points, relieve French and British divisions, and participate in operations to blunt the German attacks. Once these forces were deployed to the Woëvre region, they would become the nucleus of the new American army. The First Army headquarters became operational on 10 August and was making preparations to receive and employ the American units.[24] However, neither Pershing nor his American staff had any experience running an army-level operation. For Pershing, it was imperative that this new army be given a task to gain experience. Additionally, Pershing's men had to do well with their inaugural fight. An attack against a German pocket east of Verdun had been selected earlier in the summer to accomplish this end.

Called the St. Mihiel salient after the village in the center of the bulge, this protrusion formed in 1914 when the Germans attempted to outflank the French defenses around Verdun. Over more than four years of fighting, the Germans had fortified this area. Pershing's plan was to deploy 550,000 men of his army, supported by more than 100,000 experienced French forces, to retake St. Mihiel between 12 and 15 September and set conditions to continue the attack toward Metz, if the circumstances on the ground favored that.

The American Expeditionary Forces, with French support, began to prepare for the attack in late August 1918. On 30 August, Marshal Foch met with Pershing and laid out his plan for the broad front attack that the Americans would commence on 26 September (the Meuse-Argonne campaign). Foch suggested that Pershing abandon the St. Mihiel campaign and instead focus on preparing for the Meuse-Argonne. However, Pershing asked that he proceed with a limited attack at St. Mihiel. He pledged to then pivot the AEF one hundred kilometers back to the northwest to support the Meuse-Argonne campaign the following week.[25] Such a notion was a herculean effort even for an experienced army, yet in the end Foch agreed to Pershing's plan and allowed him to proceed with both the St. Mihiel Offensive and the Meuse-Argonne campaign.[26]

Pershing took considerable strategic risk in his St. Mihiel offensive, as the morale of the AEF was tied to the plan. But at far greater risk was the view of the AEF by the Allies and Germans. Because of this, most of the AEF's most experienced units would fight at St. Mihiel, making them unavailable for the beginning of the Meuse-Argonne. The price paid would be sending several divisions of inexperienced American troops into the initial attack in the Meuse-Argonne against seasoned and combat-hardened German soldiers.

5

St. Mihiel

The Risky Plan before the Meuse-Argonne

> You must establish the fact that American tanks do not
> surrender. This is our big chance; what we have worked for . . .
> —Lieutenant Colonel George S. Patton

The salient east of Verdun, protruding deep into the French Woëvre region, was referred to simply as St. Mihiel, after the largest town in this bulge. The St. Mihiel salient formed in 1914 as the German Army attempted to outflank the French defenses at Verdun. After an initial breakthrough, the French Army blunted the German advance. The French launched a series of counterattacks over the next year to reduce the German bulge. However, despite intense fighting and heavy losses, the Germans held firmly.

The St. Mihiel salient was forty kilometers wide (east to west) and twenty-six kilometers deep.[1] From a strategic point of view, it gave the Germans several advantages. The chief among these was that it made movement by the French Army on the Paris–Nancy rail line difficult, as German artillery was used to interdict this essential line of communication and troop movement. The German position also occupied a portion of the rail line leading across Lorraine to Verdun.[2] Finally, the salient provided a buffer zone for the Germans to safeguard the city of Metz and, more importantly, the Briey Iron Basin, which was a vital resource for war production.[3]

As the debut attack of the U.S. First Army, it was imperative that the St. Mihiel operation succeed. Ever the reliable ally, the French did all they could to ensure American victory. They provided tanks, aircraft (augmented with British bombers), and four of their

French soldiers marching in a French village near St. Mihiel. The French Army provided a substantial number of soldiers, aircraft, and tanks to support the victory of the large Franco-American offensive at St. Mihiel. (Private collection)

experienced divisions to support the fourteen American divisions poised to participate in this offensive. "More than 550,000 Americans and about 110,000 French were involved in the offensive. The air force concentrated for it, 1,481 airplanes, was the largest ever brought together up to that time and consisted chiefly of French and British planes. The Army had about 400 French tanks available, of which 350 were light . . . and 144 were manned by Americans. About 3,000 pieces of artillery were used and approximately 3,300,000 rounds of artillery ammunition were brought into the area."[4] The St. Mihiel operation began on 12 September.

As nearly 700,000 French and American troops moved to their positions around the St. Mihiel salient, the Germans deliberated on what to do. They had three layers of elaborate defensive positions from which to fight. Yet the German High Command was not sure that, in the face of overwhelming numbers, the cost of trying to hold St. Mihiel was worth it. Finally, on 9 September, orders were issued to begin the evacuation of the salient. This evacuation order would take eight days to execute, in that it consisted of destroying everything in the sector that could provide an advantage to the French and Americans. German general Erich Ludendorff declared that the evacuation order should have been given the week before, when it was clear that the Allies were planning on launching a large operation to liberate the region.[5]

The Franco-American attack at St. Mihiel was brilliantly

planned and executed. It included a three-pronged strike against the salient, with the main effort being in the Allied center, and supporting attacks into the eastern and western flanks of the bulge. Colonel William "Billy" Mitchell masterfully planned the application of air power to strike the German defenders across the depth of the line, while American and French armored formations, supported by artillery strikes,[6] swung into action.[7] While the Germans were in the middle of their elaborate and complex evacuation, the Americans attacked. One of the participants, Corporal Alvin York of the 82nd American Division, wrote of the beginning of the St. Mihiel operation: "It done opened with a most awful barrage from our big guns. It was the awfulest thing you ever heard. It made the air tremble and the ground shake. At times you couldn't hear your own voice nohow. The air was full of airplanes, and most of them American planes. There must have been hundreds of them. They were diving and circling around all over the place like a swarm of birds. We seed several right-smart fights away up there above us."[8]

The American First Army offensive went off brilliantly, demonstrating the force's ability to conduct joint air-ground operations and coordinating artillery fires in support of the tank and infantry attacks. Leading the American 1st Tank Brigade was Lieutenant Colonel George S. Patton, who would become a household name for his role in World War Two. The importance of having a good show of not just the American Expeditionary Forces, but also the tank brigade was not lost to Patton. In his pre–St. Mihiel speech to his men he said, "You must establish the fact that American tanks do not surrender. This is our big chance; what we have worked for."[9]

Patton's tanks served in direct support of Brigadier General Douglas MacArthur, another American icon rising out of World War Two. MacArthur commanded the 84th Brigade of the 42nd "Rainbow" Division and worked directly with Patton during the advance. Both of these men led from the front and were literally in the thick of the action. MacArthur would receive his fifth Silver Star for his leadership during the attack.[10]

Although the Franco-American attack at St. Mihiel went off brilliantly, the challenges of fielding an inexperienced army were evident. In the case of Patton's tank brigade, the unit suffered from mechanical difficulties and inadequate logistics planning for refueling. This left portions of the tank brigade stranded on the battlefield and the men at a loss for how to move fuel forward.[11] Yet, despite

Brigadier General Douglas MacArthur with his French liaison officer, Captain Chevalier (left), and the 167th Regiment commander, Lieutenant Colonel Walter Bare (right). (U.S. Army Heritage and Education Center, Carlisle, Pennsylvania)

such shortcomings, the French and Americans achieved the primary objectives only two days later, and completed the operation by 15 September. Pershing wrote with great satisfaction, "The rapidity with which our divisions advanced overwhelmed the enemy, and all objectives were reached by the afternoon of September 13. The enemy had apparently started to withdraw some of his troops from the tip of the salient on the eve of our attack, but had been unable to carry it through. We captured nearly 16,000 prisoners, 443 guns, and large stores of material and supplies. The energy and swiftness with which the operation was carried out enabled us to smother opposition to such an extent that we suffered less than 7,000 casualties during the actual period of the advance."[12]

Pershing added with a bit of pride, "after seventeen months . . . an American Army was fighting under its own flag."[13]

Some among the Allies feared that the AEF success at St. Mihiel would codify Pershing's dangerously antiquated idea that the Americans would win the war by the rifle, bayonet, and a spirit of attack. Pershing's "cult of the rifle" eerily reminded the Europeans

The rapidity of the Franco-American attack in St. Mihiel resulted in the capture of fifteen thousand German soldiers. In this picture, medics from the 103rd and 104th Medic Companies, 26th "Yankee" Division, provide wounded German prisoners first aid near Hannonville-sous-les-Cotes on 12 September 1918. (National Archives)

of an approach used by the French Army in 1914.[14] The 1914 French tactics were based on the writings of Colonel Louis de Grandmaison. Grandmaison served as the director of the Bureau of Military Operations *(Troisième Bureau)*. His concept was from the lessons of the Franco-Prussian War (1870–1871), where the Prussians defeated the French largely due to an aggressive offensive spirit.

Grandmaison's theory was that the bayonet and fighting spirit (élan) would win the day. This theory was applied by the French Army during the opening weeks of the war in 1914, and was confronted with the new realities of advanced technology, especially machine guns. Among the French officers leading their men in a frontal charge into the face of concentrated German machine gun fires was Lieutenant Charles De Gaulle. De Gaulle was a platoon leader in the famed French 33rd Infantry Regiment. Seemingly reliving the charges of Napoleon, and in line with the ideals of

Grandmaison, De Gaulle's regiment charged the German positions across a bridge on the Meuse River at Dinant. The men attacked in a classic bayonet charge, replete with bugles, drums, and flags. De Gaulle was among the first to fall, being hit by a bullet in the fibula, and wrote of this experience: "Suddenly the enemy's fire became precise and concentrated. Second by second the hail of bullets and the thunder of the shells grew stronger. Those who survived lay flat on the ground, amid the screaming wounded and the humble corpses. With affected calm, the officers let themselves be killed standing upright, some obstinate platoons stuck their bayonets in their rifles, bugles sounded the charge, isolated heroes made fantastic leaps, but all to no purpose. In an instant it had become clear that not all the courage in the world could withstand this fire."[15] Using such tactics, the French Army lost 210,000 men in two weeks of fighting, with little to justify the loss.[16]

Yet the American commander did not heed their concerns. Relying on outdated doctrines and ideas, Pershing's AEF would learn the hard way—through the unnecessary loss of tens of thousands of men—that technology had changed the way of war. Of this, Foch commented, "[The Americans] had to learn in just a few months or even a few weeks what had taken us several years."[17] French premier Clemenceau added that "death defying courage was not enough to win a strategical success."[18] The adversary that the Americans would face in the Meuse-Argonne would indeed make them pay dearly for every foot of ground, and Pershing's outdated tactics would play precisely into the Germans' hands.

Meanwhile, the Americans in St. Mihiel could not rest on their laurels. French units moved up to replace them so that the Americans could be rushed by truck one hundred kilometers west across the French countryside to the Meuse-Argonne region. The AEF's 82nd Division was relieved in place on 21 September by the 69th French Infantry Division.[19] As they departed, it was clear that the St. Mihiel Offensive had had the desired effect on the morale of the army. Corporal Alvin York wrote, "It was a great success. The feeling of the majority of the boys was one hundred per cent, for General Pershing. As a whole, the Army . . . believed in him, and would follow him anywhere."[20]

The downside to the St. Mihiel offensive was that many of the AEF's best divisions would not be available in the opening days of the Meuse-Argonne Offensive. This included the combat-proven

Brigadier General Frank Parker of the 1st Infantry Division in a captured German position on Montsec during the St. Mihiel Offensive. Parker commanded the 1st Infantry Brigade and later would command the 1st Infantry Division during the Meuse-Argonne Offensive. The dog belonged to a German officer who was killed during the battle for this position. His blood is on the wall next to the dog. (National Archives)

1st, 2nd, and 42nd Divisions. Due to this, several woefully unprepared American divisions would participate in the opening attacks of the Meuse-Argonne. Facing dogged German defense and daunting terrain, these inexperienced soldiers would relive Charles De Gaulle's experience of 1914.

6

Meuse-Argonne

Plan for Victory or Elusive Gambit?

The regiment waited for the impending attack. Gruesome
weeks [of fighting] lay ahead.
>   —125th Württemberg Landwehr Infantry Regiment

The sector assigned to the Americans for their initial attack on 26
September 1918 was bounded by the Meuse River on their right
flank (east) and the thick Argonne Forest on their left, hence the
name Meuse-Argonne Offensive. The Americans would strike the
bottom of the German bulge that projected into France, making a
south-to-north attack. The terrain here was difficult for any army
to fight across, especially an inexperienced one. The American right
flank rested on the Meuse River, which is roughly 46 meters wide
(150 feet) in this area. It also has a canal and a marshy seasonal
flood plain, posing a significant obstacle to military operations in
the autumn. More importantly, however, on the opposite side of the
Meuse River are imposing hills. These provided excellent observation and over watch of movement across the river. The center of the
American sector was a broad valley that sits between the Meuse
River and the Argonne Forest. This area encompasses soft rolling
hills generally cutting across the valley from west to east, an ideal
terrain for the defense. The Meuse Valley contains limited roads,
modest villages, and rich farmland.

The Argonne Forest along the American left flank remains an
imposing obstacle to this day. The forest includes steep gorges, sharp
gullies, numerous artesian wells, walls of trees, and abrupt hills. So
rugged is the area that it has withstood invading armies since the
days of Noah. Julius Caesar, the Normans, Napoleon, the Prussians,
and numerous others simply avoided fighting there, as it is simply

41

too difficult to navigate. Adding to the difficulty of fighting near the Argonne is the L'Aire River. Although only fifteen meters wide (fifty feet), it is an obstacle to movement. At times, there are two L'Aire Rivers, where the French constructed a canal to help traders navigate the narrow parts of this modest river. Such terrain makes the Argonne easily defensible should any army seek to fight there.[1]

The German Army occupied the region in 1914. Although the French contested German control of the Meuse-Argonne through-out the war, the heaviest fighting occurred in 1915 and 1916, resulting in the loss of a quarter-million men. This was a war of material, where the economic might and vast industries of nations were utilized to win battles. Artillery emerged as the "king of battle." To leverage its killing effect, occupying high ground was central to success and gave one a distinct advantage. From these vantage points, an army could dominate the surrounding area with well-directed artillery fires that weakened, cut off, or destroyed an adversary. The key terrain in the Meuse-Argonne region, unsurprisingly, was a series of dominant hills. For the Americans in 1918, the important high ground in the initial attack included Hill 285, Vauquois, and Montfaucon.

Although the Argonne Forest is a series of ridges and high ground, the most important for the war was Hill 285. Situated literally along the front line for four years, the French and German armies expended considerable blood and treasure to control the hill. The famed author of Sherlock Holmes, Sir Arthur Conan Doyle, visited the front here in 1916 and wrote:

> Trenches are trenches, and the main specialty of these in the Argonne is that they are nearer to the enemy. In fact there are places where they interlock, and where the advanced posts lie cheek by jowl with a good steel plate to cover both cheek and jowl. We were brought to a sap-head where the Germans were at the other side of a narrow forest road. Had I leaned forward with extended hand and a Boche done the same we could have touched. I looked across, but saw only a tangle of wire and sticks. Even whispering was not permitted in these forward posts.[2]

The summit of Hill 285 changed hands several times in 1915 and 1916. The belligerents endeavored to obliterate the enemy on the hill through massive artillery barrages that destroyed a swath of the Argonne Forest a kilometer wide. Having failed to achieve their end, the French and Germans began tunneling under each other, laying massive amounts of explosives beneath their adversary, and ripping chunks of earth from the hill. This resulted in hundreds of dead and created a series of craters on and near Hill 285 that in effect became a no-man's-land between the lines.

Just five kilometers (approximately three miles) east of Hill 285 was the village of Vauquois. Situated along the western half of the Meuse Valley, the area is slightly higher than Hill 285 and therefore of significant military value. From here, one can observe activity not only around Hill 285 in the Argonne Forest, but also east to the crucial high ground above Verdun. Today, on clear days, one can see the French tri-color flying near Douaumont and the Ossuary, sacred landmarks of the bloody Battle of Verdun. More importantly, however, the Germans could observe the French supply networks to the south and direct barrages against any formations moving to battle. The Germans seized Vauquois in their initial invasion of France in August 1914. Shortly after this, the French launched a series of catastrophic attacks to force the Germans off of the high ground. In the end, they only managed to secure the southern half of the hill. Endeavoring to break the stalemate, the French and Germans dug seventeen kilometers of tunnels into the hill, designed to be filled with explosives (called mines). During 1915–1917, more than five hundred mines were detonated under the hill, causing the village to forever disappear, being replaced by a line of massive craters that testify to the horrors of that war a century later.[3]

In the midst of the Meuse Valley, and several kilometers behind the front lines, is Montfaucon. Rising above the surrounding hills to 315 meters in elevation, Montfaucon was also vital to control, as it dominated everything in this area of the Meuse Valley. The hill and adjacent village has a rich history going back to the medieval age, with an attractive church donning the summit. However, the area was pulverized by French artillery during the war. The ruins of the church buttresses were turned into observation platforms by the Germans to direct artillery fires against the French on Dead Man's Hill (le Mort Homme) and Hill 304, five kilometers to the southeast. Both were key areas of terrain during the 1916 Battle of Verdun.

These hills, supported by the natural east-west ridges crossing the Meuse Valley, gave the German Army a highly defensible

Devastated hill of Vauquois. The hill was of military value due to the vantage point it provided to direct artillery fires into the enemy lines. The Germans and French fought costly battles for the hill, with neither side gaining an advantage. Subterranean mine warfare resulted in more than five hundred explosions that split the hill asunder. The line of craters became a no-man's land, with the French (and later American) lines on the southern portion of the hill and the Germans on the northern half. (U.S. Army Heritage and Education Center, Carlisle, Pennsylvania)

position for the upcoming American attack. Using the terrain to their advantage, the Germans established four lines from which to defend, creating sixteen kilometers (ten miles) of depth to stop any attack into the region.[4] The German Army preplanned artillery fires along checkpoints and road intersections that would stem any momentum should a breakthrough transpire. Additionally, German infantry units relied heavily on overlapping machine gun fires to make any attack across this defensible terrain costly, if not impossible. So effective was this defense in depth that it prevented the French Army (and its allies) from achieving any significant breakthrough between 1915 and 1918. There seemed little chance that an inexperienced American army would be able to achieve a decisive victory here. Although the terrain and German disposition seemed daunting, General Pershing was confident of success.

The German defensive network was shallow compared to the rest of the Western Front, but it provided a series of positions from which to delay and stop any penetration of the region. From the front line to the rear of the third German defensive belt was approximately fifteen kilometers (roughly nine miles). The first line included the thinly defended front area. The lessons of the war were to leave an area of about three to five kilometers of the zone nearest the enemy devoid of large troop concentrations. This area included observation points, concealed snipers, machine gunners, trenches, and the devastated area from the prolonged war. Behind this was the first defensive belt. In the Meuse-Argonne this was called the *Hagen Stellung* (position).[5] The Hagen Stellung included prepared positions, dugouts to protect soldiers, and fortified machine gun bunkers. Directed and rolling barrage artillery fires would be used in support of any German defense and counterattack. The utility of the first line was to absorb the initial attack of the enemy. As the attackers' formations advanced, their dispersion increased and their artillery support diminished.[6] At that point in the action, the front line defense would slow or stop the advance and launch local counterattacks.[7] This was the only defense line that included continuous networks of trenches, wire, obstacles, etc., having been constructed out of necessity during the war.[8]

If the front line failed to halt an enemy penetration, the second line, called *Giselher-Etzel*, just a few kilometers farther back, would be utilized. The Giselher-Etzel was a double position in the Meuse Valley offering defense in depth along the natural ridge lines in the area. There would be no withdrawal or retreat, but the German units used the land to fight, delay, and defeat any enemy attack, with the second line being utilized should the delaying action fail.[9] This line also had prepared machine gun positions, supporting artillery, and infantry strong points that utilized the natural geography to canalize and destroy enemy formations through artillery fires and infantry counterattacks.[10]

The third line and was the *Kriemhilde Stellung*, located roughly two kilometers behind the Giselher-Etzel. The Kriemhilde Stellung arguably was the strongest due to a series of fortified positions constructed along the hilly terrain.[11] As with the other lines, it included prepared positions, preplanned artillery fires, etc.[12] This was the last line ready for use, as the Freya Stellung was to be completed over the winter of 1919. These layered defenses ensured the safety and

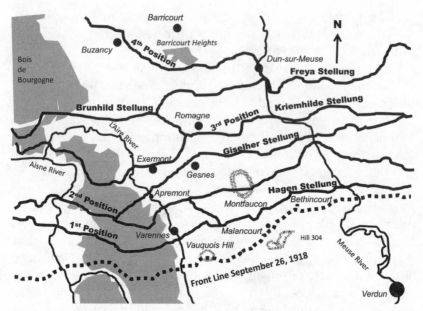

Map 6.1. German Defensive Lines in the Meuse-Argonne Region. (Josiah Mastriano)

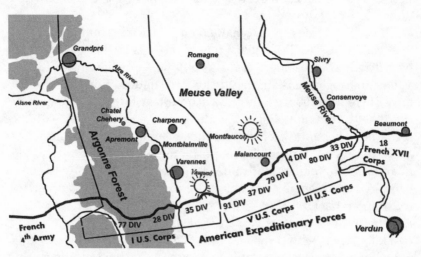

Map 6.2. Meuse-Argonne AEF Disposition, 25 September 1918. (Josiah Mastriano)

security of the vital German rail networks.[13] Of these German positions, General Pershing wrote, "The natural defenses were strengthened by every artificial means imaginable, such as fortified strong points, dugouts, successive lines of trenches and an unlimited number of concrete machine gun emplacements. A dense network of wire entanglements covered every position. With the advantage of commanding ground, the enemy was particularly well located to pour oblique and flanking artillery fire on any assailant attempting to advance within range between the Meuse and Argonne."[14]

As part of General Foch's four-prong broad front attack, the Meuse-Argonne was essential for success on the Western Front. The plan was to have Pershing's American Expeditionary Forces focus their main attack up the western half of the Meuse Valley on the eastern side of the Argonne, while the French Fourth Army advanced up the Aisne Valley to the west of the Argonne.[15] The objective for these two armies was the rail networks at Sedan-Mezieres.[16] If these were seized, the German Army to the west would be cut off from an essential supply network and thereby threatened with encirclement.[17]

Although Foch did not leave writing behind that elaborately explained his rationale with the four-pronged broad front attack that began with the Franco-Americans in the Meuse-Argonne region, his brilliance is evident. Applying the modern application of campaign analysis to his campaign design reveals what the war theorist Carl von Clausewitz called military genius. In his book, Clausewitz grapples with the ideas and strategy necessary to wage a successful war. One of the most important concepts coming from his writing is called the center of gravity: "Out of these characteristics a certain center of gravity develops, the hub of all power and movement on which everything depends. That is the point against which all our energies should be directed. Small things always depend on great ones, unimportant on important, accidentals on essentials. This must guide our approach."[18]

The German "hub and source of all power . . . on which everything depends" was its twenty-plus-division-strong strategic reserve. Over the previous four years, poor tactical adaptations by the Allies had played a role in their failure to achieve significant success on the Western Front. However, beyond this were the German reserve divisions deployed along the Western Front. Whenever the French or British achieved a breakthrough, these German divisions would rapidly deploy to the threatened sector to restore the line.

There were, in effect, two German "armies" serving on the Western Front in 1918. There were the front line divisions, whose job was to hold the line, delay, and fix the enemy during an attack. If the task proved more than the front line divisions could handle, divisions of the Western Front strategic reserve would arrive to restore the integrity of the line.[19] The key aspect of this reserve force was the rail network. The Germans constructed an elaborate and efficient line extending from Lille in the north of France down to Strasbourg in Alsace. This rail network enabled German reserve divisions to move rapidly anywhere along the Western Front within forty-eight to seventy-two hours.

The network, however, was also vulnerable.[20] There were only three rail lines from Germany supporting this force. One of the lines cut across Belgium from Cologne, another from Coblenz, and the third from Mainz. The Cologne line provided support from Germany to its forces in the northern and central part of the Western Front. The Coblenz and Mainz lines, however, converged east of Sedan, meaning that there was but one network supporting the southern part of the Western Front. It was imperative that both of these lines remain in German hands; otherwise it would be impossible for them to maintain and support their force in France and Belgium.[21]

The northern Cologne network was well behind the German lines. However, the Sedan line was dangerously close to the Franco-American attack. Because of this, the Meuse-Argonne sector had to be held at all costs, even if this meant deploying the preponderance of the strategic reserves into the sector to keep the Allies from threatening the vital rail hub.[22] The logic behind this analysis is that there were two things that the German strategic reserve divisions needed to be effective on the Western Front: (1) the frontline German divisions to hold or delay the enemy and (2) free movement across occupied France. The critical requirement for this was the extensive rail network.[23] This requirement was also vulnerable in the Sedan area north of the Meuse-Argonne. With this in mind, the Sedan-Mezieres rail lines can be viewed as a decisive point.[24]

A decisive point is "a geographic place, event, critical factor, or function that, when acted upon, allows a commander to gain a marked advantage over an adversary."[25] Attacking the German center of gravity, its strategic reserves, was not possible. However, Foch needed them unavailable to reinforce the German line in the north.[26]

With sufficient pressure by the AEF and the French Fourth Army in the Meuse-Argonne region, the German military chiefs, General Erich Ludendorff and Field Marshal Paul von Hindenburg, would be forced to commit most (or even all) of the strategic reserves to protect the vital rail network around Sedan.[27] Foch's object would be accomplished with either the seizure or threatening of this rail line once the strategic reserves were committed.[28] This delineates the importance of having the AEF attack first and rigorously create a crisis in the German line.[29] Pershing agreed with the effect that Foch intended by the employment of the AEF in the Meuse-Argonne, noting that his mission was "to draw the best German divisions to our own front and consume them."[30]

Pershing required two things to secure a decisive attack in the Meuse-Argonne: surprise and speed. As to surprise, the St. Mihiel operation worked to his benefit. The German Army expected the Americans to continue their attack toward Metz, not realizing until it was almost too late that the AEF rapidly moved to the Meuse-Argonne. With excellent French transport support, Pershing's soldiers poured into the region during the hours of darkness to prevent their detection. This, combined with an agreement to leave French units in the line, had the desired result of depriving the Germans of intelligence that the AEF had moved nearly one hundred kilometers northwest to the Meuse Valley.[31]

Speed or rapidity of advance when the attack kicked off would be difficult to achieve. The first limitation was the lack of roads. There were only three along the front line across no-man's-land.[32] It would take time to carve additional roads through the devastated areas of the front, which looked more like a moonscape than anything else in creation. The terrain, combined with the prepared German defensive networks, would also make a sustained advance difficult.

These considerations notwithstanding, Pershing's plan was to have the AEF deploy three corps composed of nine divisions (and three in reserve). This encompassed more than 600,000 Americans and 100,000 French troops, with 189 tanks (142 operated by the new U.S. Tank Corps and 46 manned by the French Army), 821 aircraft (604 manned by U.S. Airmen, 217 flown by French aviators), and 2,700 guns.[33] These forces would commence their attack on 26 September, with the objective of advancing sixteen kilometers (approximately ten miles), breaking through all three lines of the German defensive belts, and being poised to encircle the Argonne Forest.

The AEF and Fourth French Army would link up on the north end of the forest near Grandpré. The main attack would continue up the Meuse Valley, completing its reduction of the Kriemhilde Stellung and setting the conditions for a follow-on attack against the vital Sedan-Mezieres rail lines. That was Pershing's ambitious concept of operations, drafted in large part by army colonel George C. Marshall, who would be a household name in the next world war.

To make St. Mihiel successful, several of the most experienced American divisions would not be available for the crucial opening days of the Meuse-Argonne campaign. Pershing wrote of this dilemma: "some of our most experienced divisions, the 1st, 2d, 26th and 42nd were used at St. Mihiel. This prevented their transfer to the Meuse-Argonne in time to open the fight and compelled the employment of some divisions which had not entirely completed their period of training."[34] The sad fact was that most of the initial Americans forces to attack in the Meuse-Argonne were inexperienced, and in some cases woefully untrained. They would be no match for the German defenders, and thus an opportunity to breach the line here was lost.

The experienced divisions included the 4th, 28th, and 77th. However, both the 28th and 77th had suffered high casualties in recent fighting, with green troops filling the vacancies. The 77th recently had received four thousand green replacements.[35] However, at least these units had veteran leaders and soldiers in the ranks. The 28th and 77th were given the most daunting task: clearing the Germans from the Argonne Forest. Meanwhile, the 4th helped to secure the vital Montfaucon in the center of the line. The remaining divisions had no significant combat competence. The 33rd, 35th, and 80th Divisions had spent minimal time in the quiet sectors of the Western Front, while the 37th, 79th, and 91st Divisions had only recently arrived in France, with many of the men lacking adequate military training. For some this would be the first time they fired a rifle.[36]

The troubling aspect of Pershing's plan for the Meuse-Argonne Offensive is that he did not designate any of his three corps as the main effort. He sought a general breakthrough across the front. Yet Pershing's preoccupation would turn out to be the capture of Montfaucon. If its capture were essential to the success of the AEF, as Pershing would later indicate, he should have designated the V Corps as the main effort and thereby given it extra support and assets to accomplish this daunting task. Instead, some of the most

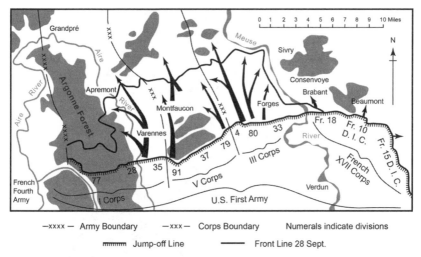

−xxxx − Army Boundary   −xxx − Corps Boundary   Numerals indicate divisions

ᴍᴍᴍᴍ Jump-off Line   ▬▬▬ Front Line 28 Sept.

Map 6.3. Plan for Day One. The Western Front, 26 September 1918. (Mastriano, *Alvin York*.)

inexperienced divisions would be assigned to this mission, encumbered by limitations of maneuver imposed by having the U.S. III Corps boundary just east of Montfaucon. These AEF-level decisions betray Pershing's inexperience in leading an army as well as the inexperience of his staff. Although President Wilson was lauded as a great communicator, great speeches are not a replacement for a realistic national strategy. Those paying the ultimate price for this lack of foresight would not be Wilson, or Pershing, but young American men from all walks of life.

Meanwhile, the Germans in the Meuse-Argonne region remained vigilant. Raiding parties and patrols were sent across the line in the Meuse-Argonne, only to find French units still facing them. Seemingly nothing had changed. The army group commander opposing the Americans in the central and eastern part of the Meuse Valley was General Max Karl Wilhelm von Gallwitz. Born in Breslau (now Wroclaw, Poland) to a devout Roman Catholic family in 1852, Gallwitz was a highly decorated and popular officer in the German Army, having served not only on the Western Front, but also in Russia and the Balkans. He received one of Germany's highest military awards, the Pour le Merite (Blue Max), in 1915 and was respected for his ability to lead and organize an army even in the most difficult of circumstances. After leading a successful defense against the

General Max Karl Wilhelm von Gallwitz, the German commander in the Meuse-Argonne region. Gallwitz, a proven and tenacious commander, was in charge of Army Group Gallwitz, which included the German Fifth Army and Army Detachment C. This included the areas from the Argonne Forest to St. Mihiel. (Mastriano Collection)

British and French at the Somme, General von Gallwitz became the commander of Army Group Gallwitz, which included the German Fifth Army and Army Detachment C. This ranged from east of the Argonne Forest to the other side of St. Mihiel.

Defending to the west of Gallwitz's Fifth Army in the Argonne were elements of the German Third Army. To ensure better command and control, the units in this area would soon be given to Gallwitz's command. There were thirteen German divisions opposite America's twelve. However, an average American division encompassed twenty-eight thousand men, twice the size of a fully manned German, French, or British division. Many of the German divisions in the Meuse-Argonne region had less than ten thousand men in the line, giving the AEF a marked advantage in size—something that the Americans would need to make up for their inexperience.

Giving Pershing another advantage was the fact that his main attack would be along the boundary of the German Third and Fifth Armies, which was near Vauquois. Boundaries between units are notoriously vulnerable, as it is difficult for commanders to coordinate and deconflict movement, maneuver, and artillery fires. This was not just the boundary between the Third and Fifth German Armies, but also the border for two different army groups. The crown prince commanded the army group that included the Third Army, while Gallwitz commanded the army group that included the Fifth Army.

Another bonus for Pershing was that the Fifth German Army received a new commander just before the attack. For several months, General Max von Gallwitz was leading both his army group and Fifth Army, a daunting task. On 22 September 1918, General of the Cavalry Georg von der Marwitz arrived, taking over the Fifth Army units deployed between Vauquois and the Meuse River. As the Fifth Army commander, Marwitz wanted his own hand-selected staff, and this resulted in gaps in reporting, missed intelligence, and delays in support and action. Although having Marwitz running the Fifth Army was good for Gallwitz, the timing could not have been worse. Changing leadership just thirty-six hours before the largest ever American attack in history caused the Germans added friction, indecision, and delay. The timing could not have been better for the AEF and the French. Despite the numerous tactical reports from across the line, Gallwitz wrote, "Up to the evening of the 24th, I did not receive any enlightenment from our supreme command."[37] Neither the Fifth Army nor the Imperial German Headquarters in Spa anticipated the Meuse-Argonne Offensive yet.

However, one of Gallwitz's liaison officers reported to him that the Third Army anticipated an enemy attack at dawn on 25 September near the Argonne Forest. Gallwitz thought that the main American attack would continue from St. Mihiel toward Metz and the Briey-Longwy Iron Basin, and that they merely had paused there to bring up the men, supplies, and support necessary for this. The German general speculated that the attack into the Meuse-Argonne was merely a feint designed to weaken the St. Mihiel front. However, to support the Third Army, Gallwitz shrewdly ordered his 5th Bavarian Reserve Division to move toward the center of the Meuse Valley and be prepared to stop any enemy attack. His 37th Division was also ordered forward.[38]

Hauptman (Captain) Drück of the 2nd Württemberg Landwehr Division inspects the main defensive line in the Argonne. By 1918, the Germans adopted a flexible defense that included a thinly manned front that was backed by a fortified main defense line. The trenches in the main defense line were constantly improved and meticulously maintained by the Germans, making any attack by the Americans in the Argonne a costly affair. (Mastriano Collection)

Defending the Argonne Forest was the German 2nd Württemberg Landwehr Division. Imperial Germany was ruled by the Prussian emperor. It comprised the Prussian-ruled states and the kingdoms of Saxony, Bavaria, and Württemberg, all of which had their own kings and armies, but which swore loyalty and fidelity to the Prussian emperor. These were the last vestiges of the Holy Roman Empire.

The Landwehr were comparable to American National Guard units. Manned and recruited from the southwestern kingdom of Württemberg, the 2nd Landwehr Division had three regiments in the Argonne. In the western half of the Argonne was the 122nd Württemberg Landwehr Regiment, in the center of the forest was the 120th Württemberg Landwehr Regiment, and along the eastern edge of the forest, the 125th Württemberg Landwehr Regiment.

These Württembergers had proved their worth in numerous battles over the previous four years and were considered by General von Gallwitz to be reliable and tough. They were the right soldiers to defend the forest. They had spent the greater part of the last four years here. Their postwar history described the Argonne Forest as their "second home." They knew the ravines, hills, slopes, and ridges well and would make the Americans pay dearly.[39]

The 120th Württemberg Landwehr Regiment had a rich history dating back 245 years, to 1673. One of its company commanders was *Oberleutnant* (First Lieutenant) Paul "Kuno" Vollmer. He had joined the 120th Regiment more than ten years previously and spent most of his time before the war in the quaint Württemberg city of Ulm, where he worked as the assistant postmaster.[40] Situated along the Danube River, and close to the Bavarian border, Ulm is surrounded by gentle hills and lush forests, perhaps adding to the appeal of the Argonne to the men in this unit.[41] However, before joining the Landwehr, Paul Vollmer moved to Chicago. There he worked on the railroads, grew to love American culture, and became very fluent in English. Although many of the officers learned English, Vollmer was rare in that he could speak it with an American accent. Vollmer spent the first two years of the war working in the 125th Regiment, after he was asked to temporarily transfer there to fill a critical shortage in that regiment. He agreed, serving as a supply officer, but he never lived down deploying the regiment to war in August 1914 without its field kitchen, a running joke with his men.[42] Vollmer was transferred back to the 120th Regiment in 1916 to serve as a company commander. He demonstrated extraordinary bravery in the war and was awarded the Iron Cross 2nd Class in 1914 and the Württemberg Knight's Cross 2nd Class in 1915. In 1918 he was awarded the Iron Cross 1st Class and the Queen Olga of Württemberg Medal. Vollmer's closest friend in the 120th Regiment was Leutnant Fritz Endriss. Fritz had a successful leather factory in Goppingen, an attractive city east of Stuttgart. They served in the army together for more than ten years. During the war, Endriss built a reputation of being fearless and reliable, much like the motto of his unit, "Furchtlos und Treu" (Fearless and True).[43]

The three regiments of the 2nd Landwehr Division were efficient units, having gained experience in several campaigns along the Western Front dating back to August 1914, when they defeated a strong French position near Eton (north of Verdun). One of the

Leutnant Paul Vollmer served in the Great War since 1914, achieving numerous awards for heroism and superior service. He would achieve the position of battalion commander in the 120th Württemberg Landwehr Regiment. (Collection of Dominique Lacorde)

commanders in the 125th Württemberg Regiment was Leutnant Paul Lipp. Lipp started off the war in 1914 as a noncommissioned officer, but after demonstrating superb leadership and being wounded in action he was promoted to leutnant. In civilian life he was a merchant in Stuttgart and a family man, with a wife and three young children. He looked forward to the war being over and returning to his family. Lipp, like Vollmer, spent the latter half of September trying to ascertain the composition of the enemy force south of them in the Argonne.[44] There were eerie noises of equipment, vehicles, and men moving in the evening, but no sign of the enemy in the day. Reports were sent up the chain of command about these strange noises to the division and army intelligence sections, but

Leutnant Paul Lipp of the 125th Württemberg Landwehr Division had served with Vollmer since the beginning of the war. Lipp was promoted from a sergeant to an officer after two years for demonstrating superb leadership, bravery, and tenacity in combat. (U.S. Army Heritage and Education Center, Carlisle, Pennsylvania)

the Württembergers and their 1st Prussian Guards counterparts in the valley to the east of the Argonne were told that there was nothing to fear.[45]

In early September, German intelligence reported correctly that the AEF was deployed east of Verdun. On 11 September 1918 the assessment was that the Württembergers were opposed by Italian units who were not preparing for an attack. Having Italians in the region was not unusual, as only a few years before the famed Garibaldi Legion fought there with great effect. After having received tactical reports that French, not Italian, was being spoken in the opposing trenches, the German intelligence section issued an assessment saying that the Italians were using French to deceive the Germans.[46]

After receiving various updates and reports, the next German assessment came out on 21 September. It said that the Württembergers were facing the French 86th Infantry Regiment, not Italians.

The report added, "No attack is expected." Meanwhile, 600,000 Americans were arriving in the Meuse-Argonne region. Finally, an "intrepid" German pilot managed to penetrate the French air screen over the Meuse-Argonne and flew over "mountains of supplies" and enemy troops being positioned for the impending attack. On 23 September, the German Third Army headquarters announced that it expected an attack by the Americans at any moment.[47] Meanwhile, as late as 24 September, General von Gallwitz had yet to receive intelligence from the Fifth Army headquarters about the impending attack, thanks in large part to the new commander's abrupt staff changes.[48]

Despite this, the Third Army and Army Group Gallwitz began taking precautions to ameliorate the effect of the impending Franco-American attack. The plan was to prevent any major penetrations and to make any American assault into the Argonne and Meuse Valley costly. General von Gallwitz ordered the 5th Bavarian Reserve Division to prepare to move forward into a position that could support the defensive line of the German 117th Division and 7th Reserve Division. The movement order was issued at 7:00 P.M. on 25 September, with the Bavarians moving forward to positions around Montfaucon.[49] The deployment of the 5th Bavarians was to ensure that this vital high ground remained in German hands and to prepare for a large counterattack to restore any penetrations of the line. This was not good news for the Americans, as the 5th Bavarians were an experienced and motivated division.[50]

The German 37th Division served as Gallwitz's reserve unit. He issued orders at 6:30 P.M. on 25 September that they make all preparations to be ready to move on a moment's notice.[51] The movement order was issued a few hours later to deploy north of Montfaucon, a position from which the division could counterattack any America penetration between the Argonne and Meuse River.[52]

The frontline German divisions would employ an elastic defense, allowing the Americans to make some gains and then force them back with the combined effects of artillery, devastating machine gun fires, and fierce counterattacks. The French and British had learned during the war that if you attack the Germans, they will counterattack. The Americans would learn the same lesson. As for the Württembergers, they had no intention of giving up the Argonne without a fight.

7

The Americans Attack!

> We are being attacked from all sides by large masses of the
> Americans. We will fight to the last man. Long live the king!
>   —2nd Prussian Guards (Foot) Regiment,
>   defending Vauquois

The Franco-American artillery barrage that kicked off the Meuse-Argonne campaign commenced late on 25 September with 2,775 guns (more than half manned by French crews). These fired on the frontline German defenses, ammunition depots, roads, barracks, headquarters, and artillery positions.[1] Thirty kilometers (nineteen miles) behind the lines, General von Gallwitz wrote, "During the course of the evening, artillery became so active along the front, that at my headquarters at Montmedy window panes began to rattle."[2]

American corporal Chester E. Baker, a printer from Huntington, Pennsylvania, was abruptly awakened when the artillery barrage commenced: "We were awakened about midnight to all hell breaking loose; our own artillery had commenced the battle without bothering to warn us. Some of the new recruits got the wind up temporarily but soon quieted down. I must confess, even us old vets of the Marne and Vesle campaigns were rattled by the suddenness of the assault."[3] Baker marveled at the artillery barrage when a German ammunition depot was hit, resulting in spectacular secondary explosions in the Argonne Forest. He was in the 28th Division, a Pennsylvania National Guard unit. He soon would face the battle of his life in the Argonne, fighting the German Württembergers defending the forest.

The long-range American and French artillery engaged targets deep behind the German lines from 11:30 P.M. to 2:30 A.M. This included the major roads, intersections, and choke points across the Meuse Valley. In the midst of this, the Allies fired tens of thousands of poisonous gas rounds into the German line, with a thick, deadly gas settling in the Meuse Valley just east of the Argonne Forest. After 2:30 A.M., a heavy barrage was fired against the Germans' main defensive line.[4] It was at its most intense between 3:00 A.M. and 6:00 A.M., preparing the way for the American infantry attack. A German eyewitness in the 120th Württemberg Regiment wrote of his experience of enduring the heaviest three hours of the barrage: "The battle was upon us, raging in the western part of the Argonne Forest. With ferocity it breaks upon us at 3:00 am. Coming from all directions the howling, suddenly above, suddenly below, it is like meeting your fate with death himself. The sky jerks around, while the soil shudders. The tumult penetrates your ears. . . . From 3:00 am to 6:00 am the explosions of hundreds of guns, mortars and howitzers are thrown into the ridges and valleys around us."[5]

The German 1st Guards Regiment, defending the part of the Meuse Valley nearest the Argonne, forward of Varennes, was devastated by the barrage. The poisonous gas was so thick that after 3:00 A.M. there was not a man without a gas mask on. The barrage tore through their barracks, field support facilities, the headquarters, and defensive positions. German eyewitnesses testified that there was a heavy artillery explosion every ten meters in their sector, killing many men.[6]

One of the American artillerymen firing into the German positions was a Missouri farmer and future president, Captain Harry S. Truman. Commanding a battery of artillery in the 35th Division, Truman's men fired 2,018 rounds in the opening hours of the Meuse-Argonne Offensive. Of this, Truman recounted, "I was as deaf as a post. It looked as though every gun in France was turned loose and the sky was red from one end to the other from the artillery flares."[7]

The infantry of the French Fourth Army, west of the Argonne, and the AEF began their advance at 5:30 A.M., while it was still dark. As the soldiers advanced, the artillery support shifted and turned into a creeping barrage, gradually hitting behind the German forward defense. The Allies had learned over the previous three years that infantry troops needed to follow the barrage closely. This would increase the chances of capturing the enemy's trenches before they had a chance to reoccupy them from the bombardment shelters.

At about the same time that the infantry advanced, the 821 French and American aircraft began their missions. The first targets were the large number of German sausage-shaped observation

Battery A of the 108th Field Artillery fires in support of the American attack. The crew of this gun is wearing gas masks, indicating that they are firing gas rounds into the German lines. (National Archives)

The celebrated French general Henri Gouraud led the French Fourth Army on the western border of the American Expeditionary Forces. Gouraud did a superb job advancing his army on the other side of the Argonne Forest. (U.S. Army Heritage and Education Center, Carlisle, Pennsylvania)

balloons flying above the Meuse Valley. One of the pilots assigned this task was Captain Eddie Rickenbacker, America's most celebrated ace. Rickenbacker was well known in the United States before the war for being a daredevil race car driver at the first Indianapolis 500 in 1911 and for setting a ground speed record that same year while, ironically, driving a German-built Blitzen Benz at 134 mph.[8] Rickenbacker captured the American imagination early in the war when he survived a dogfight with the famed Red Baron (Manfred von Richthofen) and then went on to shoot down four German observation balloons and twenty-two confirmed enemy aircraft. As Rickenbacker took to the air that early September morning, he marveled at the sights: "A terrific barrage of artillery fire was going on ahead of me. Through the darkness the whole western horizon was illumed with one mass of sudden flashes."[9]

As the barrage lifted, the Württembergers hurriedly crept out of their bomb shelters and underground hideouts to man the defensive positions. A mist settled on the Argonne and Meuse Valley, making it difficult to see the advancing enemy. The fog was so thick that several forward observation detachments of the 125th Württemberg did not see or hear the Americans advancing and were quickly overwhelmed and captured when the Pennsylvanians seemingly literally popped out of the mist upon them.[10]

Finally, at 7:20 A.M., Vollmer's 120th Württemberg had its first glimpse of the advancing Pennsylvanians of the 28th Division. German artillery fire was directed against the American columns then moving through the devastated portion of the Argonne. The forward units slowed the American advance with well-directed machine gun fire and artillery support. However, the Württembergers slowly pulled back to their main defensive line several kilometers rearward as part of the elastic defense plan. One of the Americans advancing here with the 28th Division was Corporal Baker, who commented, "We advanced rapidly through the shell-pocked terrain, dodging barbed wire barriers . . . before we came smack against more machine-gun and rifle fire." Baker's men had arrived at the main German defensive line in the Argonne, and hundreds of casualties would be paid by the end of the day to try and wrestle control of it from the German Württembergers.[11] The Germans marveled at the costly frontal assault that the Americans launched to try and break the line. Fighting entirely in the thick forest of the Argonne, the 77th Division only made paltry gains in its initial attack. Both the 77th

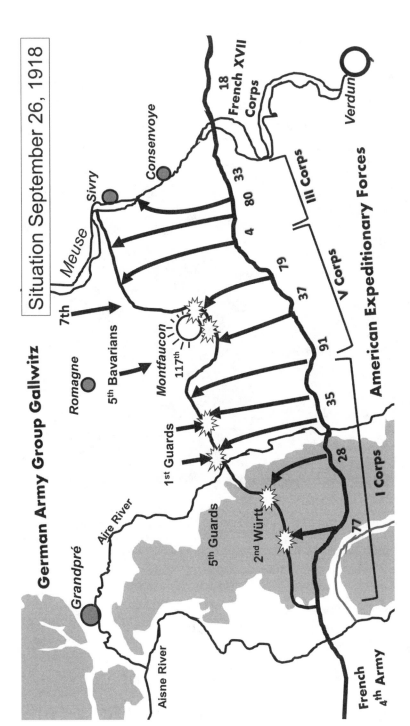

Map 7.1. Situation 26 September 1918. (Josiah Mastriano)

Soldiers of the U.S. 77th Division on the first day of the Meuse-Argonne Offensive take a break from their attack. Although only gaining a portion of its objective, the 77th Division did place considerable pressure on the German defenders of the Argonne. (U.S. Army Heritage and Education Center, Carlisle, Pennsylvania)

and 28th Divisions failed to break the German frontline defenses in the Argonne during the first day of fighting.

Meanwhile, observers from Leutnant Lipp's 125th Württemberg Regiment identified a column of Renault tanks advancing east of the Argonne, in the Meuse Valley, toward the German lines at Varennes and Vauquois. The terrain in the Argonne did not make it possible to use tanks against the Württembergers defending there,

Lieutenant Colonel George Smith Patton commanded a tank brigade during the first day of the Meuse-Argonne Offensive, until he was wounded. (U.S. Army Heritage and Education Center, Carlisle, Pennsylvania)

but the terrain in the Meuse Valley suited them well.[12] These tanks were from the 304th Tank Brigade under the command of Lieutenant Colonel George S. Patton.[13]

Although the 28th and 77th Divisions failed to achieve their objective in the Argonne, the crucial fight was in the Meuse Valley. Just east of the Argonne is the modest village of Varennes-en-Argonne, nicely situated on the edge of the Meuse Valley. Varennes has a rich history dating back hundreds of years, with the most important event occurring during the French Revolution. In 1791, French king Louis XVI and his wife, Marie Antoinette, managed to escape from Paris and attempted to reach a loyalist stronghold at Montmedy. During their brief stop near the Argonne the king was recognized. The royal family was detained in Varennes, just a few hundred yards from reaching a military escort sent out to rescue them (the detachment stopped in the north side of town, just across the bridge on the L'Aire River). The royal couple were returned

Varennes was largely destroyed by French artillery. The town has historic significance to the French Republic, as it was here in 1791 that King Louis XVI and his wife, Marie Antoinette, were captured after fleeing Paris. The Pennsylvanians of the 28th Division would liberate the town on 26 September 1918 after four years of German occupation. (U.S. Army Heritage and Education Center, Carlisle, Pennsylvania)

to Paris and executed, forever changing the course of history in Europe.

The task of liberating Varennes fell to the 28th Division (which was also fighting in the Argonne). The neighboring 35th Division would clear the eastern portion of the town up to the L'Aire River. Varennes was a vital point, as it was the hub for the four roads in the western Meuse Valley and thus controlled access to the Argonne and continued movement up the Meuse Valley. Additionally, it was a command and communication center for the German Army. Its trains used Varennes as a supply depot, and the station contained plentiful rolling stock and even small locomotives to move supplies. If Varennes were captured, it would unhinge the German defensive line in the Argonne and give the Americans momentum to continue their advance up the Meuse Valley.[14]

To ensure success, about thirty of Patton's tanks were sent in support. These were largely American-manned Renaults and several French-manned Schneider tanks. By the time the Americans reached the village around 10:00 A.M., the thick fog had burned off. It was then that the 125th Württemberg Regiment artillery observers saw the large formation of American infantry and tanks advancing toward the village. Varennes was defended by the famed Prussian 1st Guards Regiment. However, the Franco-American artillery barrage devastated its command and control, leaving only 130 German soldiers holding the line forward of Varennes.[15] Reinforcements were used to defend Varennes.

As the Americans approached the village, intense machine gun fires and German artillery fires smashed into their ranks. Adding to the chaos, many of the tanks broke down or were stuck in the marshy ground south of Varennes. However, the effects of the artillery barrage and the thick early morning fog made it impossible for the German machine gunners to hold back the masses of Americans. The forward line of the vaunted 1st Prussian Guards Division began to collapse south of Varennes. Requests for support went to the 125th Württemberg Regiment in the Argonne Forest. The 125th Regiment responded quickly. Holding the line against the U.S. 28th Division in the forest, the 125th positioned machine guns along the edge of the forest to pick off Americans and then directed artillery fire on the advancing enemy troops.[16]

During the advance, the 28th Division commander, Major General Charles H. Muir, moved forward with his men, directing troops against German strongholds delaying the advance.[17] The American attack continued with the support of Patton's tanks under heavy German fire. During the advance, the intensity and accuracy of the German artillery and machine guns increased. A Renault tank commanded by Lieutenant John Castle, of Morristown, New Jersey, and driven by Corporal Donald Call, a stage actor from New York City, was ordered to eliminate a 125th Württemberg Regiment machine gun nest that was tearing into the flank of the U.S. 28th Division. As Call's tank advanced, the Württembergers called for artillery. Suddenly, Call's tank was ripped open by a direct hit. Gasping for breath, Corporal Call fled the tank, finding refuge in a nearby crater. However, upon realizing that his lieutenant was still in the tank, Call ran back to the wreckage under heavy machine gun and artillery fire, freed the lieutenant, and carried him a mile back to the nearest aid station. For this act of heroism, Call was the first American "tanker" to receive the Medal of Honor.[18]

Still under heavy artillery and machine gun fires, the U.S. 28th Division continued to advance, breaking the left flank of the 1st Prussian Guards. The situation for the 1st Prussian Guards was quickly becoming a crisis. The fog masked the advance of the Americans. The 1st Prussian Guards Regiment commander, Eitel Friedrich Prinz von Preussen, was in the village of Varennes bracing for the attack.

Eitel Friedrich was the second son of Kaiser Wilhelm and had the honorific title of the prince of Prussia. He had commanded the 1st Prussian Guards in combat since 1914, fought on both the Western and Eastern Fronts, and had an excellent military record. His regiment was one of the best in the German Army. Of the attack, Eitel Friedrich wrote, "With the enemy appearing suddenly out of the fog caught us by a complete surprise. So rapidly did the enemy advance that by 7:00 A.M., they had surrounded and cut-off all of our forward machine gun nests. It looked like the Americans were already in our main defense positions and were about to overrun our positions." After suffering heavy losses and being overwhelmed by the Americans, the order was given for the Germans to withdraw to the second (Etzel) defensive line. A battalion (Battalion Wedel) of 120 men volunteered to delay the Americans as the rest of the regiment pulled back from Varennes, thus preventing the Pennsylvanians from continuing forward beyond Varennes that afternoon.[19] They used the ruined buildings in the town to delay the American advance.[20]

Battalion Wedel was armed with several machine guns, two 77mm field guns providing direct support to the infantry, and a detachment armed with the new German antitank rifle, the Mauser 1918 T-Gewehr. The M1918 T-Gewehr was a large-caliber rifle that fired armor-piercing rounds that could penetrate tanks.[21] Using the ruins of Varennes for cover and supported by the antitank rifles and two field guns, Battalion Wedel put up a robust defense against the American attack. Several tanks were disabled and the Pennsylvanians suffered high casualties. Wedel's men delayed them long enough for the other units to pull back to the Etzel Line, and thus maintained the "Guard Honor."[22]

The Americans of the 28th Division's 110th Regiment continued to advance, outflanking and overwhelming the German defenders.[23] Lieutenant Joseph Ferguson led his men of H Company in clearing the houses of Varennes, capturing more than one hundred Germans, mostly from Battalion Wedel.[24] The regiment continued its advance behind a large group of retreating Germans, and by early afternoon it secured the high ground north of Varennes, placing the unit more than two kilometers forward of its sister regiment (the 109th), which was stopped in the Argonne by the Württembergers.

Varennes was mostly in ruins, having been bombarded by French artillery earlier in the war. The recent barrage to support the Meuse-Argonne attack added to the destruction. Yet, the Pennsylvanians were amazed at the number of shelters and the accommodations that the Germans constructed into the northern slopes (safe from American artillery) around Varennes. These included paneled walls and electric lighting provided by generators. The officers' quarters had lunch laid out, and another dugout had a piano. The striking thing to the Pennsylvanians was that on the piano was American sheet music published during the war. The Americans were at a loss as to how the Germans acquired this. More importantly, there were crates of live hares, which were handed over to the division's supply section to supplement their rations. There was plenty of rabbit stew to go around that night.[25]

Meanwhile, just to the east of the Pennsylvanians, the battle for Butte de Vauquois was unfolding. The dominant hill along the western portion of the Meuse Valley was Vauquois. The inexperienced U.S. 35th Division was assigned the task of capturing this key terrain. The division had only limited training and time in the quiet sectors of the Western Front. It was imperative that they capture Vauquois by the first day of fighting; otherwise the American attack could stall in this portion of the Meuse Valley. As already described, Vauquois was heavily fought over during the war, resulting in the center of the hill literally being blown asunder by German and French subterranean mine warfare. Opposing the advance of the division was the Prussian 2nd Guards (Foot) Regiment.

The fierce artillery barrage and the thick fog assisted the American 35th Division in advancing up the slope and around Vauquois without being detected by the German defenders. The conditions also confused the advancing Americans, with units losing their bearing in the mist, and severely broke down command and control. As the fog began to burn off, nearby German observation balloons saw the U.S. soldiers and directed artillery fire onto Vauquois. Artillery exploded among the advancing Americans, who were trying to traverse the moonscape that comprised Vauquois. American

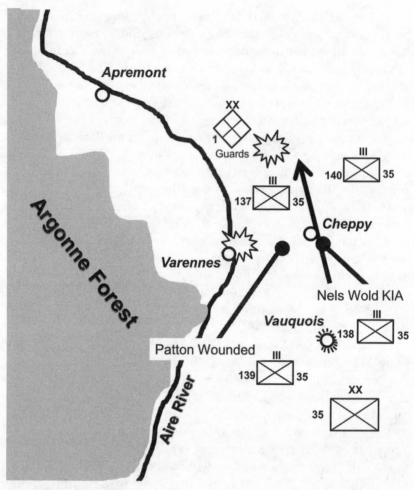

Map 7.2. Advance of U.S. 35th Division and Its Regiments, 26 September 1918. (Josiah Mastriano)

and French aircraft went to work providing close air support to the advancing infantry as well as attempting to shoot down the six massive German observation balloons deployed to the north.[26]

Sergeant William Triplet of the 35th Division described the scene as he reached the torn summit of Vauquois: "Our planes were buzzing all about . . . one fighter sailed in close over the crest, made a tight turn and exploded." At some point a German plane made it through the Americans' air screen to strafe the 35th near Vauquois. Sergeant Triplet said, "He came on a thirty degree slant from our left rear. The dirt was boiling and jumping through our platoon." A group of Americans crossed the cratered half of the hill carrying the American and French flags, to the amazement of everyone in the area.[27]

The Prussian 2nd Guards offered a robust defense of Vauquois, but there was little hope of holding, especially in the face of overwhelming numbers of American soldiers led by daring officers. Among these was Major James E. Rieger from Kirksville, Missouri. Rieger was the commander of the 35th Division's 2nd Battalion, 139th Regiment, and was assigned the daunting task of clearing the western slope of Vauquois. Rieger was the son of German immigrants and an attorney in his hometown. He was a National Guard officer and had participated in the military operations on the Mexican border in 1916. Rieger was a devoted Christian and a deacon in the First Baptist Church in Kirksville. He led his men from the front in a daring sweep across Vauquois, eliminating German resistance. His aggressive leadership threw the Prussian 2nd Guards Regiment off balance, inflicting heavy casualties on them that forced the survivors into the tunnels beneath the hill. Rieger's Distinguished Service Cross citation states, "On the morning of September 26, Major James E. Rieger with his battalion made the frontal attack on the heights of Vauquois, capturing this almost impregnable position in forty minutes."[28] This would be the first of three heroic actions that Rieger led over the next three days. Although the 35th Division was losing control of its units, there were thousands of soldiers swarming the hill. However, many of these American soldiers simply waited in trenches for someone to tell them what to do.

Meanwhile, Lieutenant Colonel George S. Patton sat in the 35th Division headquarters waiting for news from his men. Patton became impatient at the lack of news and decided to take matters into his own hands. Advancing on foot, Patton, two officers, and ten enlisted men followed fresh tank tracks into the Meuse Valley, endeavoring to find out what was holding up the advance. They followed a rough road past the western side of Vauquois that headed in a northern direction toward Varennes. However, after Vauquois, Patton's group headed northeast, toward the village of Cheppy (east of Varennes). Occasional artillery fire greeted the group, as well as ineffective machine gun fire.[29]

As they advanced toward Cheppy there were large groups of U.S. 35th Division soldiers retreating. Patton stopped them and asked why they were headed back. They said that they could not find their officers. Patton ordered them to join his small group and wait in a nearby railroad cut for orders. Patton's force soon grew to 150 men, drawing the attention of German artillery and machine guns. Growing impatient as he waited for his tanks to advance, Patton was told that they were blocked by a wide trench. With machine gun fire and artillery erupting nearby, Patton walked to the tank crews, handed them the shovels mounted on their vehicles, and ordered them to fill in the trench.[30] Patton and his aide, Private Angelo, also helped dig free several tanks stuck in the mud.[31]

After a few minutes the five tanks crossed the trench and slowly resumed their advance toward Cheppy. Patton yelled to the 150 soldiers from the 35th Division, "Let's go get them! Who is with me?" Patton waved a walking stick in the air, and the men rallied and followed him up a slope. After about seventy-five yards they passed the crest of the hill that had afforded them some shelter and were immediately engaged by an onslaught of machine gun fire. Patton later wrote, "I felt a great desire to run, I was trembling with fear when suddenly I remembered my progenitors. . . . I became calm [and said] 'It is time for another Patton to die.'" With that, Patton got to his feet and shouted, "Let's go, let's go," and continued to advance against the Germans. Of the 150 men, only six followed. Five of the group were gunned down, leaving only Patton and his orderly, Private First Class Joseph T. Angelo, walking slowly toward the enemy. Before long, Patton also was thrown to the ground as a German bullet slammed into his upper left thigh, passing through his body and exiting just inches from his scrotum. Private Angelo dragged him to a shell hole.[32] Patton directed Angelo to guide the advancing tanks into position. Under heavy fire, Angelo made several trips across the battleground and back to Patton's shell hole over the next two hours.[33]

As the tanks slowly arrived, Patton refused to be evacuated and instead directed their fire against the German machine gun nests from the vantage point of the shell hole. The tanks eliminated the enemy opposition from the area, enabling the 35th to resume its advance to liberate the village of Cheppy. With Cheppy secured, Patton agreed to be moved from the field of battle. He was carried to a hospital and remained out of action for the next four weeks to recover from his wound. His contribution to the Meuse-Argonne campaign had come to an end. Patton was interviewed after the war about this incident, and of Joseph T. Angelo he said, "without doubt the bravest man in the American Army. I have never seen his equal."[34] For his heroism, Private Angelo was awarded the Distinguished Service Cross.

As Patton engaged the Prussian Guards on the western side of Cheppy, a group of soldiers from the 35th Division advanced to dislodge the Germans from the southeast. The thick morning fog continued to have a debilitating effect on the command and control of the division's soldiers. The chaos and disorder grew particularly after the division swept across and around Vauquois. However, the regimental scout officer for the 35th's 137th Regiment, Lieutenant John Wingate, continued to advance forward of the division trying to locate enemy positions. As the fog burned off, he crossed paths with a platoon of soldiers led by Sergeant Joe Britton and another led by Sergeant Eckhardt north of Vauquois. Lieutenant Wingate took command of this group of some sixty soldiers.[35]

Lieutenant John Wingate, like many of the men in the 35th, was new to the army. However, he was not how many view lieutenants, as he was fifty years old and was remembered for his "long drooping mustache and a sort of swaggering, undaunted air."[36] Lieutenant Wingate was well liked, known as "the best loved man in the division." This affection for Wingate was due to his Christian faith. He had confidence that was not encumbered with arrogance or superiority. It was a belief and trust in God's plan and protection for his life. Lieutenant Wingate lived out his Christian faith with humanity "and a gentle kindly heart of pure gold." His leadership style was, ironically, the complete opposite to how Patton led his men, but was reminiscent of another great American. During the Civil War, Joshua Lawrence Chamberlain of Maine led a daring bayonet charge at Little Round Top during the Battle of Gettysburg. In 1864, a year after the Battle of Gettysburg, General Horatio Sickel gave Chamberlain perhaps the best compliment a leader can receive. Contemplating Chamberlain's Christian kindness and love for his men, while remembering his unsurpassed courage, Sickel told him that he had the "soul of a lion and the heart of the woman."[37] In an army full of inexperienced men, and some glory seekers, Wingate stood out as a point of light and someone that soldiers respected and trusted, even with their lives. Those who knew him best saw him as a leader that a soldier could follow, even against the gates of hell.[38]

Lieutenant Wingate guided his group of sixty soldiers toward the eastern side of Cheppy. As they advanced, a German machine gun opened fire from the underbrush of a copse of trees. Wingate led his men in a charge against the Germans, killing the crew and capturing the gun. They continued to advance and cleared several German dugouts and machine guns. As Wingate's men approached Cheppy, a German position that was impossible to charge without great loss of life opened fire on the men. One of the men, Private Nels Wold, volunteered to take out the German machine gun. Wingate gave the okay, and Nels Wold disappeared into the thicket, killed two of the German machine gunners, and captured three.[39]

The son of Norwegian immigrants, Nels was a farmer from Minnewaukan, North Dakota. Like Lieutenant John Wingate, he too was a Christian, whose faith and personal character was appealing to the soldiers he served with.[40] Although refusing to join in the excessive drinking of French wine and not flirting with the mademoiselles during his time off made him seem a bit uncommon, the other soldiers respected Nels for living out his faith and beliefs. It was such strength of character that made Nels a man of courage. Courage and bravery are not attributes that suddenly spring forth from the soul of a man, but are outward manifestations of the type of person he is on the inside. Nels developed his moral character by endeavoring to do the right thing in life, by choosing the right over the expedient. This, in effect, gave him "the soul of a lion," as it took moral courage to maintain his Christian faith in the face of countless temptations and opportunities to compromise.

After Nels cleared the German machine gun nest near Cheppy, Lieutenant Wingate led the men further into the enemy lines. As the Americans advanced, another German machine gun opened fire on the men. Private Nels Wold again volunteered to attack the enemy position. Again he succeeded, killing or capturing its occupants. Lieutenant Wingate and the other men were amazed by the selfless determination of this North Dakota farmer. Nels volunteered over and over to risk his life in attacking enemy machine gun positions holding up the advance of Wingate's men. On four different occasions during that late morning of 26 September 1918 Private Wold demonstrated uncommon valor by single-handedly attacking German machine guns holding up the advance of his unit.[41]

As Wingate's group faced yet another German machine gun position on the outskirts of Cheppy, again Private Nels Wold requested and received permission to attack. As Nels ran across the road to outflank the Germans, he was delayed by a camouflage net that he had to cut to get through. This delay was all that the enemy needed. They opened fire, fatally wounding the heroic soldier. Lieutenant Wingate ordered his men to stealthily advance, and once close enough to engage the enemy they charged, killing all of the Germans in the position. Lieutenant Wingate ordered Private Chris Antonson and Corporal Julius Vonderlieth to carry Nels Wold to the rear for medical treatment. Knowing that his death was quickly approaching, Nels asked Antonson and Vonderlieth to "pray for me boys and write my folks and tell them I love them all."[42] Corporal Vonderlieth wrote a thoughtful letter to Nels's mother, saying:

> My dear Mrs. Wold, I am sure the death of your dear son Nels was a shock to you all. I am sure you must feel very badly. However, you are not alone for all his pals in the Army miss him and feel the loss of a friend and true comrade. I was with Nels when he died and his last words were of you and his loved ones. He requested that I write you and say that he truly loved you all and was ready to go. While we all miss him, we must not grieve, for he died for a noble cause. It was the Lord's will that he be taken out of this world of sorrow into the heavenly realms above. In this hour of your sorrow I send you my sympathy and a wish that your future days may be bright and happy ones. Very sincerely J. E. Vonderlieth[43]

Thanks to Private Wold, Cheppy was taken. The liberation of Cheppy came at a high price, but this advance, led by Lieutenant Wingate and made possible by the selfless service of Nels Wold, weakened the German position in front of the U.S. 35th Division. Private Wold would be posthumously awarded the Medal of Honor for his action, with the citation reading:

> He rendered most gallant service in aiding the advance of his company, which had been held up by machine gun nests, advancing, with 1 other soldier, and silencing the guns, bringing with him, upon his return, 11 prisoners. Later the same day he jumped from a trench and rescued a comrade who was about to be shot by a German officer, killing the officer during the exploit. His actions were entirely voluntary,

and it was while attempting to rush a 5th machine gun nest that he was killed. The advance of his company was mainly due to his great courage and devotion to duty.[44]

With Cheppy and Varennes in American hands, the 2nd Prussian Guards Regiment was surrounded. The survivors planned on holding out and fighting from the many subterranean tunnels (twelve kilometers exist on the German side of the hill alone). Their last message, before their communications line was cut: "We are being attacked from all sides by large masses of the Americans. We will fight to the last man. Long live the king!"[45]

The Prussian 5th Guards was the reserve force providing support to the German defenders on the eastern portion of the Argonne Forest, deployed north of Varennes near the village of Apremont. The soldiers received the battle reports from the Prussian 1st Guards and the Württembergers in the Argonne of the masses of infantry and columns of tanks moving up the valley and prepared for a counterattack to drive the Americans back. However, when the Prussian 5th Guards Division was ready to attack (around 11:00 A.M.), the Americans had already captured Vauquois, were in Varennes, and were advancing north toward Charpentry. The decision was made to man their defensive positions, to bring up the artillery to provide support to the forward German units, and to prepare for a major battle with the Americans.[46] This was a major setback for the German forces in the western part of the Meuse Valley and exposed the flank of Gallwitz's forces to being encircled.[47]

Although the Americans had failed to drive the Germans from their main defensive line in the Argonne, the key ground of Vauquois was firmly in American hands. This was an important accomplishment and something not achieved over the previous four years of war, though the cost of this was that the 35th U.S. Infantry Division was in considerable disarray. Had the Germans launched a concerted counterattack here, the tables could have been turned on the Americans and unhinged their advance. The 35th had the 28th Division to thank, as the latter's success in rapidly securing Varennes forced the Germans to pull back from Vauquois and Cheppy. The American I Corps commander, General Hunter Liggett, remarked, "The war was a succession of lost opportunities on both sides."[48] Meanwhile, the U.S. 91st Division, on the right of the collapsing 35th Division, gained considerable ground in its sector. However, the 91st slowed its advance due to the lack of adequate progress that the 35th was making. The next important piece of terrain that had to be liberated was in the center of the Meuse Valley, Montfaucon (Falcon Hill).

Situated in the center of the Meuse Valley, Montfaucon dominated the entire American line. Three divisions were committed to reducing the German defenses on and around the hill. Assigned the sector west of Montfaucon was the 37th Division, and the sector to the right of the hill was the 4th Division. The 79th Division had the onerous burden of assaulting and taking the hill from the front. Montfaucon was three kilometers (two miles) behind the German line. Before the Americans could begin their advance against Montfaucon they had to clear a series of ridges and high ground in their immediate front. This included Dead Man's Hill and Hill 304, which had been the epicenter of unimaginable death and destruction in 1916 during the Battle of Verdun. So much artillery had crashed into Hill 304 that it was now seven meters lower in elevation than it had been before the war. The area that the three American divisions had to traverse and capture was a literal no-man's-land, littered with the shattered accoutrements of war, tangled heaps of barbed wire, and a complex maze of trenches in various stages of disrepair. It was a man-made wasteland of craters and devastation difficult to move across even while not under fire. The tens of thousands of craters—created by millions of artillery explosions—made it impossible to advance in any order. Making matters worse was that the shell holes were filled with mud and water that at times became deathtraps for men heavily burdened with equipment. Finally, the Germans retained the high ground and took advantage of the devastation to canalize any American movement into kill zones covered by machine guns and artillery.[49]

Adding to the challenge was that the 37th and 79th Divisions were green units. Both had barely two months of training as a division and were ill-prepared for the realities of modern warfare. Of all the AEF divisions leading the attack, the 79th was the least experienced, but it was given one of the most difficult missions. Although the 4th Division to the right of the sector was a combat-experienced unit with veteran leaders, it was part of a different corps. The 37th and 79th were part of the American V Corps, while the 4th was part of the III Corps. Dividing the advance against Montfaucon between two corps was a colossal error by Pershing's staff, as this meant that coordination of fires, movement, and maneuver would be greatly hampered between the 4th Division and the 79th, resulting in more lost opportunities. Despite this, Pershing expected the 79th to capture Montfaucon on the first day of the Meuse-Argonne Offensive and advance several kilometers past it to the village of Nantillois. The French Army commander, General Pétain, told Pershing that he would not be able to capture Montfaucon before winter. Pershing disagreed and decided to assign this difficult task to his least ready division in the line.[50]

The German 117th Division defended Montfaucon, having deployed there on 12 September to recover from heavy losses suffered near the Somme. The unit was augmented by other units; in all, 6,665 men were defending Montfaucon.[51] Although significantly outnumbered by the U.S. 79th Division facing them, the hardened and overlapping defensive positions made the region a veritable fortress. Making matters worse, the AEF intelligence staff had a propensity to discount the enemy's strength and capabilities. For instance, they reported that the Württemberg division in the Argonne was mostly composed of old men and convalescing soldiers and therefore of limited capacity. It was these same old and lame men that blunted the 77th and 28th Divisions' advance in the Argonne, holding more firmly than their highly vaunted Prussian Guards counterparts in the Meuse Valley. In a similar poor assessment, the intelligence staff reported that the 117th Division was weak and unable to man the line around Montfaucon. The intelligence staff was unaware that the 117th was augmented by several units, bringing up its strength.[52]

Like the other units of the AEF in the line, the 37th, 79th, and 4th Divisions "went over the top" at 5:30 A.M. As the 79th attacked, it was supported by a flame and gas regiment that laid down a smokescreen to cover the advance. This, combined with the thick natural fog and the crater- and trench-filled terrain, broke up the cohesion of the division.[53] However, due to the limited visibility the division faced only ineffective German artillery and machine gun fire as it crossed no-man's-land into the enemy trench network. As the 79th Division approached its first objective, the forest around the destroyed village of Malancourt, enemy defense stiffened. Many of the American officers were killed or wounded as they advanced through the woods and up a two-kilometer (1.5-mile) open slope leading up Montfaucon.[54]

After the morning fog had burned off and as the division attempted to advance up the long slope, it was greeted by a wall of artillery and merciless machine gun fire from several directions.[55] The 79th stalled and fell back into the woods to reorganize and to eliminate pockets of German resistance it unknowingly bypassed in the thick fog. At 4:00 P.M. a column of French-manned tanks arrived to support another attack up the slope. The division nearly reached the outskirts of Montfaucon village, but the advance was stopped well short of its objective due to heavy casualties and darkness. The lead elements that reached Montfaucon were called back down the slope.[56] German snipers had picked off the unit's runners throughout the day, adding confusion and a further breakdown of command and control. Among those to fall were runners from the corps headquarters ordering another assault.[57]

Meanwhile, the 37th made good progress against the enemy on the 79th's left flank. More importantly, however, the experienced U.S. 4th Division had a particularly impressive advance, to a position where it could bypass and cut off Montfaucon. The unit swept forward, clearing the Germans from the village of Nantillois. They were in an excellent position to outflank the German defenders from Montfaucon and thereby aid the 79th Division in achieving its objective. Yet, Lieutenant General Robert Lee Bullard's III Corps failed to act, and this opportunity slipped away due to concerns about crossing into another corps' boundaries. Crossing the corps boundary would take coordination and time to ensure that the III Corps men would not be bombarded and killed by the 79th Division's artillery. Had the 4th exploited this opportunity, it would have forced the Germans off of Montfaucon by the end of 26 September and saved thousands of lives.[58]

The two American divisions nearest the Meuse River, the 80th and 33rd, performed superbly in their initial push. This was made possible by the excellent use of terrain and the incredible heroism of several of the soldiers. The line was defended by the German 7th Reserve Division. Composed of soldiers from Prussian Saxony, the division had fought at the Battle of Verdun, the Somme, and in the 1918 German Spring Offensives.[59] It arrived in the Meuse Valley nine days before the attack and was given a relatively long line to defend.[60]

Like along the rest of the line, the attack was preceded by a devastating artillery preparation, with the infantry "going over the top"

The rapidity of the U.S. 4th Infantry Division's advance enabled it to capture these German officers near the village of Cuisy on 26 September 1918. (National Archives)

at 5:30 A.M. The heavy fog gave the soldiers of the U.S. 80th and 33rd Divisions a tactical advantage by concealing their movements from the enemy. Unlike their counterparts in the 35th and 79th Divisions, these two units managed—thanks to more experience—to maintain at least some of their command and control despite moving in the dense fog. The U.S. 33rd Division was commanded by Major General George Bell Jr. The son of a career army officer, Bell was born at Fort McHenry, the home of the Star Spangled Banner, in 1859. He went on to participate in the Spanish-American War, the Philippines, and the 1916 intervention with Mexico. General Bell was given command of the 33rd Division in 1917. It was an Illinois National Guard division. Bell quickly earned the respect of the men and of General Pershing, who praised the division, saying that it was "one of the most competent, one of the best appearing and one of the best disciplined divisions in the A. E. F." Indeed, it had the lowest cases of courts martial and one of the highest for valor, and rightly earned Pershing's respect.[61]

General Bell used turning movements, in lieu of frontal attacks, to maneuver around the German positions in the thick forest on the high ground in the center of the division's sector. The plan was to hit the enemy line from the west and outflank the German positions in a wheeling movement all the way down to the Meuse River. As the division advanced behind the rolling barrage, it wheeled into the western portion of Bois de Forges, a thickly wooded area slightly northwest of Forges sur Meuse. The German 7th Reserve Division had fortified this forest with bunkers and machine gun firing positions as well as trenches to restrict access to the area. The terrain was just as difficult as the rest of the Meuse Valley, perhaps a bit more challenging due to the limitations posed by the Meuse River and a series of marshy streams that bisected the sector. Impressive effort and preparations were made by the Americans to employ their engineers to construct crossings over both the natural and man-made obstacles that could impede progress.[62]

The U.S. 33rd Division's 131st and 132nd Infantry Regiments advanced across the marshy Forges Brook, with its engineers quickly building nine crossing points to support follow-on movements. The men continued their advance behind the American artillery barrage up the thickly wooded ridge of Bois du Forges, where they encountered heavy German machine gun and artillery fires. Yet, thanks to the unit's quick movement, and the effect of the fog, the 33rd advanced with impressive speed. The U.S. 80th Division, on the 33rd's left, however, failed to keep up, causing concern that the Illinois men had an exposed flank. Despite this, the division continued to advance, taking some precautions to safeguard its vulnerable left.[63]

It was the rapidity of the advance and the cover of the fog that gave the 33rd the advantage. As the lead elements of the division advanced into the Bois du Forges, they were adjacent to or behind the German lines. This had the effect of multiplying the results by overwhelming the defenders with surprise, adaptation, and audacity. As the division advanced, quick-thinking junior officers ordered a change to the attack. Instead of trying to sweep the Germans from the Bois du Forges in a line of attack (similar to tactics of Napoleon and Grant), small groups were formed to infiltrate the forest. This quick adaptation was suggested by the French liaison officers working with the unit.[64]

As the 33rd's small combat groups entered the Bois du Forges, they were able to overwhelm the defenders by having troops armed with grenades and mortars suppress the Germans while the infantry picked off snipers hiding in the brush and trees.[65] For this tactic to work, the unit needed innovative leaders and soldiers willing to exercise independent initiative. Developing soldiers capable of executing individual initiative proved decisive and was later called *Auftragstaktik* by the Germans, and Mission Command by the modern U.S. Army. Mission Command is defined as "the exercise of authority and direction by the commander using mission orders to enable disciplined initiative within the commander's intent to empower agile and adaptive leaders in the conduct of unified land operations."[66] Although the idea was alien to the AEF in 1918, the example of the 33rd Division slowly changed how the U.S. Army would fight over the next one hundred years.

This ability to adapt and use individual initiative to accomplish the mission was aptly demonstrated in many instances by the 33rd Division. The commander of Company E, 132nd Infantry Regiment, Captain George H. Mallon, and First Sergeant Sydney G. Gumpertz made an unusual but dynamic duo. Captain Mallon, an Irish Catholic street brawler, and First Sergeant Gumpertz, a Jewish descendant of California Gold Rush prospectors, had met the year before in Camp Logan, Texas, where their unit was assembled. They made an extraordinary leadership team, inspiring their ethnically diverse mix of soldiers from Illinois and Iowa. These two men would personify the future army ideals of Mission Command.

Following closely on the heels of the rolling barrage on the morning of 26 September, E Company crossed the marshy and waist-deep Ruisseau de Forges (the small stream in the middle of the valley). The regimental chaplain, Father John L. O'Donnell, carrying a Colt M1911 pistol in each hand, joined the attack. As the men advanced up the hill to attack the German positions in the Bois du Forges, many soldiers became disoriented or lost in the fog. Captain Mellon and First Sergeant Gumpertz were separated, but both knew what had to be done.

With just nine soldiers, Captain Mallon pressed forward, where he ran into several dug-in German machine gun positions. Captain Mallon skillfully led his men in reducing, capturing, or eliminating nine different enemy machine guns and an antiaircraft gun. The ten men continued forward until they reached a clearing in the woods where four German 150mm howitzers were in action firing against distant American soldiers. Captain Mallon led his men in a

Captain George H. Mallon *(left)* and First Sergeant Sydney G. Gumpertz *(right)* of Company E, 132 Infantry Regiment, made an unusual but dynamic duo. Captain Mallon, a devout Irish Catholic and street brawler, and First Sergeant Gumpertz, the Jewish descendant of California Gold Rush prospectors, were unstoppable on the battlefield. Both would be awarded the Medal of Honor for their fearless leadership during the Meuse-Argonne Offensive. (National Archives)

charge against the surprised German artillerymen. As he attacked, Mallon's sidearm ran out of bullets. Undeterred, he used his fists to debilitate one of the German soldiers. Such audacity resulted in the capture of the German howitzers and the crews. After the position was secured, Captain Mallon continued to lead his men to their objective, where they were stopped by two more German machine guns. Mallon ordered four of the men to flank the Germans from one side and the other five men to move against the opposite flank, while he would charge them head-on to draw fire. When the enemy gunners instead focused on the two groups moving against their flanks, Captain Mallon captured the German machine guns. By the end of the day he and his men had captured four 155mm howitzers, eleven machine guns, one antiaircraft gun, and one hundred German prisoners.[67]

Meanwhile, First Sergeant Gumpertz took charge of about

fifty men from E Company's 4th Platoon. They moved up the slope toward Bois de Forges and came under enemy rifle fire. One of the first men in Gumpertz's group to be hit was Corporal Joseph Prazak. The corporal had wanted to have plenty of ammunition for the fight, so in addition to his belt of one hundred rounds he carried two bandoliers of extra ammo, crisscrossed over his chest like one of Pancho Villa's bandits from the Mexico intervention of 1916. Additionally, Prazak tied a row of hand grenades to his belt. When the German gunners shot at Prazak, the enemy's bullets struck his ammunition belt, igniting several of the rounds, which began popping off. Fearing that this would set off the grenades on his waist, Prazak performed amazing "acrobatic" skills to free himself of his grenades and ammunition belt, much to the laughter of the other soldiers.[68]

After Prazak's antics, Gumpertz's group came upon a German trench that seemed empty. However, just to be sure, the stalwart first sergeant threw a smoke grenade into a dugout. Fifty Germans scrambled out "sneezing and coughing." The prisoners were sent to the rear, and the advance continued into the forest. Suddenly the front came alive with machine gun fire. Gumpertz asked for two volunteers. One volunteer was an American Doughboy of French-Canadian extraction, Corporal Paul Siclar. The other was an Italian immigrant, Private Sebastian Emma. The three blindly charged into the woods toward the flashes of the machine gun and a parapet. They killed the machine gun crew and captured fourteen others. After a brief pause, Gumpertz's platoon of fifty men continued forward, only to again be stopped by another German machine gun. This enemy position seemed better defended and had supporting artillery fire exploding in front of it, slowly creeping toward the Americans.[69]

Calling for volunteers resulted in Siclar and Emma both coming forward again. The three charged in "artillery formation" (single file with five yards between men). A shell burst in the midst of them, throwing Gumpertz and killing Siclar and Emma. Through a brief break in the fog Gumpertz saw the enemy machine gun. He threw a grenade and then charged it alone, with enemy bullets piercing his tunic. The grenade exploded just before he reached the enemy position, temporarily stunning some of the German gunners. Gumpertz stood over the enemy position and killed two soldiers who threatened to fire their weapons at him. The remaining sixteen surrendered; there were two machine guns in that position.[70]

Gumpertz and his men resumed the advance, running into yet another machine gun. This one was in a concrete bunker. With no regard to his safety, the daring first sergeant worked his way to the flank of the enemy position and threw a grenade into the narrow firing slot, killing all of the bunker's occupants. The advance continued, and soon a forest sniper opened fire. He was quickly dispatched, and the platoon advanced through an artillery barrage and then into a German encampment full of cooks and kitchen hands making lunch for their unit. Upon seeing the Americans, the German soldiers surrendered. Gumpertz sampled the soup and secured a box of cigars. After lighting one of the cigars, Gumpertz ordered his men to continue forward, where they spotted a battery of German artillery already captured by Captain Mallon. Mallon was standing over the German commander, who was trying to recover from the blow to the face that Mallon had landed on him just moments before. "Captain Mallon, in capturing the battery . . . had used his own unusual and peculiar method. He had swung his right and captured the battery with his fist." Captain Mallon and First Sergeant Gumpertz were delighted to see each other, and both would be awarded the Medal of Honor.[71] Gumpertz would be one of only five Jewish Medal of Honor recipients in the AEF during World War One.[72]

The advance of the 33rd Division was one of the most impressive for the Americans. The actions of Mallon and Gumpertz, combined with the incredible feats of many others, made the difference. This, combined with experienced and competent leadership, resulted in impressive results. For instance, the 132nd Regiment reached its objective by 10:00 A.M. and advanced well beyond it. In so doing, they unhinged the German position, resulting in the capture of eight hundred prisoners, four 150mm howitzers, ten 77mm field artillery pieces, ten trench mortars, two antitank guns, eight railroad cars, and massive quantities of ammunition, stores, and supplies.[73] This was postgraduate-level fighting. As demonstrated by the green 35th and 79th Divisions, the war was merciless to inexperienced troops. But the 33rd, with skillful planning and experienced leaders, used the weather and terrain to its advantage.

Across the Meuse River from the U.S. 33rd Division was the French XVII Corps, which also conducted an artillery preparation and advance to support the AEF. Facing the French in this sector was the 1st Austro-Hungarian Division, the 15th German Division, 33rd

German Division, and the 27th Württemberg Division. The French attack here was not designed to be a major push but rather a supporting attack. As a supporting attack, it began with a heavy artillery barrage followed by a major infantry and tank attack designed to both deceive the Germans regarding the location of the main attack and support the right flank of the AEF. This would prevent the Germans from focusing their counterattacks against the Americans and would also keep the enemy off balance.

The fighting here was across the land devastated by the nine-month Battle of Verdun, the longest engagement of the First World War. Lasting most of 1916, the battle had consumed an unbelievable amount of blood, resources, and treasure from Germany and France. By the end of the fighting, between 600,000 and 1 million casualties had been inflicted, and the land in the region was utterly devastated. It was a devastation and horror never seen before. After the Battle of Verdun, the area gradually became a "quiet" sector, but even a century later much of the land remains too dangerous to use.

On the receiving end of the French XVII Corps artillery barrage and subsequent infantry attack was the German 33rd Division, deployed on the man-made moonscape northeast of Verdun. Describing the attack, a survivor wrote, "This probably was the most terrifying moment that resulted in the complete collapse of the regiment. There were bloody casualties with most of our men falling into the hands of the enemy. The leadership of two companies as well as the unit's baggage and supplies fell into the enemy's hands. Of the 2nd Battalion, only Leutnant Laeger was saved." The French infantry stormed across the shattered remnants of the German 33rd Division, crossing into its third defensive line and into its rear. So rapid was the French penetration that the day was remembered as a catastrophe for the 33rd German Division. The Germans wrote of one of its units, "The whole of the regiment following the attack of 26 September was not more than a company after the greater portion of our 2nd and 3rd Battalion was destroyed. In addition to the baggage, our kitchen cooks, and even the commander of the 2nd battalion, Captain Paul von Broecker, who unluckily just returned from leave, was captured."[74]

The French XVII Corps did a splendid job maintaining liaison with the AEF right flank. Things did not, however, go so well on the American left flank. To the west of the AEF was the French Fourth

Army under General Henri Gouraud. General Gouraud was a celebrated French Army officer before World War One. He was best remembered for his impressive military actions in 1898 as a captain, when he captured the rebel African leader Samori (Samory) Ture, ending organized African resistance to French colonial rule. Gouraud was wounded during the failed landing at Gallipoli (Dardanelles), losing his right arm. After convalescing from his injury, Gouraud took command of the French Fourth Army in June 1917. He proved to be a master at innovation and brilliantly overcame the German attack against his army during the Second Battle of the Marne using "elastic defense" in July 1918.

Gouraud's Fourth Army bordered the AEF along the western edge of the Argonne Forest. The AEF unit fighting along Gouraud's right flank was the 77th Division. To ensure better liaison between the two armies, General Pershing tasked the 92nd "Buffalo" Division to provide a regiment to the French XXXVIII Corps. The 92nd was one of two divisions composed of African Americans (the other being the celebrated 93rd). The men of both divisions faced troubling bouts of discrimination in the segregated American army. Roughly 50,000 of America's 200,000 black soldiers served in combat units; the rest performed support tasks.[75]

The 92nd assigned the 368th Infantry Regiment to support the French 1st Dismounted Cavalry. The 368th went into the line with a mix of American and French gear. This included French helmets, American uniforms, and an assortment of French small arms. This had nothing to do with racism, as it was normal for American soldiers to use the weapons of their French or British counterparts when they were assigned to foreign command. It made logistic support possible since the Allies could not provide American-specific ammunition for the AEF weapons of choice, the M1917 Enfield and M1903 Springfield. Serving in the French sector, the 368th simply had to use French equipment.[76]

The objective for the Franco-American attack was Binarville. Binarville is at the end of a road that cuts across the Argonne Forest. Just under ten kilometers east of Binarville is Apremont. Control of either of these villages gave access to the forest. The Americans in the 368th began their attack in synchronization with their counterparts in the AEF and the French Fourth Army early on 26 September. However, being poorly led and lacking adequate training, their attack quickly unraveled. The fog and the tangled masses of barbed wire and trenches turned the unit into a disorganized mass of men. Things became worse when the fog burned off at 10:00 A.M. and the Germans began to engage the Americans. The 368th only gained two kilometers (just over a mile) of ground before it could no longer advance.[77] The veteran 77th Division fared only slightly better, reaching the fringes of the German main defensive line.

The end of the first day was bittersweet for Pershing. Although the AEF made impressive gains in the first day, it fell woefully short of his objectives. There were several areas of considerable concern. The 77th and 28th Divisions failed to penetrate the German main defensive line in the Argonne. The Germans used the high ground to inflict casualties on the Americans and French. German artillery fire, being directed by forward observers positioned on the Argonne hills and observation posts in the trees, wreaked havoc on efforts to move supplies and support forward on the few roads in the Meuse Valley. This added greatly to the AEF's troubles, which meant that the attacks of the next day would lack sufficient artillery support. Simply put, the 77th and 28th U.S. Divisions had to clear the Germans from the Argonne.

Additionally, word was arriving at Pershing's headquarters of the breakdown of the 35th U.S. Division. This could be a point of weakness that the Germans could exploit. Making this concern a real danger was the location of the Prussian 5th Guards Division, just a few kilometers from the 35th Division. If a counterattack was launched here, it could unhinge the gains of the day. Pershing's greatest concern was that Montfaucon, the most important piece of terrain in the AEF sector, was still in German hands. He was aware that time was against him, as the German strategic reserves would start arriving in the Meuse-Argonne in less than two days. It was imperative that the offensive renew on the next day, 27 September, with vigor and determination. The Americans had to break through the German defensive belts before reinforcements arrived to stop them. However, a far greater concern that he did not fully grasp yet was the collapse of the 35th Division. Although the unit would stay in the line until 29 September, the semblance of effective leadership did not exist. It was largely the initiative of small unit leaders that held the division together, but this meant that any success would be tactical and not the result of a coordinated division-directed action. This placed the flank of the 28th and 91st U.S. Divisions at risk as they continued to advance north. Although Pershing was justifiably concerned about controlling the key terrain in the middle of the Meuse Valley, the campaign could fail in the 35th Division's sector.

Meanwhile, Germany's General von Gallwitz ordered his reserves forward. The integrity of the main defensive line had to be held where it was not broken and restored where the Americans penetrated it. It was all about time. Messages were sent to the German Army headquarters regarding the severity of the attack. However, Hindenburg and Ludendorff had other concerns. Reports were arriving that the British First and Third Armies would attack near Canal du Nord and Cambrai. Although land could be traded for time in this sector, the loss of Canal du Nord would be a major blow to the German defensive scheme. Several divisions were ordered to prepare for movement to Army Group Gallwitz, but units had to be held back to ascertain the intentions of the Allied armies northwest of the Meuse-Argonne. Army Group Gallwitz had to hold on and prevent further American penetrations of the line. The Sedan-Mezieres rail line had to be protected at all costs; otherwise, the German Army in France could be cut off and flanked.

The German units facing the AEF had to absorb another American push and then prepare to deprive them of the initiative by launching a series of counterattacks. This meant that the units in contact with the enemy could not simply pull back into their prepared positions, but rather had to conduct an active defense that delayed the AEF at every ridge, every copse of trees, every hill. The reliable and deadly German Maxim machine gun would be the centerpiece of this plan. Making the job easier for the German gunners was the AEF's propensity to use frontal attacks, which played into the hands of the defenders.

It was a race against time for both the American and German commanders. If Pershing's AEF advanced with the same audacity as it had on the first day, there was hope of breaking the Germans' defensive network. But the lack of roads, German harassing fires, and air attacks made moving support and follow-on units north to the front difficult and at times impossible. Montfaucon had to be taken. If the AEF did not maintain the initiative, the Germans would grind them down into costly trench-like warfare in front of one of the defensive belts. Pershing's response was to issue clear orders that threatened the leaders with demotion. He expected his generals and colonels to get to the front and make what seemed impossible happen. The opportunity to break the German line—and perhaps end the war in 1918—was rapidly slipping away. Pershing's orders for 27 September 1918 were explicit:

> Division and Brigade Commanders will place themselves as far up toward the front of advance of their respective units as may be necessary to direct movements with energy and rapidity in any attack. The enemy is in retreat or holding lightly in places, and the advance elements of several divisions are already on the First Army Objective and there should be no delay or hesitation in going forward. . . . All officers will push their units forward with all possible energy. Corps and Division Commanders will not hesitate to relieve on the spot any officer of whatever rank who fails to show in this emergency those qualities of leadership required to accomplish the task which confronts us.[78]

8

Grinding to a Halt in the Argonne

27–30 September 1918

> The Commander in Chief commands that division commanders take forward positions and push their troops energetically and the corps and divisions commander be relieved of whatever rank who fail to show energy.
> —General John Pershing, orders for 27 September 1918

Pershing's directive for 27 September 1918 ordering division commanders to position themselves in the front of their units to drive the AEF forward by sheer willpower had almost a desperate tone. However, as he was soon to discover, the opportunity to break through the German line had almost passed. Germany's General von Gallwitz, demonstrating his characteristic superb ability to lead an army in a crisis, shifted sufficient forces to the Meuse-Argonne sector to limit any further breakthroughs. These additional forces also gave him the ability to launch several counterattacks to deprive the Americans of the initiative.

Yet, despite the intensity of the attack in the Meuse-Argonne, Gallwitz still believed that the main AEF attack was yet to come from the St. Mihiel area and then advance toward Metz. Gallwitz wrote regarding 27 September 1918, "I was of the opinion that I must not weaken my wing to the west of Metz too much."[1] This idea grew from the successful Franco-American attack at St. Mihiel a week and a half earlier. It made perfect tactical sense that the AEF would continue its drive toward Metz and on to the iron ore basin at Briey. Holding on to this notion during the first three days of the Meuse-Argonne campaign deprived the German Fifth Army of enough forces to stop the American advance. Trying to hold the line in the Meuse-Argonne while maintaining strength in the St. Mihiel region forced Gallwitz to request that the *Oberste Heeresleitung* (OHL), the German High Command, located in Spa, Belgium, send several strategic reserve divisions. This would provide the forces needed to blunt the American penetration while maintaining enough strength near St. Mihiel to stop the anticipated attack there (which never transpired). Led by Field Marshal Paul von Hindenburg and General Erich Ludendorff, OHL had considerable authority on military matters.

Born in Prussia in 1847 to an aristocratic family, Hindenburg enjoyed a lineage that was truly rich in German culture, having connections to both the nobility and Martin Luther, the celebrated leader of the Reformation. During his pre–First World War service, Hindenburg fought in the 1866 Austrian-Prussian War and was decorated for heroism in the Franco-Prussian War (1870–1871). He retired from the army in 1911 but was recalled in 1914. He and Erich Ludendorff brilliantly led a series of victories against the Russians. In 1916 Hindenburg became the chief of the General Staff and thereby the titular head of Imperial Germany while it was at war.

Erich Ludendorff was born in 1865 near Posen, Prussia, not far from Hindenburg geographically. However, his family was not from nobility, but descendants of wealthy merchants who achieved the status of Junker.[2] Ludendorff made up for his lack of genetic connections with an incredibly intense Protestant work ethic. To this was added the ability to think fast on his feet. After leading a series of brilliant attacks in Belgium, Ludendorff was awarded the Pour le Merite and transferred to the Eastern Front, where he served as Hindenburg's chief of staff. In many ways, Ludendorff would be the brains behind the success that Hindenburg enjoyed. He joined Hindenburg as the defacto deputy commander of OHL, with the title of *Generalquartiermeister* (first quartermaster general, or vice chief of staff).

The situation on the Western Front late in September was not a promising proposition for Hindenburg and Ludendorff. The price in blood and treasure for the year's failed Spring Offensives meant that the German Empire was running low on manpower, while the Americans gave the Allies a considerable advantage.[3] There were sufficient German reserves on the Western Front to contain the Franco-American attack in the Meuse-Argonne region. However, the ability to hold the Americans at bay was put at risk on

27 September when Field Marshal Haig's First and Third British Armies began their attack near Cambrai and Canal du Nord. Led by the Canadian Expeditionary Forces (CEF), Haig's plan was to breach the Germans' formidable defense along the Canal du Nord and then continue advancing beyond Cambrai. If successful, this would open the way for an all-out assault against the Hindenburg Line. Unlike in the Meuse-Argonne, the Germans could trade space for time in the British sector, and perhaps these two offensives could be blunted with the available twenty strategic reserve divisions.

However, the situation for OHL became increasingly untenable when the forces of Belgium's King Albert attacked north of Ypres on 28 September 1918. Albert's Army Group included the Belgian Army as well as the British Second and French Sixth Armies. This was followed on 29 September by a Franco-British offensive near St. Quentin.[4] The combined effects of these four massive attacks would eventually overwhelm the German Imperial Army. In the midst of this daunting crisis on the Western Front that stretched from the English Channel to Verdun, the challenge that Hindenburg and Ludendorff faced was how to stave off a penetration by the Allies. The most threatened sector involved the attacks by the AEF and French Fourth Army in the direction of Sedan-Mezieres. OHL made the decision to begin committing its precious strategic reserves to blunting the attacks there. Hindenburg wrote of the crisis that the American attack posed:

> In the following days [after the spring offensives failed], we essentially held the front against the enemy attacks. However, the situation changed with the expansion of the enemy offensive . . . on 26 September [the day that the American Meuse-Argonne Offensive commenced], which expanded the threat from the coasts to the Argonne. There [in the Argonne region], the Americans penetrated our lines between the Argonne and Meuse River. Here, the . . . American power made itself manifest on the battlefield in the form of an independent army for the first time and validated itself there decisively.[5]

The decision was made to commit forces against the Americans, exactly as the Supreme Allied Commander, Ferdinand Foch, had hoped.

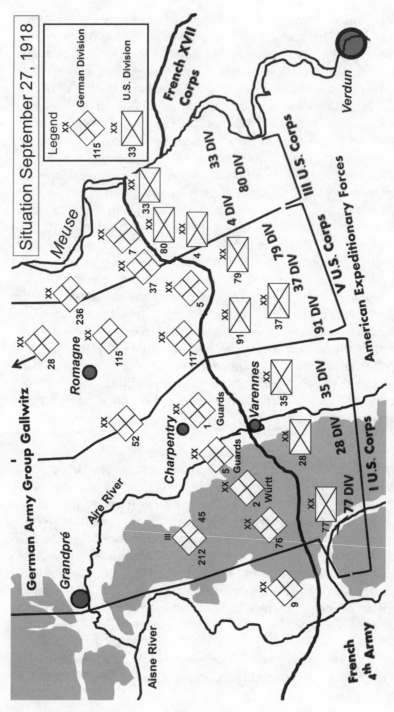

Map 8.1. Situation 27 September 1918. (Josiah Mastriano)

General von Gallwitz's concept of operations for 27 September 1918 (in conjunction with the German Third Army in the Argonne, still under Army Group Crown Prince) was to blunt further American gains, prevent breakthroughs, and retake the critical portions of the line. Among his concerns were both flanks. In the Argonne, the Third Army's 2nd Württemberg Landwehr Division had done a magnificent job stopping the American 77th and 28th Divisions. However, in the valley east of the Argonne, along the L'Aire River, the Prussian 1st Guards were pushed back and the Prussian 5th Guards had yet to launch a counterattack to stabilize the line there.[6] The 5th Guards had to attack early on 27 September to regain the ground lost by the 1st Prussian Guards; otherwise, the 2nd Württemberg Landwehr Division's position in the Argonne Forest could be vulnerable to encirclement. If the Guards could not stabilize the line along the L'Aire River, the 2nd Württemberg Landwehr Division would be ordered out of its strong position and pulled back several kilometers.[7]

Gallwitz's forces on the west bank of the Meuse (the 7th Reserve Division) and in front of Montfaucon (the 117th Division) were reeling from the beating they took the day before and needed immediate support.[8] The 5th Bavarian Reserve Division arrived to defend Montfaucon in support of these two divisions, with the 37th German Division. However, the advance of the American 4th Infantry Division the day before around Montfaucon to the east made it impossible for Gallwitz to hold Montfaucon late into 27 September, as he feared the forces there could be cut off. Montfaucon would have to be abandoned, ceding a vital piece of terrain to the Americans.[9]

Sensing the danger of a Franco-American breakthrough, OHL ordered four divisions to move into the Meuse-Argonne region to shore up Army Group Gallwitz. These would arrive between 27–30 September and included the 52nd, 115th, 236th, and 28th Divisions. The 52nd would deploy around the L'Aire River (east of the Argonne) to secure the ruptured flank along the German Third and Fifth Army boundary, and the 115th near Gesnes.[10] The 236th Division was committed to support Gallwitz in the center of the Meuse Valley. The 28th Division would move from German Army Detachment C to the Meuse Valley. Finally, the 45th Prussian Reserve Division's 212th Regiment was ordered to deploy from its position in front of the French Fourth Army and move east of the Argonne near

The ability of the Germans to hold the line in the west hinged upon a mobile and lethal force of some twenty-four reserve divisions. These troops were transported to crisis areas along the Western Front by trains and then moved by truck to the battle areas. (National Archives)

Apremont to be prepared to conduct a counterattack. The rest of the 45th Prussian Reserve Division's units would follow over the next week.[11]

With these German units moving into the sector, time was running out for the AEF. Pershing's intelligence section (G2) provided a fairly accurate assessment on the arrival of German reinforcements into the region. If there were further delays in the advance, the AEF could find itself stuck in the type of fighting that the French and British experienced earlier in the war: slow and brutal slogging against stalwart German defenses. To avert such an eventuality, Pershing's orders to the AEF were to press the attack with all rigor and determination. This would be easier said than done. The AEF would face not just the German Army, but also increasingly difficult terrain and rainy weather that gave the enemy added advantages. This notwithstanding, Pershing issued Field Order Number 25 giving his guidance for the day: "The enemy without opposing serious infantry or artillery resistance has been driven back on our whole front. The First American Army will continue its advance to the Combined Army First Objective [the Kriemhilde Line still ten kilometers to the north near Romagne]. The advance will be continued at 5:30 A.M. September 27."[12]

Pershing expected all of his divisions in the line to go over the top at 5:30 A.M. He retained command of the French 5th Cavalry Division, which he deployed to Varennes. It was to serve as the AEF's exploitation force. Pershing planned on rushing the French cavalry into any point of the line where the Americans secured a breakthrough. Should this occur, the French cavalry would rapidly advance into the German rear in classic Napoleonic style.[13]

Pershing seemed to lack situational awareness concerning the ability of his divisions to coordinate action in the Meuse-Argonne. Communication from Pershing's headquarters to the three corps headquarters and from the corps headquarters to their subordinate divisions was already difficult. Add to this the order for commanders to move their headquarters to the front. It was a recipe for disaster. Obeying Pershing's edict, the division commanders moved their command posts forward. This put them in a place to influence the actions of only a portion of their units, and resulted in a series of uncoordinated, unsynchronized American attacks. Additionally, this deprived Pershing of the situational awareness that he demanded and needed as the AEF commander.

General Hunter Liggett planned for three of his I Corps divisions to attack along the western third of the Meuse-Argonne front at 5:30 A.M. on 27 September. Yet, as Liggett's aide-de-camp noted, "Attack scheduled everywhere for 5:30 was slow in starting by an hour or so in each division and did not go fast anywhere. The difficulties of getting reports with even substantial accuracy continue, and . . . are most derelict."[14] The breakdown in timely reporting in the AEF was due in large part to Pershing's orders for division commanders to move their headquarters forward, where they were in a poor position to lead their large units and where no infrastructure existed to provide timely reporting to the AEF headquarters.

To the west, the French Fourth Army continued its deliberate and cautious advance along the flank of the AEF. The 368th Regiment of the U.S. 92nd Division again attempted a general advance up the valley west of the Argonne Forest and began a series of uncoordinated attacks toward the German main defensive line.

General Hunter Liggett (right) and General John Pershing. General Liggett commanded the U.S. I Corps, which included the 77th, 28th, and 35th Divisions along the western third of the Meuse-Argonne Offensive. Although Pershing was not happy with the progress of Liggett's corps in the first week of the offensive, he would promote Liggett to First Army commander in October. (U.S. Army Heritage and Education Center, Carlisle, Pennsylvania)

However, German artillery and machine gun fire quickly broke up the attack. By the end of the day the unit had advanced less than two kilometers and was still outside of the German defensive line held by the 9th Landwehr Division.[15] The U.S. 92nd's 3rd Battalion commander, Major Benjamin Norris, attempted to rally his men for another advance in the afternoon, ordering "Commence advance at once," but, after achieving negligible gains, the push ended with the 368th Regiment showing signs of collapse.[16] By 28 September, two-thirds of the 368th Regiment had become combat ineffective. Only a battalion under Major John Merrill was able to attack, joining the French 9th Cuirassiers in taking Binarville on 30 September. Despite this success, the reputation of the 92nd Division was irreparably damaged.

The U.S. 77th Division also failed to make sufficient progress penetrating the Argonne Forest. This created a gap in the line

General Robert Alexander, commander of the U.S. 77th Division, which fought in the Argonne Forest for the first two weeks of the Meuse-Argonne Offensive. (Fort Lewis U.S. Army Museum)

between it and the 28th Division.[17] The 77th's commander, Major General Robert Alexander, was pressing his men to gain some momentum. Alexander was a determined leader, but careless in tactics. He started off his army career in 1886 as a private, worked his way through the ranks, and demonstrated superior leadership skills, receiving a commission to lieutenant in 1889. He gained experience on the American frontier and in the Spanish-American War, the Philippines, and the 1916 Mexican intervention. It would, however, take more than tenacity to break the fortified lines of the German 76th Reserve and the 2nd Württemberg Divisions blocking his way.

However, as a result of the penetration by the Pennsylvanians east of the Argonne, along the L'Aire River, the Germans were forced to pull back three kilometers to their main defensive line in the late hours of 27 September and early on 28 September.[18] Upon gathering intelligence of the German withdrawal, General Alexander ordered a general attack to commence at 5:30 A.M. with a one-hour barrage, followed by two turning movements to envelop German strong points scattered along the high ground in the Argonne. The attack began as planned, with the 77th finally making headway across its front.

The plan for the U.S. 77th Division was to conduct a double envelopment to cut off and surround German positions on the high ground in the Argonne. This included the Abri du Crochet, Abri St. Louis, Bagatelle Pavilion, Moulin de L'Homme Mort, and St. Hubert Pavilion. These positions were manned by large groups of Germans and were centered on dugouts, subterranean living areas, and unit rest camps used when the line was stagnant earlier in the war. The accommodations were fairly plush here for the German soldiers, with tiled floors, paneled walls, electricity, and other amenities of life. Farther back in the forest, the German soldiers constructed small wooden huts, not unlike what one sees in the Bavarian outback today. The soldiers used these when out of the line to relax as well as for hunting the large amount of wild game in the Argonne Forest.

These German strong points were difficult to overcome. The U.S. 77th Division attempt of a double envelopment failed due to German resistance and the terrain, which made command and control difficult. Resolved to gain some ground, General Alexander ordered a general attack across the front. The attack worked, driving back German machine gun posts. A fierce battle ensued for Abri St. Louis, with the Germans offering stiff resistance. Alexander's men were fighting elements of two German divisions in this part of the forest. The determined 2nd Württemberg Landwehr Division was along the eastern portion of his line, and the 76th Reserve Division was along the western half. Manning the Abri St. Louis was the 76th Reserve Division. Of the difficulty that the U.S. 77th Division encountered, Lieutenant Colonel Stackpole wrote: "Abri St. Louis had been a tough nut for them, but they had smoked it out and killed occupants. Germans came out with 'Kamerad' to surrender, threw bombs and caused losses and disorder, increased by a cry of 'Retire.' No prisoners taken, and General Liggett said under such circumstances all should be killed as combatants and not taken, and particularly the officers responsible for such a trick; also that anyone, friend or foe, shouting 'Retire' or attempting to cause stampede should be immediately shot."[19]

Along the western edge of the forest, a battalion of soldiers under the command of Major Charles Whittlesey found a gap in the German defense and penetrated six hundred meters ahead of the French and American units, seizing Moulin de L'Homme Mort. In civilian life, Charles Whittlesey was a scholarly type, excelling in academics and earning a degree in law from Harvard. He flirted with socialism as a young man, but rejected the ideology when he saw that it fomented violence and class jealousy. When America entered the war, Whittlesey answered the call and joined the army. He was assigned to the 308th Infantry Regiment in the 77th Division. Being recruited from New York City, the 77th was one of the most ethnically diverse units in the AEF, with a high number of Irish, Italians, Poles, and numerous others in its ranks.

Moulin de L'Homme Mort was key terrain in the Argonne, overlooking the valley to the west and controlling movement in the forest. During the evening, Whittlesey sent out runners to establish liaison with the surrounding units, only to find that he was surrounded by Germans. He ordered the men to dig in and hold the ground in fulfillment of Pershing's orders that ground once taken should be held. The Germans were not aware of this breach in their line until the next day, but only offered paltry efforts to dislodge the Americans. The 77th Division launched a push on 30 September that broke the German encirclement of Whittlesey's men. They had no idea that this was a dress rehearsal for a five-day siege that this same unit would experience in only two days.

Meanwhile, in the center of the Argonne, the 77th Division found itself under fire from two regiments of the 2nd Württemberg Landwehr Division, the 122nd and 120th. Unlike their counterparts in the Prussian 76th Division, these Germans did not resort to tricks, but rather raw and bitter fighting. The Württembergers used machine gun fire and artillery to break up the formations of the Americans, and riflemen to pick off those surviving the onslaught.[20]

Hauptmann (Captain) Haug, the commander of 1st Battalion, 120th Württemberg Regiment, moved to the front to ensure that his line held. However, a group of Americans penetrated close to his headquarters, wounding him. Nearby was Leutnant Paul Kuno Vollmer, the assistant postmaster of Ulm, Germany, before the war. With the wounding of Haug, Vollmer assumed command of the battalion, with Leutnant Fritz Endriss taking command of his company.[21] Endriss was regarded as a particularly brave officer, and he rallied the men to hold their positions despite the overwhelming number of Americans pressing the line.

The Württembergers committed their reserves to prevent

penetrations and to shore up the defenses. Leutnant Vollmer managed to break up the American attack by coordinating artillery support across the front and integrating his machine gun strongholds and infantry. Leutnant Schmid held a forward outpost and was virtually surrounded during the attack. He had a case of grenades and threw at least a hundred of these into the advancing Americans. With such reckless abandon, Leutnant Schmid held his position.[22] Although the Germans were holding in the Argonne, it came at a high cost. Not only was Hauptmann Haug out of the war, but *Feldwebelleutnant* (temporarily commissioned sergeant major) Holzwarth, one of the most beloved soldiers in the regiment, died during the fighting this day. Holzwarth was forward of the line calling in artillery fires and reporting the location of the Americans when he was killed in action. He was the oldest warrior in the regiment and its first man to receive the Iron Cross First Class—in 1914 for heroism and bravery.[23] He was loved and respected throughout the regiment for his no-nonsense approach to leadership, and for his care of the troops. He never asked a soldier to do something that he would not do himself. This is why he died during this action, as he volunteered to occupy a forward observation post, a job normally reserved for a junior soldier. Both the Americans and the Germans soaked the Argonne with their blood.

The experience of the U.S. 77th Division was similar to that of the Pennsylvanians of the 28th attempting to advance in the Argonne. In one attempt to penetrate the German defense in the forest, a battalion in the 28th's 111th Infantry Regiment failed to advance since most of its officers had been wounded or killed the day before. Upon seeing this, the regiment's chaplain, Lieutenant Charles G. Conaty, took command. Holding pistols in both hands, he stood up in the forest, walked to the front, gave commands, and the men rose up and followed him into battle. Although a wall of German machine gun bullets slammed into the ranks, the Pennsylvanians advanced and pushed the Württembergers back several hundred yards. Conaty was a leader who cared for others and whom the soldiers would follow anywhere. The chaplain rallied the men, and with his leadership they gained a valuable foothold in the forest.

Even before this incident in the Argonne, Chaplain Conaty was respected for his bravery. He already had been awarded the Distinguished Service Cross two months earlier near the Marne River, where "Without regard for his personal safety Chaplain Conaty,

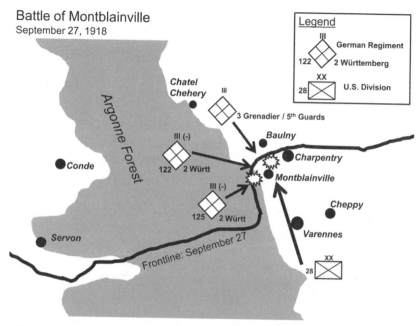

Map 8.2. Battle of Montblainville, 27 September 1918. (Josiah Mastriano)

under intense shell fire, following the attack of his troops from Crezancy to the Marne River, attended the wounded and throughout the night searched and assisted in carrying wounded to the dressing station."[24]

However, it was the progress east of the Argonne that proved to be decisive. The Pennsylvanians advanced up the L'Aire River east of the forest. Concealed from observation by a heavy fog in the Meuse Valley, the U.S. 28th Division attacked at 5:30 A.M. Supported by tanks in the valley north of Varennes, the 28th drove back the remnants of the Prussian 1st Guards. The Americans penetrated the German lines, liberating Montblainville by 8:00 A.M. The 110th Regiment of the 28th Division led this advance and had both flanks "in the air," as neither the 35th Division to the right nor the rest of the 28th on the left (in the Argonne) kept up with their advance. German gunners and snipers hidden in the edge of the Argonne (from the 2nd Württemberg Division) took a toll on the Pennsylvanians as they pushed forward. After Montblainville was secured, the Pennsylvanians continued their advance. They progressed only three hundred meters beyond Montblainville before German machine gun fire from the northwest and west stopped them. The U.S. 28th Division dug in, waiting for the 35th Division to advance and secure their eastern flank.[25]

Even today, Montblainville is a modest village by any standard. Its importance during the Meuse-Argonne campaign was simply that it was a crossroads for east-west and north-south traffic, a necessity for an advancing army. More dangerous for the Germans was that one of the roads headed into the Argonne. The capture of this village threatened the Württembergers, who were still holding firm in the Argonne, with encirclement. The capture of Montblainville put in jeopardy the boundary between the German Third and Fifth Armies, where the Americans could drive a wedge. To avert disaster, the 2nd Württemberg and Prussian 5th Guards were ordered to launch a combined counterattack toward Montblainville to drive the Americans back. The Germans attacked at 11:30 A.M. but were repulsed. More troops were ordered forward, and the Germans planned on renewing their attack around 1:00 P.M.[26] The Prussian 3rd Guards Grenadier Regiment (5th Guards Division) was to lead the attack, with support from the 125th and 122nd Württemberg Regiments (both of the 2nd Württemberg Division) and the 2nd Guards Reserve Pioneer Company. Their objective was to retake Montblainville.[27]

Concerned about their precarious position of having both flanks exposed, the Pennsylvanians made use of captured enemy weapons. Captain John Dunkle ordered his noncommissioned officers to put the German machine guns into the line to strengthen their position. This may have saved them. Beginning around 1:00 P.M. and lasting well into 4:00 P.M., the Germans launched their second strong counterattack to retake Montblainville, hitting the Americans from the east and west.[28] After several minute of intense fighting, it looked like the Prussian Guards would indeed retake Montblainville. However, the Pennsylvanians managed to establish direct communication with an artillery unit via telephone, and the subsequent fire broke up part of the German advance.

While the American artillery crashed into part of the advance, the Prussian 3rd Guards Grenadier Regiment's machine gun company commander, Leutnant Humpert, advanced with his men around the eastern side of Montblainville to control crossing points along the L'Aire River. This put him behind the Americans and cut

French Renault tanks advance along the eastern edge of the Argonne to support the American attack. Tanks often proved decisive in successful operations, such as the action of the U.S. 28th Division at Montblainville. (National Archives)

them off from support. The Pennsylvanians trapped in Montblainville were under fire from all directions, and it was now just a matter of time before they would be forced to surrender. However, when all hope seemed lost, a column of seven tanks advanced toward the town. German forward observers saw the tanks advancing and directed artillery against them. Three of the tanks were disabled by German artillery, with the crews able to escape. Two others were hit and exploded like "hell's flames." However, the last two broke through Leutnant Humpert's position, wounding him and forcing his men to fall back.[29] This broke up the German attack and saved the Pennsylvanians in Montblainville.

It was a close battle, but thanks to the use of the captured equipment, the integration of artillery fire, and tanks, the Americans repulsed the German attack.[30] The Württembergers were critical of the lack of coordination with the 5th Guards. The 125th was told that the Guards would be in a position near the town when the attack kicked off. As the Württembergers attacked, they found "the soldiers of the 5th Guards were not there. They were not where they were supposed to be; instead we encountered people from America."[31] In the defense of the Guards regiment, it lacked sufficient time to coordinate the move, having just arrived in the area. This fog and friction of war would continue to have a debilitating effect on both friend and foe.

The cost of the battle for Montblainville was heavy, with the Pennsylvanians suffering 43 killed in action and 269 wounded. One survivor noted, "It was a long night before all the wounded were evacuated and it was probably the most treacherous position that the regiment occupied during its service."[32] The Germans likewise suffered high casualties. Although outnumbered, the Americans were able to hold in large part due to a rare execution of combined arms warfare. The integration and coordination of infantry, machine guns, artillery, and tanks was truly an advanced war-fighting skill, and the Pennsylvanians did it magnificently while defending Montblainville. Although new to modern warfare, the Americans, thanks in large part to French military advice and equipment, were proving to be quick learners.

The failure of the German counterattack was a serious setback. The Americans were in a position to outflank and cut off the German 2nd Württemberg Division, who had held firmly in the Argonne Forest. However, the Americans' advance along the eastern face of the Argonne put them almost five kilometers behind the Württemberger positions in the forest. If the Germans had had sufficient reserves, they could have attacked into the flank of the Americans from the Argonne down into the Meuse Valley below. This could have unhinged the American offensive completely. However, they did not have enough forces to pull off such a risky gambit. Because of this, the 2nd Württemberg Division was ordered to execute a three-kilometer withdraw in the Argonne, pulling back into its main defense belt (*Argonnenriegel*).[33] Of this, one of the 2nd Württemberg Division units, the 125th Regiment, wrote: "Due to the further penetration of the enemy in the Aire River Valley [western edge of the Meuse Valley], the position of the division could no longer be held. The Americans were already far behind us; in our back. So, on the evening of 27 September, we were ordered to pull back 3 km to the Argonne Bolt [*Argonnenriegel*, the German main defense line in the Argonne Forest]."[34]

The withdrawal of German forces in the Argonne was hampered by a heavy rain during the night of 27 September, which would exacerbate a flu epidemic that the Württembergers were combating. From their perspective, it was difficult enough that they were fighting superior numbers of American forces, but add to this the flu epidemic, and it was a cause for concern. Adding to this, the use of gas during artillery barrages resulted in weakened respiratory systems, which made the men more susceptible to the effects of the flu.[35] Despite this, the Württembergers still had two kilometers of the eastern flank open to the Americans. To prevent a flanking action, the village of Apremont had to be held at all costs. Apremont, much like Montblainville, was a gateway to the Argonne, controlling a road crossing the forest from east to west.

After two days of fighting, neither the 77th Division nor the 28th had dislodged the 2nd Landwehr Division from the forest. Only success in the Meuse Valley opened the way for American progress in the Argonne.[36] Both American divisions would later claim in their histories that they forced the Germans back via aggressive offensive operations. This was verifiably not the case.[37] Thanks to the German withdrawal necessitated by the loss of ground in the Meuse Valley, General Alexander's 77th Division could finally report significant progress in the Argonne. But the German main defense belt was still occupied. This would prove to be a costly obstacle for the Americans. It would take a "lost battalion" and the actions of a conscientious objector in the U.S. 82nd Division to finally force the Germans out of their Argonne fortress more than a week and half later. Until then, there would be a lot of death and destruction in the ancient forest.

Meanwhile, the U.S. 28th Division was ordered to continue its advance up the Meuse Valley after its victory at Montblainville, with the mission of seizing the village of Apremont and the Argonne high ground west and north of it. Only slightly larger than Montblainville, Apremont is situated on the eastern slope of the Argonne Forest, with stunning views of the Meuse Valley below. The surrounding hills were a dream come true for German forward observers, who used these vantage points to direct deadly artillery fire on the Americans below. The abruptly rising ground surrounding Apremont was also ideal for defensive infantry and machine gun units. It was against such a formidable obstacle that the Pennsylvanians would advance.

With their artillery finally fully able to support, the Pennsylvanians continued their attack at 6:30 A.M. after a one-hour artillery

barrage on 28 September 1918. The advance was slow and deliberate, with the Americans adeptly reducing German machine gun
positions and snipers along the way. By late afternoon the men had
advanced more than three kilometers and swept the Germans out
of Apremont. Defensive positions north and west of the town were
established as they waited for additional forces to arrive. This position was entirely exposed to the west in the Argonne, as the stubborn Württembergers had again thwarted the division attack in the
forest, where the Americans failed to make any significant gains.
This meant that the soldiers of the 28th Division's 110th and 109th
Regiments in Apremont were exposed to flanking fires.

Not helping the daunting task at hand for the Pennsylvanians
was Pershing's draconian policy to relieve any officer not reacting
instantly to orders to advance. In the midst of this difficult mission
of seizing and holding Apremont, the division's 55th Brigade commander, Brigadier General Thomas Darragh, was fired and replaced
by Brigadier General Dennis Nolan. This triggered further delays
and inaction as the new leader had to figure out what was occurring
before taking action. The relief of Darragh was a result of his hesi-
tation to order the 28th Division's 110th Regiment to continue the
attack past Apremont around midnight on 28 September. Darragh
rightly was concerned about conducting a night attack, especially
as both his flanks would be open and exposed to German counterattacks. He delayed the order, giving time for the 109th Regiment to arrive on the left flank of the 110th. This would shield their
advance from German flanking action and was the right thing to do.
Nolan would also fail to conduct a rapid attack up the L'Aire Valley beyond Apremont. As the new commander, Nolan needed time,
and the cost of this was delay and inaction. This gave the Germans
time to organize for a counterattack.[38]

Pershing's penchant of forcing success by imposing his will,
demanding unrealistic results, and enforcing draconian policies
added to the delays and lack of progress for the AEF in the waning days of September 1918. His approach seemed just short of desperate and had a stifling effect on his army. Fearing a similar end,
division and brigade commanders in the AEF were quick to fire a
leader for not quickly executing an edict from his headquarters. Pershing did have cause for concern, as his intelligence staff accurately
reported the arrival of more German reserve divisions, which had
the potential to completely stop his progress. Pershing resorted to

micromanagement, leaving little room for personal initiative and discretion, but demanded results in line with his vision of the battle, which was increasingly detached from reality. Although Pershing proved proficient at handling the strategic issues of fielding an independent American army, he was less capable of leading that same army in coordinated and synchronized action. Much of this had to do with the inexperience of his force as a whole, but his constant meddling in tactical affairs hampered the little momentum that the AEF still had.

The Americans planned on continuing the attack past Apremont early on 29 September. However, the firing of the brigade commander caused delays and confusion. Adding to the interruption were the tanks that were to support the attack. They arrived late, delaying the action. As the Americans waited for their armor support, and for clear guidance from their new brigade commander, the Germans launched an attack at 7:30 A.M. to force the Americans out of Apremont.[39] Supported by artillery fire and devastating machine gun fire from the flank, the Germans advanced out of the Argonne Forest from the west and northwest. The German mission was to recapture the town and take control of the important Apremont road that provided access to the Argonne and a clear route to the village of Chatel Chehery to the north.

This German counterattack was to include units of the 120th Württemberg led by Rittmeister (Captain of Cavalry) von Sick and soldiers of the 125th Württemberg Landwehr Regiment. It was planned to be a larger attack; however, the morning push of the American 77th and 28th Divisions in the Argonne drew off portions of the forces that were to be used to retake Apremont, with the 1st and 5th Prussian Guards focused on stopping the American breakthrough in the Meuse Valley. The burden of the attack fell largely to the 2nd Württemberg Division. The plan was for a two-hour barrage to wear the Americans down, followed by an attack out of the Argonne Forest from the west and northwest.[40]

The attack began splendidly for the Germans, who quickly drove the Americans from the shell holes that they were using as fighting positions outside of Apremont. It was vicious, and at times hand-to-hand, with the Pennsylvanians making the Württembergers pay dearly for the ground. Within a few minutes, however, the Württembergers broke the American line and rapidly pursued the Americans into Apremont. As the American line broke north of

Sergeant Andrew Lynch from Philadelphia personally planned, organized, and led the assault to retake the village of Apremont. (Victory Liberty Loan Committee)

town, Lieutenant Meyer S. Jacobs ordered his one-pounder (37mm Model 1916 cannon) back. He also directed Platoon Sergeant Andrew Lynch from Philadelphia and Corporal Robert Jeffrey of Sagamore, Pennsylvania, to pull the men and equipment to Apremont. Sergeant Lynch and the men made it out of the area just as the Germans overwhelmed the nearby infantry platoon. Lynch did not know that Lieutenant Jacobs was captured. The Germans were on the cusp of a daring victory that had the potential to stall the American push up the Meuse Valley.[41]

The Germans rushed into Apremont, driving the Americans to the lower slope of the village. The command post of the

Pennsylvanian 109th Regiment was in the basement of one of the village's ruined houses. Captain Mackey, with the American unit's adjutant and chaplain, only realized that they were overrun when the lines were cut and they could hear German yelling in the house above them. The three remained still and quiet, hoping not to alert the Germans to their presence.[42] About this time, Sergeant Lynch heard that Lieutenant Jacobs had been captured. Infuriated by this news, Lynch and Corporal Jeffrey gathered five men and dashed back through Apremont to free their commander. Believing that he would still be near their original position, the Americans saw a platoon of thirty-six German soldiers with Lieutenant Jacobs in their midst. Lynch and his men charged into the fray, killing fifteen Germans, capturing three others, and rescuing Jacobs. The group dashed back around Apremont to the relative safety below the town, where a reserve company of seventy-five Pennsylvanians was waiting for orders. Sergeant Lynch pulled out his sidearm and ordered the men to follow him to retake Apremont.[43]

Captain Charles L. McLain, of Indiana, Pennsylvania, was in a similar position. His own company was in reserve, and while moving back through Apremont he discovered that the survivors of C Company were leaderless and at a loss as to what to do. Captain McLain took command and led the men in a counterattack back into Apremont. Leading from the front, McLain was shot in the leg, but he stayed with the men until they had cleared Apremont of Germans. The combined attacks of Lynch and McLain drove the Germans back to their starting positions. As the smoke cleared, Captain Mackey, his adjutant, and the unit's chaplain emerged from their basement shelter, happy to see friendly faces. Lynch would receive the Distinguished Service Cross for his actions.[44] After securing the village, the Pennsylvanians established strong points along the western and northern approaches of Apremont to prevent further German breakthroughs. The Americans prepared to resume the attack on 1 October.

The firing of Brigadier General Thomas Darragh had no other effect but to give the Germans time to organize for this almost devastating counterattack against Apremont. Even after two days of being in command, the new commander, Dennis Nolan, still was not ready to resume the offensive. Pershing's dysfunctional command climate had a negative impact on the AEF's leadership and compromised the ability of the Americans to maintain momentum.

Brigadier General Dennis E. Nolan served with Pershing in the Philippines before the war and was selected to lead his intelligence staff (G2) in 1918. During the first day of the Meuse-Argonne Offensive, Pershing fired the 28th Division's 55th Brigade commander, Brigadier General Thomas Darragh, and replaced him with Nolan. (National Archives)

Apremont was only saved due to the individual initiative and courage of Sergeant Lynch and Captain McLain. It was they who averted disaster. It is this type of soldier that the modern U.S. Army seeks to develop in its force one hundred years later—the type that seizes the initiative to accomplish the mission. Their actions echo across the generations to us today and remain examples of how individual initiative is a trait valued in any successful organization.

9

Stalling in the Meuse Valley

27–30 September 1918

Thick lines of American Soldiers advanced towards us. . . .
The entire land swarmed like an ant house of Americans.
—Hans-Oskar Rosenberg Lipinsky,
3rd Guards Grenadier Regiment

The 35th Division, despite its disorganization, was able to advance several kilometers to liberate Charpentry and Baulny. This was likewise due to the individual initiative of small unit leaders rather than the division staff. The commander of the 35th Division, Major General Traub, was close to a nervous breakdown in the midst of trying to lead his division while facing growing stiff German resistance. He appealed to Hunter Liggett for reinforcements, and Liggett offered a regiment from the U.S. 92nd Division. However, this order was countermanded by Pershing's staff, which was planning on replacing the 35th with the experienced U.S. 1st Infantry Division. The 1st Division would move into the line on 30 September. Until then, the 35th had to continue to attack with the forces it had.[1]

General Pershing issued orders that the AEF would resume the attack at 5:30 A.M. on 27 September. However, his demand that leaders locate their headquarters forward made the order impossible to carry out. Traub, like the other division commanders, obeyed Pershing's mandate. But the only real effect of this was a breakdown in command and control. This placed the division commanders too far forward to properly command their divisions. This was exacerbated by the disruption of communication lines (by both poor-quality wire and wire being cut by German artillery). Traub followed Pershing's directive to the letter and gave his officers a speech ordering them

Major General Peter E. Traub, commander of the 35th Division, speaking with Major D. C. Gardiner (right). Traub lost effective command and control over his division during the first few days of combat. (U.S. Army Heritage and Education Center, Carlisle, Pennsylvania)

to stay at the front. As a witness rightly observed, however, "Those things sound fine in a speech, but in a battle, a general can do his work much better from a known and established headquarters than he can while wandering around the field."[2]

Pershing's 5:30 A.M. attack order did not arrive until it was too late to coordinate or plan a proper attack. Fearing that he would be fired for disobeying an order, General Traub insisted that the 35th Division attack with or without artillery support or adequate planning. This resulted in a series of uncoordinated and largely unsupported probes that the Germans easily beat back.

The division's regiments that spearheaded the attack on the first day of the Meuse-Argonne were the 137th and 138th. Both of these lost many officers, resulting in a breakdown in command and control. The plan for the 35th Division was to resume the attack by bringing up the 139th and 140th Regiments. The 139th would pass through the 137th Regiment near the L'Aire River while the 140th would pass through the 138th Regiment to the east.[3] However, neither regiment could complete its passage of lines before the 5:30 A.M. attack. Furthermore, the preponderance of the division's artillery needed at least eight more hours to move forward to support the attack. These units were caught in massive traffic jams along the few roads available in the area and also had difficulty navigating across the shattered remnants of no-man's-land. The two major roads in the sector used by the division were narrow and heavily damaged. The biggest challenge was that the engineers needed time to build a new bridge and to create a bypass around a massive crater that the Germans detonated to prevent the Americans from advancing. Thousands of African American troops were used to help maintain the roads, as "automobiles of all kinds and innumerable motor trucks . . . [pulling] wagons, rolling kitchens, ration wagons, machine gun carts, staff cars" clogged the roads.[4]

Adding to Pershing's woes was that the German lines were bolstered by additional forces. Portions of the Prussian 5th Guards deployed to the area to support the weakened 1st Guards and 117th Divisions. Elements of the Prussian 212th Reserve Infantry Regiment of the 45th Reserve Division also arrived to shore up the vulnerable flank of the 1st Guards. This deprived General Traub's 35th U.S. Division of any chance of driving the Germans back. The best that the division could do for any sort of organized attack was at 8:30 A.M. Even this was risky, as neither attacking regiment would have time to plan its attack, and artillery support would be spotty at best. Colonel Hamilton Hawkins, the 35th Division chief of staff, issued orders to that effect. However, General Traub feared Pershing's wrath and told his commanders to attack at 5:30 A.M., saying, "It is General Pershing's order, it must be done."[5] Traub briefly left the headquarters as the staff feverishly tried to execute Pershing's impossible order. Colonel Hawkins was beside himself on how to put together the plan with such short notice, and even worse, there was no way that the message would make it to all the units.

The division headquarters was in a fortified bunker captured

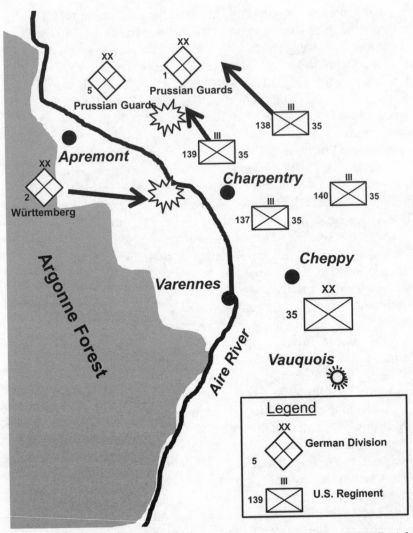

Map 9.1. Advance of the 35th Division, 27 September 1918. (Josiah Mastriano)

from the Germans the day before. It was in a position safe from artillery fired from the American lines, but not from the north, where the Germans were. Candles were lit to give ample light to allow the Americans and the French liaison officers to work. As a throng of soldiers rushed about and Colonel Hawkins gave guidance on how to pull off the 5:30 attack, an artillery barrage pounded the area. The Germans knew the precise location of this building, and with amazing precision a German artillery round "came through the window of the headquarters and exploded inside the room with a great crash."[6] The explosion extinguished the candles and created sheer chaos. Much to everyone's amazement, only one man was slightly wounded—a truly miraculous event. Colonel Hamilton did not have time to offer thanks to God, however, as the explosion got Traub's attention, and he stormed into the building, not to ask if anyone was hurt, but to demand to know if his orders to attack at 5:30 were being followed.

Traub's reaction to simply follow Pershing's order seems to have been driven out of fear. Pershing was merciless when it came to firing commanders who did not deliver results. Traub had reason to be concerned, as his attack on 26 September had failed to achieve the objectives assigned by Pershing, and two of his regiments were in disarray. Yet, to expect the division on such short notice to attack was entirely unrealistic, as the only way to communicate with the forward battalions was via runners, who simply could not get the orders to the attacking units in time.

This episode brings into question Pershing's command climate. His severe and inflexible approach to leading the American Expeditionary Forces was a mixed blessing. He had a difficult task to be sure. It was not easy leading a new and growing organization in a complex and dynamic environment, facing an adversary bent on the AEF's destruction. Pershing's leadership style was further tainted by his belief that an American soldier with a rifle and bayonet could overcome whatever the Germans threw at him. Such folly was attempted in 1914 by the French, and at a great cost they learned that no amount of bravado would stop German machine gun bullets. Yet Pershing rejected any lessons of the war offered by the French or British. Finally, relieving commanders without cause or justification created a command climate where subordinate leaders were oppressed by fear of punishment and being fired rather than encouraged to do the right thing. Thus was the case with Traub, whose division simply could not attack in any organized or effective manner until the late afternoon.

President John Adams said, "Facts are stubborn things; and whatever may be our wishes, our inclinations, or the dictates of our passion, they cannot alter the state of facts and evidence." Despite the facts, Traub demanded that his division follow the letter

Lieutenant Colonel
Delaplane was the
commander of the
U.S. 140th Regiment,
35th Division, during
the vicious fighting of
the Meuse-Argonne
campaign's first week. His
unit was held together by
three chaplains after the
regiment was driven back
by a counterattack from
the Prussian 1st Guards.
(National Archives)

of Pershing's order even though there was no way that any such attack could succeed. Unsurprisingly, the attacks failed to achieve any results. The historian of the 140th Regiment said of 27 September: "This was the day of the famous 'mixed orders.' The first plan was to attack at 8:30 after a three hours' artillery fire. Apparently the final plan was to advance at 6:30, but the commander of the 140th, Lieutenant Colonel C. E. Delaplane, received orders at 5:05 a.m. to advance at 5:30 after a five minutes barrage on machine gun nests. It seemed impossible to notify his command in the darkness, but the regiment began moving as directed, however, the five minute barrage failed to materialize."[7]

The German defenders were ready. Machine gunners from the Prussian Guards positioned a series of strong points across the front of the 140th. The only way to overcome them was by a combination of maneuver, artillery fires, and tanks. All the regiment had available was infantry maneuver, which was not enough to defeat

Lieutenant Colonel Carl
Ristine, the celebrated
commander of the 35th
Division's 139th Regiment,
spent the night of 27
September evading capture
behind German lines.
(U.S. Army Heritage and
Education Center, Carlisle,
Pennsylvania).

the German machine guns. Additionally, the Germans commanded
the heights of the Argonne Forest overlooking the Meuse Valley.
Using the vantage points in the Argonne hills, German artillery
was directed against the 140th Regiment with a combination of gas
shells and high explosives. When the men of the regiment began
advancing up the Meuse Valley, they were greeted by a wall of German machine gun fire and explosions from German artillery that
crashed into their ranks. Additionally, they faced piles of barbed
wire around one of the vital pieces of terrain, Hill 218. The attack
stalled as quickly as it began, but with heavy casualties.

Meanwhile, the 139th Regiment tried to make sense of contra-
dictory orders to attack at 5:30 A.M., 6:30 A.M., and 8:30 A.M. The 8:30
A.M. attack was the most realistic, as all of the units would have time
to make ready and, additionally, there would be artillery to support
the push. However, a runner arrived passing on to the commander
of the 139th, Lieutenant Colonel Carl Ristine, that the attack must go
at 5:30 A.M. This was simply impossible. The best that the regiment
could do was 6:30 A.M. As Ristine's men prepared to attack, they

saw their sister regiment to the east, the 140th, begin its forward movement only to be stopped by German artillery and machine gun fires. By the time the 140th's push stalled, the 139th began to move. It experienced a similar fate.[8]

Ristine's 139th attacked at 6:30 A.M. and, just like the 140th, hit a wall of fire from the Germans dug in on the high ground near Baulny and Charpentry. Yet the men advanced through the maelstrom. The casualties mounted as German artillery ripped gaping holes among the troops. By 10:00 A.M., Ristine ordered the men to dig in. The 35th Division's attack had failed to achieve any appreciable ground due to the lack of command and control, adequate division leadership, and inadequate coordination of artillery and tanks. Instead, lives were thrown away by hasty orders and weak leadership.

The 35th was composed of a fair number of veterans who saw service in 1916 on the Mexican border. Several of these so-called "Cactus Veterans" were proud of their experience and often boasted of how much better they were than the recruits of 1917 and 1918. As the men lay under withering fire near Charpentry, "A tall red-headed sergeant rose from his foxhole, and looking about the prostrate lines, yelled, 'what have you Cactus birds got to say about this?' Needless to say, there was no more boasting from the Cactus Veterans after this day."[9]

Ristine tried in the early afternoon to continue the attack after he secured armor support. However, after facing stronger German opposition, the tanks withdrew and the attack floundered. As the afternoon progressed, the division's artillery offered increasing support in countering German fire and suppressing German machine gun nests. Meanwhile, General Pershing was growing frustrated at the lack of progress. At 4:30 P.M. the following note arrived at General Traub's headquarters: "[General Pershing] expects the 35th Division to move forward. He is not satisfied with the Division being stopped by machine gun nests here and there. He expects the Division to move forward now in accordance to orders."[10]

Fearing the ire of General Pershing, Traub quickly issued orders to the division's unit to prepare for an attack at 5:30 P.M. Most of the units received the order at 5:00 P.M., giving them only thirty minutes to prepare. The lack of time notwithstanding, all four of the division's regiments planned on advancing at the designated time. The attack was an all-or-nothing gambit and the last chance that the 35th would have to make appreciable headway.

Renault tanks advance in support of the 35th Division. The French tanks were central to American success in the Meuse Valley. (U.S. Army Heritage and Education Center, Carlisle, Pennsylvania)

Unlike the uncoordinated and poorly supported attacks of the morning, the 5:30 P.M. push would include supporting artillery fires and a detachment of tanks. The plan was for the 140th Regiment, with support of tanks and elements of the 138th Regiment, to attack north toward the Serieux farm west of Cote (Hill) 231 and Eclisfontaine. Simultaneously, the 139th, supported by the 137th Regiment, would advance north to liberate Baulny and Charpentry.

The Germans reported that the attack actually commenced between 3:00 P.M. and 4:00 P.M. This was due to the volume of artillery that began crashing into their lines to prepare the way for the 5:30 P.M. step-off.[11] Throughout the afternoon the Prussian 5th Guards Division noted increased volume, duration, and effectiveness of the American artillery. To make matters worse for the Germans, a column of Renault tanks was reported by the 125th Württemberg from its high position in the Argonne. The tanks were moving north from the village of Very. Although the 5th Guards had antitank rifles, the tanks had a shock effect on the men.[12]

As the division waited for the time to attack, American artillery played among the German positions, and nine tanks slowly worked their way from the liberated village of Very to support the 140th's advance to the right. The tanks arrived on time and the infantry followed. The 139th and 137th stepped off at the same time, although without tank support. The entire division was greeted by German machine gun fire and artillery but advanced without regard for losses. A German eyewitness, Leutnant Beckmann of the 3rd Guards Grenadier Regiment, wrote of what he saw from his position above Baulny when the U.S. 35th Division attacked: "Thick lines of American Soldiers advanced towards us. One after the other they disappeared into the folds of the terrain and one after the other at brief intervals reemerged from the canyon and continued to advance. . . . Moving with and behind them were platoons of men carrying cases of ammunition and material that were being brought forward. . . . The entire land swarmed like an ant house of Americans."[13]

The American soldiers that Leutnant Beckmann saw were led by the dauntless Major James E. Rieger, the aforementioned deacon of Kirksville, Missouri's First Baptist Church. Rieger's objective was to liberate Charpentry. Rieger led his battalion in a brilliant assault into the town, quickly overrunning German positions. The audacity of Rieger's attack trapped a large group of Germans, who ended up being captured. The official report says, "[Rieger] pushed forward and on the evening of September 27, without regard for his own safety, personally led the charge into Charpentry with such speed and dash that a large body of the enemy were cut off and captured."[14] After four years of occupation, Charpentry was liberated. Rieger once again turned the tide of battle. Although he had played a key role in liberating Vauquois the day before, and now was the first American in Charpentry, Rieger still had one more important task to accomplish.

By 7:00 P.M. the 4th Guards (Foot) Regiment was driven out of Baulny and Charpentry. This compromised the flank of the 5th Guards Division, forcing the commander to order all of his units back to the next line, which was anchored on the 2nd Württemberg Division position near Apremont (in the Argonne) east toward Exermont. The order to retrograde units back to this line went into effect at 7:25 P.M. German artillery laid down a barrage to delay the Americans and prevent them from exploiting the withdrawal.[15] By 8:00 P.M. the German line was broken, and both Charpentry and Baulny

Major James E. Rieger, the commander of 2nd Battalion, 139th Regiment, 35th Division, was called "hopelessly useless" due to his gentle Christian approach to leadership. He would be dubbed the "Hero of the Argonne" after he led his battalion in seizing the hill of Vauquois, liberating Charpentry, and advancing beyond Exermont. (U.S. Army Heritage and Education Center, Carlisle, Pennsylvania)

were liberated. Groups of Doughboys remained behind to clear the villages and to root out concealed German machine gun positions.[16]

Several contemporaneous accounts of this action state that the attack was successful due to the cover of darkness.[17] This is simply false. The attack began at 5:30 P.M. and the majority of the fighting ended with the setting of the sun. The sun sets around 7:30 P.M. in this part of France in late September, with some light still in the skies as late as 8:00 P.M. Several small units continued advancing into the darkness, adding to the ground gained, but this was minor in comparison.

As the sun set, Lieutenant Colonel Carl Ristine moved forward to the regiment's front, advancing with his skirmish line, hoping to maintain the momentum. Before long he was alone and just south of Exermont. He called out to a body of nearby troops, which turned out to be Germans. Ristine slowly disappeared into the darkness to avoid capture, eventually finding a 35th Division lieutenant and five privates, also lost in the darkness. The group settled into a position on a hill only to be discovered by a nearby group of Germans. Ristine surveyed the situation and determined that they were better off trying to get away individually. Of the seven, only Ristine escaped without being killed or captured. As he evaded capture, suddenly massive explosions lit the skies north of him near Chatel Chehery and Fleville. The withdrawal of the 5th Prussian Guards to positions around Exermont meant that massive ammunition depots were threatened with capture. To prevent this, the German command ordered their destruction.[18] Ristine witnessed this amazing display as he meandered back toward the American lines. He hid during the day of 28 September and finally made it back to American lines on the 29th. His absence exacerbated the ineffectiveness of his regiment those two days.[19]

Pershing ordered that the 35th Division continue to attack on 28 and 29 September. The attacks on the morning of the 28th were haphazard and uncoordinated. Although disjointed, the Americans seized the Montrebeau Woods and progress toward Ruisseau d'Exermont was made. The U.S. 35th Division was increasingly in disarray. This condition gave the Germans an opportunity to drive a wedge into the American lines. The history of the 138th U.S. Regiment honestly describes the condition of the 35th, writing: "The division was a division in name only now. Brigade and Division Headquarters had almost ceased to function. . . . The 35th Division was in effect a number of small units, companies, battalions and regiments, waging little individual wars against a well organized and well directed enemy."[20]

General von Gallwitz needed to blunt the American advance up the Meuse Valley. There was a risk of a breakthrough, and that had to be prevented. An American breach of the German line here would threaten half of the German forces on the Western Front. The survivors of the beleaguered 1st Guards Division were ordered to make one more daring attack before being pulled out of the line for a respite. Hoping to exploit the degraded condition of the U.S. 35th

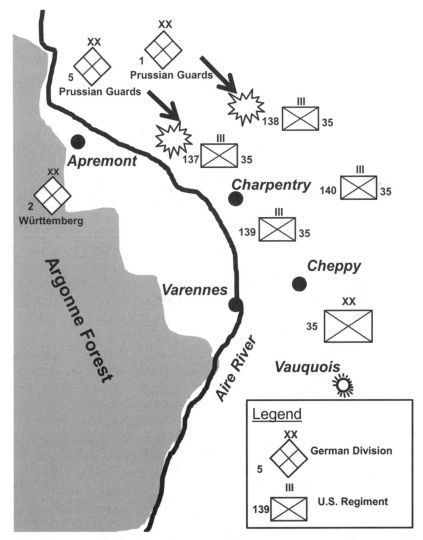

Map 9.2. Advance of the 35th Division, 28 September 1918. (Josiah Mastriano)

Division, the 1st Guards focused on knocking the Americans off of the high ground below Exermont.

Sunday, 29 September, was cold, dark, and rainy, as most days in the Meuse-Argonne campaign would prove to be. The Germans had to achieve success today to blunt the Americans. However, before the Germans attacked, the commander of the U.S. 140th

German prisoners were usually eager to help a wounded American off the battlefield. This ensured their safety as they passed through the lines to the first aid areas. In this photograph, a severely wounded American from the 35th Division has stopped to brief a passing officer of the situation at the front. (National Archives)

Regiment, Colonel Delaplane, was ordered to seize Exermont. Supported by a group of tanks and a small element of the 139th to the left, the 140th and 138th stormed through high explosive shells and poison gas, and into German machine gun nests. The advance was costly, and the dismal weather played into the Germans' hands. Lieutenant Henry L. Rothman, of the 140th's medical unit, advanced with the men and noted, "We went over at 5:30 A.M. and walked into a most awful barrage of H.E. [High Explosive] shrap [shrapnel] and gas which was penetrated by the rat-tat-tat of the Maxim and the vicious zip-zip of the bullets as they cut the grass at one's feet—or head. It was through this inferno that we swept down into Exermont."[21] The first unit to attempt the capture of Exermont was led by Major Parker Cromwell Kalloch of the 35th's 137th Regiment. As Major Kalloch led his men north, across an open field, the Germans unleashed the heaviest fires upon the men that they experienced. Kalloch's unit "was beaten back."[22] But there was hope.

Delaplane's attack would possibly have failed if not for the detachment of the 139th Regiment advancing in support to his left. The detachment striking forward on Delaplane's left was commanded by none other than Major James Rieger, the hero of Vauquois and Charpentry. It was ironic that this devout Christian found himself leading yet another charge on the Sabbath. Despite the heavy rain, mud, artillery explosions tearing into his line, and the deadly poisonous gas fog that the Germans poured into his ranks, Rieger was unmoved. He prayed for God's protection as he led his men forward.[23]

Many of the men in the division had first met Major Rieger in Camp Doniphan a year earlier. Their introduction to him was not on the rifle range, but in a popular Sunday school class that he organized and led each week. Rieger noted that the men lacked opportunities to study the Bible and for Christian fellowship and came up with the idea of the Sunday school class to fill this need. Rieger's class was immensely popular, with about three hundred men attending each week. His Bible teaching was relevant and powerful, focusing on the need for each man to accept Jesus as his personal Lord and Savior for Salvation and then to live a life that honored God. The admiration and respect that the men had for him grew as they saw that Rieger's Christian faith was genuine and he "walked his talk." It was clear that Rieger loved his men, and this was demonstrated by his care and concern for them. There was no surprise when in combat Rieger fearlessly led them into battle from the forefront and in the most dangerous position. He was indeed a fearless Christian whose faith carried him and his men through the fiercest barrage and even seemingly against the gates of hell itself.[24]

Rieger led his men north, across a wide-open field, where the German artillery and machine gun fires intensified. This was the same field where Major Kalloch's attack had failed a few minutes earlier. The division's history records what happened next as the men advanced against the fierce German resistance. "As if they were walking forward through a driving hailstorm they turned their faces leeward and, leaning forward against the blast, pushed ahead."[25] Rieger, with elements of the 140th Regiment, led the men down the clearing, across the small stream below Exermont, and through the village. His men eliminated or captured the German defenders and then continued the advance north to control the high ground overlooking the town. It was about 9:00 A.M. when he secured Exermont.

Delaplane arrived with his troops and ordered the men to dig in even as his tank support withdrew under heavy fire.[26]

Under Rieger's leadership, his battalion seized two important locations (Vauquois and Charpentry), and he was the first American in Exermont. Rieger then led his men beyond Exermont to the furthest point of advance of the entire division. The irony of this is that during their days of training at Camp Doniphan in Oklahoma, Rieger was told that he would not amount to much. Then, in 1917, the aspiring commander of the division's artillery brigade, Brigadier General Lucien Barry, was given the task of getting the 35th Division ready for war. However, Barry, a Regular Army officer, used his time more to root out National Guard officers that he disapproved of than to focus on training the men for combat. Barry apparently had designs to force Major Rieger out of the unit, ostensibly because he disapproved of the officer's Christian faith and his leading the popular Sunday school for the men. Rieger's overt Christian faith was not something that Barry wanted in his officers. However, Rieger was too popular with the men for Barry to fire him outright. On one occasion Barry blurted out that Rieger was "hopelessly useless."[27]

The "hopelessly useless" Major James E. Rieger would be lauded in France and the United States as the "Hero of the Argonne" for the series of heroic feats he accomplished during the first three days of the Meuse-Argonne Offensive. As a result, he was promoted to lieutenant colonel, given command of the 138th Regiment, and awarded the Distinguished Service Cross (DSC), the Purple Heart, and the French Croix de Guerre. Rieger's DSC citation states:

The Distinguished Service Cross is presented to James E. Rieger, Lieutenant Colonel, U.S. Army, for extraordinary heroism in action near Charpentry, France, September 27, 1918. Lieutenant Colonel Rieger commanded the battalion which had, with conspicuous gallantry, captured Vauquois Hill and the Bois-de-Rosignel, and which was later held up for some hours in front of Charpentry by severe artillery and machine-gun fire. He placed himself in front of all his men, and thus starting them forward, led them to the attack with such speed and dash that a large number of the enemy were cut off and captured. General Orders No. 59, W.D., 1919.[28]

Rieger, a humble and genuine man, would cite I Corinthians 1:27 to explain his heroism: "But God hath chosen the foolish things of the world to confound the wise; and God hath chosen the weak things of the world to confound the things which are mighty."

Brigadier General Lucien Barry proved less successful in his leadership during the Meuse-Argonne. His inability to provide the division's infantry with consistent artillery support came under severe scrutiny both during and after the battle. General Barry disregarded targeting information, even as his guns fired into the men of the 35th Division, causing scores of American casualties. Liggett told General Traub to fire Barry, saying, "If your artillery Brigade Commander is not giving you full support and is not to you a satisfactory and loyal commander you are authorized to relieve him." General Pershing met Brigadier General Barry on 28 September and wrote of the meeting, "General Barry inspired me with grave doubts as to whether he might not be a millstone about the neck of General Traub."[29] Barry also refused to adjust his fire based on reports from the Air Service, which would have spared the division's men being bombarded by his guns. AEF aircraft provided reports on the location of the friendly and enemy positions during the offensive, which Barry refused to use. His negligence was cited in an investigation led by the AEF chief of staff, General H. A. Drum, a month later.[30] Considering this assessment, one wonders about Barry's judgment on Rieger's being "hopelessly useless."

However, the Germans were far from done. Gallwitz needed to break the momentum of the American push up the Meuse Valley, and the focus of this counterattack was the American vulnerable point, the 35th Division. As the 35th dug in around Exermont, German artillery began firing around 11:30 A.M. into their positions. Using a combination of high explosives and gas rounds, the German artillery endeavored to isolate the forward American units and prevent reinforcements from moving up. A barrage of conventional artillery rounds and poisonous gas fired behind the Americans boxed them in.[31]

The most devastating artillery fire came from the German units hidden in the Argonne Forest. The 2nd Württemberg Landwehr Division had artillery forward observers posted on the hills and high in the trees of the rugged Argonne overlooking the Meuse Valley. Traub directed that his artillery could not fire into these German positions since it was outside of his divisional sector. This gave the Germans a free hand in dealing out death to Traub's men. The German Landwehr's division artillery, as well as other heavier caliber guns, fired into the flank of the 35th Division. The fires were particularly accurate and unhinged the American infantrymen in and around Exermont. As the Americans were smashed by poison gas and artillery shells, the Prussian 1st Guards launched a series of infantry attacks to outflank and break the 35th Division's hold between Baulny and Exermont.[32] The main body of the 1st Guards was made of up the 4th Guards (Foot) Regiment, which crossed the L'Aire River below Apremont and attacked into the left flank of the 35th Division. The 4th Guards (Foot) Regiment was reinforced with two storm trooper units and a company of the 122nd Württemberg Landwehr Regiment. Other 1st Guards units struck the front and right flank of the exposed lead elements of the 35th around Exermont.[33]

Additionally, the Germans had the advantage of controlling the skies with more than a dozen aircraft that strafed, bombed, and harassed the Americans at will. This, with the German advantage in volume and accuracy of artillery fire, ensured the destruction of the 35th.[34] The German counterattack was devastating. Germany had the advantage in air to ground aircraft. It developed the Junkers J1 in 1917 specifically for ground attack. This was followed by the production of yet another ground attack aircraft, the Hanover C-III. The Americans would experience the wrath of these machines daily in the Meuse-Argonne.[35]

Lieutenant Henry L. Rothman of the 140th's medical company established a dressing station in the ravine south of Exermont to treat the scores of injured men. As he bandaged wounded soldiers, German artillery crashed along the line, and soon retreating Americans streamed past telling him to leave with them. Rothman refused and remained with the injured. A German machine gun cut down a group of Americans retreating past Rothman. Seeing the mass of wounded, he crawled to them and began treating their wounds until the concussion of an explosion knocked him out. When Rothman came to, he realized that the Germans had advanced past his position; he was surrounded by the enemy. Instead of panicking, Rothman merely resumed treating the wounded until a second wave of Germans advanced toward him. The Germans had thus far done no harm to the wounded, until a soldier in the second wave held a pistol to the head of one American. However, a German sergeant intervened and told Rothman that the men "would be well cared for and asked [him] not to judge them all by the one who wished to shoot the wounded." The third wave of Germans to advance joked with Rothman, saying that he "would be better off with them than with the Americans." Rothman was moved to a prisoner-of-war camp in the heart of the Black Forest, near Villingen-Schwenningen, Germany. He returned to American hands on 29 November 1918 after two months of captivity.[36]

Major Rieger, from his forward position on the high ridge above Exermont, saw the Germans preparing to attack and alerted Colonel Delaplane, the 140th Regiment commander, who established his headquarters in Exermont, requesting reinforcements. However, instead of getting the support required, Rieger was told to withdraw his men. The stalwart major brilliantly organized his men to conduct a fighting retreat, which was more like a delaying action. His men were pressed at times on three sides, but, under the inspiring leadership of Rieger, held their ground until ordered to make an organized withdrawal. When the men arrived in Exermont they were surprised to see that Delaplane's 140th had already vacated the village. Rieger's men arrived at the new line (two kilometers south of Exermont) later that evening with only two officers (Rieger being one of the two) remaining and 65 percent of his men killed or wounded.[37]

It was a moment of great crisis for the 35th Division and potentially the U.S. First Army in the Meuse-Argonne region. Only three battalions in the entire division were fighting as organized units to impede the German advance (Rieger, O'Connor, and Brightfield). If any of these failed to do their utmost this day, the line would be broken. Captain Thompson, commander of the 3rd Battalion of the 138th Regiment, was appalled by the disorganization and breakdown of cohesion in the 140th Regiment as it retreated through his position below Exermont. He had witnessed a similar tragic collapse of another unit just the day before, where a retreat turned into a rout. When Thompson was ordered to pull his men back, he feared that the unit would join the retreat. Instead of pulling back, Thompson ordered his men to advance. They attacked through the German barrage and momentarily blunted the German progress. But the 35th was no longer an effective fighting force. Word of the withdrawal spread across the division, and that was enough for the dispirited men to leave their positions and units to seek safety in the rear. One eyewitness wrote, "across the road came the worn-out infantry. . . . By the time each unit reached the . . . line, the confusion and disorganization was about as bad as it could be. In the absence of officers, orders and rumors of orders drifted about from man to man, and many of them thought the place they were to stop was much further back. In no case that I have heard of did the men fail to stop and take position when they had a recognizable order to do so."[38]

The Americans were quickly driven back to the line they held the day before, and something had to be done to prevent this from turning into a rout. Even Traub was affected and feared he was about to be captured. In the midst of the crisis, individual officers rallied the broken units. All of the 140th Regiment's chaplains stood in the gap to bring order out of the chaos. One of these was Chaplain Hart, doing what Traub failed to do. He saw the masses of broken men filtering to the south and stood on the new line, acting with confidence and boldness. One eyewitness wrote, "It was interesting to see [Chaplain Hart] suddenly become Division Headquarters. 'You are a Captain,' he would say to one doughboy. 'You are a Lieutenant,' to another, 'take charge of these men.'" Colonel Delaplane, who was "no lover of chaplains," was amazed by this and offered the highest praise to Chaplain Evan Edwards during this incident, "Well Chaplain, I thought I had three chaplains, but I have not. I have three SOLDIERS!" All of the regiment's chaplains were awarded citations for their selfless courage.[39]

The only reserve that the division had remaining was the 110th Engineer Regiment. It was ordered forward to establish a line along the east-west Apremont–Eclisfontaine road just above the Chaudron farm. The engineers deployed along this line were the only thing between the Germans and disaster. Captain Thompson's battalion maintained contact with the enemy and slowly retrograded to high ground just forward of the engineer line, and it was the only infantry unit of battalion strength to support this final position. When the Germans arrived, the 110th Engineers held the line and saved the 35th from a complete breakdown.

The collapse that the 35th experienced on 29 September truly began two days earlier when the division had culminated. Culmination is a military term that marks the point when an attacking force can no longer continue offensive movement. The 35th Division's culmination after just forty-eight hours came about for many reasons. Heavy losses of men as well as the mixing up of units plagued

Chaplain Evan A.
Edwards was one
of several chaplains
who rallied the
men of the 140th
Regiment after it
was driven back
by the Prussian 1st
Guards Division on
29 September 1918.
(National Archives)

the division. But the chief reason for this was the lack of leadership from the division commander down to the company and platoon level. General Traub's shortcomings have already been described. Throughout the brief five days that the 35th was in the line, Traub was continually in a react mode to both the demands of General Pershing and the battle that his soldiers faced. The matter was not helped by Hunter Liggett, who merely carried forward the messages and orders of Pershing without analysis or consideration. But the failure fell on Traub, who was woefully out of touch with the realities and instead merely forwarded Pershing's orders to his subordinate leaders to follow.

The failing of Traub notwithstanding, a far greater problem was the high loss of junior leaders at the company and platoon levels. Pershing demanded that his officers lead from the front, and this is exactly what thousands of captains and lieutenants did, with an overwhelming number of them being killed or wounded in action by the end of the second day. The division went into the fight without enough junior leaders, which was exacerbated by the loss of those they had. As the division's history notes, "The most serious loss, from the cold military viewpoint, was in the officers. There were plenty of men left to do the work, but the division had started in woefully short of Lieutenants, Captains and Majors, and every loss of that kind hurt."[40] It was the loss of these junior leaders, combined with the loss of a number of majors and lieutenant colonels, that caused the ultimate failure of the 35th to conduct any further significant offensive action during the remaining three days it was in the line. There were several small advances made over the next two days; however, effective command and control ceased, and organizing attacks on the grand scale as seen on 26 and 27 September was simply impossible.

Additionally, Traub's propensity to pass along orders without contemplation or consideration of their effects on his division is noteworthy. Much has already been said of this. But even General Pershing was astounded that Traub blindly followed orders without requesting clarification or modifications when the situation necessitated it. On 28 September, General Pershing wrote, "I decided to go out and see the situation toward the front myself." He made his way to the 35th Division. After a disturbing meeting with General Barry, Pershing met with Traub. He was concerned about the condition of the 35th and its lack of progress. Traub attempted to explain what caused these problems and explained that the Germans were delivering devastating flanking artillery fire from their positions in the Argonne Forest. He went on to say that he could do nothing about it due to Pershing's order not to fire outside of the divisional sector. Pershing was stupefied by this and said, "But surely you do not obey that order?" Traub bluntly answered in the affirmative, saying, "It is the order."[41] Traub's conduct and poor leadership were brought into question after the war, and he was ordered to testify to the House of Representatives Rules Committee to explain his actions.

The 1st Infantry Division was ordered to quickly move via mechanized transport to assembly areas near Varennes and Vauquois to replace the collapsing 35th. The 1st Infantry Division, known as the Big Red One, moved into the 35th's sector on 30 September. It seems that nothing could now save the 35th. The combination of poor leadership and inexperienced soldiers could not overcome the German forces that they faced.

10

Securing Montfaucon and the Center of the Meuse Valley

27–30 September 1918

> Montfaucon was not taken. . . . About noon I gave . . .
> instructions that it should be taken.
> —Diary of General Pershing, 27 September 1918

The failure of the U.S. 79th Division to take Montfaucon was a grave concern for General Pershing. Continued German possession of this key terrain threatened the continued advance of the American Expeditionary Forces in the Meuse Valley. Montfaucon had been an integral part of the German defense of the western half of the Meuse Valley since 1914 thanks to the incredible observation it afforded those who held it. From the crest of the hill, and from the old church tower (later destroyed by French artillery), one has a clear view of every major terrain feature ten kilometers west to the Argonne and fifteen kilometers east to the high ground above Verdun. The Germans used this hill with some effect in directing artillery barrages against masses of enemy formations during the war. The hill simply had to be taken and taken quickly.

The saga of the 79th Division's battle for Montfaucon is one of missed opportunities. American units both to the east and west of the hill advanced past it and were positioned to bypass and take the hill from behind. To the west was the 37th Division, which made excellent progress the day before and was in a good position to strike behind the German positions on Montfaucon. Elements of the 37th's 145th Regiment made an uncoordinated attempt to attack

Colonel Claude B. Sweezey, commander of the 313th Regiment, 79th Division, whose men captured Montfaucon. When a soldier reported that the advance could not continue, he responded in his characteristic stammering way, "Y-e-s y-y-ou will, b-b-y God." (U.S. Army Heritage and Education Center, Carlisle, Pennsylvania)

into the flank of Montfaucon, but inexperience and lack of artillery support doomed it to failure. Had the push occurred when the 79th Division's 313th Regiment attacked, the results would have been far better. As described earlier, Colonel Claude Sweezey gallantly led his men forward, but inexperience, concealed German machine gun nests, lack of artillery support, and the morning fog fragmented the unit. By the time the men reached Montfaucon, their ability to drive the Germans from this so-called "little Gibraltar" was nigh impossible.

On the other side of Montfaucon were the combat-experienced men of the 4th Division. The 4th Division made excellent gains east of Montfaucon and was in a good position to strike the German position from the rear. However, this was no easy endeavor. Recent scholarship on the subject asserts that some sort of personal agenda prevented the 4th Division from assisting in the capture of Montfaucon. Nothing could be further from the truth.

The 4th Division was part of the U.S. III Corps. Montfaucon and the 79th Division were in V Corps. Conducting cross-unit attacks over corps boundaries is not an easy endeavor, even for well-trained and experienced combat units. To conduct cross-boundary operations, the key is having unencumbered communications between all units. Crossing a corps boundary without clear and effective communications could result in your units being fired upon by friendly forces. Additionally, direct liaison was required between the 79th and 4th to support a cross-boundary operation, but there were no contacts between these units.[1] Finally, the authority to conduct a cross-corps operation would require the planning and support of the American army headquarters, something that was not possible at that time. Knowing the risk of such an endeavor, General Pershing strictly forbade cross-border operations unless authorized by his headquarters, despite his retort to Traub to the contrary.

The U.S. 4th Division advanced four kilometers ahead of the 79th Division on 26 September, reaching the Bois de Septsarges. The division was ordered to continue its advance north, which it did with considerable loss. Although the U.S. First Army *discussed* the possibility of bypassing Montfaucon and attacking it from behind, the ability to actually execute such a maneuver with mostly inexperienced forces seemed daunting at best. Instead, ambiguous orders arrived at the 4th Infantry Division headquarters suggesting that it support the 79th in securing Montfaucon. The 4th Division's chief of staff, Colonel Christian Bach, was at a loss as to how his division would actually do this, saying that the order was "as clear as mud." Colonel Bach discussed the matter with his counterpart at III Corps, Brigadier General Alfred Bjornstad, and they agreed that the 4th would support the 79th attack on Montfaucon "not by an advance into the [79th's sector] . . . but by a steady progression to the front."[2] This would result in the German defenders of Montfaucon being threatened by encirclement and hopefully force them back. In the end, this is what triggered the German withdrawal of their forces from Montfaucon on 27 September, justifying the decision of the 4th Division and III Corps chiefs of staff. But this occurred after the 79th Division suffered hundreds of casualties attempting to assault the hill.

Like the other units in the line, Pershing demanded that the 79th Division push its headquarters forward, making it impossible to maintain contact with subordinate units or to coordinate the movement of the entire force. The orders from Pershing arrived at General Joseph E. Kuhn's headquarters shortly after midnight on 27 September. They said:

> Division and Brigade commanders will place themselves as far up toward the front of the advance of their respective units as may be necessary to direct their movements with energy and rapidity in any attack. The enemy is in retreat or holding lightly in places, and advance elements of several divisions are already on First Army objectives and there should be no delay or hesitation in going forward. Detachments of sufficient size will be left behind to engage isolated strong points which will be turned and not be permitted to hold up or delay the advance of the entire brigade or division. All officers will push their units forward with all possible energy. Corps and Division Commanders will not hesitate to relieve on the spot any officer of whatever rank, who fails to show in this emergency those qualities of leadership, required to accomplish the task which confronts us. This order will be published to all concerned by the quickest means possible. Pershing.[3]

Pershing's 27 September order belied his lack of understanding of the situation, or of commanding an army in the field for that matter. Advancing the headquarters forward in the field of combat was befitting of the Napoleonic wars of the nineteenth century, in his "frontier campaigns" in Cuba, the Philippines, or Mexico, but not on the Western Front. Pershing's divisions encompassed more than twenty thousand men, which required that their respective headquarters be located not forward, but farther back, so as to provide command and control of the massive formations and divergent subordinate organizations. Well-placed division, brigade, and regimental headquarters enable the synchronization and coordination of attacks that include planned artillery support and mutually supporting maneuver to bypass and outflank enemy positions. Instead, by pushing headquarters forward, these massive American units would launch uncoordinated, piecemeal attacks that lacked adequate artillery support and included little, if any, maneuver. More times than not, local commanders resorted to outdated frontal attacks that achieved some ground, but at horrific costs in lives. Even the Germans were appalled to see these amateurish attacks charging headlong into the merciless sting of their machine guns. By clinging to the old style of fighting, Pershing would only achieve small, tactical victories, and lose the chance of an early breakthrough in the Meuse-Argonne.

Pershing's reputation as a ruthless leader, firing generals for the slightest infraction, had the added detriment of compelling his subordinate commanders to not seize the initiative or try innovative maneuvers. The 27 September order had just this sort of effect. His subordinate commanders dutifully advanced forward, exacerbating their inability to maintain contact with their subordinate units. Not only were the forward headquarters virtually impossible to find in the darkness, but telephone lines were cut by artillery fire, and runners often failed to find the units they were sent to pass messages to. This forced General Kuhn, the 79th commander, to bypass unit commanders and issue orders directly to any of the subordinate units that he could contact. Although such an adaptation helped the 79th continue its forward movement, it was detrimental to the division as a whole. Entire units were cut out of the unit's plans, resulting in lack of synchronization and coordination of movements. Instead of a massive division-level attack on 27 September, the advance would be a series of disjointed probes directed at dislodging the Germans from Montfaucon. Even Kuhn and his chief of staff, Colonel Tenney Ross, were forced to set out

Major General Joseph E. Kuhn, the 79th Division commander. General Pershing was concerned that the 79th Division failed to capture Montfaucon on the first day of the Meuse-Argonne campaign and ordered that everything be done to secure it on 27 September 1918. Other than putting immense pressure on Kuhn, Pershing offered no material assistance or support to capture the vital hill. (U.S. Army Heritage and Education Center, Carlisle, Pennsylvania)

on horseback early on 27 September to figure out what his division was doing. This is how far command and control had disintegrated after less than a day of combat.[4]

Conflicting orders were given to the 79th Division's units on when to attack. Orders arrived from Pershing's headquarters demanding that the division push throughout the night to catch up to the advance of the 4th Division. This caused the 314th Regiment on the right flank of the division to begin slowly advancing after 4 A.M. The darkness served the 314th well. Its men listened to the advice of the French liaison officers on the importance of maneuver. Using darkness as cover, several of the German machine guns that halted their advance the previous day were destroyed. Others were bypassed in the darkness, leaving them to the follow-on regiment, the 315th.[5]

After only one full day of fighting, the Americans were proving to be fast learners. This type of assault, advancing by small unit infiltration tactics and bypassing enemy strong points to be mopped up by follow-on units, was an innovation from 1916 that forever changed the way infantry maneuvers and attacks on the battlefield. Until 1916, most attacks were arranged largely in line formations, with masses of men marching into battle to overwhelm an enemy. However, the advent of the machine gun made such an approach obsolete. As is so often the case, military tactics lagged behind technology. More than a year of using linear attacks of massed men would pass before this innovation was integrated into Western Front tactics.

French captain André Laffargue wrote in 1915 of the need to transition to infiltration tactics instead of using Napoleonic linear attacks. Laffargue called for small groups of soldiers to maneuver across the battlefield, destroying enemy positions with machine guns and grenades. Strong enemy positions would be bypassed and destroyed later as these small groups advanced forward. Such an approach called for decentralized command and control and relied on the individual initiative of each soldier. The French Army would embrace his ideas during the Battle of Verdun, where, after tens of thousands of men died attempting traditional frontal attacks to retake the vital Fort Douaumont, the French leadership employed Laffargue's ideas with great effect. The Germans studied the French success in retaking the lost ground north of Verdun and also had copies of Laffargue's book. In 1918, the Germans used their perfected version of this tactic in the form of storm troops.[6] Without formal training in Laffargue's approach, the soldiers of the 79th were quickly adapting to the realities of war on the Western Front in an astounding fashion.

As the remainder of the division prepared to attack around 7 A.M., a battalion of field guns was finally in position to support the advance. This unit managed to navigate through the immense American traffic jams behind the lines and over the rough roads to co-locate with the 313th Regiment to provide timely and effective support for the attack. This was welcome, especially when the guns went into action an hour before the advance began. The infantry was thankful for this support, and it was the only artillery that it would have, as a false report from the First Army prohibited fires on Montfaucon, believing that American soldiers were already on the hill.[7] Tank support was promised as well, and with this the 79th had a good chance of taking the hill.

Pershing and his staff were increasingly frustrated by the breakdown of communication and by the uncoordinated action. One staff officer wrote, "Attack scheduled everywhere for 5:30 was slow in starting by an hour or so in each division and did not go fast anywhere. The difficulties of getting reports with even substantial accuracy continue."[8] Pershing, his army, and the corps staff had no idea that the lack of synchronized action was due in large part to their orders for commanders and headquarters to deploy too far forward. When the 35th Division's 313th Regiment (to the left of the sector) began its attack at 7 A.M., it did so more than an hour after the rest of the army and more than two hours after its sister regiment, the 314th, which had been advancing since 4:30 A.M.

Had the two regiments coordinated their attack, more ground could have been gained. General Kuhn only added to the chaos when he fired one of his brigade commanders: Brigadier General Robert Noble. Although Noble was not a very good leader, the timing of his sacking, during a day of important attacks, only ensured that the 79th Division would soon find itself in the same state as the 35th. Some viewed Kuhn's decision to fire Noble as a way to deflect the blame for failing to seize Montfaucon the day before, and this seems to be the case.[9] It seemed that both Pershing and Kuhn were conspiring to destroy the combat effectiveness of the 79th Division with their disjointed and unrealistic demands and orders. In addition to this, more conflicting orders arrived. To compound matters, the division's four regiments were ordered to break from their normal brigade formations to form provisional brigades. The 313th and the 316th fell under the leadership of the 157th Brigade, while the 314th and 315th Regiments came under the 158th Brigade. This disrupted the unit organization that had been in existence since 1917. Since the founding of the division, the 313th and 314th were under the 157th Brigade, and the 315 and 316th were part of the 158th Brigade. This last-minute reorganization was extremely disruptive to command and control and demonstrates the lack of rational leadership at the senior level of the 79th Division.[10] New command relationships were imposed over units, which had to work under unknown leadership teams, a new staff, and with support units with which they were not familiar. Success or failure of military operations are frequently determined by how well a unit works for a specific command team, and personal relationships between the staff and support elements often make the decisive difference.[11] To make matters worse, Kuhn ordered this reorganization just an hour before the entire division would assault Montfaucon. It was an-all-or-nothing gambit for Kuhn, and this green division would mirror the fate of the 35th, where poor leadership and inexperience would necessitate its replacement in the line by another division.

On paper, Major General Joseph Kuhn had the experience to succeed as a division commander. He had been commissioned as an officer in the U.S. Army in 1885 and graduated first in his West Point class. As an engineer officer, Kuhn commanded soldiers at the battalion level. He was a military observer during the Russo-Japanese War in 1905 and in Germany in 1914–1916. He was one of only a handful of American officers to see the advent of modern war; yet Kuhn was unable to apply his experiences to his division. There are several causes for this shortcoming. One of the chief reasons for this failure was the lack of senior leader training. The U.S. Army founded the War College in 1901 and was graduating small classes of officers with some understanding of higher level warfare. The first class of the U.S. Army War College began in 1904, just ten years before the First World War.

The War College was founded as a response to the dismal performance of the U.S. Army in mobilizing, deploying, and sustaining its force during the Spanish-American War. It was created to train future generations of officers to operate at upper echelons of command and staff. However, declining budgets, a shrinking force, and a focus on maintaining a frontier-type force that policed the new American territories in the Philippines and the Caribbean shifted much of the army's attention away from planning for a conventional war. Finally, in 1916, the War College began planning for what the army would need to do should it be drawn into the European war. The president of the U.S. Army War College, Brigadier General Montgomery M. Macomb, directed that the staff and students begin planning for what a war with Germany would look like. However, President Woodrow Wilson accused him of warmongering and ordered that the Army War College cease such activities.[12] The decision to maintain an army focused on "small wars" and the lack of preparation by the Wilson administration resulted in an American field army and an officer corps not ready for the realities of modern war. Such was the case for Kuhn, and the price to be paid for the lack of prudent prewar preparation was the blood of young men.

As the remainder of the U.S. 79th Division prepared for its morning attack, Gallwitz weighed his options. Montfaucon was still in his hands, and this essential terrain could be used to stall the entire American offensive. However, the U.S. 4th Division was in a position to outflank the units defending the hill. Gallwitz's forces included the German 117th Division (11th, 157th, and 450th Regiments) and the 37th Division, which had been arriving throughout the night and morning. Without this new force, Montfaucon could not be held. The initial American attack the previous day was costly for the German 117th, as its 450th Regiment was nearly combat ineffective from the losses it suffered. It will be remembered that the lead elements of the German 37th Division counterattacked against the U.S. 79th Division the day before and was responsible for stalling the American attack. The arrival of the remainder of the 37th Division on Montfaucon had the potential to blunt and defeat the U.S. 79th Division's attack as long as the American 4th Division did not threaten to encircle the hill.[13] Despite the threat of an attack from the rear, Gallwitz directed that the Germans hold the hill until ordered otherwise.

The soldiers of the German 37th Division assigned to defend Montfaucon realized that their position was tenuous at best. The 37th Division was recruited from East Prussia and included three regiments, the 147th, 150th, and 151st. This unit had a proven record throughout the war, and was particularly noted for its excellent performance in supporting three of the five German offensives that occurred across the Western Front between March and July 1918. Although they would do their best to defend the hill from another attack, there was some confusion among the soldiers. Two battalions of the unit were told that they would be replaced, but no relief arrived, and the men remained in their positions. Colonel Georg von Harder, the commander of the 151st, personally surveyed the defenses and encouraged the men to make all preparations possible for another enemy attack in the morning. Colonel Harder had been awarded the Pour le Merite for his superb leadership during the Battle of the Marne just a few months before.[14] Harder told the 3rd Battalion commander, Hauptman Hofmeister, that his unit would remain on Montfaucon. Hofmeister had been sick with the flu and had been told earlier that his unit would be relieved. Hofmeister dutifully inspected his battalion and ended up personally guiding one of his companies back to their fighting positions when no replacement units arrived.[15]

The 37th Division's 151st Regiment was concerned about their precarious position. The southern rim of the hill below the main defensive line on Montfaucon protruded into the American lines. The unit's leadership was rightly concerned that the position would be pinched off by an American attack from the east and west. The decision was made to withdraw the men and reposition them in the main defensive belt below the southern crest of the hill.[16]

As adjustments were made to the line, it seemed that the darkness and thick fog worked against the German defenders. There was, however, some good news for the Germans. During the night, two Bavarian companies arrived to bolster the defenses of Montfaucon. But as they were moving into their positions "in the night and fog, [they] suddenly disappeared." An officer from the 37th (Lieutenant Linde) was detailed to find them, but he could not locate them.[17] As the Germans finalized their defensive plan for Montfaucon, the attack commenced. The 151st Regiment of the German 37th Division recorded how it began: "Under the protection of the fog were made our final adjustments. Suddenly, the Americans attacked with strong forces supported by tanks. The brave and impetuous actions of the enemy were hard to defend against. However, with the help of our mortars and excellent artillery support, we were able to hold the line, but only at the cost of frightening casualties."[18]

The 7 A.M. attack on Montfaucon by the U.S. 79th Division was a crescendo of death and destruction. When the fog cleared, German resistance stiffened as the Americans made their way up the long slope. The 313th and 314th Regiments faced heavy German artillery fire that tore into the ranks. The entire slope was watched closely by German artillery observers located on the high ground to the east of the Meuse (from Hill 378) and ten kilometers to the west in the Argonne, setting the southern half of the hill ablaze in a Dante-like inferno.[19] The only reply from the U.S. 79th Division was a lone battalion of artillery from the 157th Artillery Brigade.

The division was blessed to have this one battalion of artillery get through the tangle of traffic behind the lines. The chaos that ensued on trying to advance units and support forward was hindered by a return flow of vehicles carrying the thousands of wounded. Combined with occasional German artillery fire and strafing German aircraft, there seemed no way to get things moving. It was so bad that the commander of the American Air Service, Brigadier General Billy Mitchell, commented after he flew over the rear area of the 79th Division, "Although there was some congestion in other places, it was worse in this area than I had ever seen on a battlefield."[20]

The honor of taking Montfaucon fell to the 313th Regiment. Recruited largely from Baltimore, the men were close-knit and proud. They were commanded by Colonel Claude B. Sweezey, who was an experienced officer and West Point graduate. Sweezey was known for his military bearing, for being cool under fire, and for a speech impediment. One of the traits that the men respected most was his moral courage to have frank—and at times heated—discussions with his brigade commander, William Nicholson. Sweazey was determined to succeed this day and led from the front. As part of the formation was bogged down by German machine guns, one soldier ran to him to report that the advance could not continue. Sweezey responded in his characteristic stammering way, "Y-e-s y-y-ou will, b-b-y God." The men grinned at hearing this and it was soon used by most soldiers of the 313th in response to anyone suggesting that they couldn't go on in the face of overwhelming enemy fire.[21]

As the Americans attacked, six French-manned Renault tanks burst upon the scene and, to the elation of the Americans, advanced to their front. Halfway up the slope, concealed German machine guns opened fire, with the French tanks maneuvering and returning fire to eliminate the strong points. Unlike the previous night, when the American soldiers did not support the French tanks in the late assault up Montfaucon, this time the troops kept up and used grenades and their rifles to break up the German defense. By 11 A.M. the lead elements of the 313th Regiment swept into the outskirts of the ruins of the town that once rested on Montfaucon. Among the first to enter Montfaucon was Lieutenant Joseph H. Cochran, who "showed remarkable courage and absolute disregard for his personal safety in leading his platoon against machine gun positions."[22]

The 79th pressed the attack and swept through the damaged village and over the summit of Montfaucon. The men marveled at the ruins of the ancient cathedral, where the Germans had carved holes into the remaining buttresses to use for observation and sniper fire. One of the houses in the village included a giant, fortified

In the attic of this house was a powerful telescope used to direct artillery fire against the French during the 1916 Battle of Verdun. The crown prince of Germany also used the telescope to monitor the progress of his army in 1916. The Americans found the telescope in good working order, although a Doughboy seeking souvenirs made off with the eyepiece, making the telescope useless. (U.S. Army Heritage and Education Center, Carlisle, Pennsylvania)

observation scope used to direct artillery fire. The crown prince of the German Empire himself was reputed to have been in this observation house in 1916 during the Battle of Verdun. The men at last saw the importance of Montfaucon, which dominated everything between the Argonne and the Meuse River. Artillery observers were ordered forward to use this position against the enemy, which they began to do with some effect.

Mopping up the ruined village, destroyed cathedral, and hill took forty-five minutes. With this finished, Colonel Sweezey sent a message via courier pigeon at 11:45 A.M. announcing "Montfaucon captured 1145." Pigeon 47 was given the honor of delivering the message. The bird flew the twenty-two miles back to its station in 1 hour and 43 minutes, "with its left wing torn and bleeding, evidently caused by shrapnel."[23] A runner was later dispatched to inform Kuhn, who was elated by the news that indeed Montfaucon was secured.

The Americans found Montfaucon a veritable fortress. The Germans had carved deep dugouts into the hill and often used the ruins of the houses to create bunkers, barracks, storehouses, and even fortified observation points. These were strong positions designed to survive artillery barrages, and in which the soldiers were happy to find shelter. One of the greatest discoveries, however, was a fresh water well, which the men of the 79th greedily enjoyed. No resupply of any sort had reached the men in two days, and the fresh water and captured German rations helped ameliorate their exhaustion, thirst, and hunger.

As the hill was swept of German defenders, Pershing sent orders to the 79th that the hill must be taken. He wrote, "About noon I gave energetic orders that [Montfaucon] should be taken by one means or another." The hill was indeed already taken, with the 79th Division both sweeping the town of defenders and deploying units along the northern, western, and eastern portions of the hill to repulse an anticipated German counterattack deemed to be forming north of the area. Pershing's role as army commander should have focused on coordinating and synchronizing the attacks of the three army corps that he had in combat. The damaged and limited roads, the heavy traffic, enemy harassing artillery fires, and the inexperience of the soldiers all conspired to prevent artillery from getting into the fight and furthermore prevented supplies, ammunition, and food from getting to the front. Yet Pershing was preoccupied with the immediate fight, the day-to-day tactics, instead of thinking forward in time and space about what needed to occur to maintain the army's momentum. The idea that "amateurs talk about tactics, but professionals study logistics" seems applicable. Pershing was a man of the moment, of the fight at hand, which was the responsibility of his subordinate commanders. He lacked strategic thinking and long-range plans on how to achieve a breakthrough in the Meuse-Argonne. Instead, he found himself in a reaction mode, allowing the Germans to dictate the terms of battle and thereby giving them the general initiative.

To the east of Montfaucon, the 79th Division's 314th Regiment maintained the offensive and, although facing stiff opposition, kept up with its sister regiment, the 313th. The 314th's commander, Colonel William H. Oury, conducted a masterful advance in the face of a determined enemy. After a brief pause east of Montfaucon, the 315th Regiment arrived and Colonel Oury's men resumed the

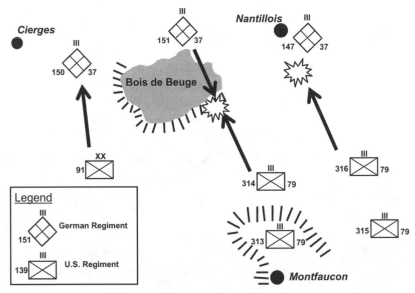

Map 10.1. Advance of the 79th Division North of Montfaucon, 27–29 September 1918. (Josiah Mastriano)

attack to the north, but only made minor gains in the face of German resistance.[24]

To the left, the 313th, now supported by the 316th Regiment, also endeavored to advance north toward Nantillois. The 313th managed to make slightly more progress thanks to French tanks that supported the advance. The defending German 151st Infantry Regiment (of the 37th Division) suffered the wrath of this Franco-American attack. The Germans reported, "Between 1235–1245 in the afternoon, there was a breach of our lines by an enemy attack that included tanks in the western portion of Bois de Beuge across the front of the 151st regiment and our left flank was set ablaze by artillery, infantry and machine gun fire."[25] This created a crisis for the two German regiments defending this area (the 151st and 147th) and threatened to exploit the boundary between the two units.

Unit boundaries tend to be vulnerable points, as they require considerable coordination and deconfliction to ensure mutually supporting operations. This is particularly sensitive at the regimental, brigade, and divisional levels. Should an enemy find a unit's boundary and attack into it, there is a higher likelihood of success.

This Renault tank was disabled during the 79th Division's advance toward Nantillois. (U.S. Army Heritage and Education Center, Carlisle, Pennsylvania)

The commander of the German 37th Division immediately identified the danger and focused all the artillery that could be mustered on the area, particularly against the French tanks.[26] This began to erupt around the advancing French tanks and American infantry. Several of the tanks were destroyed with direct hits, forcing the remaining ones to withdraw. In the ranks of the attacking American infantry plunging forward as the tanks retreated was Lieutenant Hank Welling, commanding F Company of the 316th Regiment. As he led his men down the gentle north slope of Montfaucon toward the breech in the German lines, he was severely wounded and fell to the ground. One of the junior noncommissioned officers, Corporal Paul Runkle, saw the lieutenant fall and took charge, leading the men forward until he was relieved by an officer. The officer was none other than Lieutenant Welling, who refused to be removed from the battle. Despite such sacrifice and courage, the attack stalled just a kilometer north of Montfaucon.[27]

Many of the 313th and 314th's officers were killed or wounded leading the charge up and around Montfaucon. Considering the condition of these units, General Kuhn ordered the 315th and 316th to take the lead in the advance that would begin on 28 September. Although the previous two days were merciless for the division, it was a learning organization. Unlike the 35th Division, which was nearing culmination and collapse, the 79th was adapting well to a tough situation. Kuhn learned the importance of maintaining control over his force and deployed his headquarters in an excellent location where he could communicate with his commanders. Orders began to flow in a timely fashion and, although his division had suffered considerable casualties, better communication helped the division synchronize and coordinate its upcoming advance.[28]

However, there was a material lack of artillery. Only four batteries were available to support the attack thanks to the massive traffic jam behind the lines. Meanwhile, the Germans had dozens of guns and howitzers of all calibers in position to lay waste to the front from their concealed positions along the heights of the Argonne to the west, the heights of the Meuse to the east, and the high ground to the north behind Romagne. The German barrage along the American line commenced at 5:00 A.M. and continued in earnest throughout the day. The scant artillery units that the Americans had in action provided meager support in comparison.[29] The 79th Division history records: "The lines dropped; automatics opened a spluttering reply, here and there a group rushed, dropped and crawled cautiously; the lines crept on—forward; delayed, harassed, terribly punished—but on, their dead behind them, their tortured wounded moaning to the winds that most heartbreaking cry of the battlefield: 'First aid, this way; first aid, this way.' German artillery, some of it from beyond the distant Meuse, dropped a hail of shrapnel and high explosives; machine guns spewed the ground with a deadly shower—the Regiment crawled on."[30]

The 3rd Battalion commander sent the following message to his headquarters, "Being fired at point blank by field pieces. For God's sake get artillery or we'll be annihilated."[31] Kuhn asked his men to hang on, as both heavy and light French tanks would soon arrive to support the attack. Twelve tanks arrived in the afternoon, in the nick of time to bolster the wavering attack by the 316th Regiment. Thanks to the tanks and the leadership of the 316th commander, Colonel Oscar Charles, the men managed to advance several hundred yards, clearing Bois de Beuge and advancing north of Nantillois.

The Germans took measure of the terrain and created kill zones in any areas where the movement of soldiers could be canalized. One such area was a cup-like valley between Montfaucon and Nantillois, which the 315th Regiment advanced through. Passing the survivors of Oury's 314th Regiment, Colonel Alden Knowles, the 315th commander, identified the location of the enemy artillery firing into this kill zone and requested counterfire to destroy or disrupt them before his men passed through.[32] The message from Knowles stated:

Have [Artillery]. pound 10.2–80.2, 13.1–80.5, 12.6–81.5 and line 10.0–82.3 to 11.0–82.6. These hostile positions form a cup into which we cannot advance without serious losses. Some guns to be directed on Nantillois. [Artillery]. must get busy fast if they are to assist Inf. Tanks circled right of Nantillois last night going 500 meters north that town. No tanks now assisting on our front. We are in touch with 4th Div. on right. Our disposition 10.6–78.6 to 12.3–79.2 Please rush artillery fire.[33]

What minuscule support that could be provided was so insignificant that Knowles and his men reported that no American or French counterfire was evident. Although the attack was to go at 7:00 A.M., Knowles waited thirty minutes hoping against hope for some effective artillery support. It never materialized, and with that he ordered his men forward, using rushes to dash through the German artillery. Adding to the horror, a squadron of German aircraft attacked them from the skies, pouring hot lead into the earth around the men.[34]

The Germans surged more than twenty aircraft into the area. In addition to strafing the ranks of men attacking below, one of the German aviators shot down the single balloon that the 6th Balloon Company had in the sky for observation and artillery support. However, forward observers arrived at the crown prince's old observatory on Montfaucon and quickly filled that gap, despite being under constant artillery fires themselves.[35]

The German aviator who shot down the observation balloon was *Unteroffizier* Hans Heinrich Marwere. After successfully eliminating the balloon, he returned to strafe the Americans. However, the infantry would have none of that and turned their weapons on

German pilot Hans Heinrich Marwere flew over Montfaucon to shoot down the single American observation balloon airborne near there on 27 September 1918. This photograph shows the burning balloon. (U.S. Army Heritage and Education Center, Carlisle, Pennsylvania)

Marwere was rescued from his plane and captured after crash landing in the American lines on 27 September 1918. (U.S. Army Heritage and Education Center, Carlisle, Pennsylvania)

Marwere's aircraft, disabling his engine. He was forced to land his plane among the Americans. As the plane alighted on the ground, a wheel came loose and the plane flipped over. Hans Marwere was rescued and captured by soldiers of the 315th Regiment.[36]

German pilot Hans Marwere's plane flipped onto its back as he tried to land. It was damaged by American ground fire on 27 September 1918. (U.S. Army Heritage and Education Center, Carlisle, Pennsylvania)

At dawn, the German 147th Regiment reported a heavy enemy barrage. This is interesting in that, from the American perspective, the barrage was ineffective. However, although it paled in comparison to the size of the corresponding German barrage, it still was noted as preceding a general American attack, which occurred between 7:00 A.M. and 7:30 A.M. across the front south of Nantillois. The plan was to focus heavy artillery fires against the field upon which the Americans had to cross to continue their advance. From the German perspective, they repelled several attacks until "suddenly, around the noon, two enemy battalions and tanks advanced toward Nantillois."[37]

By now, one-third of the Americans attacking with the 79th Division were killed or wounded, and the combined effects of the German artillery, machine gun fires, and incessant aerial strafing created significant disorganization. But the men had their orders, so they advanced north toward Nantillois. Two of the tanks were Saint-Chamond heavy tanks. Equipped with a 75mm cannon and four Hotchkiss machine guns, this vehicle packed considerable punch and had quite a psychological impact on the battlefield. The

Two French Saint-Chamond heavy tanks supported the American push toward Nantillois. The tank in this photograph was knocked out by German artillery. The tank's crew was buried adjacent to the wreckage. The Saint-Chamond was one of the most heavily armed tanks made during the First World War. (U.S. Army Heritage and Education Center, Carlisle, Pennsylvania)

squadron of French-manned tanks performed magnificently, but in the ensuing combat nine were knocked out by German artillery.[38] Yet the 79th continued to attack. Additionally, the 79th now had direct liaison and contact with the 4th Division on its right, enabling the two divisions to conduct mutually supporting maneuvers. The men of the 315th attacked through a deadly German barrage and swept into Nantillois in style. German machine gunners and snipers peppered the Americans from the flanks, but this only stiffened their resolve to hold on to this costly and important prize, and in their zeal the soldiers swept north to capture a battery of six German 77mm field guns, twenty-three prisoners, and five machine guns. Nantillois was liberated at 11:00 A.M. on 28 September.[39]

The German 147th Infantry Regiment (of the 37th Division) was given the mission of blunting any American progress beyond Nantillois. However, its position was precarious from the start of the day. Defending to its east was the German 36th Division, which was

Leutnant Wolff (center of photo, #6) of the German 151st Regiment blunted an American breakthrough at Nantillois. When the 79th Division, supported by French tanks, broke the German line, Leutnant Wollf (a battalion commander in the 151st Regiment, 37th German Division) rallied his men and led a counterattack, driving the Americans back. (Plickert, *Infanterie Regiment Nr. 151*)

being driven back to Brieulles, exposing its left flank to American envelopment. One of the officers, Leutnant Wolff (of the 151st Regiment) rallied two of his companies and four heavy machine guns to attack into the breach to blunt the Franco-American penetration of the line. Leutnant Wolff had the heavy machine guns lay down covering fires, and the two companies alternatively bounded forward. As one company advanced, the other provided supporting covering fires. Wolff's fearless counterattack temporarily halted the French tanks and American infantry and gave the 147th and 151st Regiments time to withdraw their men.[40] The Germans reported that the "enemy suffered heavy bloody losses in addition to three destroyed [French] tanks left on the battlefield." The price for this temporary victory, the Germans added, depleted their already thinning lines.[41]

After recovering from Wolff's counterattack, the Americans continued their attack north. However, the German 37th Division's 147th Regiment occupied strong positions along the woods and ridges north of Nantillois. The Germans laid down another heavy barrage between the town and high ground and additionally massed their machine guns and employed their *minenwerfer* (heavy

German soldiers of the 151st Infantry Regiment, 37th Division, man a 170cm minenwerfer. The American 79th Division fought this German regiment outside of Montfaucon. (Plickert, *Infanterie Regiment Nr. 151*)

mortar) units to break up the American formations attempting to advance up the slope. Despite these measures, several American companies managed to penetrate the German line. This compelled the 147th Regiment to launch a series of counterattacks around 8:00 P.M. to drive the Americans back. The 147th's 4th Company, under the command of Cavalry Captain Mullenweber, led these counter-attacks. His personal bravery inspired the men, and they broke up the American attack. However, during the assaults this "courageous hero" suffered a mortal wound.[42] Late on 28 September, Gallwitz ordered that the 5th Bavarian Reserve Division move into the line to bolster the 37th Division.[43] The 79th was in large part responsible for the destruction of two German Divisions, the 117th and 37th. The 37th would remain in the line for most of October but would never recover from the losses of these three days.[44]

The U.S. 79th Division would launch one more attack on 29 September before being replaced by the famed 3rd Division (Rock of the Marne) on 30 September. Despite coordinating artillery and tanks,

Murphy, the beloved mascot of the 313th Regiment, 79th Infantry Division, was adopted at Camp Meade, Maryland, and stayed with the regiment throughout the war. (Thorn, *History of the 313th Infantry Regiment*)

the attack was stopped and the Americans were forced back to their positions at a horrific price. The "fresh" Bavarian 5th Reserve Division proved ready to do its duty to stop further progress by the 79th. The Bavarians performed superbly and rendered the 79th incapable of further offensive action.[45]

To blunt American progress in the 79th sector, the Germans laid down a heavy barrage laced with poisonous gas. This toxic German barrage crashed among the men of G Company, 313th Regiment, near Montfaucon, wreaking havoc. More concerning for the men, however, was the safety of their beloved mascot, Murphy. Murphy was a stray dog that the men found at Camp Meade, Maryland, in 1917 during their training. The "little brown pup" was nursed to health and considered a member of the regiment. Although a female, she also had the nicknames Mike and Michael. Murphy was given (ironically) "dog tags" and a Khaki coat with 313th stenciled on it when they sailed for France. She served with the regiment throughout the war, with her place of duty being the G Company field kitchen. As the German gas rounds exploded near the field kitchen this day, several of the men saved Murphy from being gassed by "nearly smothering her with blankets." Murphy gave birth to two pups in France, which the men named "Montfaucon" and "Verdun." The 313th history says both "followed a military career." After surviving a war wound, she returned to Maryland with the men in 1919.[46]

At 7:30 P.M. on 30 September, the 79th commander, General Kuhn, wrote to the V Corps commander describing the condition of the division and the need for immediate replacement:

Commanding General, Fifth Corps.

I am informed that my telephone message to you regarding the situation of the 79th Division which was relayed through two intermediate stations, reached your headquarters about 1630 today. I am not sure that you have in fact received this message. I therefore deem it my duty to inform you by an orderly officer that the remaining troops of the 79th Division have been ordered, to take up a holding position along the northern edge of the Bois de Beuge in front of NANTILLOIS. Due to casualties and straggling, the effective force now available for holding this position is less than 50 percent of the original strength of the command. All of these troops are completely exhausted and incapable of effective action. They have been under a terrific shell fire, mixed with gas, for more than 24 hours. They have twice attempted to advance and capture the BOIS de QUONS. Both times they were driven back by artillery fire from the front and flanks, principally the right, and from combined machine gun fire. The tanks co-operated in the first attack towards the MADELEINE FARM, losing three. In yesterday's attack nine tanks were lost at the same point. The command has been on very short rations since the beginning of the advance and has suffered greatly from lack of water, which it has been impossible to supply during the last 36 hours because of the artillery fire before mentioned. I am informed that a somewhat similar situation exists on my right and left. It is my opinion that no advance by infantry is possible until effective counter battery work has been instituted. It has been impossible for the divisional artillery to cope with the situation. I deem it my duty to bring these matters to your attention in order that proper action may be taken in the premises. Identification of prisoners show that the Fifth Bavarian Reserve Division is now on our right.[47]

The 79th Division (minus its artillery) spent October in quiet sectors rearming, resupplying, and receiving reinforcements. It would rejoin the fight in November, applying the hard-learned lessons of September 1918. The 79th had come a long way in just five days. It had started as a green and inexperienced division, and now it was a proven fighting machine. But the experience came at a high price. Thus is the cost of a nation not prepared for war, and thus is the price for civilian and military leaders disconnected from the realities of the world.

Although the Americans were making only minor gains, the Franco-Anglo attacks elsewhere along the Western Front were proceeding. Foch's Grand Offensive (as it would later be called) put the Germans on their heels, and the expanding torrent of attacks from the Meuse-Argonne to the English Channel was too much for Ludendorff and Hindenburg to contend with. This was especially true since increasing numbers of their strategic reserve divisions were diverted to fight the Americans.

There were also signs that Germany was beginning to fracture politically. On 29 September 1918, the Social Democrats formed a government that took control of the Reichstag. They demanded that the Kaiser seek an end to the war. President Wilson offered the Germans a way out via the Fourteen Points. Wilson had outlined his view on what he envisioned for the world after the war in a speech that he delivered in January 1918. That view would form what some later referred to as "Liberal Imperialism."[48] Beyond calling for the end of colonial empires (via self-determination), Wilson's Fourteen Points focused on five key considerations:

1. Democratic states provide peace and stability.
2. Free trade is key to global prosperity.
3. International laws and international institutions are essential to maintain order, peace, and security.
4. Collective security is necessary to maintain peace.
5. The United States is "chosen" to lead this new world order.[49]

The key aspect of Wilson's lofty rhetoric was that it gave Kaiser Wilhelm hope of being able to negotiate. Such a thought was impossible with the French or British. But time was not on the Kaiser's side. The tide had tilted decidedly against the Germans. To compound matters, Bulgaria capitulated on 30 September, and Germany lost its key ally in the Balkans. Additionally, British, French, and Arab forces had fractured Turkish Ottoman control of the Middle East. It would be just a matter of days before this empire founded in the Middle Ages would collapse. There was even talk in Vienna of Austro-Hungarians seeking a negotiated end to the war. The irony could not have been lost on the Kaiser, as it was the Austro-Hungarians that he went to war to protect. Soon the Germans would be alone.

11

Stagnation and Stalemate

The war was a succession of lost opportunities on both sides.
—General Hunter Liggett

October was a hard month for the American Expeditionary Forces and the French Army in the Meuse-Argonne. Bolstered by additional strategic reserves, the Germans made it difficult for the Americans to achieve substantial gains. General Pershing tried to overcome this by pouring more men into the line. However, the casualties merely mounted without delivering the victories he needed to regain the momentum. In desperation, he issued draconian orders that stated "ground once-gained will not be lost" and fired any senior officer who was not delivering victory. Despite these endeavors, the promise of breaking out of the Meuse-Argonne seemed all but lost.

Adding to the dismal situation on the ground was the weather, which was cold and rainy for most of the month. This hampered movement and contributed to many of the men in the line suffering from various illnesses and viruses. This created the need to begin rotating units in and out of the line to give soldiers the opportunity to dry out their clothes, rest, and take care of hygiene. But the worst element facing the Franco-American forces in the Meuse-Argonne was the terrain.

The terrain in the Meuse-Argonne gave the Germans a marked advantage. The east to west range of rolling hills that crossed the Meuse Valley created natural lines from which the Germans could offer a robust and costly defense. Integrating these natural terrain features into prepared positions was a boon for the German Army. The sluggish advance of the Americans into the Argonne added to the German position. The German 76th Reserve Division and the 2nd Württemberg Landwehr Division (respectively defending the western and eastern half of the Argonne) executed a brilliant defense of the forest, denying the Americans the vital high ground overlooking the Meuse Valley. This meant that the American advance had on its west flank the German-occupied high ground of the Argonne Forest. From here, German forward observers directed lethal artillery into American units moving across the valley below. Additionally, the Germans deployed snipers and machine gun units along the high ground commanding the Meuse Valley, picking off American soldiers who moved within range of their weapons. The most lethal weapon employed here against the flank of the American forces was artillery firing poisonous gas. The Germans deployed additional batteries into the Argonne to increase the volume of fire into the American advance up the Meuse Valley.

Massive stockpiles of artillery ammunition were hauled up the north-south road in the Argonne Forest. The north-south road was the main supply network in the forest. The Germans had constructed it in 1915 to support their fighting units along the southern portion of the Argonne. It was a large logistic artery twenty to thirty feet wide and capable of two-way vehicular and horse-drawn traffic. Along the eastern side of the road the Germans had an active small-scale rail line. This miniature train moved continually up and down the north-south road, delivering soldiers, ammunition, supplies, mail, and anything else the army needed to maintain its position in the Argonne.

The train used on the north-south road was inspired by Paul Decauville. French engineer Paul Decauville had designed a small-scale rail system in the late 1800s. It was quickly purchased by the French Army, then adopted by the German Army and the British Army. The tracks were easily assembled and it facilitated the movement of military units and assets smoothly and rapidly. The Decauville system was particularly well suited for trench warfare, serving fortresses, and supplying a stationary field army.

The American First Army area of operations included the Argonne Forest along the western flank, and then east to the Meuse River. The Meuse served as an easily identifiable boundary between the Americans and the French XVII Corps, which was deployed east of the Meuse. The XVII Corps conducted a supporting attack up the Meuse River, to secure the American flank. However, this advance ended by the third day of the Meuse-Argonne Offensive. As the American army continued to advance up the western bank of the Meuse, it soon found itself under the German occupied Meuse

The German Imperial Army used every scale of rail to supply its units on the Western Front. The preferred small scale rail of the German Army was the French-designed Decauville network. This photograph is of the German north-south road in the Argonne, their only supply artery in the forest. It provided everything that was needed to supply the military units in the area for the war effort. (Mastriano Collection)

Heights on the eastern side of the river. The situation was similar to the experience of the Americans advancing under the observation of the German-controlled Argonne.

To reduce the lethality of the artillery and enfilade fires, the American units operating close to the Argonne were directed to only conduct movement at night. This helped to ameliorate the losses; however, the Germans knew the location of the roads in the Meuse Valley and periodically fired barrages at the key intersections even at night. German control of the Argonne high ground proved disastrous for the American offensive, as it restricted movement, delayed attacks, and created significant "Clausewitzian friction" for the American and French armies. Carl von Clausewitz was a Prussian military officer who fought against Napoleon a hundred years before the First World War. Even today his book *On War* has a profound influence on military thinkers. In his book, Clausewitz wrote of the concept of friction:

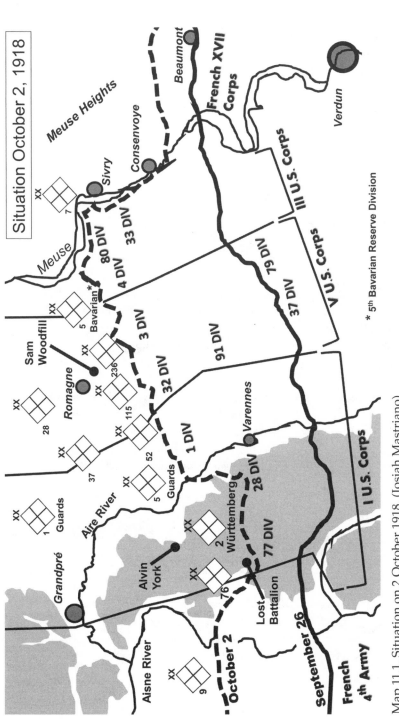

Map 11.1. Situation on 2 October 1918. (Josiah Mastriano)

Everything is very simple in war, but the simplest thing is difficult. These difficulties accumulate and produce a friction, which no man can imagine exactly who has not seen war. . . . Friction is the only conception which, in a general way, corresponds to that which distinguishes real war from war on paper. The military machine, the army and all belonging to it, is in fact simple; and appears, on this account, easy to manage. But let us reflect that no part of it is in one piece, that it is composed entirely of individuals, each of which keeps up its own friction in all directions.

Friction, according to Clausewitz, is the accumulation of unforeseen events and actions by the enemy that delay or hinder your plans. In this case, German command of the Argonne and Meuse Heights added considerable "friction" to the American advance. This, combined with the inexperience of the American army and the weather, changed everything. Pershing was now facing the type of warfare that he was critical of the Allies for waging. The success or failure of the American advance now hinged on the individual heroism of soldiers.

The crisis for Gallwitz's line was far from over, but the situation was stabilizing. His main defense line, the Kriemhilde Stellung, was not penetrated at any point. His units were suffering high casualties but were inflicting considerably more on the French and Americans. Although this brought some hope to Gallwitz, each of his losses was irreplaceable, while the Americans seemingly had an endless supply of men to pour into the line.

Gallwitz had the support of the German High Command, as both Ludendorff and Hindenburg understood the threat that an American breakthrough in the region posed to the German Army on the Western Front. To ensure a robust ground defense, Hindenburg and Ludendorff committed a growing number of their limited strategic reserves to reinforce Gallwitz. In the end, the preponderance of Germany's twenty-plus divisions of strategic reserves would serve in the Meuse-Argonne. Additional resources, artillery and aviation assets, were ordered to support the Germans in the Meuse-Argonne region as well. Ludendorff and Hindenburg provided two of their elite pursuit (fighter) squadrons to reinforce the front there. The Germans created four of these in 1917. Each included twelve aircraft, flown by Germany's best pilots. These were dubbed "flying circuses" because the units could quickly pack up and deploy anywhere along the Western Front.

The German High Command deployed two of these squadrons to the Meuse-Argonne. One was Manfred von Richthofen's renowned Flying Circus (*Jagdgeschwader* I).[1] Dubbed the Red Baron, Richthofen had been killed in action five months earlier, but his famed aviation unit continued to fight with considerable effect. When the Flying Circus arrived in the Meuse-Argonne region, it was commanded by Oberleutnant (First Lieutenant) Hermann Göring. Göring would leverage his fame to become a leader of the National Socialist (Nazi) Party and go on to command the German Air Force (*Luftwaffe*) during World War Two. The Richthofen Circus had the distinctive red-painted noses on its aircraft. The other elite squadron deployed to the region was the Loezer Circus (Jagdgeschwader III). Under the command of Hauptmann Bruno Loezer, this unit had the notorious "yellow-bellied fuselages" on its Fokker D.VII aircraft. Loezer was one of Germany's leading aces, with forty-four victories.[2]

The German surge of aircraft to the region was hinged upon two considerations. The first was to safeguard the German flank around Sedan. The other was to have the aircraft in a position to defend German cities on the Rhine, which the Allies were bombing via their strategic bombing campaign. British general Hugh Trenchard was one of the leading thinkers on the use of airpower. Taking a page out of the German bombing of London, Trenchard was now bringing the fight to German cities. It had the effect of drawing off German aircraft to defend the homeland.[3]

Ludendorff ordered the realignment of Army Group Gallwitz. Until now, the German forces in the Argonne were part of the Third Army under Army Group German Crown Prince. Gallwitz's Fifth Army boundary now included most of the Argonne Forest, and Ludendorff assigned "Group Argonne to Gallwitz's Fifth Army and included the transfer of the German LVIII Corps" (the 2nd Württemberg Landwehr Division, 5th Guards, 52nd Infantry, and 1st Guards). This gave Gallwitz better command and control over the German forces in the region, especially as the Argonne high ground was key to blunting the American advance.[4]

The situation for the Germans in early October was tenuous at best. By now, most of the Western Front, from Verdun to the English Channel, was under attack as Ferdinand Foch had planned. The

Grande Offensive was Foch's plan to overwhelm the Germans with a broad-front attack. The most dangerous location for the Germans was the Franco-American attack in the Meuse-Argonne, where a breakthrough would sever the vital rail network at Sedan and spell the end of Berlin's plan to hold through the winter of 1918.

Although Gallwitz needed more men and units, thus far the defenders of the Argonne were holding firmly. The 76th Reserve and 2nd Württemberg Landwehr Divisions had prevented an American breakthrough and were brilliantly leveraging the high ground to punish the Americans with artillery in the valley below. The Württembergers were singled out for praise by the Third Army commander, General Karl von Einem, who wrote on 4 October 1918, "In the sector of the 2nd Landwehr Division all attacks failed in the face of the bravery and stubborn tenacity of the Württemberg Land-wehr."[5] The next day, now in Army Group Gallwitz, the Württem-bergers were praised by their new commander, who wrote, "After a strong artillery preparation, the enemy renewed his attacks against Group Argonne and Meuse Group West. In the sector of the 2nd Landwehr Division they were completely repulsed."[6]

However, the situation for the German units in the Meuse Valley was not quite as certain. The Prussian 1st Guards Division had per-formed superbly, but by 29 September it was a shadow of its former self and had to be withdrawn from the line. It was replaced by the Prussian 5th Guards and the 52nd Division. The 117th Division was withdrawn from the line after being brutalized during the battle of Montfaucon. The 117th, 236th, and 5th Bavarian Reserve Divisions occupied the line here. Additionally, the German 37th Division was pulled back five kilometers to prepare defenses near the village of Exermont, where there would soon be a significant fight. The Ger-man 28th Division also arrived in the north of Cunel to likewise pre-pare the area for a large battle. Gallwitz was promised additional reinforcements later in the month.

The casualty rates for the Americans were too much to contem-plate, necessitating the replacement of several divisions. Pershing's concept of fielding the large 28,000-man divisions to enable the units to endure high casualty rates proved untenable. The U.S. 35th and 79th Divisions were already withdrawn from the line and replaced by some of the best units that the Americans had in France. The 35th was replaced by the 1st Division. This was the first American unit to arrive in France in 1917, and it had seen considerable action on the Western Front. It was well led and highly motivated. However, the U.S. 1st Infantry would face the wrath of Gallwitz's more experienced and better-trained forces.

In the center of the American line, in V Corps' sector, the U.S. 32nd Division took the lead in the 91st Division's area of operations, while the 3rd replaced the 79th Division. The 3rd Division was one of the most celebrated American units in France and was praised for its role in stopping the Germans on the Marne River earlier that summer. This resulted in the division receiving the moniker "Rock of the Marne." Although Pershing now had more experienced units in the line, the opportunity to break through ended after the second day of the Meuse-Argonne Offensive, 27 September. After that, the Germans successfully stabilized the line in several areas with the arrival of the initial group of reinforcing units.

It would take the personal initiative of soldiers in the American Expeditionary Forces to break the German grip on the region. This would come at a great cost in lives, but it would help wear the Germans down and create conditions for the Americans to regain some momentum. One such case was Private John Barkley, of the 3rd Infantry Division's 4th Regiment. Barkley was pushed forward alone to establish an observation post a half-kilometer behind enemy lines. He reported German activity from a shell hole on a ridge overlooking a wood and hill leading into Cunel. At daybreak, his telephone line was severed due to a German artillery barrage. While he considered how to return to American lines, the Germans began to form for an attack.[7]

A brief American bombardment of the Germans gave Barkley the cover that he needed to secure a German machine gun and ammunition from nearby dead soldiers. He carried these to a derelict French Renaut tank and waited for the Germans to resume their advance across the nearby fields. The gun originally mounted in the French tank was missing, so Barkley set up his captured German MG 08/15 in its place. He made several trips to secure ammunition from the dead, acquiring some four thousand rounds. Once the Germans advanced, he opened fire from a position behind them, killing about one hundred and breaking up a regimental-level counterattack. This engagement lasted the greater portion of the day and included German assault units trying to kill Barkley with grenades, return fire, and even a German 77mm field artillery piece, which temporarily stunned him. However, once recovered, Barkley killed the artillery crew and continued firing. He survived this action and was awarded the Medal of Honor.[8]

Barkley's is but one of hundreds of such heroic feats accomplished in the Meuse-Argonne. General Pershing hinted at the importance of these individual acts of heroism and how they helped the American army regain the initiative. In his 1931 memoirs, Pershing wrote:

> Deeds of daring were legion. . . . There were thousands . . .
> who bore themselves with equal gallantry but whose deeds
> are known only by the victorious results they helped to
> achieve. However, as typifying the spirit of the rank and
> file of our great army, I would mention Lieutenant Samuel
> Woodfill, 5th Division, who attacked single-handed a series
> of German machine gun nests near Cunel and dispatched
> the crews in turn until reduced to the necessity of assault-
> ing the last detachment with a pick; Sergeant Alvin C. York,
> of the 82d, who stood off and captured 132 Germans after
> his patrol was literally surrounded and outnumbered ten to
> one; and Major Charles W. Whittlesey and his men of the
> 77th division, who, when their battalion was cut off in the
> Argonne, refused to surrender and held out until finally
> relieved.[9]

Pershing's choice of Woodfill, York, and Whittlesey for special mention among so many other heroes is telling. By early October it seemed that the American advance would be limited to minor gains at a great cost in lives. For the greater part of the month, this is precisely what transpired. However, the individual actions of these three soldiers, and others, had significant strategic effects across the American front.

The honor of Pershing's recognizing Woodfill, York, and Whittlesey is significant in many aspects. The foremost is that these three played important roles in helping the American army regain the initiative. But there is more. In a time when Regular Army officers had a dislike for National Guard soldiers and a general distrust of National Army recruits, the admission by Pershing demonstrates professional growth. These men represented the three types of American soldiers on the battlefield. Woodfill was a professional Regular Army soldier who began his military service in 1910. York was a member of the National Army, which was formed in 1917 mainly from the pool of draftees and conscripts called upon when the United States entered the war.[10] Whittlesey was a member of the 77th, a National Guard division largely recruited from New York City. National Guard divisions tended to have a regional flavor. Despite the preconceptions, soldiers from all three of America's "armies" shaped the outcome of the war.

The impact of these three soldiers, and so many others in the Meuse-Argonne, echoes across the generations. These soldiers were faced with a stronger enemy, overwhelming odds being against them, and all hope seemingly being lost. Yet each of these men faced the darkness and conquered the enemy strongholds. This had the cascading effect of breaking the enemy's hold across the front and slowly shattering his ability to blunt further attacks against his lines.

As General Pershing correctly stated, there were thousands of heroic deeds, some recognized and rewarded, many others lost or forgotten. In a general history of the Meuse-Argonne, it is impossible to tell the story of all the divisions and regiments that played a key role in breaking the German defenses. The same is true for the individual soldiers—there are too many stories to capture in a humble survey of this important campaign. To give a flavor of the heroism, sacrifices, and valor of the 1.2 million Americans fighting in the Meuse campaign, several key soldiers will be highlighted, as their role seemed particularly important. They will include Pershing's three, Woodfill, York, and Whittlesey, as well as the dauntless Captain Charles Harris, the determined Brigadier General Douglas MacArthur, and several others. Additionally, the heroism and sacrifice of several key German defenders in the Meuse-Argonne will be highlighted, men who fought for their country no less valiantly than the Americans did for theirs.

12

The Siege of the Lost Battalion

If ever the patriotism of our country should wane and the national pulse beat slow, let a veteran of the Argonne arise and tell the story of courage, self-sacrifice and endurance that carried the Liberty Division through this wilderness of France—to victory. Hearts will beat quicker at the telling, eyes will glisten, pride in America and her sons will be stimulated anew—for, in the annals of the nation, the "spirit of the Argonne" must be placed alongside the "Spirit of 76."
—*History of the Seventy Seventh Division*

The beginning of the end for the German occupation of the Argonne commenced on 2 October 1918. Until then, the American 77th and 28th Divisions had achieved only negligible progress in the forest. But this was about to change based on the leadership of an American major and a battalion of soldiers. The concept of operations to drive the Germans from the Argonne Forest during the Meuse-Argonne Offensive was to be a series of turning movements by the 77th and 28th Divisions (in coordination with the French Fourth Army to the west). However, the adage that no plan survives first contact proved true. The lack of progress made by the French and Americans, combined with the terrain, the inexperience of the Americans, and the robust German defense, made flanking movements little more than a well-intentioned fantasy. In effect, the undergraduate American forces in the Argonne were fighting on Ph.D. terrain—not a good thing when lives are at stake. Being outclassed, the American leadership resorted to frontal attacks in an effort to overwhelm the German defenses.

The U.S. 77th Division included men from New York City and the Lower East Side. The Lower East Side was composed of

European immigrants living in slum-like squalor. One of its largest groups consisted of Italians who had arrived en masse over the preceding decade. Intelligence reports that the German 125th Württemberg Regiment received prior to the Meuse-Argonne Offensive that wrongly said that an Italian unit was deployed to the area were due to the large number of native Italian speakers in the U.S. 77th Division. German listening posts heard Italian being spoken from the French trench lines and assumed that an Italian unit had returned to the Argonne sector. The Italians had a long association with the Argonne, going back to the famed Garibaldi Legion, which had fought a series of bloody battles against the Germans there earlier in the war. The Italian actions in the Argonne are of legend, in that Giuseppe Garibaldi II and his four brothers served here. They were the grandsons of the Italian founding father Giuseppe Garibaldi.

In addition to the Italians, the 77th Division also included a significant number of Eastern European Jews, Poles, Greeks, Romanians, and Russians. This was a tough bunch of men to train and lead. Many had recently immigrated to the United States and worked some of the toughest jobs. For many of the Italians, working the strenuous and difficult jobs on the railroads was the norm. Others worked dangerous and toxic factory jobs. Like other American divisions, there was a problem with soldiers understanding English. Additionally, it took considerable effort to keep the men from associating only with their ethnic faction. These ethnic groups within the division often ended up in fights against one another, especially when alcohol and women were available in the French cafes behind the lines.

Since the division included men largely from Manhattan, it was often referred to as the "Metropolitan Division" by the officers. However, the men of the 77th preferred the "Liberty Division." For the recent migrants filling the ranks of the division, the memory of first seeing the Statue of Liberty upon arriving in the United States evoked profound meaning to them. In the end, "Liberty Division" stuck despite the efforts of the unit's leaders to retain the more sophisticated sounding "Metropolitan Division."[1]

The fate of the division would soon be indirectly caught in the middle of a clash between the American and French leadership. German control of the Argonne was having a deleterious effect on the French Fourth Army to the west and the U.S. First Army to the east. The Supreme Allied Commander, Ferdinand Foch, was concerned that if the Germans were able to bog the French and American attacks down in the Meuse-Argonne region, it would free up the strategic reserves. The German reserves were needed in northern France to stop the Canadian-led British Expeditionary Forces attack, which had already broken through the German line.

Foch learned with a degree of dismay that instead of making progress by maneuver and the application of combined arms (infantry, artillery, armor, and aircraft), Pershing just poured more and more men into the line. Of this, Foch wrote, "[The Americans] tried to overcome these difficulties by increasing its forces in the first line; but this only intensified them, resulting in a complete blocking of its rear and the bottling up of communications."[2] Foch was convinced that Pershing could not handle the task at hand and that his lack of experience threatened the entire advance on the Western Front. Thousands of American lives were being thrown away needlessly.

Foch saw what needed to happen; the Argonne must be cleared of German forces and the Meuse Heights secured. He discussed how to execute this quickly with General Pétain. They agreed that several American divisions should be withdrawn from General Pershing and tasked to support the French Fourth Army west of the Argonne and the French XVII Corps. Under seasoned officers, and with experienced French units, the Americans would be able to outflank the German positions on the high ground and thereby break the enemy control in the region.[3] Foch decided that a new Franco-American Second Army would be created to clear the Germans from the Argonne. He wrote:

> To remedy this situation, I decided, in agreement with General Pétain, to withdraw a certain number of divisions from the American sector of attack and to use them in part east of the Meuse and in part west of the Argonne. To avoid all loss of time, it was proposed to incorporate them in the French Army Corps already in line. General Pershing was then to take under his orders the Franco-American forces operating on both flanks of the Meuse, while a new French army commander would take command of the Allied forces operating on each side of the Argonne.[4]

Foch's chief of staff, General Maxime Weygand, was given the grim task of convincing Pershing to go along with this decision.

The fate of the Lost Battalion was indirectly caused by pressure from the French High Command on General Pershing to produce results in the Meuse-Argonne Offensive. Here, the Supreme Allied Commander, Ferdinand Foch (left), speaks with his chief of staff, General Maxime Weygand (center), and French 6th Army commander Jean Degoutte. Weygand would pass along the concept to reduce the size of the American command. (Bibliotèque nationale de France)

Pershing described his conversation with General Weygand in his diary in considerable detail. Pershing seems to have agreed with the logic, as Weygand reported to Foch that Pershing accepted this concept of operations. However, after considering what this meant, the reassignment of his U.S. I Corps to the French Second Army (one-third of his engaged forces), Pershing changed his mind. Pershing wrote a letter to Weygand and Foch outlining his objections to the idea.[5] Foch was not pleased with Pershing's response and thought that an experienced French commander in the Argonne would quickly overcome the German defenses in the forest, but he decided that it was in the best interests of the alliance to respect the views of the American commander. Foch wrote, "In order to satisfy him I agreed to maintain the organization of the command as it was, 'provided the American attacks should be resumed and once started, continued without pause.'"[6]

Foch faced difficulties similar to those that the second Supreme Allied Commander would encounter during the Second World War. Then, General Dwight Eisenhower would have to manage the conflicting national interests and divergent views in his own multinational organization. Like Foch, he often deferred to the national interests of the allies. One example is Eisenhower's supporting Bernard Montgomery's Operation Market Garden, the failed armored and airborne offensive across the Netherlands in September 1944. There were viable reasons why the British earnestly campaigned for this, but in the end, the attack fell short and depleted limited resources for the rest of the Allied armies, forcing the advance in France and Belgium to stall in 1944. Foch took a similar risk in 1918 with Pershing. It no doubt would have been better from his perspective as the Supreme Allied Commander to mandate the creation of a Franco-American Second Army in the Argonne. However, keeping national leaders in common purpose and common cause was far more important. Foch, clearly with this in mind, acquiesced to the wishes of Pershing.[7]

Pershing wrote of this, saying, "Received short letter from Marshal Foch that he agreed to the modifications which I proposed to the plan . . . submitted on September 30th . . . provided that my attack should be resumed at once, and that there be permitted no halts."[8] Pershing had to achieve results in the Argonne, or risk losing a third of his command to the suggested French-led Second Army. Pershing issued orders demanding that the offense be resumed and that ground once taken would not be lost. Orders were communicated to General Hunter Liggett, who in turned passed them to the 77th Division commander, Major General Alexander. Liggett also dispatched his aide-de-camp, Lieutenant Colonel Stackpole, to speak personally with Alexander to ensure that he understood the importance of the early October attacks.

Stackpole recorded what Alexander and he discussed during their meeting: "Visited Alexander, 77th, at his P.C. in Bois de Batis. He claims that his division has never lost any ground gained, that it has been steadily plodding along through very difficult country that the experience has been invaluable, and the men have done well, with very slight losses—300 or so. He said he had canned a good many at the rear echelon (Florent) among the officers showing incompetency, timidity or neurasthenia. He has changed his mind about General Johnson, whom he does not now want to relieve."[9]

This was not completely true, in that the 77th Division did make some progress but frequently was driven back from ground gained by German fire and counterattacks. Additionally, Alexander's focus on firing officers was a way to deflect blame from himself for the lack of clear progress, similar to Major General Kuhn's firing Noble on 27 September to shift blame and focus away from himself on the failure to capture Montfaucon on the first day of the offensive. Pershing set the tone and standard by resorting to rash and often unjustified firings of officers that only worsened the command climate and bred distrust in the ranks, but he seemed to not understand that loyalty works both ways and that it is built on trust, not fear of retribution.

The key remark of the conversation between Stackpole and Alexander regarded the fate of Johnson. Alexander was considering sacking him, but for some reason had a change of heart. It would be Johnson's men who would soon break through the German lines and save both his reputation and that of the American army. The demand from Pershing on the leadership of the I Corps and the 77th Division for tangible success in the Argonne was not lost on any officer in the chain of command. Knowing Pershing's and Alexander's reputations, they would precipitously fire anyone not meeting their expectations.

Late on 1 October, orders were issued to the 77th Division's two brigades (the 153rd and 154th) to attack at 6:30 A.M. on 2 October. The 153rd Brigade was composed of two regiments, the 305th and 306th, and occupied the right half of the division's sector in the Argonne. The 154th Brigade also had two regiments, the 307th and 308th. Major Charles Whittlesey commanded the 1st Battalion of the 308th Regiment. The 308th's regimental commander was Colonel Cromwell Stacey, a combat-experienced Regular Army officer. Stacey had a colorful career, seeing action in Nicaragua, the Spanish-American War, the Philippines, and, more importantly, recently on the Western Front. Stacey had proved heroic and decisive in battle, especially in July while serving with the 3rd Division, the "Rock of the Marne." He was awarded French and American medals for bravery. Colonel Stacey took command of the 308th Regiment on the second day of the Meuse-Argonne Offensive (27 September) and was an unknown quantity to the men in the 77th.[10]

The 154th commander, Brigadier General Evan Johnson, was a well-respected leader, but he was constantly undercut by Alexander, who had a penchant for blaming him for the division's shortcomings. Alexander reserved his particular wrath for Johnson. Thus, it was natural that when Pershing turned his gaze upon the lack of progress being made by the 77th Division, Alexander shifted the blame to Johnson.[11] The pressure to make substantial gains was intense, and Alexander cast caution to the wind and directed that the divisions attack without regard to friendly unit progress on the flanks. The men were to attack toward the objective and not stop until they were on it. The division's "objective was the ridge traversing the divisional zone of action just north of the road and railroad, La Viergette-Moulin de Charlevaux (Charlevaux Mill)."[12]

This objective was the road and railway that cut across the width of the Argonne, serving as one of the few east-west routes through the unforgiving land. It connected the village of Apremont on the eastern edge of the Argonne with Binarville to the west. The Germans had considerably improved the road over the previous three years, making it wide enough for two-way traffic and, more importantly, adding a Decauville rail line to the road. This line branched off from the main route along the north-south road in the midst of the Argonne proper. The logic to seize the road and rail line was sound, as it would hinder German lateral movement considerably and cut off a vital line of communication.

There were two German divisions defending in the U.S. 77th Division's sector. Covering the western portion of the Argonne was the 254th Regiment of the German 76th Reserve Division. The unit

The 76th German Reserve Division arrived in the Argonne just days before the American attack. This photograph is of the 254th German Regiment, 76th German Reserve Division, on its way to fight in the Argonne. These men would lay siege to the Americans in the Lost Battalion. (Private collection)

was composed of men from the grand duchy of Hesse, many of whom hailed from around Frankfurt. It had an excellent record as a defensive division and had arrived in the Argonne the day before the American attack.

Defending the central and eastern portion of the Argonne was the 2nd Landwehr Division. This militia-type unit was similar to the U.S. National Guard and was composed of men from the south-western German kingdom of Württemberg. They had been in the war since 1914 and had spent much of the conflict in the Argonne. The 2nd Landwehr had three regiments: the 122nd, 120th, and 125th. The Americans in the 77th Division faced the 122nd Württemberg and a portion of the 120th. The Württembergers waged a successful defense against the Americans. In fact, at no point thus far had these Germans lost significant ground by pressure from the American 77th or 28th Divisions. They had received several orders to fall back to prepared positions to avoid being encircled by penetrations along the eastern rim of the Argonne, after the Prussian 1st Guards was driven back. Due to this, the corps commander sent the following telegram to the king of Württemberg in Stuttgart, "The 2nd Landwehr Division has particularly distinguished itself by its bravery and intrepidity during the recent fighting in the Argonne and has thus contributed toward the failure of the enemy's attempt to break through."

Colonel Johnson asked Alexander to delay the attack, as his two regiments needed time to reorganize before another major push. The series of failed attacks over the previous week had taken a toll, not to mention that there was no time to integrate the replacements into the unit. In the context of Pershing demanding progress in the Argonne, Alexander balked at Johnson's request for a delay and replied: "You tell General Johnson that the 154th Brigade is holding back the French on the left and is holding back everything on the right and that the 154th Brigade must push forward to their objective today. By 'must' I mean must, and by 'today' I mean today and not next week. You report heavy machine gun fire, but your casualty reports do not substantiate this. Remember that when you are making these reports."[13]

General Johnson was appalled by this reply from Alexander and called him personally to explain the situation, which resulted in another harsh rebuke. Alexander said, "There will be no dallying, or delaying! Headquarters wants action and they shall have it. Either attack on schedule or I'll relieve you on the spot and put in somebody with guts! Do I make myself clear?"[14] The 308th would attack regardless of the condition of the men, or of the enemy situation.

The orders from the division were to attack at 6:30 A.M. Alexander added that all units would continue to advance regardless of losses and without concern for their flanks.[15] As one officer wrote of the day's mission, "each assaulting unit would try breaking through individually—regardless of flank support. Once an advance element, like a spearhead, could be flung out into hostile territory, flanks could be swung up to connect with it."[16] However, confusion reigned among the Americans. While the 153rd Brigade attacked at 6:30 A.M., the 154th Brigade did not step off until thirty minutes later, at 7:00 A.M. Such uncoordinated attacks enabled the Germans to throw back the Americans in turn. There was a splattering of supporting artillery playing on suspected German positions near the front, especially for the 153rd Brigade.[17] However, neither of its regiments (the 305th and 306th) made any progress and were stopped by German machine guns, thick bands of wire, and German artillery. The U.S. 28th Division to their east likewise was unable to advance against the determined German defenders and was driven back by the Württembergers yet again. The Germans often sent out details to ambush the Americans in the forest, while concealed machine guns and snipers also took a toll.[18] There was another push to gain some ground in the early afternoon, but it was likewise stopped by the Germans.[19]

Johnson's 154th Brigade began its attack at 7:00 A.M. The 307th Regiment to the right hit a series of wire obstacles covered by robust German machine gun fires. Groups of Germans maneuvered through the heavy brush and terrain and drove back most of the 307th with grenades and small arms fire. German artillery soon joined the battle and prevented the Americans from making any appreciable gains.[20] A company of 307th soldiers under the leadership of Captain W. Kerr Rainsford advanced through a gap in the lines and was within a few hundred yards of the objective and not far from where Whittlesey would later advance. Captain Rainsford, however, needed more men and dispatched a runner, Private Patrick Gilligan, to find the platoons and guide them forward. Private Gilligan was one of the fastest men in the unit and a reliable soldier. He was a likeable red-headed Irishman. As Captain Rainsford waited for his two support platoons, a preplanned American artillery barrage ripped into the German lines to his front.[21] Captain Rainsford described the scene:

The barrage was stunning to watch for those twenty minutes, there within forty yards of it—the thick smoke among the leaves, the black fountains of earth, and the great yellow trees crashing down in front. Then it ceased, and at once the whole forest began to echo with a sound like a hundred pneumatic riveters at work. We moved forward into a close wall of foliage, combed and re-combed by the traversing bullets, and we fired blindly into the leaves as we went. The noise was deafening, and I could hear "H" and "E" going into action on our right rear, but nothing from the left. Then Gilligan came up with the other two platoons and saluted with a grin. I told him that I had thought he was lost or headed home, though in reality I didn't see how they had come so quickly nor found me so directly.

"Never fear, Captain," he answered, "and praise God it's here that we are and in time for it all, and yourself so safe." And even as he spoke he was down with a bullet through the brain. I think he was the first to be killed.[22]

Captain Rainsford's company continued their advance, penetrated the German wire entanglements, and scooped up several prisoners. He dispatched patrols to link up with the 308th to the west and also men to the east to ascertain where the rest of the 307th was located. As he organized for a second advance, written orders arrived via a runner to withdraw to the jump-off line and prepare for a German counterattack. This ended the only successful advance by the 307th during the 2 October morning assault.[23] The rest of Captain Rainsford's 307th Regiment was stopped in front of the German wire obstacles. Their exposure in front of the enemy position had resulted in a disaster when the Germans unleashed "a furious barrage from the 77s, trench mortars, reinforced by showers of hand grenades and rifle grenades from the enemy's trenches."[24] The report of this disaster to headquarters is what triggered Rainsford's premature withdrawal.

Meanwhile, as Rainsford withdrew, the 308th Regiment found a way partially through the German lines. The 1st Battalion (Whittlesey) and 2nd Battalion (Captain George McMurtry) advanced into the forest. The U.S. 77th Division provided a creeping barrage that helped the Americans make some headway. However, the men were again stopped just a few hundred meters in front of their start line. Major Whittlesey sent out scouts to find a way around the German strongholds deployed on the high ridges. As the 308th probed cautiously forward, reports circulated among the Germans that the French Fourth Army had penetrated part of the 76th Reserve Division line to the west. This posed a danger for the German 245th Regiment, which was compelled to shift a portion of its forces west to drive back the French.[25] The Germans had no reason to be concerned about the Americans as it seemed that their advance was already blunted. The experience of the past week was that once the American advance was stopped, they withdrew to their lines.[26]

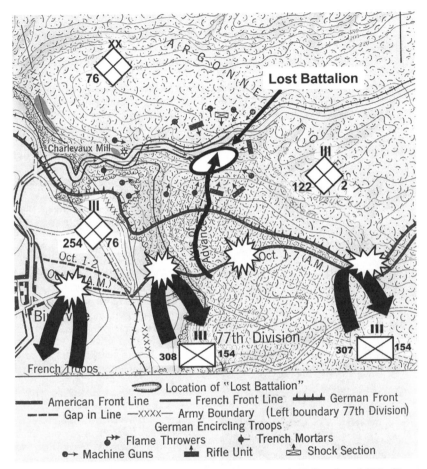

Map 12.1. Lost Battalion in the Argonne Forest, 2–7 October 1918. (Base map courtesy of American Battle Monuments Commission)

As the German 245th Regiment shifted forces west, a runner reported to Major Whittlesey that Brigadier General Johnson had ordered another attack that would be supported by the division's artillery. The barrage would begin at 12:30 on suspected German positions and then begin rolling back against the enemy at 12:50. It was at that time that Major Whittlesey was directed to continue his advance toward the objective. Advancing in a ravine, Whittlesey led his battalion, followed closely by three companies under the leadership of Captain McMurtry. As the barrage lifted, the Americans

Major Charles Whittlesey was a New York lawyer in civilian life. His natural leadership abilities held the nearly seven hundred men of the Lost Battalion together despite horrific living conditions and incessant German attacks. (U.S. Army Heritage and Education Center, Carlisle, Pennsylvania)

advanced, constantly delayed by snipers. In exasperation over the costly delays, Whittlesey ordered the men to "Advance until the last man drops!"[27] With that the Americans swept aside minor German resistance in the forest and then advanced up the ravine to an open field bounded on the north side by a small stream. The men dashed over this field, across a small wood bridge, and up the steep hill in front of them that included the much sought-after road. By late afternoon the six companies of the 308th and a detachment of nine machine guns from the 306th Regiment had arrived at the objective, the Viergette-Moulin de Charlevaux road. Whittlesey took stock of the terrain, deciding where to deploy his men as they waited for support to arrive. They were more than a kilometer behind German lines.

The Viergette-Moulin de Charlevaux road was about ten meters (thirty feet) wide and cut into the hill above, leaving a small jagged cliff above the road. The road was winding and the area thickly wooded. Below the road, the hill was steep and difficult to traverse. Being at a 60-degree angle, it took considerable effort to climb. At the base of this steep incline was the Ruisseau de Charlevaux (Charlevaux Creek), a shallow, narrow stream. The soldiers found a small foot bridge here that many used during the advance. On the other side of the stream was a seasonally marshy open space used by the Germans as a ceremonial parade field for unit formations as well as a place to gather and interrogate French prisoners of war. From there, the French prisoners were marched on the Viergette-Moulin de Charlevaux road to detention camps. Just west of the pocket was Hill 198, which provided the Germans a dominating view of the American position. The high ridges south of the position gave the Germans a marked advantage. Whittlesey decided on deploying just below the road in an area about 75 meters wide and 350 meters long.[28]

The nine machine guns were deployed to the left and right flanks of the perimeter. Major Whittlesey then had the six companies dig in. The companies were deployed in the following order (from west to east), H, B, C, A, G, E.[29] He located his headquarters near the center of the pocket. For communications, Whittlesey left a series of runners along his axis of advance to maintain contact with the regiment as well as to guide reinforcements forward. Should this fail, he had several courier pigeons and signal rockets. Scouts were sent out to recon the surrounding area, in the hope of establishing liaison with the 307th on the right and the French on the left. Additionally, Whittlesey sent a report via runners on the exact location of his unit to General Johnson.

The imagination of reporters and the public was captured when news broke of this unit trapped behind enemy lines, later called the "Lost Battalion." It was never lost and it was not a battalion. It was actually a task force that included elements of three battalions, a machine gun detachment, a team of five medics, and three artillery forward observers.[30] This notwithstanding, the term "Lost Battalion" still stirs the imagination and will be used in this chapter accordingly.

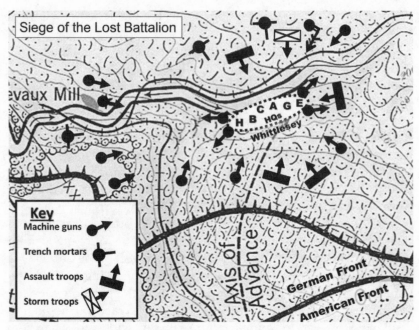

Map 12.2. Siege of the Lost Battalion. (Base map courtesy of American Battle Monuments Commission)

Although the location that Whittlesey selected to deploy his men was not ideal, it had some advantages. What would end up being the most important consideration was access to water. The Ruisseau de Charlevaux provided a reliable water source. The men came into the fight with little food, and should the wait for follow-on forces be longer than anticipated, at least they would have water. The steep slope provided some protection from German artillery. However, German mortars would be another matter altogether.

The breakthrough was possible due to three considerations. The first was the gap created in the ravine below Hill 198 when the 254th German Regiment shifted its focus to the west to blunt the French penetration west of the Argonne. The second was that Whittlesey and his men stumbled upon the boundary between two German units. As discussed, unit borders at any level are a potential weak point. Maintaining liaison between the bordering units is the only way to ensure that unit boundaries are not weak. The shifting of the 254th German Regiment without coordination with the 2nd Landwehr Division resulted in a gap in the line, which Whittlesey exploited to great effect. This lack of coordination amplified the effect of Captain Rainsford and his men of the neighboring 307th Regiment. Rainsford's penetration of the 122nd Regiment front just west of where Whittlesey would later deploy drew the attention of the Württembergers away from the vulnerable German Army boundary. Thus, the way to the Charlevaux was open, and exploited by the men of the 308th Regiment. This series of German blunders would have strategic effects that changed their situation both in the Meuse-Argonne region and on the Western Front.[31]

As the day ended, the German soldiers of the 254th Reserve Regiment (76th Reserve Division) and 122th Württemberg Regiment (2nd Württemberg Division) repositioned to seal off the gap in the line. It was touch and go, as it was yet unclear to the Germans that there was a large group of Americans dug in along the vital Charlevaux road/rail. However, it soon became painfully clear that there was a problem. American machine guns and riflemen tore into a group of Germans moving along the road. The reaction of the 254th to the crisis was slower than usual, as its commander, Major Emil Hünicken, had been summoned to meet with the grand duke of Hesse, Ernst Ludwig Karl Albrecht Wilhelm (Duke Ernest Louis). The grand duke had requested a report on the performance of the soldiers of Hesse in the 254th. Major Hünicken was granted an audience with the grand duke on 2 October at the duke's palace in Darmstadt. The duke was the grandson of Queen Victoria. Command of the 254th in the Argonne went to Hauptman (Captain) Hansen. Hansen was a courageous officer recommended for the Pour le Merite for his leadership in recent battles. However, assuming temporary command of the regiment in the midst of perhaps the single most important battle it would experience was no small endeavor. That night, the Germans started receiving reports on the location of the American penetration.[32]

The American brigade commander, Brigadier General Johnson, received confirmation that elements of the 308th U.S. Regiment were on the objective and awaiting reinforcements. He ordered the 307th U.S. Regiment to advance to Major Whittlesey. The attack was quickly broken up by the 122nd Württemberg, except for the lead unit, K Company, under the command of Captain Nelson Holderman, who linked up with Whittlesey early on 3 October.[33] This brought the total number of Americans in the pocket to 694 men.[34]

Meanwhile, Hauptman Hansen (the acting 254th commander)

Major Emil Hünicken, the commander of the German 254th Regiment, opposed Major Whittlesey and the Americans trapped in the Argonne. (Hünicken, *Reserve Infanterie Regiment Nr. 254*)

was growing concerned about the condition of his line and the potential size of the American penetration. He reviewed the reports with the regimental staff and discerned that there was a one-kilometer gap between his regiment and the 122nd Württemberg. The regimental history says that "they had considerable luck that the division's 76th Reserve Pioneer Battalion" was available to cover this gap before the Americans discovered and exploited it.[35] However, it was too late; Whittlesey and his men were already through the gap. To compound matters, the position of the "Amerikanernest" (the Germans would refer to this pocket as the "American Nest") was behind the Giselher Stellung. This was the German first main defense network, and should the Americans not be driven back, the German defense of the Argonne would be compromised.

Late on 2 October, the 254th worked with the 122nd Württemberg to infiltrate around the American pocket and sever their link with the rest of the U.S. 77th Division. The 122nd was not as responsive to Hünicken's requests as he hoped, but their assistance would be forthcoming. In the meantime, he deployed machine guns and trench mortars around the perimeter. The 76th Reserve Pioneer Battalion was reinforced by two infantry companies and given the difficult task of covering the southern edge of the Amerikanernest. Later on 3 October, two companies of the 122nd Württemberg manned the line adjacent to the 76th Pioneers. This was followed by several more companies of the 245th Regiment. These units were engaged in two directions, north toward the Amerikanernest and south facing the U.S. 77th Division. Time was of the essence. The Amerikanernest had to be eliminated quickly.[36]

Whittlesey received confirmation in the morning from his line of runners and the patrols that he sent out to link up with the French that they were indeed surrounded by the Germans.[37] Meanwhile, early on the morning of 3 October, Hauptman Hansen met with his regimental command and staff to discuss the situation. The regiment assessed that the unit trapped in the Amerikanernest included "two reinforced combat companies, trapped on the [Charlevaux] mill meadow."[38] The importance of eliminating the Amerikanernest was not lost to the 76th Reserve Division commander (*Freiherr* Quadt Wyckradt Hüchtenbruck), or, *Generalmajor* Wellman (the I Reserve Corps commander). Hüchtenbruck directed his divisional staff to work out a plan where the other two regiments (253rd and 252nd) could occupy more of the front so that Hansen's 245th Regiment could focus on the reduction of the Amerikanernest. This relief in the line of most the 245th, combined with the recent departure of key staff from the German leadership, delayed a timely counterattack.[39]

As Hansen prepared his men for an attack on 3 October, the I German Reserve Corps commander, Generalmajor Wellman, received written congratulations for driving back the French the day before, in addition to eliminating a French "Lost Battalion" west of the Argonne. Meanwhile, across the lines, the U.S. I Corps commander, General Hunter Liggett, asked his chief of staff to send the following written congratulations to General Alexander: "The Corps Commander has directed me to extend to you and to the entire 77th Division a most cordial expression of his gratification at the steady, solid progress made since the beginning of the operation now under way. The difficulties of the terrain are fully understood and the amount of ground gained is noticeable."[40] Despite the kind

Freiherr Quadt Wyckradt
Hüchtenbruck commanded the
76th Reserve Division. He led a
brilliant defense of the western
Argonne and exploited
American inexperience to
delay their advance into the
region. (Hünicken, *Reserve
Infanterie Regiment Nr. 254*)

words on both sides, the most important battle in the Argonne was
being waged one kilometer behind German lines.

The plan for the reduction of Whittlesey and his men began
when German trench mortars began pounding the American position late in the morning. This would be complemented by machine
gun fire and snipers from Hill 198, as well as from the ridges to the
south and east. Finally, a series of counterattacks would be launched
to finish off the Americans by the end of the day. The plan was supported by the 122nd Württemberg Regiment.[41] The German counterattack force included one battalion from this regiment, a portion
of the 376th Pioneer Battalion, and the 3rd Uhlan (Lancers) Foot
Battalion.[42]

Brigadier General Johnson took on the burden of rescuing his
trapped men and planned on doing this largely with his own unit.
Oddly, there was no appeal to Major General Alexander for the division reserves to be thrown into the assault as part of the rescue. It is
not clear why Johnson did not ask for additional support. We can
surmise that Alexander's toxic leadership style had much to do with
this. Whatever the reason, Johnson said during a meeting on 3 October with his officers, regarding Whittlesey and the other trapped
Americans, "This is a family affair and as such, we will handle it

ourselves."[43] This would lead to Johnson ordering attack after attack to break through to the trapped Americans. His men would conduct two to five attacks each day. Several of these assaults were personally led by Johnson, who became increasingly desperate to save his men. The casualties that his men sustained during these abortive frontal attacks were staggering, with one hundred Americans falling in just one of them.[44]

The Germans planned on crushing the Amerikanernest on 3 October, just as they had forced a similar French pocket to surrender the day before. As the acting regimental commander, Hauptman Hansen, planned the elimination of Whittlesey and his men, the 77th Division launched an attack at 9:00 A.M., followed by a heavy artillery barrage and another unsuccessful attack at 11:45 A.M. The frontal attacks by the 77th Division disrupted Hansen's plans to finish off the trapped Americans. Instead, he was compelled to divert most of his soldiers to the south to blunt the strong American push, and then to follow up with counterattacks to break up and repel any American penetrations.

Because of the attacks largely from the 77th Division's 154th Brigade (under Johnson), Hansen failed to eliminate the Amerikanernest. A series of minor German probes against them did drive up casualties, however. The German attacks, combined with the harassing machine gun fire from the hills overlooking the pocket and the trench mortars, cost the Americans in the pocket about one hundred casualties. The situation for Whittlesey and his men was becoming desperate. After twenty-four hours of sitting on the objective, they were nearly out of food, were running low on medical supplies, and had lost 20 percent of their men.[45] The Americans held onto hope that their rescue was forthcoming, just as they had a week before when they were trapped for a day. The surrounded Americans had no idea that they had four more days of siege to endure. One of Whittlesey's officers, Lieutenant William J. Cullen, who commanded a company on the left side of the pocket, described a typical scene in the day of the life of the Lost Battalion:

We could hear the Boche around us shrieking and trying to intimidate us with their schrecklichkeit [terror].

We have the Americans just where we want them, they yelled. They closed in on us. From the direction of his voice the leader was just behind my post of command. He would call out: "Eitel," and a voice over to the left would answer "Hier." Then: "Adolph." Another voice now on the front would answer: "Hier." Then: "Sind deiner men da?" [are your men there (ready)] and the answer: "Ja, Ja!" Then the son of a gun would shout: "Alle zusammen!" (All together), and thereupon it seemed that the law of gravity had been reversed and everything went up in the air. They simply piled high explosive grenades in on us. Their trench mortars rained their infernal shells. We couldn't see them, of course, due to the heavy brush, and waited for them to rush us. During a lull their leader called out:

"Kamerad, vill you?"

He seemed to think that we were ready to surrender. That was about the last straw for me. "Come in and get us, you blankety-blank-blank!" I yelled at him, using the few cuss words that I knew of his language. Then we opened fire on where we judged they were and gave them hell. That settled that little attack. There was blood all round us the next day, and we knew we got some of them.[46]

Knowing that his men were in a desperate fight, the 245th commander, Major Emil Hünicken, did all he could to get back to the front as soon as possible. His audience with the grand duke of Hesse was on 2 October in the ducal palace in Darmstadt, Germany. Duke Ernest Louis was sincerely interested in the well-being and conduct of his citizens. He also inquired as to the situation in France. The duke was concerned that the fortunes of war had turned against Germany and that time was running out. He listened intently to Major Hünicken. Duke Louis thanked the major for his frank discussion and then asked that he pass along to his countrymen sincere greetings and best wishes to the 254th for its bravery and honorable service on behalf of the Grand Duchy of Hesse.[47]

Major Hünicken appreciated the duke's kind words, but he had a sense of urgency to return to the Argonne. He wasted little time, and instead of enjoying the hospitality of the Duke, Hünicken politely asked to be excused to return to his men. Following the meeting he rushed to the Darmstadt main train station and spent a day and a half working his way back to the Argonne. After a full night of traveling, he arrived at the 254th's headquarters at 7:00 A.M. on 4 October, where he received a detailed

The grand duke of Hesse, Ernst Ludwig Karl Albrecht Wilhelm. Duke Ernest Louis summoned the 254th Regiment commander, Major Emil Hünicken, to Darmstadt, Germany, for an update on the war. As a result, Hünicken missed the first two days of the Lost Battalion siege and the only real chance of defeating it. (National Archives)

situation update from Hauptman Hansen and the regimental staff. The task at hand was clear, Hünicken needed to finish off the Amerikanernest today, otherwise risk losing the advantage of the Giselher Stellung.[48]

Ironically, the two senior officers opposing each other were both majors. The two majors could not be more different, other than their care for their men: the Harvard-educated lawyer Major Charles Whittlesey and Major Emil Hünicken, a highly decorated officer in the German Imperial Army. Hünicken had served with his regiment in East Prussia, Russia, and the Balkans, receiving several awards for heroism during the campaign in Romania. He was considered one of the unit's most capable and reliable officers. The regiment was transferred to the Western Front for the first time in March 1918. Together with their division, they fought in the German Spring Offensives and the particularly brutal fighting near St. Quentin. Hünicken was appointed to the position of 254th Regiment commander on 25 April 1918 and remained its commander through the end of the war.[49]

By now, General Alexander was growing concerned and ordered a general attack across the front of the U.S. 77th Division to rupture the German line and save the besieged Americans. As usual, the American attacks were poorly planned and poorly executed. A series of disjointed advances were attempted through the morning of 4 October with little appreciable gains.[50] The French Fourth Army endeavored to gain headway to the west but was also stopped by the Germans. The seemingly incessant (yet ineffective) American pushes in the Argonne did, however, disrupt Hünicken's plan of quickly reducing the Amerikanernest, as once again the reserve units had to be rushed to the front in lieu of attacking the American pocket.

To his credit, Major General Alexander was moved to action. Johnson was wrong; this was more than a family affair. The trapped Americans put not just the honor of the division at stake, but also that of the entire American Expeditionary Forces. The story of the Lost Battalion quickly caught the imagination of both the American and French armies and was beginning to take on a life of its own, with many of the myths told about this five-day siege still perpetuated a century later. The saga was one of heroism and bravery. The 77th Division's staff was directed to find a way to support the trapped men. The staff developed a three-pronged approach to save the "Lost Battalion." The first part encompassed continuing attacks across the division's front until the unit was saved. Coordination was conducted with the Fourth French Army to also apply pressure on the Germans west of the Argonne to drive them back via a flanking action from the valley into the Argonne. The second prong included using aircraft to resupply the Americans by air. This would include drops of ammunition, food, and other supplies. This was the first time that aerial resupply would be attempted by the fledgling U.S. Army Air Service, a significant military adaptation of the time. The third aspect was focusing the division's 152nd Field Artillery Brigade in creating a wall of fire around the flanks and northern approach to the pocket where the Lost Battalion was deployed. The idea was to at least partially protect the men from German attacks.[51]

The frontal attacks by the American 77th Division continued, with a growing sense of urgency. The French Fourth Army to the west of the trapped Americans, as well as the U.S. 28th Division to the east and southeast, endeavored to likewise drive the Germans back. Despite the crescendo of pressure, both the German 76th Reserve Division and the 2nd Württemberg were unmovable, offering a robust and costly defense. The U.S. I Corps commander, General Hunter Liggett, ordered a general attack across the front by his three divisions in the lines (the 77th, 28th, and 1st Divisions). All three attacks failed to achieve results "and revealed once more the folly of trying to overthrow machine guns by sheer weight of human bodies, without adequate support or surprise."[52] Lack of liaison and cooperation between Liggett's divisions did not help matters, and he did little to ameliorate this shortcoming. Liggett's aide-de-camp observed on 3 October 1918, in the midst of the Lost Battalion siege, "Liaison between 28th and 77th is supposed to be established on about this line, but there is entire distrust of each by the other, and an unfortunate amount of back biting and argument. (The time of one accurate and conscientious observer spent in determining the facts would quickly resolve the uncertainty—but then there would be nothing for the staff to argue about)."[53]

Despite the lack of progress by the I Corps, General Pershing was impressed by Hunter Liggett's leadership style and told him that he would be given command of the First Army.[54] Up to this point, General Pershing had been serving as both the American Expeditionary Forces commander and the First Army commander, and that was certainly a bad situation, as that made him responsible for American strategy in Europe generally and for American military operations in the Meuse-Argonne. Because of this, he lacked adequate time to perform either task well. He was caught up in the politics of the alliance and interaction with the Supreme Allied Commander, the French premier, American politicians, the secretary of war, and the president, all while trying to run an army. It was now necessary for him to relinquish command of the First Army, and Liggett would prove to be an excellent choice. The creation of the U.S. Second Army was necessary since there were now so many Americans in the Meuse-Argonne region. The Second Army would become operational on 10 October 1918.

At 1:30 P.M., the 77th Division's 152nd Field Artillery Brigade began to fire a "protection barrage" in support of Whittlesey and his men. This was at first welcomed by the men, until the artillery smashed into their position. The position that Whittlesey had selected for his men provided considerable protection from German artillery. However, being on the southern slope of the hill below the Charlevaux road placed his unit in a position where American artillery from the south could lay waste to the pocket, and this is exactly what it did. The dead and dying mounted as the American artillery ripped gaping holes into the slope, staining it with blood. To make matters worse, Whittlesey's only means of communication was carrier pigeon, of which he had two remaining. Whittlesey scribbled a message and passed it to Private Omer Richards to attach to one of the birds.[55] The message read:

We are along the road parallel 276.4
Our own artillery is dropping a barrage directly on us.
For heaven's sake stop it.
Whittlesey, Major 308

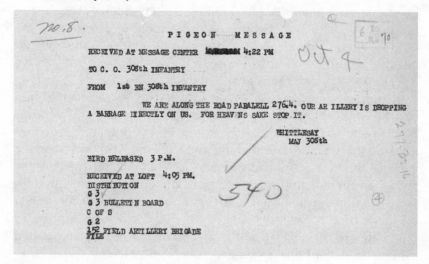

Whittlesey's last courier pigeon, Cher Ami, saved the unit from destruction by delivering this message to headquarters. (National Archives)

As Richards reached into his pigeon basket, one of the birds escaped, leaving their last bird, Cher Ami, with the responsibility of stopping the American barrage. Richards attached the message to Cher Ami's leg and released the bird. Cher Ami was terrified to fly in the midst of the barrage that was exploding all around the besieged men of the Lost Battalion and quickly landed on a tree. Major Whittlesey was appalled to see this and ordered Richards to get the bird on its way. Richards yelled at the bird and threw rocks and sticks, but Cher Ami refused to budge. In desperation, Richards climbed up the tree in the midst of the artillery barrage. Cher Ami

Cher Ami is the most celebrated American "war bird." It delivered the message that saved the Lost Battalion from being obliterated by friendly fire, at the cost of an eye, a leg, and hole in the breast. (National Archives)

simply fluttered to higher branches, compelling Richards to climb near the top until finally the bird flew off.[56] As Cher Ami headed back to the 77th Division line carrying its life or death message, suddenly a shell "exploded directly below the bird, killing five of our men and stunning the pigeon so that it fluttered to the ground."[57] All hope seemed lost. Meanwhile, an American observation plane from the 50th Aero Squadron circled above, seeking visual confirmation on the location of the trapped Americans. Flying an aircraft into an ongoing artillery barrage was more evidence of the fledgling American army's lack of experience, as the barrage masked any chance of the American pilot or his observer seeing the men below, who were hunkered deep into their "funk" holes trying to survive the torrent of steel. During this time, Cher Ami came to and struggled to fly. Off the ground Cher Ami slowly flew. The pigeon made it back to its loft more than twenty minutes later, having lost an eye and a leg and gained a hole in the breast. But the message got through. The American barrage finally lifted after nearly two hours. It caused 110 casualties, of which thirty died.[58]

For decades the horror of this "friendly fire" incident was a closely guarded secret. There was no investigation or dialogue as it was thought that it would trigger public outrage. Yet, covering up this tragic episode prevented the U.S. Army from learning valuable lessons, and it lost a chance to evaluate ways to avoid a repetition of this horrible experience in the next world war, when there would be numerous similar instances of fratricide. Whittlesey had provided the 77th Division with the precise location of his unit. The error was not his, but committed by the fire direction artilleryman in the 152nd Brigade. By all rights, this experience should have broken the fighting spirit of the Lost Battalion. It is one thing to suffer losses from the enemy, but something else altogether to lose men by fratricide. The men by now were out of food, only had access to the water at night (when German snipers or machine gunners could not shoot at them), and were running low on ammunition and grenades. A third of the original force was now either dead or wounded, and the greater number of these by American artillery.

It is a testament to the leadership of Whittlesey, McMurtry, and Holderman that they held the men together in the midst of the unthinkable predicament that they endured. Whittlesey's calm and reassuring manner steadied the men. He spent much of his time moving around the perimeter to check on the soldiers, even while under fire, to converse with them and to bolster their confidence. Whittlesey's most important attribute was not his sharing their suffering, but his caring for each soldier and constantly risking his life to assure them. Each time he moved along the side of the hill he was exposed to German sniper and machine gun fire. This gave the soldiers the ability to hang onto hope that under his leadership they would get out of their situation with honor.

As the barrage lifted, the Germans attacked, inflicting even more casualties. The Germans opened up an intense machine gun grazing fire and tossed scores of grenades into the American pocket. This was followed by an assault to finish off the surviving Americans. Remarkably, the Americans refused to relent and drove the Germans back. However, the Americans of E Company, located in the eastern portion of the pocket, were overrun by the attacking Germans. The Germans were repelled from this position after intense fighting, but only after they had killed or captured a significant number of the Americans in E Company. Two of the men captured by the Germans were Lieutenant Victor Harrington and Lieutenant James Leak. Before being segregated for questioning, Leak and Harrington concocted a plan to deceive the Germans as to the size and condition of the "Lost Battalion."[59]

The 254th German Regiment reported gleefully on the results of their attack. Although they were repelled, the prisoners were a boon and would provide the information needed to finish off the Amerikanernest. The report said, "The loot of the day included one heavy machine gun and two light machine guns. One officer [there were actually two: Leak and Harrington], and thirteen men captured."[60] An interesting aside is that the Germans reported that they killed both a French and an American soldier near the front. This was likely a Franco-American liaison team trying to establish coordination for an impending attack. The German report described the French officer bedecked in his "steel-blue colored uniform."[61]

During questioning, Leak and Harrington provided the Germans all manner of false information. They said that there were twelve hundred men in the pocket (twice the number who walked into the area two days before) and that they had plenty of food and ammunition, having been given extra before the attack. Leak played upon the stereotype images of the Americans, adding, "I do not think that there are less than 1,200 [Americans] now. New Yorkers. The gangster type; very ruthless and good shots. They will never give up."[62] This disinformation had the desired effect and caused the Germans to believe that the Amerikanernest actually outnumbered them. Leak and Harrington bought Whittlesey time. The Germans were a bit more cautious on 5 October and relied on trench mortars, grenades, and harassing machine gun fire to inflict casualties on the Americans, rather than a direct assault. The frontal attacks by the American I Corps and French Fourth Army did not achieve any breakthroughs this day.

The German 76th Reserve Division reinforced the 254th Regiment with an assault unit equipped with flamethrowers to finish off the Amerikanernest. They resumed their attacks on 6 October. The 254th Regiment reported that they launched four attacks against the Amerikanernest, all of which were amazingly repelled by Whittlesey's men. The casualty figures of the Americans and Germans grew daily.[63] The U.S. 50th Aero Squadron also began their air resupply efforts on this day.[64] The Germans fired on the American aircraft as they flew over the pocket "low and slow," shooting down three of them.[65] None of the packages landed in the pocket. Rather, most of the drops ended up in the hands of the Germans. The 254th Regiment reported that "enemy aircraft flew across the sector dropping supplies. It would not be an understatement of the pure joy that we [the 254th Regiment] experienced as these supplies fell into our hands. We were greeted by packages of chocolate and tobacco pouches . . . these were gifts fit for a king."[66]

Two intrepid American aviators from the 50th Aero Squadron would give their lives in doing everything possible to confirm the location of the Lost Battalion. The pilot of one of the DH-4s was Lieutenant Harold Goettler. He and his aerial observer, Second Lieutenant Erwin Bleckley, took off on 5 October to ascertain the precise location of the cut-off Americans. Their first attempt did not bear fruit, and although their plane received considerable damage from German ground fire, they set off on a second sortie later that day in another aircraft. The Germans were waiting for them, and after a second pass the DH-4 was hit forty times. Although receiving a mortal head wound, Goettler managed to keep the airplane airborne long enough to crash land in friendly territory. Bleckley was thrown from the crash and died from his wounds. However, his map survived with the precise location of the Lost Battalion. Both would receive the Medal of Honor for their actions.[67]

Meanwhile, Major General Alexander was on a rampage at the U.S. 77th Division headquarters. He was mortified when he learned that his 152nd Artillery Brigade fired on the men in the pocket. Additionally, his entire division had failed to make any progress in saving Whittlesey. General Hunter Liggett met with Alexander at his headquarters to discuss this. The following observations were recorder by Hunter Liggett's aide-de-camp:

> Alexander said he was about at the end of his rope. He had tried coaxing and kicking and every expedient to make his men move. He had sustained losses, but not heavy, and he had many stragglers and men drawn from the city, who knew nothing about the woods and fighting of this character, but he thought they were not all in, and was greatly distressed that he could report no better progress. . . . He has just canned another colonel [Cromwell Stacey] after two days' trial and given the regiment to a captain; he has an

average of about one officer to a company. He seems to be having an unusual amount of trouble with officers and to act very hastily in their shortcomings. I have heard him say nothing commendatory about any of them.[68]

General Alexander was not the right man for the task ahead. His toxic leadership style of threatening, bullying, and firing officers at the drop of a hat did more to disrupt his military operations than perhaps even the Germans could have achieved. The division needed a leader who could inspire, not yell and threaten men into action.

Liggett was not pleased with the lack of progress made by the 77th in clearing the Argonne, or in saving the Lost Battalion. Finally, after four days of fruitless frontal attacks, an original plan was contrived. The I Corps had the U.S. 82nd Division in reserve. The 82nd would push up the eastern flank of the Argonne behind the U.S. 1st Division, which recently had made progress up the valley. The 82nd would launch an attack on 7 October into the Argonne (in a westerly and northwesterly direction). The concept of operations encompassed the 82nd advancing into the Argonne by Chatel Chehery and Cornay. The object would be the German north-south road just a few kilometers into the forest. If successful, this would threaten the 2nd Württemberg and 254th German Reserve Regiment with encirclement, forcing them to draw back from the Amerikanernest. The attack would commence early in the afternoon on 7 October. The 77th and 28th Divisions (as well as the French Fourth Army) would continue their respective frontal assaults as well. The attack order was issued late on 6 October.[69]

In the meantime, the Germans planned an all-out assault to finish off the Amerikanernest. The attack would be launched from all sides, commencing with grazing machine gun fire, a hail of grenades, and trench mortars. Following that would be the largest infantry attack yet, reinforced by the assault unit with flamethrowers.[70] As the Germans prepared for their late afternoon coup de grâce, another group of prisoners was scooped up near the Amerikanernest. The soldiers had left the perimeter to secure food from the airdrops.[71] One of the prisoners, Private Lowell Hollingshead, was interrogated by German leutnant Fritz Prinz. Prinz directed Hollingshead to deliver the following letter to Major Whittlesey:

Sir:

The bearer of this present, Private Lowell R. Hollingshead has been taken by us. He refused to give the German Intelligence Officer any answer to his questions, and is quite an honorable fellow, doing honor to his Fatherland in the strictest sense of the word.

He has been charged against his will, believing that he is doing wrong to his country to carry forward this present letter to the officer in charge of the battalion of the 77th Division, with the purpose to recommend this commander to surrender with his forces, as it would be quite useless to resist any more, in view of the present conditions.

The suffering of your wounded men can be heard over here in the German lines, and we are appealing to your humane sentiments to stop. A white flag shown by one of your men will tell us that you agree with these conditions. Please treat Private Hollingshead as an honorable man. He is quite a soldier. We envy you.

The German Commanding Officer[72]

Private Hollingshead returned to the pocket and delivered the letter to Major Whittlesey. The surrender request was rejected, which unleashed the final German torrent. The battle was the fiercest of the previous five days. The soldiers of the Lost Battalion refused to capitulate. This mixed group of diverse nationalities from New York City and the Midwest came together to fight off the intense assault. Indeed, although out of food for days, suffering some 70 percent casualties, and with their ammunition nearly exhausted, they fought with incredible determination and ferocity. The inspirational leadership of Whittlesey enabled the men to perform more than they could have imagined. This is how a leader truly leads—not by the bombastic approach of Major General Alexander, but by the humble and unassuming style of Major Whittlesey. Of the 694 Americans in the Lost Battalion, 493 were either killed or wounded. The Medal of Honor would be awarded to five of the soldiers in the Lost Battalion (including Whittlesey, McMurtry, and Holderman) and the two aviators, Lieutenants Goettler and Bleckley, who lost their lives locating the Lost Battalion.[73]

The daily attempts by the 77th Division to save the Lost Battalion were noble, but they accomplished little more than adding to the casualty figures. The wave of attacks gained little ground and were poorly planned and executed. Coordination between the American units was disjointed at best and virtually nonexistent with the French to the west. Within the 77th Division, there was a lack of clarity on what the objective was, little coordination between the regiments, and a penchant for attacking the strongest point of the German line. These frontal assaults often attacked into German kill zones, where the Americans would be stopped by bails of barbed wire and then chopped to pieces by machine guns, grenades, and artillery. This is how a green military organization responds to a crisis—without imagination or reason.[74]

The relief of the Lost Battalion would come early on 8 October. The U.S. 82nd Division began its attack into the Argonne on 7 October and struck deeper into the Argonne on the 8th. This threatened the German units deployed around the Lost Battalion with being encircled, and they were forced to pull back, opening the door for the 77th Division to finally link up with its men. Lieutenant Cullen described what happened next:

On the morning of October 8th, about 1 A.M., I was in my bunk hole when I heard a voice calling, "Lieutenant, Lieutenant!" I thought it was time to repulse another Boche attack. But it was my battalion runner with a little gunny sack containing bread and two cans of bully beef. He brought a message from the Major that our right flank had come up and that a patrol had reached us with a few rations. I opened up the bully beef, took a fork from my mess kit and went around my posts on a tour of inspection. I told the men what had happened and, to prove the truth of what I said—it seemed so incredible—I gave each man a forkful of bully. We were ready to go on for another six days then. So it was that relief came to the "Lost Battalion"—its whole significance, like the significance of the great moments of life, being epitomized in a very little thing, "a forkful of bully."[75]

As the men of the Lost Battalion beat back the last German attack, the U.S. 82nd Division attacked into the eastern half of the Argonne. With the support of the 28th Division, the "All American"

82nd boys stormed the vital German position guarding the gateway to the Argonne, called "Castle Hill." Once in American hands, the way was open to attack and cut off the north-south road, the only German resupply route in the Argonne. The German army group command saw that this threatened the 2nd Württemberg and 76th Reserve Division with encirclement, so they were ordered to pull their lines back several kilometers in the late evening of 7 October.[76] The Germans saw the remainder of the 82nd "All American" Division preparing for a large assault into the Argonne that would continue in earnest on 8 October. The Americans of the 82nd knew the plight of the Lost Battalion and had no idea that it was already saved. Although the Battle for the Argonne was far from over, this impending American attack would produce another hero of epic proportions, Corporal Alvin York.

13

Alvin York

A Conscientious Objector Wins the Day

Le plus grand exploit jamais réalisé par un simple soldat de
toutes les armées en Europe.
— Maréchal Ferdinand Foch

Sergeant York, you are the greatest civilian soldier of the war.
— General John J. Pershing

As the Allies continued their offensive in the West in early October,
things were happening in Berlin that would forever change the face
of the war. Politically, a Reichstag controlled by the Social Democrats rose to power, in large part due to the collapsing domestic situation. The four-year blockade of the German ports led to severe
shortages and even starvation among portions of the populace. The
Social Democrats were among the first in the leadership to see that
there was no longer a chance for Germany to win the war, and they
put considerable pressure on the Kaiser to seek its end.

Strategically, things were taking a turn for the worse. The Austro-Hungarian Empire, never a reliable military power for Germany in the First World War, was publicly speaking of seeking a
negotiated peace. In addition to this, Germany's ally Bulgaria had
withdrawn from the war the week before. Meanwhile, the Ottoman
Empire was reeling from a series of military defeats in the Middle
East as the number of American soldiers even in Europe was nearing 2 million. There was simply no way that the German Imperial
Army could long stem the rising tide.

As the siege of the Lost Battalion entered its fourth day, General
von Gallwitz was facing an increasingly dangerous situation across
his front. In the near-term, the situation was generally improving.

The arrival of the German Western Front reserve divisions slowed and in some instances stopped the Americans. Although the Americans would not break out of the Meuse until 1 November, the attack in the region was having the desired effect: drawing off German units from across the Western Front. This included twenty-one divisions pulled off of the British and French portion of the line. However, Gallwitz knew that this was just buying time, time that the Germans were running short of. The Allied Grand Offensive was in full motion. The Western Front was ablaze from the English Channel to the hills north of Verdun. This was stretching German resources. Gallwitz received the preponderance of the reserves due to the danger that the Franco-American attack posed to the vital German rail lines. The concern for Gallwitz was that the Americans were more than ten kilometers closer to the Sedan-Mezieres rail than they had been two weeks before. The main threat in his sector was the western portion of the Meuse Valley, as the most experienced American unit, the 1st Division, pushed north. But the German positions on the high ground in the Argonne were causing considerable harm to the Big Red One through flanking fires.

There were three essential pieces for General von Gallwitz's defense. The most important was his control of the Argonne Forest in the western portion of the American push. This high ground was proving an excellent platform from which to engage the Americans with flanking fires. The second vital part of Gallwitz's defensive plan was the control of the Meuse Heights along the eastern portion of the American attack. This had the same effect as the Argonne farther to the west. The third consideration for Gallwitz was the prepared German defensive belts. The Americans penetrated portions of the second belt. Once the third, and most powerful, was breached—the Kriemhilde/Siegfried Line—it would be difficult to hold the Americans and French back. The Allies often referred to the Siegfried as the "Hindenburg Line." The Siegfried Line was the strongest defensive belt that the Germans constructed behind their lines on the Western Front. The Kriemhilde Stellung was the southern sector of the overall Siegfried Stellung. Ironically, what the Allies called the Siegfried Line in World War Two was never called that by the Germans. Then, the Germans called it the West Wall. This was a legacy name by the British, French, and American veterans who fought on the Western Front in 1918.

Gallwitz had to decide whether to commit additional forces to the Argonne Forest or to reinforce his units in the valley. His decision was to bolster the Argonne Forest defenses. As the Germans recorded:

The General HQ was concerned about these occurrences and committed elements of the 1st Guards Infantry Division, a portion of the 52nd Reserve Division, the 210th and 212th Regiments of the 45th Reserve Division, the 47th and 58th Machine Gun Sharpshooters. However, fighting in the woods around Sommerance and Romagne became intense, so that one could not support both locations. We had to stop the enemy's main attack, which was now east of the Aire [in the Meuse River valley]. So our artillery around Hohenbornhöhe was used to provide fires against his flank.[1]

This meant that the Prussian 5th Guards and 2nd Württemberg Divisions were to be reinforced by the Prussian 45th Reserve Division's 210th and 212th Regiments. The 45th would begin movement on 7 October and support the 2nd Württemberg in the Argonne as part of a counterattack force to drive the Americans out of the eastern portion of the forest. If successful, this would threaten the flank of the American main attack in the valley below and unhinge its forward movement. This had the possibility of setting the Americans back significantly.[2]

Meanwhile, after several days of frontal attacks to relieve the Lost Battalion, the U.S. Army's 82nd Reserve Division was tasked with the mission to advance up the eastern portion of the Meuse Valley and attack into the Argonne Forest. The division had been in reserve since it was moved from St. Mihiel more than a week earlier. The division had performed well in St. Mihiel, but Pershing decided to fire the division commander, Major General William B. Burnham, whom he viewed as not aggressive enough with his unit's subordinates.[3] The division's new commander was Major General George Duncan, who was a friend of Pershing. Duncan was in Paris when he received his orders and hurriedly packed and "had no idea" where the division was. He arrived shortly before the unit was ordered forward.

The 82nd "All American" Division was in the ruins of Varennes on Sunday, 6 October, when Major General Duncan, the new commander, received the order "to seize the eastern slopes of the

General George Duncan was given command of the 82nd Division just days before its fateful attack into the Argonne in early October 1918. (National Archives)

Argonne Forest."[4] Liggett's entire I Corps would participate in this attack, beginning on 7 October. The plan was for the 77th Division to attempt another frontal attack in the Argonne, for the 1st Division to continue its pressure on the German forces in the Meuse Valley, and for the 82nd and 28th Divisions to attack into the eastern flank of the Argonne Forest.

Major General Duncan's mission "to seize the eastern slopes of the Argonne Forest" seemed impossible.[5] Of this, Duncan said, "I was just handed the problem of making the attack. . . . There were no intelligence reports of the enemy."[6] Duncan was new to the 82nd and to Liggett's I Corps. Pershing's propensity to fire or reassign officers before major combat operations demonstrated his lack of experience in administering an army and his immature leadership style. Duncan's response to this was, "We were all rather depressed. It seemed to commit a large body of troops to an assault without thorough orientation; careful placing of troops in

Map 13.1. York Attack Plan. (Mastriano, *Alvin York*)

an assault and a thorough coordination with artillery presented very grave difficulties."[7] In the end, Duncan's plan was to attack on 7 October into the Argonne through Chatel Chehery, to drive the Germans off of the high ground, and then to push into the forest. The mission for the attacking force was the German north-south supply road that was roughly three kilometers west of Chatel. If the attack failed on 7 October, it would be followed by a larger three-pronged attack designed to dislodge the German hold on the eastern Argonne.

As Duncan and the 82nd U.S. Division staff planned the attack into the Argonne, Chaplain Daniel Smart led a worship service for the men awaiting orders in Varennes. It was a rare sunny day and a Sunday. Chaplain Smart was a lieutenant who hailed from

Cambridge, New York. The chaplain read from II Timothy in the New Testament:

> I charge thee therefore before God, and the Lord Jesus Christ, who shall judge the quick and the dead at his appearing and his kingdom; Preach the word; be instant in season, out of season; reprove, rebuke, exhort with all long suffering and doctrine. For the time will come when they will not endure sound doctrine; but after their own lusts shall they heap to themselves teachers, having itching ears; And they shall turn away their ears from the truth, and shall be turned unto fables. But watch thou in all things, endure afflictions, do the work of an evangelist, make full proof of thy ministry. For I am now ready to be offered, and the time of my departure is at hand. I have fought a good fight, I have finished my course, I have kept the faith: Henceforth there is laid up for me a crown of righteousness, which the Lord, the righteous judge, shall give me at that day: and not to me only, but unto all them also that love his appearing.[8]

This was Smart's last sermon. He would die a few days later while tending the wounded. Among the men listening to the sermon was Corporal Alvin C. York, a conscientious objector from Pall Mall, Tennessee.

The division moved slowly through the night to attack positions east of Chatel Chehery. The 1st Battalion of the 82nd's 328th Regiment attacked through Chatel Chehery and into the Argonne, seizing a foothold on the hill overlooking the village. The hill (called 223 by the Americans or Castle Hill by the Germans) was a gateway into the Argonne and was key terrain. The Germans spent the day and evening trying to push the Americans off of it. Although suffering high losses, the Americans managed to hold on to a narrow portion of the hill.[9]

As the battle for Castle Hill raged on through 7 October, the forward elements of the 120th Württemberg Landwehr Regiment were ordered to pull back from their positions around the embattled village of Apremont, where they had been fighting the 28th Division for nearly a week. Among the Germans redeploying near Chatel Chehery was Leutnant Paul "Kuno" Vollmer. Vollmer was promoted to commander of the 120th's 1st Battalion on 29 September after the

Leutnant Paul Vollmer commanded a battalion in the 120th Württemberg Regiment and found himself face to face with Alvin York during the morning of 8 October 1918. (U.S. Army Heritage and Education Center, Carlisle, Pennsylvania)

previous leader was wounded in action. His mission west of Chatel Chehery was to (1) prevent an American breakthrough into the
Argonne, and then (2) lead a counterattack to drive the Americans
out of the area and retake the high ground overlooking the Meuse
Valley. However, Vollmer's march along the north-south road was
observed by American aviators, resulting in harassing artillery fire,
of which he wrote: "While marching [on] 7 October . . . we passed
a great number of artillery positions that had been shot to bits and
were in a state of chaos. Part of my own company, the 5th Company 120th Landwehr, was lying on the North South Road; some
dead and others wounded, these men were the victims of one single shell."[10] When Vollmer finally arrived at his position, the battle
for Castle Hill was raging, and soon claimed the life of one of his
friends (Hauptman Müller) and the loss of another, Dr. Kugel, the
surgeon for the 125th Württemberg Regiment. Kugel was captured
as he tended the wounds of the mortally wounded Hauptman Müller and refused to fall back.

The Germans prepared for the main American attack that they
expected to occur on 8 October. The German plan was to have the
survivors of the German unit on Hill 223 fight until they ran out
of ammunition. After depleting their ammunition, the men would
retreat to a series of prepared positions about a kilometer west of
the hill. The Americans would be allowed to enter the valley, which
was covered by two regiments of the 2nd Württemberg Division,
the 120th and 125th. These two regiments were to be reinforced by
the 210th and 212th Prussian Reserve Regiments, and would turn
the valley into a kill zone.[11] The Germans would finish off the surviving Americans with a four-regiment counterattack at 10:30 A.M.
Leutnant Vollmer would lead the counterattack along the southern
half of the valley.[12]

As Vollmer organized his men for the defense early on 8 October, the 82nd All American Division completed its plans for a second push into the Argonne, which would include an attack from
Hill 223 into the Argonne and two additional attacks north of Chatel
Chehery. Corporal York and the other men in his battalion moved
during the early morning hours up the steep slope to Chatel Chehery under the watchful eyes of the Germans, who barraged the
Americans with poisonous gas, making their climb all the more difficult. As the men clumsily advanced to Chatel Chehery, Corporal
Alvin York reflected on the moral dilemma before him.

Alvin York, in Hoboken, New Jersey, after he returned from France in 1919. (National Archives)

York grew up in the mountains of north Tennessee near the Kentucky border in a devout Christian family. Things forever changed for Alvin when his father died in 1911, leaving him responsible for the family, his mother, and a farm on which it was virtually impossible to make a living. To augment the income from the farm, the York men hunted to put meat on the table and to sell the pelts of the animals. York was perhaps the best shot in the region, thanks in large part to his father's influence. Growing up in a large family, Alvin had quickly learned that the only way to spend quality time with his father, William, was to join him on hunting excursions. William, a crack shot, taught his son everything he knew, and Alvin soon exceeded his father's marksman skills.

However, the steadying influence of William York ended after he was kicked by a mule he was shoeing. The burden of running a family, farm, and household suddenly was thrust upon Alvin—a burden for which he was not ready. To escape from the cares of his world, Alvin soon found himself joining friends and a few of his brothers on the Kentucky border in drinking establishments known as "Blind Tigers." The Blind Tigers were built literally on the state line, with half the building in Kentucky and the other half in Tennessee. This enabled the proprietors and drinkers to circumvent state laws on alcohol regulation.

The Blind Tigers were rough places, with men going there to get drunk, gamble, and chase women. This volatile mixture of conflicting interests often led to violent fist, knife, and gun fights. One of the Blind Tigers that York frequented was called Marder's Place. It was renowned for monthly deaths from the shootouts between drunken customers. York initially joined his friends at the Blind Tigers to gamble and to have fun. However, he gradually found himself consuming more and more alcohol, and before long he spent entire weekends drunk. York's favorite drinking game was last man standing, where York, his friends, and several brothers would buy all the alcohol that they could afford and then drink until they passed out. The winner, which was the last one still coherent, was rewarded with the remaining booze. His life was spinning out of control. Alvin later wrote:

> At the beginning we used to have a few drinks of a weekend and sit up nights, gambling our money away; and of course, like most of the others, I was always smoking and cussing. I don't think I was mean and bad; I was jes kinder careless. But the habits grew stronger on me. Sorter like the water that runs down a hill at first it makes the ravine, and then the ravine takes control of the water that's the way it was with me. I jes played with these things at first, and then they got a-hold of me and began to play with my life. I went from bad to worse. I began really to like liquor and gambling, and I was 'most always spoiling for a fight.[13]

Hope seemed lost for Alvin, especially after the law was after him for an array of infractions. His attempts to stop the cycle of wild living failed. York recalled this difficult period, "When you get used to a thing, no matter how bad it is for you, it is most awful hard to give it up. It was a most awful struggle to me. I did a lot of walking through the mountains and thinking. I was fighting the thing inside of me and it was the worstest fight I ever had."[14] However, his life would take a new direction after a local girl caught his eye. Gracie Loretta Williams was from a nearby farm, and when York saw her he was instantly smitten. Since Gracie and her family were strong Christians, the only place where Alvin could openly see her was church. He began regularly attending worship services just to see Gracie.

On New Year's Day 1915, York attended a revival service in his church. The minister, Reverend Melvin Russell from Indiana, preached the Christian salvation message, which highlights the sinfulness of man and the promise of salvation by accepting Jesus into one's heart and life as your personal Lord and Savior. York said it was as if lightning hit his soul. He went forward to the mourner's bench (below the podium) and asked for God's forgiveness and accepted Jesus into his life. He stood up a changed man.[15] Alvin's new faith would be put to the test the next day, which was Friday. His drinking buddies called on him to join them in a weekend of carousing at the Blind Tigers. "Sometimes Everett or Marion or some of the other boys would drop around and tell me they were putting on another party and invite me to join them. Then it was that I was most sorely tempted. I prayed most awful hard and got a good hold on myself and didn't go. Each time I refused, it was so much easier next time; and every day it became easier. In a few months I got them there bad things out of my mind."[16]

This was the most important period in York's life, where he developed his moral character. As he struggled with sin and endeavored to do the right thing, York built his "character muscle," becoming a brave and courageous man in his heart and soul. "And that is the greatest victory I ever won. It's much harder to whip yourself than to whip the other fellow, I'm a-telling you, and I ought to know because I done both. It was much harder for me to win the great victory over myself than to win it over those German machine guns in the Argonne Forest. And I was able to do it because . . . God . . . showed me the light, and I done followed it."[17]

Corporal Murray Savage was Alvin York's only true friend in the U.S. Army. They read and studied the Bible together and prayed together. Savage was among the first to fall when Lipp's machine gun opened fire, sending York into action. (East Bloomfield Historical Society)

York's life was radically changed. Instead of getting drunk on weekends, he became a leader in his church, teaching Sunday school, leading the choir, and even preaching on Sundays. However, his world turned upside when he received a draft notice. York saw this as a violation of "thou shall not kill." York's request to be categorized as a conscientious objector was disapproved, and he was compelled to report to duty at the 82nd Division at Camp Gordon, Georgia. Thankfully for York, his company commander, Captain Edward Danforth, and his battalion commander, Major G. Edward Buxton, saw potential in him and took time to discuss his concerns. Since his performance as a soldier was impeccable and he was the best shot in the unit, York was promoted to corporal, but he still wrestled with the idea of killing for his country even after his unit leadership made a convincing case for serving in the army when they read to him from the Old Testament book of Ezekiel, chapter 33.

As a conscientious objector, York's time at Camp Gordon was difficult. He was ostracized by several of the other junior NCOs (Bernard Early and William Cutting). Furthermore, his refusing to join the men in downtown Augusta, Georgia, to chase women and get drunk further alienated him. Although the temptation was difficult, he stayed true to his Christian life. York was encouraged when another Christian, Corporal Murray Savage, from upstate New York, befriended him.

As York's unit prepared to attack the Germans in the Argonne on 8 October 1918, he was still convinced that he could not kill for his country. The plan for the American offensive was to kick off with a ten-minute artillery barrage, followed by the infantry assault at 6:10 A.M. However, no barrage materialized. The unit's leader decided to attack as planned without the barrage. For the Germans, this was too good to be true. At precisely 6:10 A.M. the soldiers of the All American 82nd Division swept down Hill 223 and into the open valley along the edge of the Argonne Forest. As the Americans advanced across the valley, the Germans opened fire, of which York wrote:

> The Germans met our charge across the valley with a regular sleet storm of bullets. I'm a-telling you that-there valley was a death trap. It was a triangular-shaped valley with steep ridges covered with brush, and swarming with machine guns on all sides. I guess our two waves got about halfway across and then jes couldn't get no further nohow. The Germans done got us and they done got us right smart. They jes stopped us in our tracks. Their machine guns were up there on the heights overlooking us and well hidden, and we couldn't tell for certain where the terrible heavy fire was coming from. It 'most seemed as though it was coming from everywhere.[18]

York watched in horror as men all around him were hit by German machine gun and rifle fires. Not far from him, the unit's platoon leader, Lieutenant Kirby Stewart, had his legs cut out from under him by a hail of bullets, and then he was hit by another volley that killed him as he tried to crawl forward.[19] Command fell to Sergeant Harry Parsons, a vaudeville actor from Brooklyn. Parsons was well liked for his sense of humor and outgoing personality. German artillery suddenly began tearing holes as it erupted among the ranks. With this, the attack wavered and stalled. All hope seemed loss. However, Parsons observed a cut in the valley five hundred meters to the south where it just might be possible to get behind the German lines. He yelled orders to Acting Sergeant Bernard Early and Corporals York, Savage, and Cutting to lead their squads through this cut to get behind the machine guns holding up the advance. Of the four squads, only seventeen men remained,[20] including Bernard Early, Corporal York, Corporal Savage, Corporal Cutting, and Privates Maryan Dymowsky, Carl Swansen, Fred Wareing, Ralph Wiler, Mario Muzzi, William Wine, Percy Beardsley, Patrick Donohue, Thomas Johnson, Joseph Kornacki, Michael Sacina, Feodor Sok, and George Wills.

The seventeen men moved haphazardly toward the notch south of them, between exploding artillery and through a hail of bullets right under the guns of the 2nd Württemberg Machine Gun Company and the 7th Bavarian Mineur (miners). The 7th Bavarians were experts at digging under the enemy during the days of trench warfare and laying explosives that would be detonated to tear a hole in the lines. Now that the stagnant days of fighting were over, the 7th Bavarians were fighting as infantry. The unit's commander, Leutnant Max Thoma, had reported to Paul Vollmer only a few hours before. Thoma was a dedicated and serious soldier who intended to do his duty for the Fatherland. However, as the Germans prepared to open fire on the seventeen Americans crossing below their guns, suddenly American artillery crashed upon them. This was the belated artillery barrage that providentially arrived at the precise moment it was most needed. When the barrage ended, York and the other Americans safely made it behind German lines.

As the senior enlisted soldier, Early did a brilliant job leading the group behind the lines. They moved slowly and deliberately, endeavoring to not be observed. They meandered behind German lines for quite some time, and Early held several short discussions with the other squad leaders (York, Savage, and Cutting).[21] After more than an hour, the seventeen Americans happened upon a two-hundred-year-old trench in the forest that once marked the border between communal lands and royal lands (under French king Louis XIV). The group followed this trench down the hill to a German supply road. Near the supply road were two German soldiers carrying large tin cans. Leutnant Vollmer had ordered them just minutes before to retrieve water for wounded soldiers. Upon seeing the Americans, the two German soldiers dropped the tin containers and ran straight back to Vollmer's headquarters, yelling that the Americans were behind the lines.[22]

Just before this episode, advance elements of the Prussian 210th Reserve Regiment had arrived near Vollmer's headquarters. Vollmer was set up in a modest hunting hut that the Germans built earlier in the war. This part of the Argonne had been quiet over the previous

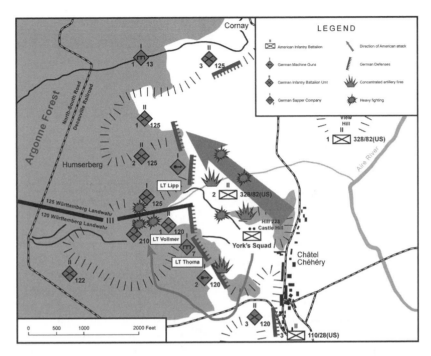

Map 13.2. York's Unit Attacks into the Argonne Forest, 8 October 1918. (Mastriano, *Alvin York*)

three years and offered those German soldiers not in the line a place to relax. In German fashion, cabins (huts) and other structures were built in the forest for shelter during hunting expeditions. It was at one of these huts in the meadow below the large German-occupied hill called "Humserberg" where Vollmer stationed his battalion headquarters. It was a challenging day for Vollmer, who received the brunt of the American attack. Despite the overwhelming nature of the enemy, the 82nd Division was inexperienced and effectively stopped in the valley. Vollmer, in the midst of battle, was preparing to lead the counterattack in his part of the valley to finish off the Americans. The key ingredient of this counterattack was the 210th Prussian Reserve Regiment.[23]

The 210th had marched through the night, and as soon as they arrived near Vollmer's headquarters they cast aside their equipment and began to eat breakfast. Their move across the Meuse Valley and into the Argonne was not an easy endeavor. The men were constantly forced off the road to make room for artillery and field ambulances. To make matters worse, French and American observers saw their movement and harassed them with artillery. The Prussians were physically exhausted. Once they stopped, the men passed out canned meat, bread, and marmalade and sat on the damp meadow ground to catch their breath. Vollmer arrived and rebuffed them for their sloppiness, but the leader of the group responded, "We hiked all night and first of all we need something to eat."[24] As Vollmer contemplated what to do next, suddenly from the south he heard the two medic soldiers yelling something about the Americans. Before he had a chance to do anything, the Prussians suddenly jumped to their feet with their hands in the air, yelling, "Kamerad! Kamerad!" Vollmer turned around and was captured by a "large and strong American man with a red-mustache, broad features and a freckle face." It was Corporal Alvin C. York.[25]

The seventeen Americans bagged about seventy Germans in the meadow through the shock of their sudden appearance. Bernard Early ordered the men to compress the large group of Germans into a manageable mass and then move them out to the American lines. However, some of the Germans deliberately dragged their feet in the hopes that the machine gun on the hill above would notice their plight. As the prisoners slowly moved, the Germans above noted the slackening of fire below. The German machine gun commander, Leutnant Paul Lipp, saw the dilemma. He ordered his machine gun repositioned, then motioned to the prisoners to fall to the ground, upon which Paul Vollmer yelled "get down" and the German prisoners fell to the ground, leaving the seventeen Americans exposed. Lipp's machine gun sprayed the area, killing six Americans and wounding three. The surviving eight Americans huddled on the ground with the German prisoners, trying not to get shot. There was a moment of chaos for the Americans, trying to figure out who was now in command. The soldiers yelled to each other, and it was discerned that York was the only noncommissioned officer not dead or seriously wounded. The conscientious objector York was the only leader left, and the burden of command fell to him.

York contemplated what to do. The main thing was Corporal Murray Savage, York's only real friend, who had been torn to pieces by the German machine gun.[26] Scanning the environment, there were nine dead or wounded Americans scattered across the meadow, with German prisoners huddled on the ground. In that instant, York had clarity of mind and knew exactly what to do. After ordering the

other seven soldiers to keep down, York charged up the hill, crossing the German supply road to occupy a spot lateral to the two lines
of German fighters. The lower old sunken road included the German machine gun, and above this a platoon of German riflemen
was shooting into the American throng below.[27] York yelled for the
enemy to surrender. York then fired forty-six rounds into the flanks
of the enemy, killing all nineteen of them.[28] Just before York charged
up the hill, the German commander, Leutnant Paul Lipp, ran up
the hill to bring another platoon of riflemen to support the attack.
York looked up and saw Lipp returning with about thirty German
reinforcements and decided that it would be better to return to the
prisoners and other seven Americans. However, as York ran down
the hill, he passed behind a trench containing Leutnant Fritz Endriss
and eleven soldiers. Endriss glanced back to ascertain why Lipp's
machine gun was no longer in action and saw York running behind
the line and down the hill.

Endriss ordered his men to fix bayonets and follow him. He
blew on his command whistle and led them toward Corporal York.
Of the dozen Germans, only Endriss saw York. The other men had
no idea why Endriss was leading them in a bayonet attack in the
wrong direction. As the Germans charged, York slid on his side,
dropped his rifle, and pulled out his M1911 Colt pistol and began
picking off the Germans from back to front. This was a skill he
had learned while hunting turkeys in Tennessee. If he shot the
lead bird, the flock scattered. He could bag more than one bird if
he shot the last birds first. Private Beardsley was adjacent to York
and attempted to fire his Chauchat light machine gun to stop the
bayonet attack, but it jammed. With that, Beardsley flung aside the
Chauchat, joining York in firing into the charging Germans with his
own sidearm. The last German to fall, just a few feet from Alvin,
was Leutnant Endriss. York shot him in the abdomen, throwing
Endriss back several feet.

Endriss was alive, crying out for help. Leutnant Paul Vollmer,
captured earlier in the action, was lying on the meadow floor with
the other prisoners. He desperately wanted to help Endriss. They
had been friends for more than a decade and had survived some of
the most horrific epochs of the First World War together. Vollmer
knew what to do. He stood up in the midst of the firefight (York
was exchanging shots with Paul Lipp and his reinforcements) and
walked over to York, saying, in perfect English:

Leutnant Fritz Endriss died leading the bayonet attack against Alvin York in an attempt to save the captured Paul Vollmer and the other seventy Germans. (Family photograph of Alexander and Friedrich Bruesch)

> Vollmer, "English?"
> York replied, "No, not English."
> Vollmer, "What?"
> York, "American."
> Vollmer, "Good Lord! If you won't shoot any more I will make them give up."[29]

York was astounded at the turn of events and told Vollmer to "Go ahead and do it," whereupon the German commander pulled out his field whistle and blew on it. Paul Lipp heard the whistled command to surrender and directed his men to lay down their weapons and move down the hill. York and the seven other Americans now had roughly one hundred German prisoners.

York used Vollmer as an interpreter and managed to push the mass of prisoners into a manageable group rather quickly. The wounded Americans and Germans (including Fritz Endriss) were moved into the formation, and the group began to move toward the American lines. They followed the road where the Americans had encountered the two German soldiers earlier. York placed Leutnants Lipp and Vollmer at the head of the formation, and he followed closely. The Americans still had to pass through the German line. Leutnant Max Thoma, the commander of the 7th Bavarian Company, saw the formation moving toward him and that the Germans were prisoners of the Americans. Thoma yelled to his men to fix bayonets and follow him. However, the Bavarians could not get a shot at the Americans. York had his pistol in the small of Vollmer's back and told him to order the Bavarians to capitulate. In the end, Vollmer ordered Thoma to surrender, giving York a total of 132 prisoners.

The capture of Leutnant Vollmer's battalion created a gap in the line, which Captain Danforth rushed his men into, and by early afternoon the 82nd All American Division severed the north-south road. This action had a devastating effect on the German grip over the Argonne. Although the Germans launched a lethal counterattack in the northern part of the valley, it was for naught. The 2nd Württemberg Division commander, General Anton Franke, received orders to withdraw from the Argonne. The news was heartbreaking for the Germans. "It was now that . . . the leader of 5th Army, gave the last word. We needed to occupy the secondary defensive positions further back. In the evening of 9/10 October, the regiment departed from the Argonne. The German soldiers gave so much after hard battles since 1914—more than 80,000 dead were left here. American artillery briefly hit the Humserberg line during the retreat and always there were the shrapnel. By Cheviers, the Regiment was in shelters. We were dead tired, too tired to contemplate, but able to hold onto hope."[30] The stalemate that Pershing faced was gradually being lifted, thanks to the men of the Lost Battalion and the heroism of a good-for-nothing drunk turned Christian from Tennessee.

The unsung heroes of the York saga are Major Buxton and Captain Danforth, who saw potential in this conscientious objector. They were willing to discuss his reservations about serving in the army and killing for his nation. More importantly, however, they

This photograph was taken as York marched his 132 captured Germans to a prisoner holding area. In the front of the formation are three of the four German officers that York captured. The German officer on the right front is Leutnant Paul Lipp, who commanded the German machine gun and supporting infantry that killed many Americans in the attack. In the center is Leutnant Max Thoma, the commander of the 7th Bavarian Mineur Company. To the left is Leutnant Paul Vollmer. Behind Vollmer is Alvin York. (U.S. Army Heritage and Education Center, Carlisle, Pennsylvania)

were willing to openly discuss his and their Christian beliefs. This boldness was the prime driver for York's staying in the army despite his moral dilemma. Thanks to their leadership, he was in the line on 8 October 1918.

Alvin York charged into the Argonne a conscientious objector and walked out a hero. He remains the model of an ideal soldier to this day for the U.S. Army and is featured in its leadership manuals. York personifies the "warrior ethos" and how one soldier can hold the key to victory, or defeat. But there is more to his life than this. The most important aspect is that of his moral character. York did not suddenly become a hero, but over the course of three years he established a pattern of choosing the right thing in the small decisions in life. In doing this, he developed his "character muscle." What happened on that one day in October was merely an outward manifestation of the man he had become in his heart and soul. When all hope was lost and while facing overwhelming odds, he knew exactly what to do, and it changed history.

14

Cracking the Siegfried Line

Give me Chatillon, or a list of five thousand casualties.
—General Charles Pelot Summerall's orders
to Brigadier General Douglas MacArthur

With the Argonne liberated, the French and American soldiers still had the heavy task of breaking the German grip in the Meuse Valley. The Imperial German Army had one last prepared line in the sector as part of the Western Front's Siegfried Line. The Siegfried Line was dubbed locally the Kriemhilde Stellung. This defensive network used the hilly terrain to channelize the Americans into kill zones. Although the Kriemhilde was not a continuous line of wire and trenches, it was formidable and backed by bunkers, prepared fighting positions, machine gun emplacements, and plenty of artillery. The Germans began work on a fourth line, called the Freya, in 1918, but it was far from complete. Once the Kriemhilde Stellung was broken, the Franco-American attack in the Meuse Valley could finally begin a swift advance.

Breaking the Kriemhilde Stellung would not be easy, as German reserve divisions continued to arrive to blunt an American breakthrough. Additionally, the German command of the high ground on the eastern side of the Meuse River proved devastating to the Franco-American advance. From here, the German Army directed deadly artillery fires into the ranks of the advancing soldiers. Despite this, the situation was improving, as there were no longer flanking fires from the Argonne along the western portion of the line. The combined actions of the Lost Battalion and Corporal Alvin York had forced the German defenders of the Argonne Forest to withdraw on 9 October.

Gallwitz was troubled by the progress of the Americans and French in his sector. Although his soldiers were performing superbly, the supply of men to fill the ranks of his army was drying up. More concerning for him and the German High Command was the progress of the Allied armies farther north. A force of British, French, and American troops attacked near Cambrai and crossed the embattled Canal du Nord on 27 September and then shattered the Siegfried Line on 29 September after crossing the St. Quentin Canal. The combined Allied force was making steady gains in the north. For the Germans, there simply were not enough forces to contend with every crisis on the Western Front. Therefore Hindenburg and Ludendorff took risks in the north and continued the flow of reserves to the Meuse-Argonne region, where a breakthrough would threaten a third of the German forces with encirclement.[1]

The stubborn German defense of the Meuse-Argonne region threw Pershing's plans into disarray. Pershing entered the campaign with ideas of an unstoppable Franco-American advance and instead found his army slowed to a crawl, slugging it out with the Germans in a brutal fight for every ridge, valley, and village. Instead of adapting his leadership style and doctrinal approach to war, Pershing had a low tolerance for mistakes (aside from his own) and resorted to sacking generals for the slightest errors. The saving grace for the Americans was the thousands of French military advisors (liaison officers) scattered throughout the AEF. These experienced military professionals helped the Americans adapt and innovate in the face of stubborn German defenses. In addition to this, the individual initiative of junior officers and soldiers often snatched victory from the jaws of defeat. Such was the case with the Lost Battalion, Alvin York, and Lieutenant Sam Woodfill.

General Pershing ordered an army-wide attack for 15 October. He envisioned that this attack would break the German Kriemhilde Line and finally lead to open warfare. The plan was classically Pershing: overly ambitious and detached from reality, envisioning an advance across the front that had not been the norm since 26 September. To compound the troubles, the AEF did not confer or coordinate its attack with the French Fourth Army to the west. When coordination was belatedly made, the French insisted that the attack occur on 14 October, to which Pershing's staff hurriedly adjusted, depriving the subordinate French and American divisions assigned to the AEF sufficient time to make their plans.[2]

The French Fourth Army made some gains in its advance west of the Argonne Forest. The western half of Pershing's front, composed of the American I Corps (77th and 82nd Divisions), endeavored to

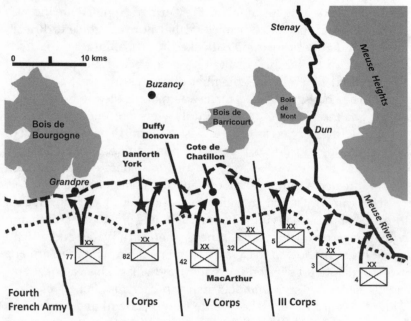

Map 14.1. Meuse Front, 14–20 October 1918. (Josiah Mastriano)

advance into the Kriemhilde north and northeast of the Argonne. But after a series of German counterattacks drove them back, these forces only achieved minor gains and failed to break the enemy's main defensive line. The two divisions would spend the next two weeks slugging it out with the Prussian and Bavarian divisions holding tenaciously to the Kriemhilde.[3]

In the center of the American line, the V Corps' 42nd and 32nd Divisions achieved considerable success. Although falling far from the ambitious objectives of Pershing, these two divisions were among the first to crack the Kriemhilde. The 32nd launched a well-coordinated and deliberately executed attack that enabled the division to advance north several kilometers, resulting in the liberation of the village of Romagne and the securing of a foothold beyond the Kriemhilde Line. The conduct of the 32nd in this attack showed all of the signs of a division that had learned considerably from its experiences and was able to plan and fight a modern battle on the Western Front. Using well-planned and coordinated artillery fires and innovative ground maneuver, the 32nd drove the Germans from La Cote Dame Marie and Hill 287, vital high ground fortified as part of the Kriemhilde Line. The 32nd fought off a series of German coun-terattacks and continued an impressive advance that secured the high ground around Romagne.[4] This was the same ground that Per-shing believed the AEF would seize on 26 September, the first day of the Meuse-Argonne Offensive. Although more than two weeks later than planned, Pershing wrote, "The main objective of our ini-tial attack of September 26th had now been reached.[5] . . . Failing to capture it on our first attempt, the army had deliberately, systemi-cally and doggedly stuck to the task in the face of many difficulties and discouragements."[6]

To the left of the 32nd, the 42nd Division also performed well. Although the 42nd's gains pale in comparison to those of the 32nd, it too punched a hole in the Kriemhilde Line and drove the Germans off a vital hill necessary to control the Meuse Valley. The 42nd Divi-sion was formed near Garden City, New York, in 1917 and was one of the first American divisions to arrive in France. The commander of the 42nd Division was Major General William A. Mann, and its chief of staff was Brigadier General Douglas MacArthur.[7]

The 42nd Division was composed of men from twenty-six states and the District of Columbia. Encompassing Americans from across the nation, it was called the "Rainbow Division." Of this, MacAr-thur wrote, "The outfit soon took a color, a dash, a unique flavor that is the essence of that elusive and deathless thing called soldiering. It has always held a special place in my affection and to this day I feel a thrill whenever I see a Rainbow's colorful patch."[8]

The MacArthur family was a household name even before American entry into the Great War. His father, Arthur MacArthur, was awarded the Medal of Honor for his leadership in capturing Missionary Ridge, Tennessee, in 1863 during the American Civil War. He went on to serve on the frontier and in the Philippines, where he would serve as the military governor and ultimately rise to the rank of lieutenant general.[9] Although it would seem impos-sible for a son to surpass the reputation of such a father, Douglas MacArthur would do so after two world wars and the Korean War. In World War One, MacArthur would be one of the most highly decorated soldiers in the AEF, receiving two Distinguished Service Crosses and six Silver Stars.[10] He would be awarded the Medal of Honor during World War Two, making him and his father one of only two instances of a father and son receiving America's highest award.[11]

MacArthur was renowned for leading from the front, an attribute that Pershing required of his leaders at all levels of command. This was precisely the sort of leader that the new commander of the V Corps wanted. Major General Charles Pelot Summerall had been appointed commander of the V Corps on 11 October. Summerall had an exemplary record thus far in France and was particularly noted for his leadership of the 1st Division, which he commanded until being appointed to corps command. He had only three days to plan and coordinate the V Corps' 14 October attack.[12]

Summerall surveyed the terrain that the 42nd fronted and quickly realized that the key terrain was the German-controlled Cote de Chatillon. This hill was on the right half of the 42nd Division's front, and the burden of taking it fell to the 84th Brigade, commanded by Douglas MacArthur. Knowing this, Summerall said to MacArthur, "Give me Chatillon, or a list of five thousand casualties." Douglas MacArthur recorded his reply to the corps commander, "we'll take it or my name will head the list."[13] However, taking the hill would require more than bravado.

MacArthur's brigade included two regiments, the 167th (composed of men from Alabama) and the 168th (from Iowa). The commander of the 167th, Lieutenant Colonel Walter E. Bare, wrote, "Cote de Chatillon was key to the situation and was very strongly fortified with concrete machine gun emplacements."[14] Despite this, MacArthur planned on a frontal attack to seize the hill on 14 October. As the attack kicked off, the men of the Rainbow Division were faced with bands of barbed wire, fortified German fighting positions, and deadly artillery fires. Because of this, the 42nd Division did not achieve appreciable gains anywhere on its front. MacArthur's 84th Brigade did make some progress, mostly up the adjacent Hill 288. The 83rd Brigade, to the left, failed to make any headway. The inability of the 42nd Division's 83rd Brigade to make any progress threatened the right flank of the 82nd Division to its west, where recently promoted Sergeant Alvin York and the survivors of his fight in the Argonne faced German counterattacks from two fronts. Summerall was appalled by the failure of the 83rd Brigade and quickly fired its commander, Brigadier General Michael Lenihan. MacArthur faced a similar fate if he did not produce results quickly.[15]

MacArthur ordered his two regiments to launch a night attack during the early morning hours of 15 October to seize Cote de

Chatillon. The plan was to unload the rifles and have the men assault Cote de Chatillon by using only bayonets. Although priding himself on understanding the situation the men faced at the front, MacArthur was increasingly becoming detached from reality. The thick bands of barbed wire, each thirty to forty feet wide, made such a desperate measure impossible to accomplish. Additionally, the darkness would not last long. The Germans would fire illumination rounds at the first sign of trouble and lay waste to the Americans with machine guns and artillery fires. Lieutenant Colonel Walter E. Bare contacted MacArthur to explain the foolishness of such an order and managed to convince him to rescind it. MacArthur consented but demanded that the hill be taken that day.[16]

The attacks on 15 October fared no better than those of the previous day. Although MacArthur's brigade made minor gains, the hill, with its reinforced bunkers, was still in German hands and threatened to repulse the success of the 32nd U.S. Division east of the Rainbow Division. Summerall demanded results. If the hill was not taken soon, MacArthur would be fired just as Brigadier General Lenihan had been the day before. Lieutenant Colonel Bare told his regiment to prepare for another frontal attack. Although MacArthur would receive the credit for seizing the hill, Captain Ravee Norris, the commander of Bare's combined 1st and 3rd Battalions, was responsible for the coming victory.

Norris bristled at the folly of MacArthur's idea of the night bayonet attack and was now confronted with another failed concept: the third frontal assault of Cote de Chatillon. Norris wrote:

Quite elaborate plans had been made for the capture of the hill. They included a frontal attack. After listening for some time to all the details without being asked my advice I finally became impatient and said, "I have been up there forty-eight hours! I am to make the attack. Am I to have nothing to say about it?"

"Well, what have you got to say about it?" replied Bare

"We will never take that hill by just attacking it from the front," I said. I then went on to explain that while the overhead machine gun and artillery concentration were keeping the Germans down I would send about 100 men whom I had in support to infiltrate along the hedge which ran from the edge of my wood up to the gap in the wire.[17]

Late on 15 October, MacArthur summoned the unit's commanders to his headquarters. Lieutenant Colonel Bare (167th Regiment) was joined by the 168th Regiment's commander (Colonel Matthew A. Tinley) and the 151st Machine Gun Battalion's commander (Major Cooper D. Winn). MacArthur discussed the importance of seizing the hill and highlighted that it had to be captured the next day, and if not, all of the men, including him, must fall on the battlefield as casualties trying to take it.[18]

The men discussed how to take the hill, and the result entailed a third frontal assault. Bare suggested that they try Norris's plan. To do this, Bare would need the support and permission of Tinley's 168th Regiment for Norris to cross into their sector. Although Tinley outranked Bare, he said, "I will be delighted to not only cooperate in every way I can but will take orders if necessary from Col. Bare."[19] MacArthur agreed to Norris's plan to suppress the German defenders frontally and then to infiltrate one hundred soldiers through the gap on the flank.

Norris assigned one of his company commanders, Captain Tom Fallow, to lead the one-hundred-man infiltration detachment and decided that he, too, would be present to lead it since success or failure hinged on this one action. As planned, the American preparatory barrage went in around 10:00 A.M. Using the cover of the barrage, Norris, Fallow, and the rest of the detachment successfully infiltrated the wire. When the barrage lifted, Fallow blew three blasts on his whistle, which was the signal for the men to charge up the hill. Just then a German machine gun opened fire, with a bullet hitting Norris in the heel, throwing him to the ground. Fallow led the men up the hill, where they drove the Germans from this vital high ground.

As the 167th's Alabamans swept Cote de Chatillon of Germans, Colonel Tinley ordered his 168th Regiment of Iowans to advance, and they secured the high ground to his front. The strongest point of the Kriemhilde position was taken and the German Siegfried Line was cracked open. Although the Germans launched several counterattacks to dislodge the Americans, their attacks failed in large part due to the heroism of the soldiers on the hill and also, in great measure, thanks to the advance of the American 32nd Division just east of this action. However, the Germans were far from quitting. Nearly a month of bloody fighting remained, and although the Kriemhilde was fractured in the Cote de Chatillon and Romagne

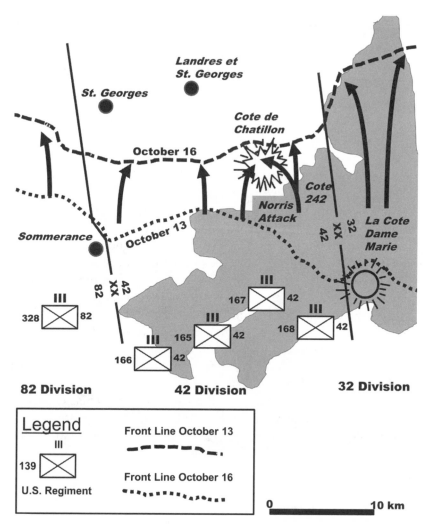

Map 14.2. MacArthur and the Battle of Cote de Chatillon, 13–16 October 1918. (Josiah Mastriano)

region, thousands of Americans would fall endeavoring to dislodge the Germans from the remainder of the line.

During the initial assault, Captain Ravee Norris lay where he was shot, anxious for some news on the outcome of the attack. "Finally a sergeant . . . came back to me and said or rather yelled. 'Captain, we've got the hill and a lot of these . . . Heines as well.' I laughed with relief and also had tears in my eyes."[20]

In one of those rare moments, history hung in the balance at Cote de Chatillon. Had MacArthur launched a third unsuccessful frontal attack, chances are that he would have been sacked and his future in the U.S. Army would have been all but over. The history of the Second World War from the fall of the Philippines to the surrender of Japan would have had a different name associated to it and perhaps even a different outcome. Additionally, the famed Inchon Landings during the Korean War likewise would not have occurred. The alternate futures where Brigadier General Douglas MacArthur's career ended at Cote de Chatillon are seemingly endless. But the hill was captured, and MacArthur's future in American history was secured. Yet, it was not his brilliance that saved the day, but rather the idea of a junior officer. An attribute of a good leader is not thinking that one has a monopoly on ideas. MacArthur knew a good plan when he saw one and was willing to try it even in his hour of greatest need.

Ravee Norris perhaps deserves one more comment. He displayed significant moral courage in pushing back against the foolhardy plan to conduct a night bayonet attack. In fact, he was sure that he would be removed from command for expressing his disapproval. Norris risked his position to save his men from a flawed plan. When faced with the concept for a third frontal attack against the hill, he displayed moral courage by offering a better approach to the problem, one that he would personally lead. This is the type of leader that people are willing to follow. For the capture of Cote de Chatillon, Ravee Norris was promoted to major and awarded the Distinguished Service Cross.

15

The Battle for the
Siegfried Line Continues

In honor of our dead heroes let us maintain the pledge and
vow to ensure that the reason why they died, for "a better
more beautiful fatherland" will remain our truth after the war.
—Major Friedrich von Pirscher, commander of
459th German Infantry Regiment,
defending the Kriemhilde Line
between Romagne and Cunel

The saga of Lieutenant Samuel Woodfill occurred in the center of
the Meuse Valley on 12 October, two days before the army-wide
attack. The 5th Division began arriving among the U.S. 4th Division's forward positions late on 11 October and early 12 October.
Elements of the 60th Infantry Regiment advanced toward Cunel at
6:00 A.M. to conduct a reconnaissance in force. This included the
60th Regiment's 3rd Battalion and a machine gun company. Leading this attack was Company M, under the command of Lieutenant
Woodfill.

Sam Woodfill was one of the rare Regular Army soldiers in the
ranks of the AEF. He grew up on a farm near Belleview in southern
Indiana. His father, John Woodfill, was a veteran of both the Mexican War and the American Civil War and was a crack shot. John
taught his son how to shoot, stalk game, and hunt in the forest near
their home. Inspired by the experiences that his father had in the
military, Woodfill joined the U.S. Army in 1901 and before long was
in the Philippines fighting a counterinsurgency. Woodfill found it
difficult to adjust to life in the army, and he admitted to making
every "rookie" mistake in the book when it came to marching. But
he had two traits that made him stand out.[1]

The first thing about Woodfill was his moral character. His

parents were both devout Christians and lived their lives honorably before him. Throughout his life, Sam Woodfill endeavored to do the right thing, even if it was unpopular or made him a loner. Thus, in the army a century ago, when most soldiers spent any free time "drinking, gambling and womanizing," Woodfill endeavored to follow the Christian example of his parents. He did not mind being alone or castigated for not following the crowd to get into trouble on the weekends. Much like with York and other heroes described in this book, these everyday choices built Woodfill's character muscle that made him the courageous and brave soldier that would rise to the occasion outside of the quaint French village of Cunel one day in October 1918.[2]

Woodfill's second attribute was his rare ability to hit targets with his rifle at long ranges. In a military organization fixated on developing adept shooting skills, Woodfill found a place where he could excel. After his tour ended in the Philippines, he was assigned to Alaska for several years at Fort Egbert, near the Alaska-Canada border. A few years after his Alaskan tour of duty, he served on the Mexican border during the troubles with Pancho Villa. When the United States entered World War One he was promoted to lieutenant and assigned to the 60th Infantry Regiment in the 5th "Red Diamond" Division.[3]

As Woodfill's men moved up the Meuse Valley to assume their lead position in the line, he ended up being pinned down in a shallow fighting position by a German machine gun. He was certain that this would be his last day alive. As the bullets tore into his pack, Woodfill pulled out the photo of his wife that he carried with him and wrote on the back:

> In case of accident or death, it is my last and fondest desire that the finder of my remains shall please do me a last and everlasting favor to please forward this picture to my Darling Wife. And tell her that I have fallon on the field of honor and departed to a better land which knows no sorrow and feels no pain. I will prepair a place and be waiting at the Golden Gait of Heaven for the arrival.[4]

The plan for Woodfill's men was to begin their advance at 6:00 A.M. One of his favorite men was a young Italian immigrant named Private Gianni "Johnny" Pulcino. Pulcino had recently immigrated

Lieutenant Sam Woodfill was awarded the Medal for Honor for heroic actions in and around the village of Cunel on 12 October 1918. (U.S. Army Heritage and Education Center, Carlisle, Pennsylvania)

to the United States and was a terrible shot. Woodfill took Pulcino under his wing and tried to help him shoot better, to no avail. Just before the unit began its advance, Pulcino said, "We have da beega fight." Woodfill replied, "Looks like it. Lots of shooting in this fight, maybe Pulcino." Pulcino answered, "I no care Tenente [Lieutenant]. I go weeth you."[5]

The men moved at 6:00 A.M., in skirmish lines with bayonets fixed. The advance took them over a ridge and then down a gentle slope that leveled off at the small village of Cunel. The terrain rose sharply behind Cunel, with the high ground covered with forests called Bois de Pultiere and Bois de Rappes. The morning fog masked the area in front of the Americans, enabling them to advance partially obscured from observation. Just south of Cunel a spattering of German machine gun fire slammed into the line, followed quickly by artillery exploding among them, throwing two men into

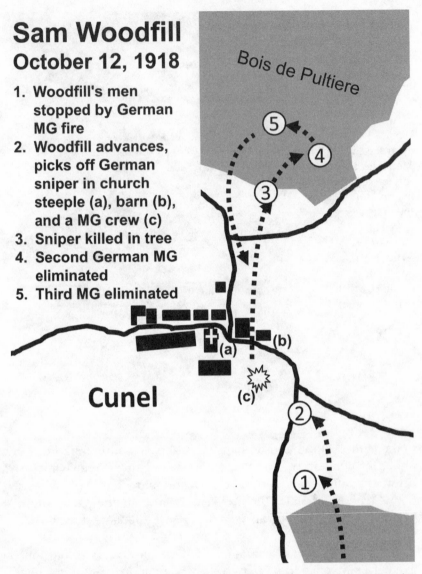

Sam Woodfill
October 12, 1918

1. Woodfill's men stopped by German MG fire
2. Woodfill advances, picks off German sniper in church steeple (a), barn (b), and a MG crew (c)
3. Sniper killed in tree
4. Second German MG eliminated
5. Third MG eliminated

Bois de Pultiere

Cunel

Map 15.1. Sam Woodfill's Actions on 12 October 1918. (Josiah Mastriano)

the air. Woodfill ran to render aid, but before he arrived they were on their feet, fumbling to pick up their weapons and equipment. Woodfill wrote, "the machine guns were spittin' a swath of fire that was cuttin' the men down like a mowin' machine'; the shelling was growing worse."[6] The advance stalled in the face of overwhelming machine gun fire, with Woodfill's men seeking cover in shell holes or the woods south of Cunel. Woodfill said, "The only thing to do was to find out where that first machine gun was and get it."

Woodfill ordered the men to stay under cover as he tried to find the German machine guns. After dropping his pack, he dashed across the field and jumped into a shell hole. German machine gun bullets rained around his position, "So close I could feel the heat of them on my face." After the German fire lifted, he surveyed the ground and identified three German positions to his north. Working from left to right, the first was a sniper in the destroyed steeple of the village church about 250 yards to the northwest. A German machine gun was in the low ground in front of him along a road, and a rifleman was in a barn to his front right.[7]

Woodfill decided to engage the sniper in the church tower first. Although he could not see the German rifleman in the church, he noticed a little window and fired five rounds into it at 250 yards. There was no more firing from the church. Woodfill next decided to engage the firing coming from the barn to his front right. He noticed that a board was missing from the gable end of the building and fired a clip of bullets into it, silencing that German rifleman.[8]

Woodfill strained to locate the German machine gun to his front, but the low terrain prevented him from seeing it. With no other option, he charged forward, diving into shell holes as machine gun fire sputtered into the ground around his feet. The third shell hole that he jumped into was filled with mustard gas, burning his eyes, nose, and throat. Knowing that the gas mask would inhibit his shooting, Woodfill simply leapt out of the shell hole and across a field, where the only refuge was a thicket of thistle. From there Woodfill crawled into a ditch and caught sight of the German machine gunner and fired a shot, instantly killing him. Three more Germans attempted to operate the machine gun, but Woodfill picked them all off. The fifth man in this position tried to flee but was also shot by Woodfill.[9]

The lieutenant waited a moment and then dashed into the German position and saw the five dead Germans and the machine gun. He darted around what he presumed to be another dead German, but then the man jumped up, yanked Woodfill's rifle out of his hand, and reached for his Luger to finish the American off. Woodfill was quicker on the draw and pulled his Colt .45 from his belt and fired. The German fell to the ground with a grunt. The dead German was an Oberleutnant (first lieutenant), the same rank as Woodfill. He took the Luger and the rank from the dead officer's shoulder and waved to the men to follow him through Cunel and up the hill to Bois de Pultiere.[10]

Woodfill was the first American in Cunel, and with a handful of his men following he continued beyond the town and into the fortified Bois de Pultiere. As Woodfill dashed into the woods, a sniper hidden in a tree opened fire on him. The lieutenant found cover but was unable to locate the sniper. One of Woodfill's runners had followed him up the hill. When the sniper began firing, the runner sought refuge beneath the tree that the sniper was using. The sniper fired at the runner, with the bullet passing close to his nose and between his feet. Before the sniper could fire a second shot, the runner opened fire, killing him. Seeing this, Woodfill continued his frenzied assault into the German line.[11]

The lieutenant's next target was a series of German machine guns manning the Kriemhilde. The machine guns were on a zig-zag line in the woods and had a commanding view of Cunel and the countryside around it. Woodfill quickly outflanked one of the machine guns and killed all five of its crew. After this, he ran into three German soldiers carrying ammunition. The three yelled, "Kamerad, Kamerad," and surrendered. Woodfill said, "Their fright was almost comical. They were nothin' but boys and they were surrendering in dead earnest. I made sure they were disarmed." He directed them down the hill to his soldiers below and continued his one-man assault of the Kriemhilde.[12]

As the prisoners trotted off to the American lines, another machine gun to his immediate left (west) opened fire on his men advancing through Cunel. The vegetation in this part of the forest was thick, forcing Woodfill to crawl all the way over to this third German machine gun. When the head of the gunner was exposed, Woodfill fired, instantly killing him. Just as at the first machine gun, the entire five-man crew fell to Woodfill's well-aimed rifle while trying to keep their weapon in action. As he made his way to the now defunct German machine gun position, German fire tore up the ground around him, whereupon he leapt into the trench, nearly on top of a German soldier. Both Woodfill and the German attempted to fire their pistols against their adversary. Woodfill won the draw and fired into the enemy's abdomen. As the soldier fell to the ground, another charged with a rifle from around a corner in the trench. Woodfill pulled the trigger of his pistol, but it jammed. As the German charged, Woodfill grabbed a nearby pick mattock that was stuck into the side of the trench and hit the enemy soldier in the head with the pointy end. As that German fell, the soldier with the abdominal wound pulled out his Luger and narrowly missed Woodfill. The American wheeled around and finished the first German off with the pick.[13]

As the German line fell into confusion, Private Blackmore caught up to Woodfill and reported that they were surrounded. Soon, other men arrived, including Corporal Sullivan, and Woodfill had his men dig in. Meanwhile, he sent runners to his battalion commander requesting support. After an hour, his commander, Major Davis, directed that Woodfill and his men fall back through Cunel as there was no support available to hold the breakthrough. As the men slowly fell back, German airplanes crisscrossed above, strafing nearby American positions. Woodfill tried his skill in shooting one down, but failed. The German aviators attacked several of the American positions and then directed their artillery onto the horses, mules, and men of the machine gun company, killing six men and all of the animals. Word of Woodfill's feat circulated throughout the regiment, and he would be awarded the Medal of Honor for it. As the entire American First Army prepared for a big push scheduled for 14 October, one in which his unit would play a central role, Woodfill was medically evacuated. Exposure to the mustard gas, combined with the flu, ended his time in the division. He spent two months in the hospital recovering.[14]

Woodfill's attack on 12 October occurred as the German 236th Division was being replaced in the line by the 123rd Saxons and 3rd Guards. There was considerable confusion among the Germans when Woodfill and his men assaulted the Kriemhilde. The Americans had that one opportunity to crack the line at a lower cost in lives on that day. The next time would not be so easy. The last German defensive belt in the region, the Kriemhilde Line was holding back the Franco-American onslaught. Along the western half of the AEF front, the U.S. 77th and 82nd Divisions could not penetrate it. Both of these divisions launched a series of attacks from 14 October to 31 October and failed to achieve a sustainable breakthrough. Even Pershing's beloved 1st Infantry Division could not breach the Kriemhilde. In the center and eastern part of the Meuse Valley, the

32nd, 80th, and 4th Divisions were making slow but steady progress against the line despite suffering from flanking fires. To maintain the momentum, the 42nd "Rainbow" Division moved forward to replace the 1st Division, while the 5th Division advanced to assume 3rd Division's sector.[15] As Brigadier General Douglas MacArthur fought to secure Cote de Chatillon and Hill 288, the 5th Division (as part of the U.S. III Corps) to the east also planned to crack the Kriemhilde Line.

The orders for the attack were issued to 5th Division on 13 October. The plan was for most of the III Corps to attack along the eastern portion of the Meuse Valley in conjunction with the V Corps' attack in the center. General Pershing's concept of this operation encompassed the following considerations:

(a) The French XVII Corps, under our army, was to continue its offensive east of the Meuse River.

(b) The III and V Corps, with fresh divisions (the 5th and 42d), were to drive salients through the hostile positions on both flanks of the Bois de Romagne and of the Bois de Bantheville.

(c) The I Corps was to hold the enemy on its left flank while advancing its right in conjunction with the left of the V Corps.

(d) The French Fourth Army, which had now come up on our left and held the south bank of the Aire and the west bank of the Aisne as far as Vouziers, was ordered by General Pétain to attack on the same day, so as to outflank the enemy opposing our left.[16]

The situation for the III Corps appeared particularly daunting. After an initial brilliant advance early in the offensive, the attack slowed to a crawl as German reinforcements poured into the line. Compounding matters was the German occupation of the high ground on the opposite bank of the Meuse River. The high ground provided the Germans with excellent observation to direct artillery fires into the flank of the advancing Americans, particularly in the III Corps. This placed pressure on the ability of the Americans not only to advance, but to receive supplies and support. The friction that the German command of the Meuse Heights posed was significant and delayed the movement of forces, and logistics, often forcing the Americans to wait to conduct large movements in hours of

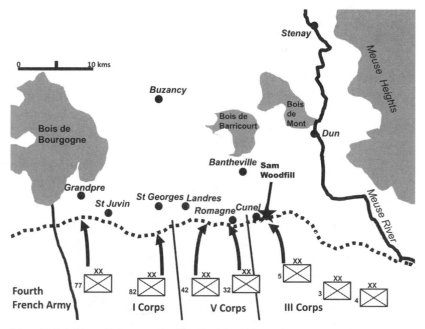

Map 15.2. Meuse Front, 12–14 October 1918. (Josiah Mastriano)

darkness, which was not an easy endeavor. Night movement was not free of German harassing fires, as the artillery frequently fired illumination rounds to identify targets along the roads.

Ironically, only two years before, the Germans faced the same difficulty. When the Germans commenced their Verdun campaign in February 1916, the German commander, Falkenhayn, focused his initial attack on the high ground on the eastern side of the Meuse River. As the German Army fought its way toward Verdun, the French Army, in control of the high ground on the western side, fired devastating artillery fires into the flanks of the German Army. This compelled Falkenhayn to launch an attack against the French-occupied high ground west of the Meuse. Now, two years later, the American army found itself in a similar situation and would soon also be compelled to drive the Germans from the high ground on their flank. Until the enemy was cleared from those positions, the American III Corps would suffer mounting casualties, and its advance would be slowed by the rain of steel pouring from east of the Meuse. Not even the experienced American 3rd and 4th Divisions could overcome this challenge.

In this environment, the U.S. 5th Division was given the task with the rest of the III Corps to attack on 14 October in an endeavor to break the Kriemhilde Line just a few kilometers to the north. The planning conducted by the leadership of the 5th Division for this attack was yet another sign that the AEF was learning and rapidly coming of age in this clash of armies. The leaders and staff of the 5th conducted continuous coordination and liaison with both the U.S. 32nd Division to its left and the 42nd Rainbow Division farther west. This was necessary as German control of Cote de Chatillon could decimate the advance of the 5th. Additionally, the division commander (Major General John McMahon) and the two brigade commanders (Brigadier General Joseph Castner and Brigadier General Paul Malone) established their headquarters where the three could rapidly communicate for mutual support during the attack. Although such measures are common to a professional and trained army, such was not the case for the AEF. The planning and coordination implemented by the 5th Division for the 14 October attack demonstrated that this was not the same army that kicked off the attack in September. It was adapting to the realities of modern war. These changes were not directed from Pershing or his staff, but rather from the tactical levels of command, where life or death hung in the balance.

The American plan was to commence a two-hour artillery barrage against the Germans at 6:30 A.M. The American infantry attack would begin at 8:30, with the artillery barrage slowly walking back into the German lines. The main attack was on the division's left and included two regiments under the command of the 10th Brigade (6th and 11th). Advancing to the right was the 60th Infantry Regiment (of the 9th Brigade). These lead units would attack in a northerly direction to dislodge the Germans from the high ground north of Cunel, which was part of the Kriemhilde defensive line. Following in support of the attack were the 61st Infantry Regiment and the 58th Infantry Regiment of the 4th Division. The problem was that the sector assigned to the 5th Division was too narrow for the four regiments to operate.

With a zone barely a kilometer in width, maneuver and flanking movements against German positions would be difficult if not impossible to execute for the 5th Division. Despite the improvements adopted at the division, brigade, and regiment levels, the corps and army command and staff still had much to learn before they would be considered ready for basic military operations against a trained and agile adversary. Such an approach to war may have worked before machine guns and massed artillery fires, but not on a 1918 battlefield.[17]

Then there were the Germans. In battle, the fog and friction of war exists and even the best-laid plans can be overthrown. As the nineteenth-century Prussian chief of the General Staff Field Marshal Helmuth von Moltke exclaimed, "no plan of operations extends with any certainty beyond the first contact with the main hostile force." The Germans had a say in the matter, and events were conspiring to unhinge the well-thought-out plans of the American 5th Division. The night before the attack, an American soldier was captured, and he provided the Germans with details of what his comrades were planning. The German 236th Division, which defended the area around the village of Cunel, requested additional artillery support to disrupt the American attack.[18] The Germans reinforced their forward positions and ensured that ammunition and supplies were distributed.[19]

The German 236th Infantry Division had arrived in the area around Cunel in late September. It had been in continuous combat against the Americans since 29 September and would remain in the line there until 17 October. The unit had been formed in 1917 and encompassed men from North-Rhine Westphalia as well as from German-occupied Lorraine. About half of the soldiers in the division were experienced men who had recovered from injuries incurred earlier in the war, and the remaining were young men from the "Class of 1918." The 236th served across the Western Front, in Flanders, Cambrai, Ypres, and Artois, and had an excellent reputation as a fighting force, especially during the 1918 Spring Offensives. Its performance against the Americans in the Meuse Valley thus far had been exemplary, inflicting heavy casualties and stubbornly holding on to the terrain assigned to it. The 236th suffered more than three thousand casualties during the eighteen days it fought the Americans, losing only 413 men as prisoners.[20]

The 236th Division had three regiments, the 457th, 458th, and the 459th. All three of these fought against the American push into the region during the first half of October. The commander of the 459th was Major Friedrich von Pirscher. Pirscher was a well-respected officer with a tendency to go forward with his men and share their experiences, risks, and dangers. He distinguished himself during the German Spring Offensives earlier in 1918 and for his fearless leadership was awarded the Pour le Mérite.[21]

The 236th Division was ordered to begin transitioning with the German 123rd Saxon Division around Cunel and with the 3rd Guards Division around Romagne on 12 October. It was to serve as the army's counterattack division, deployed sixteen kilometers to the north, near the small French village of Nouart. The lead elements of the 123rd Saxon, reinforced by the celebrated 3rd Guards Regiment of Fusiliers, relieved Major Friedrich von Pirscher's 459th Regiment late on 12 October in their positions near Cunel. The 459th had only just arrived near Nouart when intelligence reported plans of the large American attack. The 459th was halted near the Kriemhilde Line to help fight off the American attack. The 236th's two other regiments (the 457th and 458th) were already farther back, but were told to be ready to move at a moment's notice. The exhausted men of the 236th had been in near continuous combat for two weeks and were looking forward to a few days of much needed rest. Instead of rest, "the tired and foot-sore" men of the division prepared to head back toward Romagne and Cunel to once again fight the Americans.[22]

The day promised to be clear and sunny, a rare occasion for the Meuse-Argonne region in October 1918. It had either rained or been cloudy for most of the past two weeks. Most mornings the soldiers faced a thick, wet fog. As the sky transitioned from darkness to a deep blue, the Americans could see that large, sausage-shaped German observation balloons flew to the north and east. This was an ill omen for them, in that the Germans used these to guide and direct artillery fire where it could do the most harm. Thanks in large part to the advance warning that the Germans received about the attack, additional observation balloons were ordered up this morning to ensure that the planned German preemptive artillery barrage was lethal.[23]

At 6:00 A.M., German artillery pounded the Americans. A member of the U.S. 5th Division wrote of this experience: "The Boche put down the strongest counterfire our men had ever seen. For two hours the positions of the assault battalions were raked with high explosive. Losses were severe and some confusion was felt before the attack was started."[24] American artillery began firing at 6:30. The 5th Division had nearly three times the regular artillery support peppering the German lines, as additional artillery units had been brought forward to help the Doughboys break the Kriemhilde Line. Both sides of the lines were on fire with the explosions and bursting of thick waves of artillery.

Despite the fierce German barrage, the American infantry attack began promptly at 8:30 A.M. The Germans shifted their artillery to focus on the large masses of Americans emerging from the woods. Massive gaps were torn into the advancing Americans as the German artillery laid waste upon their line. One of the U.S. 5th Division's officers, Major John Muncaster, called the barrage "a band of steel across our front." For the survivors advancing through this, they were greeted on the other side with a hail of fire from the high ground to the north, northeast, and northwest that was "thickly populated with German machine gun nests."[25] The Germans had created a kill zone below the village of Cunel designed to decimate and defeat the American attack.

Despite the wall of fires, the Americans made some headway against the Germans with maneuver and flanking movements. The division's officers were leading from the front and adapted quickly. Fire was focused on German strong points as battalion and company commanders skillfully moved their men into positions to eliminate German opposition. Progress by the 5th Division's 10th Brigade was disrupted west of Cunel by a small counterattack by elements of the German 28th Division. The 28th was considered a first-class division and was given the name "Flying Shock Division" for its ability to rapidly appear on the battlefield. The 28th was fondly called by the Germans the "Kaiser's Own."[26] This division had been used to counterattack against the Americans in June at Belleau Wood. Now it was again fighting the Americans, this time to prevent a breakthrough of the Kriemhilde Line.[27]

Just as at Cote de Chatillon, success hinged on the individual initiative of the soldiers in the line. On the right flank of the U.S. 5th Division's attack, the 60th Infantry Regiment plunged ahead into the maelstrom. The volume of fire coming into their ranks was more than these soldiers had ever experienced. Most of the men were stopped or driven back. However, others continued to advance. One of the regiment's battalion commanders, Lieutenant Colonel Philip Peyton, and his runner continued to push onward and ended up on the flank of one of the German machine guns holding up the advance of his regiment. They finished off the entire crew of five Germans manning that gun and then returned to the regiment to rally the men in the valley south of Cunel.[28] By the end of the day the Americans fighting around Cunel had cut a swath into the Kriemhilde Line. From Cote de Chatillon to the Heights of Romagne and Bois de Pultiere above Cunel, the famed German Siegfried Line was finally breached in the American Meuse-Argonne sector. Two more weeks of intense fighting remained before the Germans would be driven back from the entire defensive line in the Meuse area, but this marked a significant achievement for the American Expeditionary Forces and their French allies in the region.

16

Falling Short of Glory

> I took command of the First Army on the sixteenth [of October
> 1918]. It then consisted of seventeen American and four
> French divisions . . . a total of more than 1,000,000 men.
> —Lieutenant General Hunter Liggett

General Pershing decided on 10 October to relinquish command of
the First Army to General Hunter Liggett. This was due in large part
to the creation of the Second Army. With nearly 2 million American
soldiers now in France, it was impossible for all of these to serve in
a single army. The new U.S. Second Army would be commanded
by Lieutenant General Robert L. Bullard beginning on 12 October.
Bullard was well liked by Pershing and had commanded the 1st
Infantry Division earlier in the war. Successfully leading the 1st
Infantry seemed to open doors, as a string of Big Red One veterans
were given priority advancement. The Second Army assumed control of roughly fifty-five kilometers (thirty-four miles) of the front—
between the Meuse and the Moselle southeast of Verdun. Pershing
directed Bullard to prepare for a general attack toward Metz, the
elusive objective that so many in the AEF thought should have
been the focus of the offensive. This push would commence on 10
November.[1]

Pershing's army-wide attack of 14–16 October failed to come
close to accomplishing his lofty goals. The overly ambitious concept was for all three of his corps to break out from the Siegfried
(Kriemhilde) Line and advance into open country toward the
Sedan-Mezieres rail lines. Meanwhile, the other Allied armies farther north continued to make incredible gains since their breakout
of the Siegfried Line two weeks before. The Supreme Allied Commander, Ferdinand Foch, was pressuring Pershing to make gains
in the Meuse-Argonne and asked what was holding up the French
and Americans. The problem facing them in mid-October was the

Germans. Hindenburg and Ludendorff had committed forty-one of their divisions to the Meuse-Argonne sector. Thirty-one of these were in the line, with ten more in close reserve to counterattack any Franco-American penetrations. Simply put, the German High Command was taking risks in the north and trading land for time. Hindenburg and Ludendorff did not have this luxury in the Meuse-Argonne, as the capture of the Sedan-Mezieres rail would be catastrophic to the entire German Army on the Western Front.

The German leadership identified the Meuse-Argonne as a critical vulnerability and therefore committed the preponderance of their forces to blunt the Franco-American attack. During an interview after the war, Hindenburg bluntly stated, "From a military point of view, the Argonne battle was the climax of the war and its deciding factor . . . without the American blow in the Argonne, we could have made a satisfactory peace at the end of a stalemate or at least held our positions on our own frontier indefinitely undefeated." This was a major reason for the lack of progress in the sector. But there was more to the failure than this.

Pershing's propensity to fire officers was not just against those who had faltered in their duties, but also against those for whom he had a personal dislike. Thus was the case with Major General William Burnham of the 82nd Division, who was relieved because he did not have the type of leadership style that Pershing thought was necessary in France. This was also the case for the 26th Division commander, Clarence Edwards, who Pershing never liked personally. In such cases it seemed as though the AEF commander sought reasons to remove the men from their posts. Finally, it seemed that Pershing preferred Regular Army officers over National Guard leaders, and the sacking of commanders reflected this bias throughout elements of the AEF. This created distrust in the ranks and did not help in his endeavor to forge a modern fighting force. The ultimate shaming of sacked officers was orders for them to report to the Classification Depot at Blois. Being summoned to Blooey (as the Doughboys derogatorily referred to it) meant that a leader was fired from his job and would be reassigned to an administrative or other innocuous position.

In the first week of the Meuse-Argonne campaign Pershing fired four brigade commanders, and soon after that a division commander (General Burnham of the 82nd). This was followed in October with a major shakeup when he sacked the V Corps commander and three division commanders. This "zero-defect" command climate tended to sap initiative and had the opposite effect of what Pershing hoped. The string of fired generals and senior officers deprived the army from learning and adapting at the higher levels of command and instead brought more inexperienced officers into the line, who often made the same mistakes as their predecessors.

Pershing gave command of his First Army to Lieutenant General Hunter Liggett. After reviewing Pershing's plans for the 14 October offensive, Liggett astutely asked not to assume command until after this. Liggett would officially become the First Army commander on 16 October. He used the next six days to acquaint himself with the condition of the army and was concerned with what he saw. The First Army was in deplorable condition after three weeks of fighting. Several of his divisions were combat ineffective due to low manning. Additionally, straggling was a major concern, with an estimated one hundred thousand soldiers away from their units. Finally, there was a severe lack of draft animals. This meant that scores of the AEF's artillery could not be moved, thereby reducing the lethality of the divisions in the line.[2]

These deficiencies notwithstanding, Pershing asked Liggett to continue the attack upon taking command. Liggett politely asked Pershing to let him command the First Army and give him the discretion to do what he needed to make it more effective and lethal. Pershing, to his credit, deferred to Liggett, moved his headquarters away from the front, and focused on the larger strategic issues. Such a focus should have been Pershing's priority throughout the year. Instead, he allowed himself to get drawn into the comfort zone of tactics, a problem for many senior leaders. As Pershing poured over maps on where to attack in the Meuse-Argonne, politics in Paris were conspiring against him. The French premier, Georges Clemenceau, was not impressed by Pershing's leadership and was disappointed by his inability to make significant progress against the Germans. For several weeks Clemenceau had been pressing Foch to intervene and force Pershing to allow experienced French officers to lead his staff and army. Pershing had to go, as far as Clemenceau was concerned.[3]

Le Tigre, as Clemenceau was called, did not like Pershing and was appalled by his refusal a year earlier to learn from the French experience of the war. Their relationship continued to erode as Pershing spent less and less time dealing with strategic issues. Instead,

General John Pershing escorts French premier Georges Clemenceau on an inspection of American troops. Pershing's preoccupation with the array of tasks of running an army deprived him of the time to remain strategically engaged with Clemenceau, in part causing the rift between them. (National Archives)

he allowed himself to become absorbed with the tasks of the growing American army. This was certainly more comfortable for Pershing, who was out of place in strategic discussions. Clemenceau's dour view of Pershing was confirmed on 28 September 1918. Delighted with the capture of Montfaucon, Clemenceau decided to spend his seventy-seventh birthday touring the recently liberated hill and celebrating the Doughboys who were fighting to push the Germans from French soil. The trip, however, was a catastrophe. The roads to Montfaucon were jammed to a standstill with thousands of trucks, horses, tanks, artillery, and men. Pershing's divisions were simply too large for the narrow sectors that he assigned to them. Clemenceau was furious and ended up getting out of the car and "using strong language." He never made it to Montfaucon.[4]

This experience confirmed to him Pershing's lack of ability

Marshal Ferdinand Foch, the Supreme Allied Commander, did much to shield General John J. Pershing from Premier Clemenceau's displeasure. (U.S. Army Heritage and Education Center, Carlisle, Pennsylvania).

to lead a modern army. Clemenceau pressed Foch to take action. However, Foch preferred to have an amiable relationship with his multinational leaders and shielded Pershing from the premier's wrath. The lack of American progress in the Meuse-Argonne area by mid-October was the final nail in the coffin.[5] Clemenceau wrote an impassioned letter to Foch on 21 October that demanded the removal of Pershing from command.[6] Although Foch agreed that Pershing was not performing well on the battlefield, he refused to take such a harsh and difficult action, fearing that it would have disastrous consequences for the alliance.[7] This calamitous clash was due in large part to Pershing's lack of strategic engagement and understanding. As he busied himself with tactical issues, he neglected the greater issues beyond winning the battle.

Now that Pershing had finally let go of command, he could spend more time on issues of strategic value, but it was nearly too late. He had burned bridges of goodwill with Clemenceau and squandered opportunities to think and plan for what the peace should look like after the war ended. Pershing was out of his league and running out of time. Meanwhile, Liggett developed plans to get his army back in fighting shape. Instead of continuing to bang its head against the Germans in continuous and uncoordinated attacks, with depleted forces, a new approach was adapted.

The next big offensive for the First Army would commence on 1 November (28 October was initially selected, but 1 November was preferred by the French Fourth Army). There would be no major attacks over the next two weeks. However, the divisions in the line were ordered to continue local attacks to seize key terrain, clear woods, and maintain pressure on the Germans. Liggett had an eye on securing the terrain that he needed to ensure a breakout on 1 November. Willing to learn from the French and British experience of the war, Liggett ordered better use of artillery, aviation, and tanks in the offensive. It was imperative that the attacking units employed these combat multipliers in thoughtful and deliberate ways. The use of artillery received particular attention. Liggett directed that artillery be used in the French manner and that supporting fire and gas be used to suppress the enemy during an attack. Finally, American infantry units would be trained in French small unit tactics that used infiltration to avoid strong points and maneuver to outflank enemy positions.[8]

As the French and American soldiers in the Meuse region prepared for the last big push, much fighting remained. The divisions in the line were directed to seize and hold the high ground and other positions that were deemed key terrain. It would be attritional war, the type of fighting that Pershing had hoped to avoid. This was the difference between war on paper and real war. Perhaps Pershing was finally grasping the reality of the challenge that he faced.

17

Maintaining the Initiative

I never expected such speedy developments. The Americans are becoming dangerous!

—Diary of General Max von Gallwitz

Per General Liggett's guidance, the U.S. First Army divisions still in the front line would conduct localized attacks during the last two weeks of October. It was imperative that these occur to maintain the initiative and to seize key terrain necessary to support the resumption of the army offensive on 1 November. The III Corps commander, Major General John Hines, directed the 3rd Division, supported by elements of the 4th Division, to attack German positions on the high ground to the north, seize Hill 299, and clear the Clairs Chenes Wood.[1] The 5th Division would attack to the left of the 3rd Division.[2]

The attack kicked off at 7:00 A.M. on 20 October after a five-minute artillery barrage. German machine gun fire from Bois de Pultiere and the Clairs Chenes Wood tore into the soldiers of the 3rd Division, blunting their advance. However, elements of infantry from E Company and soldiers of the 6th Engineers maneuvered to the east flank of the woods and drove the Germans out of the area. The detachment was led by Captain Charles D. Harris. When the German machine guns blunted the progress of the infantry, Harris and his men were moving across an open field with tools and wire. Harris ordered his men to drop their implements and follow him more than a kilometer forward into the enemy-held woods. In the face of fierce German resistance, Harris led his men against the enemy, capturing two German machine guns and three prisoners.[3]

Captain Harris was a recent graduate of the U.S. Military Academy and, at twenty-one, the youngest captain in the AEF. The young man's father was Major General P. C. Harris, the U.S. Army adjutant general. Charles was popular with his men for his upbeat and

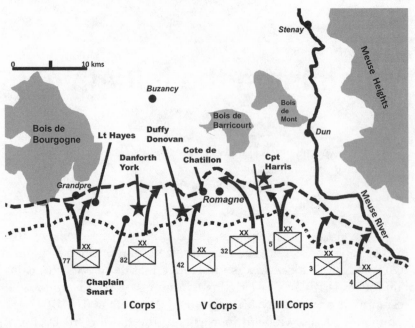

Map 17.1. Meuse Front, 14–20 October 1918. (Josiah Mastriano)

friendly disposition. More importantly, however, he was remembered for being "brave, he seemed not to know the meaning of fear. . . . He was one of the coolest men under fire."[4]

Harris and his men organized their defense against an all-but-certain German counterattack, not knowing that the 5th Division failed to advance on their left, leaving them vulnerable to being outflanked.[5] Around 1:00 P.M., the Germans began their counterattack against Captain Harris's men. Both of the captured machine guns were put in action against the enemy attack. As the Germans surged forward, Harris moved one of the MG 08/15 machine guns into the field to secure better fields of fire. His fearless actions inflicted heavy casualties on the advancing enemy and momentarily stopped their advance.[6]

As the battle raged on, Harris was hit in the left lung by a bullet. As he lay exposed in his vulnerable position, the Germans fired an artillery barrage against the Americans in Clairs Chenes Wood. When the barrage lifted, several of Harris's men ran into the field to pull him to safety and take him to an aid station. However, the German attack resumed, and Harris fell into enemy hands. The

Captain Charles Harris was posthumously awarded the Distinguished Service Cross for leading an attack that unhinged the German defenses in Clairs Chenes Wood. (Lieutenant General Theodore Stroup and Harriet Stroup)

Germans moved him to their first aid station in nearby Aincreville, where he died a short time later.[7] The Clairs Chenes Wood changed hands several times before the Americans finally and permanently wrestled it from German control. The Germans buried Harris with honors and marked his grave. He was awarded the Distinguished Service Cross posthumously. The award citation states:

> The Distinguished Service Cross is presented to Charles D. Harris, Captain, U.S. Army, for extraordinary heroism in action in the Clairs-Chenes Woods, October 20, 1918. While leading his company in an attack on enemy machine-gun nests, Captain Harris, with three of his men in advance of the remainder of the company, fearlessly attacked an enemy machine-gun nest, capturing three prisoners, and two guns, turning the guns against the enemy. He was mortally wounded while operating one of the guns in an exposed position.

Such feats of heroism and sacrifice on both sides marked the next two weeks of action across the front. The fighting was desperate and intense to the very last. Meanwhile, a few kilometers west of Clairs Chenes Wood, the 82nd Division likewise endeavored to evict the Germans from the high ground to their front.[8]

Alvin York's action that eliminated 25 enemy soldiers and captured 132 more triggered the German withdrawal from Argonne Forest. After the liberation of the Argonne was completed, the men moved to the Meuse Valley to participate in the next phase of fighting: the reduction of the Kriemhilde Line.[9] During the move out of the Argonne, the 82nd was under German artillery fire and frequently strafed by German aircraft. Undaunted by this, York's battalion chaplain, Captain Smart, rushed to the aid of wounded soldiers and died while trying to help men during their time of greatest danger and need.[10] They remembered a scripture he preached the Sunday before from John 15:13, "Greater love hath no man than this, that a man lay down his life for his friends."[11] The loss of Chaplain Smart was a severe blow to the men. His words of truth and encouragement had carried them through some of the darkest hours. He was the personification of a Christian who walked his talk. They could not help but remember his last sermon a few days before, where he preached on finishing the race of life well.[12]

The 82nd Division deployed to the center-western part of the Meuse Valley, with the 42nd Rainbow Division and the village of Sommerance on its right flank, and the 77th Liberty and St. Juvin on its left. At great cost in lives, the three divisions began a series of attacks starting on 14 October to crack the Kriemhilde Line. This portion of the Siegfried/Kriemhilde Line included thick bands of barbed wire entanglements, reinforced bunkers, strong points, and canalized terrain that led to kill zones.[13]

The sky to the front was filled with German observation balloons and aircraft. The Americans kicked off their attack at 8:30 A.M. with an artillery barrage followed by the infantry assault.[14] However, before the men began their attack, German artillery answered with high explosive and gas rounds across the 77th, 82nd, and 42nd Divisions' front.[15] The German barrage crashed on the American troops, close to Alvin York, "And then bang! One of the big shells struck the ground right in front of us and we all went up in the air. But we all come down again. Nobody was hurt. But it sure was close."[16]

The American attack went from bad to worse. German artillery continued to tear into the ranks of the men as they endeavored to advance. This dispersed the men during the attack. The 42nd Division soldiers to the right of the 82nd had it far worse. German machine gun fire from the Kriemhilde to their front and Cote de Chatillon decimated the regiment on the left flank of that division. This drove many of the 42nd Division soldiers into the 82nd's line of attack, disrupting the attack of both for some time. The 42nd's regiment operating alongside the 82nd Division was the 165th. The 165th was the 1918 designation for the famed 69th "Irish Regiment."

The 69th, as part of the Irish Brigade, has a prominent place in history, especially for its role in epic battles as part of the Federal Army of the Potomac during the American Civil War. Led by the celebrated Irish nationalist leader Thomas Francis Meager, the 69th broke the Rebel line in the Sunken Road at Antietam. During the Battle of Gettysburg, the Irish drove the Confederates from the northern part of the Wheatfield. The regiment's chaplain, Father William Corby, played a key role in that battle with his inspirational leadership. Yet, the Irish Brigade is most remember for its heroic but doomed assault against Confederate positions on Marye's Heights during the Battle of Fredericksburg on 13 December 1862. There, the Irish attacked a strong enemy position dominated by a stone wall that they could not penetrate, losing scores of men in the attempt.

On 14 October 1918, the Fighting 69th (165th Regiment) had its own modern-day version of Chaplain Corby in the form of Father Francis Duffy and its own Thomas Meagher, in the person of Colonel William "Wild Bill" Donovan. If one asked Father Duffy to sum up his life, he would say, "As for myself . . . I am very Irish, very Catholic; very American person if anybody challenges my convictions. But normally, and let alone, I am just plain human."[17] In his unique way, Duffy described the Irish men with whom he served:

> The religion of the Irish has characteristics of its own—they make the Sign of the Cross with the right hand, while holding the left ready to give a jab to anybody who needs it for his own or the general good. I cannot say that it is an ideally perfect type of Christianity; but considering the sort of world we have to live in yet, it is near as we can come at present to perfection for the generality of men. It was into the mouth of an Irish soldier that Kipling put the motto, "Help a woman, and hit a man; and you won't go far wrong either way."[18]

Father Francis Duffy remains the most celebrated military chaplain in the United States. He was awarded numerous medals for heroism by France and the United States for fearlessly serving in the front lines with the soldiers and going above the call of duty to minister to the wounded. (U.S. Army Heritage and Education Center, Carlisle, Pennsylvania)

Father Duffy is the most well-known military chaplain in American history. A renowned theologian before the war, he eagerly joined the men of the Fighting 69th when the United States entered the fight. He was respected by the men, for whom he did all he could to meet their Christian needs in time of war with messages of hope, prayer, and encouragement. Father Duffy was always where he was needed most—and more important, fearless in battle. Exposing himself to great danger, he often moved forward to rescue the wounded while under fire from the enemy. The epitaph of the Civil War chaplain Father Corby also applied to Duffy: "no spot was too dangerous or too much exposed to the fire of the enemy for the Irish Brigade's priest."[19]

The task that the Fighting Irish and all of the 42nd Rainbow, 82nd All American, and 77th Liberty faced that day in the Meuse Valley was as daunting as what their forefathers faced at Gettysburg, Fredericksburg, and Antietam. Before the Irish Brigade marched to death and glory at the Wheatfield during the second day of the Battle of Gettysburg, their chaplain, Father Corby, stopped the men to pray with them. Corby offered general absolution[20] and added, "The Catholic church refuses Christian burial to any man who turns his back to the foe or deserts his flag."[21] In his own way, Duffy did the same. When preaching a sermon before the battle he said, "Much as I love you all I would rather that you and I myself, that all of us should sleep our last sleep under the soil of France than that the historic colors of this Old Regiment, the banner of our republic, should be soiled by irresolution or disgraced by panic."[22]

Duffy was with the men that day when they assaulted the strongest part of the German line in the region. Leading the men was Lieutenant Colonel William "Wild Bill" Donovan. In the Second World War, Donovan would lead the Office of Strategic Services (OSS), and he is considered the founder of the Central Intelligence Agency. But on this day in 1918 he led men into the battle of their lives. Knowing that the men would need inspiration, Donovan did not take the usual route of officers to remove anything that would make him stand out (and thereby draw German sniper fire). Before the battle began on 14 October 1918, Donovan put on his Sam Brown Belt and double shoulder straps. He then led the men into the maelstrom.[23]

The survivors describe the scene as almost surreal, the entire unit moving forward in line like their ancestors assaulting the Stone Wall at Fredericksburg. Enemy artillery blew gaping holes in the

Colonel William "Wild Bill" Donovan led the men of the 165th Regiment into battle on the fateful day of 14 October 1918. His fearless leadership drove the men forward until he was wounded by a German bullet. Donovan would serve in the Office of Strategic Services (OSS) during World War Two and is considered the founder of the Central Intelligence Agency. (U.S. Army Heritage and Education Center, Carlisle, Pennsylvania)

line as the men advanced, and German aircraft dived upon them, with the ground boiling as machine gun bullets sprayed about them. In the midst of the men was Donovan, yelling above the din of battle his favorite phrases to encourage the men, "Come on! Come on Fellows! It's better ahead than here!" He would wrap his arm around the shoulders of the soldiers showing fear and urge them on, "Come on old sport, nobody in this regiment was ever afraid." When a spray of German machine gun bullets peppered the ground around his feet, he calmly smiled and said to the men, "Come on now, men, they can't hit me and they won't hit you!"[24] Donavan's coolness under fire seemed to reflect the ideals of the old Irish song, which goes:

I'll hang my harp on a willow tree,
I'll be off to the wars again;
A peaceful home has no charm for me,
The battlefield no pain.

But the bullets and artillery hit many of the men. When one round exploded, killing a soldier and maiming another, a nearby soldier tasked with carrying ammunition, Corporal John Patrick Furey, jumped into the shell hole, picked up the wounded man, kissed him, and said, "Me poor fellow, me poor fellow" while putting tourniquets on his severed limbs. Furey carried the injured soldier to the rear.

Despite the bravery of Duffy and the courageous leadership of Donovan, the mission proved impossible to accomplish. The Germans put up a robust defense and the Irish wavered. However, their redemption drew near as nine tanks advanced to help them vanquish their adversaries. German artillery observers saw the tanks and expertly directed the artillery barrage against them, forcing them to retreat. By then, the Irish had reached the bands of barbed wire that marked the leading edge of the Kriemhilde Line near the Landres-et-Saint-Georges Road. Supporting engineer soldiers bounded forward and labored feverishly to cut gaps in the lines, but German machine gun fire, combined with artillery and mortar fires, broke up the attack and eventually drove the Irish back. Donovan was shot through the knee during the melee and, after the attack failed, was removed from the field of battle.[25] He spoke briefly with Father Duffy, saying, "Father, you're a disappointed man. You expected to have the pleasure of burying me over here."

"I certainly did, Bill, and you are a lucky dog to get off with nothing more than you've got."[26]

Father Duffy described the outcome of the battle in the historic context of the Irish Brigade: "When the wire is deep, and still intact, and strongly defended, the infantry can do little but hang their heroic bodies on it. But we shall not dwell on this. The most glorious day in the history of our regiment in the Civil War was Fredericksburg, where the Old 69th in the Irish Brigade failed to capture the impregnable position on Marye's Heights, though their dead with the green sprigs in their caps lay in rows before it. Landres et St. Georges is our Fredericksburg and the Kriemhilde Stellung our Marye's Heights."[27]

The repulse of the 42nd Division's forces created a gap along the 82nd Division's line that would have catastrophic implications. During the fight of the Irish, to their right, the 82nd's combined 327th and 328th Regiments advanced toward their portion of the Kriemhilde Line, a few kilometers in front of them near the Landres-et-Saint-Georges Road. They too were greeted by focused German artillery, machine guns, and riflemen. The route of advance was littered with scores of casualties. On the ground was torn equipment, torn men, and the scattered accouterments of war, peppered with the darting to and fro of medics and punctuated with the exploding thuds of artillery. Yet the 82nd All American Division was able to make headway.[28]

The 82nd's Captain Danforth encouraged the men forward, and on they went, sweeping across the Landres-et-Saint-Georges Road and two hundred yards beyond into a wood and to the Ravine de Pierres. This placed the men in the midst of the Kriemhilde Stellung. Corporal York and his men fought tenaciously to drive the Germans back and, after a series of pitched battles, won the wood. Ironically, the soldiers facing York and his men were from the Prussian 45th Reserve Division, elements of which they had fought in the Argonne just days before. Despite the hard-won victory, the flanking fire from the 42nd Division's sector tore into the men, and they were ordered to fall back to the Landres-et-Saint-Georges Road and dig in for the anticipated German counterattack.[29]

Meanwhile, to the west of the 82nd, the 77th Division likewise launched its attack. The immediate objective was to clear the village of St. Juvin and then continue to attack north to breach the Kriemhilde Line. The route of advance for the 77th was particularly daunting. The men jumped off north of the Argonne village of Marcq, down a slope, across the L'Aire River, and then back up a slope to the village of St. Juvin. The Americans would be in range and line of sight of the Germans the entire way, except when they were on the east bank of the L'Aire.[30]

As the Americans commenced their attack, they were greeted by heavy German artillery and machine gun fire from the high ground around St. Juvin. The attack quickly stalled. Among the first to fall during this assault was Lieutenant Michael J. Hayes. Hayes was a well-respected leader in the unit known for his remarkable strength and endurance. Standing at six feet and one inch and weighing 190 pounds, he was unmatched in physical stamina and Christian humility. "He had a smile for everyone," "never swore or had a hard word for anyone. He was manly and strong and a soldier's soldier. His moral character was unimpeachable." Hayes always kept the New Testament in his pocket and spent most of his spare time reading it. He stood out as a leader by being willing to risk everything for his men, and he was not afraid of hard tasks.[31]

During the early part of the attack, Hayes was engaged by a German machine gun. He fell near the L'Aire River. One of his friends, Lieutenant Robert Patterson, ran to his aid, but a bullet had passed through Hayes's head. The attack wavered under blistering fire. Patterson bandaged his wound and remained with him until he passed several hours later. This was one of the rare occasions when the men cried when they heard that their lieutenant had been killed in action. Patterson wrote of Hayes, "A better soldier never lived. His purity of character, his devotion to the cause he was fighting for, his instinctive kindness, his courage, these marked a great man."[32] Hayes rests in Arlington Cemetery.

The 77th resumed the attack to secure St. Juvin in the afternoon. After using a series of flanking maneuvers they drove the Germans back. Several Germans were captured in the village during the mopping-up operations. This was followed by an attack to drive the Germans off of the high ground north of St. Juvin, which succeeded. The intensity of German artillery increased, and the attack ended north of the village.[33]

The engagements and battles experienced by the 77th, 82nd, and 42nd Divisions during 15–31 October were similar. Morning American attacks to secure high ground, or woods, were followed by fierce Germany artillery barrages and desperate counterattacks.

Little ground would be gained over the next two weeks, especially after Liggett focused on preparing the divisions not in the line for the breakout attack scheduled for 1 November. Yet, for the soldiers in the line during this period, it would be a dark time, with deteriorating weather and mounting casualty rosters.

Due to the high casualties suffered by the 82nd Division over the previous week, Alvin York's 328th Regiment was merged with the 327th. Once this was completed, they were ordered to launch another attack early on 15 October. The attack was to commence with a three-hour artillery barrage at 4:00 A.M. with large amounts of poisonous gas. The barrage would intensify shortly after 7:00 A.M., with the American infantry attacking behind it at 7:30.

However, Gallwitz ordered that the Prussian 45th Reserve Division and the 15th Bavarians launch an attack against the Americans in the area. The concept was to fire an intense barrage followed by an attack against the 82nd and 77th American Divisions to drive them back from the Landres-et-Saint-Georges Road.[34] This was to ensure the integrity of the Kriemhilde Line and to secure the west flank of Cote de Chatillon.[35]

A thick fog covered the Meuse Valley that morning. As York and the other soldiers of the 82nd Division prepared to assault the Germans, a heavy artillery barrage slammed into them, driving the men back to their shell holes and fighting positions. As the Americans sought protection in their foxholes, grey-clad figures suddenly emerged from the fog on the heels of the barrage and rushed through the American line. The Prussian 45th and Bavarian 15th Divisions had the advantage as the entire right flank of the 82nd Division was vulnerable. The fighting was fierce and soon turned into hand-to-hand as the Prussian and Bavarian attackers drove the Americans back several hundred meters, nearly to their jump-off line from the previous day.[36]

Leading the 210th Prussian Regiment of the 45th Prussian Reserve Regiment was Oberstleutnant (Lieutenant Colonel) Fischel. Fischel had been the regimental commander since 1917 and had a reputation of being a fighter. He led the first wave of men into the Americans. Working closely with the 15th Bavarians, the Germans smashed into the 82nd, driving them back. The exposed American flank in the 42nd U.S. Division sector was used with great effect. The 210th's regimental history described Fishcel's actions during this attack, saying, "The regimental commander was always in the

Oberstleutnant (Lieutenant Colonel) Fischel was in command of the Prussian 210th Reserve Regiment, 45th Prussian Reserve Division, during 1918. (Gieraths, *Geschichte des Reserve Infanterie Regiments Nr. 210*)

front line and he had a habit of being in the place of the heaviest fighting."[37]

As the 82nd "All American" was being driven back, York's company commander, Captain E. C. B. Danforth, and battalion commander, Major James Tillman, rallied the men and rushed reinforcements into the exposed right flank. This only temporarily stalled the German push. As the fighting waged across the front, German follow-on units began advancing, and Fischel was set to achieve an important victory in the center of the Meuse Valley. There was no way that the 82nd could stop the second wave of advancing Germans, and the All American Division would potentially be driven from the field of battle.[38]

The Germans' second wave began to advance across the embattled field at 7:25 A.M., precisely as the preplanned American artillery

268 THUNDER IN THE ARGONNE

intensified. This crashed into the Prussian and Bavarian ranks, scattering and dispersing them. The second wave did not make it, ending hopes of driving the 82nd from the field.[39] The survivors of the first wave began falling back when it was clear that they were on their own, and Fischel's hope for a victory was lost.[40] Fischel's Prussians and the 15th Bavarians performed a fighting withdrawal, and when the fog burned off, German aircraft commenced strafing the American line, and artillery peppered the division for the rest of the day.[41] Although the Germans were thrown back, their effort did disrupt the planned attack by the 82nd.[42]

The Rainbow Division still had not advanced to secure the right flank of the 82nd. This was due to the ongoing fierce battle for Cote de Chatillon farther to the east. Until that key terrain was taken, the Germans had de facto control of the region. To ameliorate the vulnerability, the right flank of the 82nd Division's sector was bent back. Additionally, artillery observers moved forward with two 75mm field guns and a 37mm cannon platoon to strengthen the line.[43]

When the day cleared, the soldiers had front-row seats to a spectacular dogfight that included more than three hundred French, German, and American aircraft fighting for command of the skies. A German Fokker D.VII biplane with a light gray fuselage and camouflaged pattern wings was shot down near Alvin York's position. The German pilot parachuted to safety and was captured by York's men. The Americans cut pieces from the airplane and the German pilot's parachute to keep as souvenirs. Despite the impressive air demonstration, the Germans typically controlled the skies along the front, which brought with it troublesome strafing and, worse, directed artillery fire.

The next two weeks were dedicated mostly to holding the line, and occasional attacks against the Germans. German aircraft strafing the American lines and incessant German artillery fire was the norm, both incoming and outgoing. The artillery fire often included poisonous gas. To compound matters, the weather was damp, cool, and rainy. This placed a toll on the health of the Americans now stuck living in water-filled holes. The 327th/328th surgeon estimated that virtually all of the men were sick. This compelled the divisions in the line to adopt a three-day rotation schedule, with soldiers serving one day at the front, one day in reserve, and one day in the rear. This allowed the men to tend their equipment and health.

All major attacks were called off after 21 October by the Americans, and the mission of the 77th, 82nd, and 42nd, as well as the other divisions already forward deployed, was to hold the line until the 1 November breakout.[44]

The American divisions in the line were ordered to begin aggressive patrolling and raids to keep the Germans off balance in the days before the 1 November offensive. York and the seven men who were with him on that one day in October three weeks ago, when they captured 132 Germans, were still alive and together. This included Privates Percy Beardsley, Thomas Johnson, Joseph Kornacki, Michael Sacina, Feodor Sok, George Wills, and Patrick Donohue.[45] Over the previous three weeks, the men had seen nearly continuous combat. They had fought off German attacks and counterattacks, endured attacks from the air, artillery, and poisonous gas, and even had the flu. York's regiment lost 30 percent of its men, 1,189 soldiers.[46] At long last, on Reformation Day, 31 October, they were being replaced by reinforced and ready combat divisions that would play their role in finishing the war. None of the men knew that the end was only eleven days away. Yet, the cost of this war came at a high price. York remembered his fallen comrades, saying:

> All was terribly quiet in the field. And I jes couldn't help thinking of the boys that only the day before was alive and like me. Dymowski dead. Weiler dead. Waring dead. Wine dead. Swanson dead. Corporal Murray Savage, my best pal, dead. Oh, my, it seemed so unbelievable. I would never see them again. I would never share the same blanket with Corporal Savage. We'd never read the Bible together again. We would never talk about our faith and pray to our God. I was mussed up inside worser than I had ever been. I'm a-telling you when you lose your best buddie and you know you ain't never going to see him again, you sorter know how terrible cruel war is. There was nothing I could do now for Corporal Murray Savage or any of the other boys that done lost their lives.[47]

As York and his men moved to more comfortable accommodations behind the line, he recalled the prayer he uttered a few weeks before:

O Jesus, the great rock of foundation
Where on my feet were set with sovereign grace;
Through Shells or Death with all their agitation
Thou wilt protect me if I will only trust in thy Grace
Bless thy holy name.[48]

York's prayer was answered. He made it through the tempest.

18

Planning for the Last Grand Push

Death before dishonor!
    —General Marwitz, German Fifth Army commander

The major Franco-American offensive would commence at 5:30 A.M. on 1 November. The two-week "reset" gave the soldiers time to refit, retrain, rearm, stockpile supplies, and coordinate their artillery fire plan. Although the experience of holding the line was "hellish," it bought time to deliver the knockout punch to the Germans. The concept of the operations called for the French Fourth Army to continue its attack up the valley west of the Argonne while the U.S. First Army maintained its attack up the Meuse Valley. The 1 November offensive was a milestone for the Americans. It was truly an American army. Liggett wrote, "For the first time we were on our own. In the past, French artillery, aviation and other technical troops had made up our deficiencies."[1] Although French liaison officers remained in the AEF, the attack up the Meuse Valley was now truly American. This American-only experience was short-lived, as a French infantry corps would soon arrive to support the American push on the east bank of the Meuse.

The Germans' situation on the Western Front was becoming desperate. The pressure of the broad front attack had sapped their reserves and was stretching both manpower and resources. Army Group German Crown Prince, to the west of Gallwitz, found itself in a dangerous position of possibly being rolled up by the combined forces of the Allies. Crown Prince Wilhelm issued orders to his First, Third, Seventh, and Eighteenth Armies, saying, "On all army fronts a decisive stand will be made in the present forward position."[2]

Gallwitz had not been idle and was bringing up supplies and additional forces to blunt the American attack. However, resources

271

General Georg von der Marwitz, as one of two army commanders under Gallwitz, led the German Fifth Army against the Americans from the beginning of the Meuse-Argonne campaign on 26 September. By 1 November the situation had become desperate for his men, as the numeric and material superiority of the Americans had worn his army down. (National Archives)

and—more importantly—men were running low. To add to the dilemma, the Americans had broken through the Siegfried (Kriemhilde) Line, making it difficult to blunt a breakout. Army Group Gallwitz (*Heeresgruppe* Gallwitz) still comprised two subordinate armies. Gallwitz's army extended from the Aisne River in the west to Metz in the east. The eastern half was commanded by General Georg Fuchs, a proven and capable leader. The western half was under the command of the German Fifth Army, led by General Georg von der Marwitz.

The portion of Army Group Gallwitz under incredible pressure was in the Fifth Army half of the sector. Because of this, Gallwitz deployed twenty-seven of his forty-one divisions to support Marwitz, taking considerable risk in Army Detachment C's area to the east. Fuch's Army Detachment C had been thinned down to fourteen divisions, most of which were battered units, withdrawn there for refitting and rest. This made Army Detachment C vulnerable, but Gallwitz decided to make that area an economy of force zone. The outcome of the war, for Gallwitz, would be decided with Marwitz's Fifth Army.

The terrain was considerably less defensible north of the compromised Kriemhilde Line across the Meuse Valley. But a professional and experienced leader like Marwitz still had some advantages. The defense hinged on three important terrain features. Along the western edge of the Fifth Army's zone was high ground north of the liberated village of Grandpré. As a sort of northern spur of the Argonne Forest, this high ground dominated the Aisne and Meuse Valleys and could be used as a thorn in the side of the French and American attack, much as the Argonne Forest had been during October. Additionally, this high ground, called Bois de Bourgogne, was astride the boundary of the French Fourth Army and the American First Army. This offered the German defenders an opportunity to exploit a critical vulnerability of the enemy.

The second important terrain feature that was vital to the German defense of the region included Bois de Barricourt. Like much of the high ground in the region, Bois de Barricourt encompassed a thick forest, with the southern edges offering excellent fields of fire and observation of the valley below. The third terrain feature vital to the German defense was the high ground north and west of the French village Dun sur Meuse. Sitting astride both banks of the Meuse River, Dun sur Meuse included both the river and

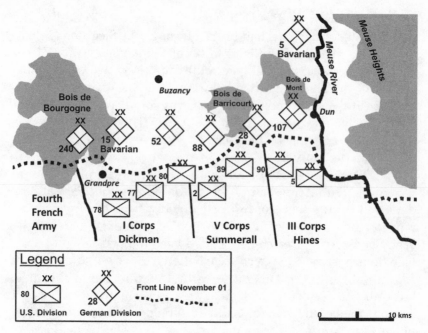

Map 18.1. German Fifth Army Defensive Plan, 1 November 1918. (Josiah Mastriano)

a canal, making the middle part of it an island. Dun sur Meuse was a gateway to Verdun and a trading town in quieter days, but it would soon find itself the center of fighting. However, the town could not be held without controlling the high ground north of it. This same high ground provided excellent control of the surrounding Meuse Valley and was essential to hold as part of an integrated defense.

To the west, a robust group of divisions were deployed on the high ground north of Grandpré. Due to the lack of manpower, Marwitz weighted the defense here in the west, where the German units on Bois de Bourgogne were his main effort and the hinge of his plan. This area was essential to hold and could blunt both the French Fourth Army and U.S. First Army from making appreciable progress. Understanding the decisive nature of this high ground, Marwitz took risks in the center of his line, planning on using flanking fires and a "mobile" reserve to plug any breakthroughs there. Based on his experience of the past five weeks, the plan was sound. Key terrain in German hands could be leveraged to break up these antiquated tactics with massed machine gun fire and focused artillery. However, this was not the same American army that he had faced just days before.

Although Gallwitz's and Marwitz's plans to blunt the American attack were sound, the German situation at the strategic level was in a crisis. Berlin's international partners were looking for a way out of the war. The Ottoman Empire capitulated on 31 October. The Austro-Hungarians quit the war on 4 November. Before the 1 November American attack, Austro-Hungarian forces on the Western Front were anticipating orders from Vienna announcing the end of hostilities, which would create gaps in the lines when their men withdrew. For Gallwitz, this meant that three Austro-Hungarian Divisions (1st, 35th, and 106th) were pulling out of the Meuse sector even as the Americans were to renew their offensive.

The Austro-Hungarian Empire not only quit the war, but would fragment on the day after the armistice into independent nations (Austria, Hungary, and Czechoslovakia) and the kingdom of the Serbs-Croats-Slovenes (forming into Yugoslavia), while Romania and Poland gobbled up large pieces of the fragmented empire to the east and north. Although the actual fracturing of the empire was a few weeks off, the diverse ethnic nationalities in its army began to leave the line for home. General Marwitz wrote on 29 October, "I had here [in the Fifth Army] many Austro-Hungarian Divisions . . . all in a blink of an eye wanted to return home to Hungary, Czechoslovakia, to a new homeland." This created no small crisis for his army group in that his staff had not anticipated this, and the time and planning required to fill the gaps were insufficient. More problematic, however, there simply were not enough German units remaining.[3]

But there were other troubles for the Germans. "There was fighting from the Dutch frontier to Verdun." The Allies were gaining ground in every corner of Europe. In Belgium, the Allies liberated "Bruges, Thielt and Courtrai" and the German "Sixth and Seventh Armies . . . abandoned Lille and Douai." Meanwhile, in France, the Allies advanced beyond the Oise to La Fere. Elsewhere in Europe, the Italians renewed their offensive, and in Serbia the Germans retreated to the Danube River.[4] A month of negotiations with the Wilson administration only gave *hope* of ending the war, but no material advantage to the Germans. Ludendorff noted an increasingly "arrogant" tone in Wilson's replies concerning German appeals for terms to end the war. Even President Wilson grasped that the tide had turned against Germany and that it was militarily, diplomatically, and economically in a weak, if not desperate position.[5]

Hindenburg and Ludendorff briefed the German leadership in Berlin. The meetings were attended by Kaiser Wilhelm and Prince Max von Baden to discuss the precarious situation on the Western Front and the overall direction of the war. The new German government was becoming inpatient to end the war and directed its hostility toward Ludendorff. In a moment of honesty, Ludendorff confessed, "There is no hope. Germany is lost."[6] The Kaiser bluntly asked for Ludendorff to step down, whereupon he submitted his resignation. Hindenburg remained in his position. Upon hearing the news of Ludendorff's resignation, Crown Prince Wilhelm wrote from his army headquarters on the Western Front, "I knew at once that this meant the end of things."[7]

For Army Group Gallwitz, the situation was becoming increasingly ominous. During the last two weeks of October, Marwitz's Fifth Army had lost nearly thirty-three thousand men fighting the French and Americans in the Argonne and Meuse Valley. Although they inflicted more casualties on their foes, the Germans simply did not have an endless supply of men to replace their losses.[8]

As the Germans grappled in Berlin with how to end the war, Marshal Foch summoned a meeting of the Allied commanders in Senlis, France. Located forty-four kilometers north of Paris, Senlis dates back to the Romans and is an attractive medieval town with a magnificent cathedral. Foch moved his headquarters from Bombon to Senlis on 18 October to be closer to the front and in a more centralized location to provide better command and control of the Allied armies.[9] He asked Marshal Haig, General Pétain, and General Pershing for their input on the terms regarding an armistice with Germany. Haig suggested "lenient" terms, while Pétain and Pershing pressed for harder terms. Pershing wrote that Foch "had no inclination toward leniency."[10]

Since Liggett took over the U.S. First Army in the Meuse-Argonne region, things had changed considerably. When Liggett took over, he called for an end to major army operations from 16 October to 1 November.[11] Although, as described, combat operations continued for the divisions in the line, the next two weeks focused on preparing for the next major multi-army operation. The ensuing two weeks were used to refit and retrain divisions for the realities of modern warfare. Of this, Liggett wrote: "There was a lull of two weeks in the major operation while we tightened up. My staff and I traveled constantly among the troops, making every effort to profit from my past mistakes and to encourage the fighting spirit of the army for the impending attack on the enemy's main positions, and never was the response more immediate or effective."[12]

Liggett was a student of history and saw that Pershing's approach was ill-advised and dangerous, saying, "The defects of the American operation in this battle were such as were humanly inescapable in a not yet fully seasoned army." Reflecting on the first large battle of the American Civil War, Liggett wrote, "I know that [Union general] McDowell had a perfect plan of battle at the First Bull Run, but that he made the mistake of assuming that he had an army instead of a well-intentioned mob."[13] The two-week "reset" gave the engineers and other support elements time to improve the roads for the transport of supplies and ammunition and to bring hot food to the front. Artillery units pushed forward, and great pains were made to improve the hygiene and morale of the men. Additionally, newly arrived soldiers (replacements) were trained in the tactics of modern war. Even showers and laundry facilities arrived, allowing the men to wash off the incessant cooties (lice).

In preparation for the big push, unit training focused on small unit tactics that bypassed strong points and used maneuver to outflank a defending enemy.[14] Additionally, objectives were designated across the front within range of artillery.[15] This would ensure supporting fires as the infantry advanced. Liggett lifted the draconian restrictions on artillery that Pershing had imposed during the campaign (as discussed in earlier chapters). These restrictions had marred the opening days of the Meuse-Argonne Offensive). Finally, the AEF's air component received new orders. Its support of the AEF had been lackluster at best. For the Doughboys, it often felt like the Germans ruled the skies and strafed them with impunity. Liggett demanded that the U.S. Army Air Service provide better support of the attack.[16] This included shifting from deep targets (interdicting German units behind the line) to focusing on supporting the attacking divisions.[17] Liggett also saw to it that he had ready access to a fleet of trucks to rapidly move units across his front to wherever they were needed.[18] At long last, the Americans had a modern combat force led by a seasoned commander and staff. When the army attacked on 1 November, it would be no mob, but a ready force.

General Pershing had difficulty staying out of Liggett's way during the planning and build-up for the 1 November offensive. Liggett's aide-de-camp, Lieutenant Colonel Stackpole, recorded that Pershing arrived at First Army headquarters on Tuesday, 29 October, "worried" and sought to immerse himself in the minutiae of the planning. Stackpole recorded that "Liggett . . . told him to forget it and not allow himself to be bothered, to give us the directive and leave us alone."[19] To his credit, Pershing complied, but he frequently appeared at Liggett's headquarters seeking updates and was eager to provide advice.

The American attack would include three corps. The I Corps would be in the west with the 78th, 77th, and 80th Divisions in the initial push, the V Corps with the 2nd and 89th Divisions would be in the center, and the III Corps would be in the east with the 90th and 5th Divisions. Liggett's assessment of his opponent's defensive plan was on target. He correctly surmised that Marwitz had anchored the German plan on the Bois de Bourgogne north of Grandpré. This created a gap in the German line in the center of the Meuse Valley. Liggett therefore directed that Summerall's V Corps serve as the main attack, with the objective of clearing the Barricourt Heights by the end of the first day. The III Corps would support the right flank of the V Corps with an attack north toward the high ground above Dun sur Meuse. Liggett directed the I Corps to make a demonstration against the reinforced German positions on Bois de Bourgogne, but not to launch a general attack until the second day of the push. This would keep German forces pinned down without the trademark Pershing frontal attacks while still enabling the V Corps to outflank the strong German position.[20]

Liggett was appalled to learn that his direction that the V Corps be the main attack was disregarded and that the new "Group of Armies" general headquarters issued orders on 28 October that directed the I Corps "to drive north as the spearhead of the army, the other corps following in echelon movement." Liggett saw the folly of this plan to attack the enemy where he was the strongest, saying that "such an attack seemed doubtful of success." Liggett directed Colonel Marshall to write revised plans to Pershing's General Headquarters (GHQ) to correct the error. This revision emphasized Liggett's concept of operations that the main attack would be led by the V Corps in the center of the line, with III Corps in support to the east. I Corps would not make an attack until the

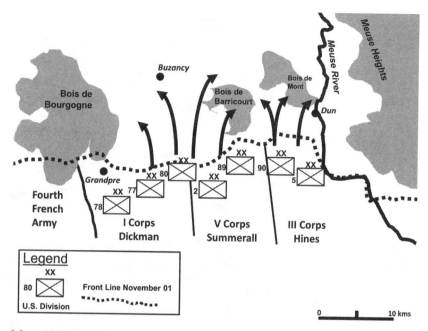

Map 18.2. U.S. First Army Plan of Attack, 1 November 1918. (Josiah Mastriano)

second day of the offensive unless it was required to advance to support the left flank of the V Corps. GHQ approved the revision.[21] However, the flurry of staff work between Liggett's First Army and Pershing's GHQ seems to have caused confusion for the V Corps commander, who wrote angrily that on the first day of the attack "First Corps on our left did not gain any ground. . . . To me, the inaction of the First Corps was unpardonable."[22] However, the confusion and attempt to change the plan was not an American error, but rather came from the French army group commander, General Andre Maistre.

As the Americans prepared for their final offensive, coordination was executed with the French Fourth Army to ensure a mutually supporting advance. The coordination of this multinational Franco-American attack fell under the purview of French general Paul Andre Maistre. Maistre had recently been appointed as the commander of the Group of Armies. This put Maistre in overall command of the French Fourth Army and the U.S. First Army. He "was charged with assuring coordination of the operations of the

General Paul Andre Maistre was appointed by Foch in late October 1918 as the commander of an army group that included Pershing's First Army and Gourmand's Fourth Army. Although the appointment complicated the command and control, it did improve coordination with French Fourth Army. (National Archives)

French troops on the right of his group and those of the American First Army."[23]

Maistre's appointment was a result of Pershing's lackluster performance in October, and thanks in large measure to the disdain that France's Premier Clemenceau had for him. He was appointed to this position on 21 October, and his introduction included "a general instruction" from Foch on what he envisioned for the French Fourth Army and American First Army. Thanks to Liggett's quick response, that misguided plan was disregarded.[24]

General Maistre was a seasoned and experienced officer who had an exemplary record in the French Army. He fought in the opening battles of 1914 and was a veteran of both Verdun and the Somme. He helped restore morale after the French Army mutiny of 1917 and played a key role in stabilizing the Italian Front after the German/Austro-Hungarian victory at Caporetto. His leadership was exceptional and untarnished throughout the war. Now, late in October, he found himself caught in a political nightmare of not just helping coordinate the Franco-American attack, but also

Pershing (left) had a preference for former 1st Division commanders, like General Pelot Summerall (right). As the V Corps commander during the final weeks of the Meuse-Argonne campaign, Summerall brilliantly planned an attack that shattered the German defenses in the area. (National Archives)

appeasing Clemenceau. This caused considerable concern for Pershing, who was now paying for his neglect of the strategic matters of command. Fortunately for Pershing, Foch did not agree to Clemenceau's demands to relieve Pershing, and further did not sufficiently empower Maistre to coopt either the French Fourth Army or the U.S. First Army.[25]

As Liggett and the U.S. First Army staff drafted detailed plans for the 1 November attack, Maistre made his rounds to visit the Americans. On 29 October, Liggett was returning from a visit to a subordinate corps headquarters and was appalled to see Maistre's entourage arriving at his headquarters. Instead of having his plans questioned by Maistre, Liggett "ducked on purpose" and suddenly found he needed to visit another of his subordinate headquarters. Pershing was left to answer Maistre's questions.[26]

Despite the small degree of consternation that Maistre's

appointment made for the Americans, his arrival was rather benefi-
cial. He insisted on better support and coordination from the French
Fourth Army to the west of the Americans. He knew what the
Fourth Army could do, and there would no longer be a gap between
the French and American advances, as in the case of the Lost Battalion. Liggett's ducking notwithstanding, Maistre made a tour of
the front and visited Summerall's V Corps headquarters prior to the
1 November offensive. Maistre doubted that the Americans would
succeed and asked Summerall if he thought that the attack would
achieve something. Maistre stated rather demurely that "the American losses were very heavy." Summerall replied with American
bravado that "if the French fought as hard as the Americans, their
losses would be heavy too."[27]

19

Heaven, Hell or Hoboken

The saying around here is; Heaven, Hell or Hoboken by
Christmas.
—Corporal Ellis James Stewart, Company G,
305th Ammunition Train, 80th Division

As the Americans made preparations to begin their final offensive
with the French Fourth Army, Gallwitz was summoned to Berlin to meet with Kaiser Wilhelm and the War Cabinet. The Kaiser
requested that the army group commanders confer with him on
acceptable terms for an armistice. This was a meeting that Gallwitz
could not miss since the fate of the empire and the future of Germany hung in the balance. However, his attendance there deprived
Army Group Gallwitz of its leader, relegating temporary command
of it to Marwitz. The military leadership discussed the possibility
of making preparations to withdraw the army to a line extending
from Antwerp to the Meuse River. This would reduce the length
of the line and use natural obstacles (rivers and canals) to structure the defense. However, Germany would lose important leverage
for the negotiations related to the armistice; thus the order was not
sent for execution.[1] As Germany's leaders deliberated on what to
do, intelligence reports indicated that the attack was imminent. One
American commented on the massive preparation being made for
the attack, writing: "During the last week in October . . . [we] were
told of the great drive that was to begin November 1. . . . Had nothing been said, it would have been easy to guess that preparation
was being made for something big. . . . Artillery was everywhere—it
seemed necessary to but shake a bush to find a cannon."[2]

With temporary command of the army group thrust upon him,
the departure of the Austro-Hungarian units in his sector, and an
enemy attack expected at any moment, more bad news arrived. Just
hours before the attack, Marwitz was notified that his adult daughter

Elisabeth had died. He was shocked by the news, which he wrote was completely unexpected. "She was the first loss in my blessed and happy family. . . . She was a strong person, a true Christian, so happy, so warm and so full of life." The news struck Marwitz deep in his heart, and the pain of her death shook him to his core.[3]

As Marwitz reeled from the loss of his daughter, French and American artillery erupted across his line. Long-range enemy artillery even crashed near the army group headquarters in Montmedy and destroyed part of the rail line. One shell exploded fifty meters behind the house where Marwitz slept, killing twenty and wounding considerably more. He wrote that the day went from bad to worse.[4] The Allied barrage was accurate and deadly against both the deep targets, such as Montmedy, and the German positions along the front line.

The main attack for the Americans was by the V Corps, in the center of the line and under the command of General Summerall. Summerall meticulously oversaw the artillery plan to ensure that "the entire corps front . . . [was] covered by a sheet of shell, shrapnel and bullets." He insisted on precision and that the artillery would fire upon every enemy position identified by his intelligence section. The plan for the preparatory barrage was to silence "every known enemy battery," pin down the infantry, and attack all enemy machine gun positions identified by military intelligence. Scores of air reconnaissance missions had been flown, with hundreds of photos taken to locate enemy positions. Those discovered were marked on maps and targeted for destruction.[5]

Summerall made his rounds to motivate the attacking units. His visit to the 2nd Division was not received well, but he did communicate his intent. Marine private Elton Mackin recorded Summerall's key points. In Mackin's recollection, Summerall emphasized the importance of maintaining the momentum to seize the Sedan rail line, saying, "Way up there north is a railroad. Go cut it for me. . . . Men, if you cut it soon enough, you may very well end this . . . war!" The 2nd Division was to advance through the Rainbow Division's sector, where the 42nd met their "Fredericksburg Stone Wall." The key to the German defense here was the village of Landres-et-Saint-Georges. Summerall admonished the men to stay clear of the village, saying, "Keep away from it because we're going to smother it with gas."[6]

Long-range artillery began firing against deep German targets at

10:00 P.M. on 31 October. Captain Charles Case, of the 89th Division's 314th Engineers, remarked that "A little Halloween joke would be played on Fritz starting at 10 o'clock . . . and we would have to get up early to help things along." Indeed, the engineers were given the daunting task of quickly repairing roads and bridges to ensure the forward movement of the division's supplies and additional troops. The lack of sufficient engineer support during the early days of the Meuse-Argonne Offensive played a part in the Americans' losing momentum early on. The engineers who pushed forward for this attack were determined to prevent a reoccurrence of that error.

For the Germans this was not Halloween, but Reformation Day. On 31 October 1517, Martin Luther, an Augustinian monk and professor of theology, was outraged at the abuses of the Pope, who authorized the selling of indulgences for assurance of heaven. This was part of an effort by Pope Leo X to raise money to build St. Peter's Basilica. Luther responded by writing and posting the Ninety-Five Theses on the Castle Church in Wittenberg. In it he rebuffed the papacy for this money-raising scheme and, citing scripture, affirmed that salvation was a free gift of God through Jesus Christ available to any who believed. It was a solemn occasion for the German Lutherans facing the Americans and French that cold and damp night. Some of the soldiers in the line recollected the importance of this day in history, and how it had forever changed the world 401 years earlier. This new attack beginning on Reformation Day 1918 likewise would forever change the Germany that they served and fought for.

The barrage commenced in incredible ferocity at 3:30 A.M. and included the corps machine guns laying down suppressive fires, mortars engaging known close enemy positions, and focused artillery against the key terrain. The high ground around Bois de Bourgogne was saturated with 41.4 tons of poisonous gas, eliminating nine of the twelve German artillery batteries there.[7] The timing was coordinated with the infantry, which began their attack at 5:30 A.M. The assaulting infantry units also had control over the creeping barrage, behind which they attacked. The barrage could be adjusted or halted based on the movement of the ground force. This corrected a deficiency of the AEF's previous barrages, which always outpaced the assaulting infantry troops. Every aspect of the barrage was so unique in the experience of the AEF that for years it was called "the Summerall Barrage."[8]

The fire support plan required artillery to maintain suppressive fire on the high ground to deny the Germans its use and soften it up for the American assault. Additionally, poisonous gas would be used extensively against all vital German positions, town intersections, and German formations. No artillery was in reserve. All of the guns were forward to support the attack. Finally, all of the machine guns in the corps were brought forward to engage the enemy.[9] In effect, Summerall was throwing everything but the kitchen sink at the Germans.

Per the plan, the I Corps, in the left of the U.S. First Army's zone, engaged the enemy with indirect fire but made no major push. They were to fix the Germans with a "demonstration" while the V Corps, as the main attack, advanced up the center of the Meuse Valley, with the III Corps in support to the east. Summerall said that the plan "was simply an application of the age-old principle of fire and movement."[10] The American soldiers occupying the left flank of the I Corps were from the 78th Division. Assembled at Fort Dix in 1917, the 78th included men from New Jersey, New York, and Delaware. Many of them were recent immigrants from Italy. Among them was Private Bernardo Rinaldo, whose English was only now becoming better thanks to help from the U.S. Army. Another immigrant from Italy was U.S. Army captain D. A. Colonna, who described the opening of the barrage: "The sky behind us was a flickering, gleaming red. The roar was as of myriad drums rolling almost in unison and the air overhead seemed almost alive with whistling visiting cards to the departing Jerry. The effect of this on the men who had heard little but shells coming in their direction was tremendous. The men walked about the hills whistling and singing and the erstwhile quiet forest was alive with conjectures as to what was happening when the winged death that was flying overhead arrived at its destination. After the firing had ceased there was extreme quietness."[11]

The U.S. 2nd Division and 89th Division were given the honor of leading the main attack for the First Army. The 2nd was dubbed "the Indian Head Division" for the image emblazoned on its patch and was one of the most celebrated American units in the AEF, rivaling even the revered Big Red One. It was a combat-experienced unit that performed superbly at the Third Battle of the Aisne, Chateau Thierry, St. Mihiel, and in the French Aise-Marne Offensive. However, its most celebrated engagement occurred at Belleau Wood. There, fighting side by side with the 3rd "Rock of the Marne"

Division, the 2nd performed superbly. As the French withdrew during the early part of the battle near Belleau Wood, the division was encouraged to fall back, with USMC captain Lloyd Williams reportedly retorting, "Retreat? Hell, we just got here." It was here too that the Marines of the 2nd Division purportedly were given the honorific title of "Teufel Hunden" (Devil Dogs) by their German adversaries. But legend has a way of distorting facts.

During Belleau Wood, the division was commanded by Major General Omar Bundy of the U.S. Army. Bundy left command later in the summer. During the Meuse-Argonne it was led by a superb Marine general, John Lejeune, and included one brigade of Marines (composed of the 5th and 6th Marine Regiments). Lejeune took command on 28 July 1918 and remained the division's commander through the end of the war. What seems to have been lost to history was that there was also a U.S. Army infantry brigade of equal size in the division, composed of the 9th and 23rd Regiments. Additionally, the division's artillery brigade and support units were all U.S. Army, meaning that only about a third of the 2nd Division was actually Marines. This notwithstanding, the unit was one of the best American divisions, and because of this Summerall designated it for the main effort in his V Corps attack, together with the likewise experienced (but lesser known) 89th Division. The 2nd Division had recently returned from supporting the French Fourth Army in the Aisne Valley (west of the Argonne), where it had valiantly captured Mont Blanc. Lejeune had employed innovative small unit tactics in that battle and arrived in the Meuse-Argonne with a stellar reputation.

As the barrage pummeled the Germans, the Marines and soldiers in the line made their final preparations for the "jump off." A common term used during World War One to denote an attack was to say, "Going over the top." This was a legacy phrase from the years of trench warfare, when soldiers literally had to climb up and out of their trenches to attack. But an officer in the 89th Division correctly said, "We just 'stepped off' as were not in trenches and had no 'top' to 'go over.'"[12] As Summerall warned the men, the village of Landres-et-Saint-Georges was shrouded in fire, smoke, and poisonous gas. Private Mackin wrote that it was covered in a "greenish-yellow, shot with coils of writhing black, with now and then a livid flame to light it all."[13]

Captain Charles Dienst of the 89th Division's 353rd Regiment

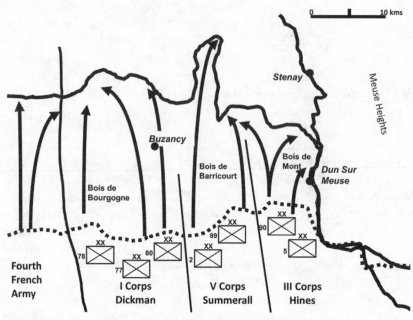

Map 19.1. Ground Gained, 1–3 November 1918. (Josiah Mastriano)

wrote, "The hours waiting for the big show to begin were nerve-racking. . . . At 3:30 o'clock in the morning of November 1st, guns of every caliber pounded away; mingled with the din and roar was the rattle and clatter of countless machine guns. The enemy was prompt with his counter artillery. There we lay listening to the shells bursting all about us in the woods."[14] As the artillerymen on both sides exchanged rounds, Dienst saw a German shell explode at the entrance of the "funk hole" used by the regimental intelligence staff. Dienst and a Lieutenant Carl Eades ran to the destroyed position expecting to find mangled bodies. Eades yelled into the black, smoky hole, "Anybody hurt." Much to their surprise the reply was "No." A candle was lit to investigate. Although all of the soldiers' packs were destroyed and shrapnel had shredded the interior of the position, the only injury was an abrasion on one soldier's chin. The survivors agreed that they came "pretty close to heaven."[15]

Nearby, the German counterbarrage slammed into the 89th Division's 314th Engineers. One of the wounded was Private Frank Victoriana from New Orleans, Louisiana, who was hit on the hip by a fragment from an exploding artillery shell and knocked to the ground. The unit's senior medical officer, Major Cassidy, rushed to his side. While rendering first aid, "soon almost the whole side of his body was swollen and of a much darker hue than 'Vic's' normal complexion." Victoriana was ordered off the battlefield to the rear for better treatment. But he "didn't want to miss any of the fun . . . and wouldn't go." Major Cassidy commended him in an official memorandum for commitment and dedication to duty. Victoriana became a legend in the unit as "the only instance of a man in our company receiving a citation for having disobeyed the lawful orders of his superior."[16]

The German 88th Division, one of the units opposing the Americans that morning, had excellent intelligence reporting on the American 89th Division. Ironically, the German 88th had fought against these same Americans at St. Mihiel in September. The German report said, "The division is again opposite the 89th American Division. . . . The division is as at that time still known as a good American Shock Division, which undertakes many strong patrol movements. . . . Its objective is the line from Buzancy Heights southwest of Stenay."[17]

As the 89th Division's 353rd Infantry Regiment commenced its attack, it immediately ran into a series of German machine guns. Although the men advanced on the heels of the rolling barrage, the Germans manned their weapons in time to engage the Americans. The 353rd's leading battalion was immediately engaged by four German machine guns as it crossed an open area below the Bois de Bantheville. The initial blast of fire killed one of the company commanders and a group of soldiers. The unit was stalled until First Lieutenant Harold Arthur Furlong seized the initiative. Upon identifying the location of the German machine guns on his flank, Lieutenant Furlong fearlessly charged across the open space and worked his way behind the German line. Using his rifle, Furlong picked off the German gunners and forced the supporting riflemen to surrender. He returned to the American lines with twenty prisoners, and the advance was resumed. For this action Furlong was awarded the Medal of Honor.[18]

As the Americans advanced, fifteen American-operated Renault tanks swept up the road to support the soldiers and Marines of the U.S. 2nd Division. Among the tanks moving into action was one driven by Sergeant Paul Postal, who had a cat with him. A few weeks before, Sergeant Postal was at the repair depot at Varennes and befriended a stray calico. The cat was quickly adopted as the

The advance of the U.S. 353rd Regiment was held up until Lieutenant Arthur Furlong outflanked the German unit defending the area. (U.S. Army Heritage and Education Center, Carlisle, Pennsylvania)

unit's mascot and named Mustard. It went into action with Sergeant Postal on 1 November. At the same time, the 89th Division "stepped off" to the east of the 2nd. The 89th's 177th Brigade spearheaded the attack, with the 354th Infantry Regiment on the eastern flank of the 2nd Division and the 353rd Infantry Regiment farther east along the right flank of the V Corps boundary alongside the 90th Division.

The key terrain that the 89th had to seize was the Bois de Barricourt, which was a wooded elevation several kilometers north of the jump-off line. American artillery tore into the German units there, but survivors remained, ready to defend the ridge. If the Bois de Barricourt fell, the German center in the Meuse Valley would be compromised. Both the 353rd Regiment and the 354th advanced closely behind the rolling barrage preceding the attack. This gave the Germans little time to recover and brace themselves for the

Sergeant Paul Postal of the 321st Tank Company is pictured here with the unit's mascot, Mustard the cat. Mustard was found by Postal in Varennes and immediately adopted. The 321st Tank Company supported attacks across the Meuse front, including the 1 November offensive. (U.S. Army Heritage and Education Center, Carlisle, Pennsylvania)

assault. However, several machine gun crews of the German 88th Division managed to get their weapons into action, cutting into the advancing American infantry formations. Using fire and maneuver, the Americans quickly eliminated these pockets of resistance.[19]

The 353rd Regiment's commander, Colonel James Reeves, expertly led the men forward from a position where he could provide

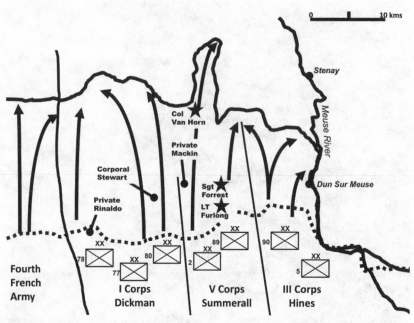

Map 19.2. Key Events, 1–3 November 1918. (Josiah Mastriano)

better command and control. This, unlike Pershing's demand that all leaders go to the front, where command and control was lost, gave him the ability to leapfrog his three battalions forward. As objectives were secured, the attacking battalion would hold the key terrain while a follow-on unit bounded through them to assault the next objective. This worked brilliantly, with the regiment advancing beyond its three prescribed objectives for the day and advancing nearly eight kilometers into German lines.[20]

Colonel Reeves applied a diamond formation for his assault troops, which included placing Chauchat light machine guns on each flank. When the diamond formation encountered resistance, the flanking elements with the Chauchats moved "forward and outward to encircle" the enemy. In addition, 37mm guns and Stokes mortars operated as a supporting heavy weapons platoon for each diamond assault formation, staying about "40 paces" behind and poised to eliminate German machine gun positions. Of all the weapons at the Doughboys' disposal, the rifle-fired grenades proved the most useful.[21] The Americans had at last come of age.

The other 89th Division unit spearheading the attack was the

354th Infantry Regiment, and its experience was similar to that of the 353rd. As the assault units advanced, they too were warmly greeted by German machine guns. The men maneuvered to eliminate the German positions, but this was no easy operation, as the Germans still had fight in them. For instance, resistance was so fierce in some areas that Company B of the 354th suffered eighty casualties in the first hour of the advance. Every officer in this company was a casualty, and more than half of the men.[22]

Thus was the case for Company D of the 354th, which followed closely behind the rolling barrage north up the Meuse Valley. The unit's company commander, Captain Kelly, thought it would boost confidence if the officers advanced with a "cigar clinched in [their] teeth." However, as the unit approached the French village of Remonville from the southeast, six machine guns tore into the formation, halting the advance. This is when Sergeant Arthur J. Forrest rose to the occasion.[23] Hailing from Hannibal, Missouri, Sergeant Forrest was but twenty-three years old, 140 pounds in uniform, and barely five feet, six inches tall. He was known as a humble and quiet soldier and after the war often was compared to Sergeant York. Forrest was a professional baseball player and a well-known sportsman of the time.[24] When the United States entered the war in 1917, he set aside professional baseball and volunteered to join the army.[25]

When the German machine guns stopped his company's advance, Forrest knew he had to do something. Captain Kelly said, "We were just a little southeast of Remonville in the Meuse-Argonne Offensive" when his unit was stopped by the German machine guns. All the men, including Sergeant Forrest, "flopped" to the ground. Forrest crawled toward the enemy position until they saw him and began to fire in his direction. "The bullets were whizzing by me like dust in a windstorm. I was just so frightened that I didn't know what to do, so I ran as fast as I could." That is, he ran directly toward the enemy, tossing two grenades into the machine gun position, and then clubbed a German survivor with the butt of his rifle. Four Germans charged him, and Forrest fought two of them off with his bayonet. The other two he shot with his rifle. Seeing another group of Germans about to charge him, Forrest threw his rifle aside and fired his pistol into the throng, driving the enemy "into holes like frightened rats." The Germans had retreated into a small network of tunnels. Forrest coaxed the Germans out, capturing six and silencing six enemy machine guns.[26] The quiet man from

Hannibal, Missouri, was awarded the Medal of Honor for this feat, which states: "When the advance of his company was stopped by bursts of fire from a nest of 6 enemy machine guns, without being discovered, he worked his way single-handed to a point within 50 yards of the machine gun nest. Charging, single-handed, he drove out the enemy in disorder, thereby protecting the advance platoon from annihilating fire, and permitting the resumption of the advance of his company."[27]

Thanks to this action, and many other acts of heroism, the 354th advanced some eight kilometers (five miles) into the German lines, driving them from the heights in the Meuse Valley and unhinging their defensive capability. In like manner, the soldiers and Marines of the 2nd Division advanced brilliantly against the German lines. The men followed closely behind the barrage, quickly overrunning the forward German strongholds. The supporting column of fifteen tanks assisted the 2nd Division in eliminating the German strong points along and north of the Landres-et-Saint-Georges Road.[28] These were the same enemy positions that had prevented the 82nd and 42nd Divisions from making progress in October. As the history of the 5th Marines recorded, "throughout the day, resistance remained light and each of the 5th's battalions had a . . . successful advance."[29] The 5th Marines, together with the 6th Marine Regiment, consolidated their gains and would spend 2 November bringing up the U.S. Army brigade to take the lead of the attack.[30] During this time, Marine private Elton Mackin recollected a comical incident:

A hidden shell hole lurked beneath the slime of mud near where we rested. The plodding men . . . stumbled into it from time to time and gave us fun. One lanky fellow stepped squarely in the middle of it and landed on the surface with a flop, just saving his face from being ducked by reaching desperately, stiff armed, beneath the surface. We watched, amused, waiting to hear him curse. He came up, standing thigh deep in the hole and glanced around to note his audience, threw back his head and roared with laughter. Men who hadn't laughed for days laughed with him. The laughter spread. It rolled across the rain soaked woods. . . . Men laughed 'til tears rolled down . . . joyously. What a strange spectacle. A little band of men. They knew the fellowship of mud, blood and rain. They knew the fellowship of laughter miles from home.

The advance of the U.S. 2nd Division was enabled by several factors. The chief reason for the quick breakout was that Germany's General von Marwitz decided to take risks here so as to better defend the high ground east and west of the position. He placed the 52nd Division here, which was considerably weakened from the heavy casualties it had suffered in September and early to mid-October fighting the Americans around Exermont. Exacerbating the situation for the German 52nd Division was the decision by the American V Corps commander, General Summerall, to fire tons of deadly gas into its ranks before the attack. This generated at least three hundred casualties in the 52nd. The next day, Gallwitz read the reports of what happened to the 52nd Division and noted, "Almost one whole battalion of the 52nd Division made the acquaintance of 'Edison Gas' a new combination resembling our 'Yellow Cross' Gas."[31] As the 52nd reeled from the chemical assault, the Americans attacked, capturing one thousand of the survivors. The German 52nd Division had barely two hundred men remaining by the end of the day and was deemed combat ineffective.[32] The Americans had a path open in the center of the German line.

The German response was uncharacteristically muted. Although the flanking divisions (the 240th and 15th Bavarian in the west and the 28th, 107th, and 5th Bavarian in the east) held, the center was fractured. The 52nd and 88th Divisions were shattered and all but combat ineffective. Forces had to be brought forward to stem the American breakout in the center. To do this, the Germans needed time. When the Americans had attacked in the Meuse Valley five weeks earlier, their inexperience and tepid efforts to exploit opportunities gave the Germans time to respond. However, now the American army showed no signs of slowing. The only concerted counterattack that the Germans offered late on 1 November was led by the 31st Division's 166th Regiment. Composed largely of ethnic French living in German-occupied Alsace-Lorraine, the 166th's attack blunted the progress of the American I Corps in the west, but it did not have enough forces to likewise attack into the flank of the American penetration in the center of the line.

General Marwitz was dismayed at what the Americans had achieved on 1 November. He wrote in his diary: "November 1st is a worse day. The supremacy of America was just too massive. The artillery fire destroyed our front line so much that it no longer existed. Because of this, the Americans easily penetrated our lines and even are advancing past those places where our men are still resisting. We were pushed back significantly across broad front and suffering very high losses that include much of our artillery. The Americans have the initiative in this new large attack."[33] Marwitz ordered that his men fall back to the planned Freya Stellung position. Although little work had been done on this final defensive line, the position was surveyed to leverage defensible terrain, to hold against the American offensive. Using wooded ridges, hills, and choke points, Freya would give Marwitz's army an interim position to blunt the American offensive. If this were not possible, then the army must fall back to the east bank of Meuse River.[34]

Marwitz contacted the army group commander, Gallwitz, late on 1 November to discuss the precarious situation. Since the American artillery had severed most of the communication lines, neither Marwitz nor Gallwitz had a clear picture of just how bad things were in the Meuse region. Gallwitz said, "I agreed with General von der Marwitz to retire his line to the Freya Position and bring back to the west bank by motor trucks the 236th Division, which had been only recently moved to the east bank of the Meuse for a short respite."[35]

The movement would commence the next day. Gallwitz wrote: "The picture that presented itself at 5 p.m. was not rosy. The break in the center deepened to 4 kilometers, inasmuch as the 15th Bavarian Division too was forced to give in, with only the two divisions on the outer wings holding their ground. The two reserve divisions . . . proved to have insufficient fighting value to bring a change in the situation."[36]

The Americans had advanced over eight kilometers into the center of the line. This meant that the Freya Line was already compromised. The Freya extended from Dun sur Meuse on the river, west to the Bois de Barricourt (Barricourt Heights), and then farther west toward Buzancy. The Americans were in possession of the Barricourt Heights and in fact were four kilometers beyond this vital high ground. The situation was becoming desperate. Once Gallwitz discovered this, he conferred with Army Group Crown Prince to his west to determine their situation and learned that the French Fourth Army under Gouraud had likewise dealt a vicious blow to the German forces there. Both Army Group Crown Prince and Army Group Gallwitz decided to make a limited withdrawal to safeguard any units threatened with encirclement. Gallwitz was concerned about the outcome of the day's events and confided, "undoubtedly, we had suffered a defeat!"[37]

For the German Fifth Army, this meant immediately withdrawing its divisions on the left and right flanks. Orders were given to the men to immediately pull back. The units had to be out of the zone of fighting before the anticipated resumption of the American attack, which they determined could begin as early as 4:00 A.M. with the preparatory artillery barrage. Moving a division in contact in such a short period of time is usually impossible, but as life or death hung in the balance, the withdrawing units largely made it out of the line before the American I and III Corps commenced their early morning attack on 2 November. The German units in the center, facing the dauntless 2nd and 89th Divisions (of the U.S. V Corps) had to remain to prevent a complete collapse of the line.[38]

The U.S. First Army commander, recently promoted Lieutenant General Hunter Liggett, was elated by the success of his men. Reports indicated that 3,602 Germans were captured, including 151 officers.[39] This was a promising start to the new offensive. An anxious General Pershing spent the greater part of the day monitoring the offensive at Liggett's headquarters. To his credit, he did not interfere in Liggett's operation.[40]

For the First Army to succeed, it had to maintain the momentum. The I Corps, on the western part of the army line, would attack in earnest on 2 November. Of the three divisions in the I Corps, only the 80th advanced in support of the left flank of the V Corps' 2nd Division. The 80th swept north with an eye toward threatening the flank of the German defenses in Bois de Bourgogne. There was considerable excitement in the ranks that this push would at last break the German grip in the Meuse Region. Corporal Ellis James Stewart, from Mercer County, Pennsylvania, said, "The saying around here is; Heaven, Hell or Hoboken [New Jersey] by Christmas." Hoboken was the major port of entry back to the United States for soldiers in France. One of Ellis Stewart's hometown friends, Tom Urmson, claimed that "he can 'lick' several Germans." However, before the Meuse-Argonne kicked off, Urmson suffered appendicitis and did not return to duty until two weeks after the end of the war.[41] Corporal Stewart wrote after the war about Tom, "I think he [Tom Urmson] was lucky. The 80th Div Doughboys sure were in the fight."[42]

The 78th and 77th U.S. Divisions only achieved minor gains, per the plan from Liggett not to needlessly waste American lives attacking frontally against strong German positions. Now the V Corps was poised to strike into the rear of the German forces facing the I Corps and threaten them with encirclement.[43] To the east, the U.S. III Corps had an excellent day in its advance along the west bank of the Meuse River. The U.S. 90th Division kept up with the brilliant advance of the 89th Division and cleared the Germans from the eastern portion of the key terrain around Bois de Barricourt, while the 5th Division cleared the zone of Germans up to the Meuse River.[44]

The advance continued on 2 November. Hunter Liggett visited the I Corps headquarters early in the morning only to find that the commander, Major General Joseph Dickman, and his staff "depressed at their failure to get in on the Big Parade of the day before. I told Dickman his opportunity to catch up with the procession would come that day."[45] But this was part of the plan. The V Corps had outflanked the Germans the day before and forced them to give up the key terrain without a fight. This was a far different army than the one that had entered the fight five weeks before.

When the I Corps kicked off its attack on 2 November at 5:30 A.M., there was no resistance from the German side of the line. Exactly as Liggett predicted, Marwitz had ordered the German divisions opposing the I Corps to fall back. The I Corps troops found the hills and forest near the front vacant. Finding no Germans in the area, Dickman ordered his units forward with all vigor and even loaded part of his infantry onto trucks to catch up with the withdrawing German units. By the end of the day, the I Corps' 78th and 77th Divisions had caught up with the rear guard of the German Army and were nearly as far forward as the V Corps. The 80th Division held its position from the day before, waiting for the rest of the corps to come up on its left flank. Watching this rare opportunity slip away, Liggett longed for the "finely trained cavalry division at San Antonio, which transport difficulties had kept in Texas chafing at the bit. . . . With American Cavalry, I believe I could have captured all of the enemy on the front of First Corps."[46]

The 80th Division's ammunition train took advantage of the pause to push supplies in motor vehicles and horse-drawn caissons to the troops. Corporal Ellis Stewart reflected on their thankless task, saying, "The A.T. [ammunition train] is to go ahead and deliver the goods no matter how much the roads and towns are being shelled. The worst thing about it is you can't shoot back."[47]

For the V Corps, conflicting orders and changing objectives prevented the 2nd Division from making any appreciable gains. The 89th, however, launched a daring attack several kilometers deep into German-held territory, seizing the village of Tailly. The 89th now had the deepest penetration into the German lines. Meanwhile, the III Corps continued its wheeling movement to the northeast to clear the Germans from the west bank of the Meuse. In this operation, both the 90th and 5th Divisions performed brilliantly.

The U.S. First Army resumed the offensive in earnest on 3 November. Meanwhile, the German High Command approved the plan to pull the German Fifth Army behind the Meuse River.[48] Great care had to be taken in conducting this retrograde operation. It was imperative that the withdrawing forces left behind strong rear guard units to prevent the Americans from breaking through. While the Germans prepared for this complicated movement, the Americans pushed on relentlessly to prevent their escape. When the Americans kicked off the attack on the morning of 3 November, Captain Colonna of the U.S. 78th Division was amazed to see two hundred American airplanes flying in support overhead.[49] All three of I Corps' divisions made excellent progress, advancing some ten kilometers that day. However, the going was not so smooth in the V Corps sector. Marwitz had deployed the recently arrived 41st Division into the center of the sector to prevent the Americans from exploiting the gap there. In addition to this, the German 236th Division also arrived to stave off an American breakthrough in the center of the Meuse Valley. However, the 236th was without its machine guns. The trucks carrying these were stuck in mud farther back.[50]

By 2 November, the Marine brigade of the 2nd Division was in reserve. The division's U.S. Army brigade, composed of the 9th and 23rd Infantry Regiments, was given the daunting task of leading the pursuit of the German Army on 3 November. The two regiments launched a series of attacks during the morning and afternoon that gained little ground and at the cost of many casualties. The two regiments, along with the 89th Division to its right, were stopped by dogged German resistance. The Doughboys of the 2nd Division could not advance beyond Nouart due to the German domination

The 2nd Infantry Division, composed of both soldiers and Marines, was one of the best divisions in the AEF. This photograph is of two of its commanders. To the left is U.S. Army general Omar Bundy, who commanded the division for most of the war, and to his right is Marine general John Lejeune, who commanded the 2nd beginning 28 July 1918. (U.S. Army Heritage and Education Center, Carlisle, Pennsylvania)

of the high ground above Belval and the Foret de Dieulet. The division commander, Major General Lejeune, issued orders for the soldiers to not only clear Belval (three kilometers north), but also to force the Germans from the Foret de Dieulet. To do this, the 9th and 23rd Regiments would have to advance nearly eight kilometers in the face of stalwart German defenses.[51]

The 9th Infantry Regiment commander, Colonel Robert O. Van Horn, came up with a brilliant and audacious plan to accomplish the mission. Colonel Van Horn was a Signal Corps officer by trade and had a colorful career. In 1897, after he failed to secure an appointment to West Point, he left the University of Michigan and enlisted in the U.S. Army as a private. His view was that through hard work and sacrifice he would eventually earn a commission as an officer. Van Horn was a natural in army life, and just as he predicted, within two years he was given a commission as a lieutenant. He fought in Cuba during the Spanish-American War and later deployed to the Philippines to fight in the counterinsurgency against Muslim separatists in 1903–1904. Van Horn proved adaptable and resilient, and because of this he was appointed a military governor in the Moro Province. With such a record, he was selected in 1907–1908 to serve as the military aide to President Theodore Roosevelt. Van Horn loved technology and innovation and soon was serving in the fledgling U.S. Army Air Service.[52]

However, Van Horn's place was with the men in the field and an assignment with the 2nd Infantry Division. He had been in command of the 9th Infantry Regiment for one day. However, this was not the first time he had faced a determined adversary in a complex environment. Relying on his experience in the Philippines, Van Horn came up with a scheme that took considerable risk but, if successful, would break the German defensive line.[53] His plan was to advance during hours of darkness. The marshy nature of the terrain, in the end, called for the 9th and 23rd Regiments to move in column up a single road that flowed north out of Nouart, through Belval, and then across the Foret de Dieulet on to Beaumont, the final objective for this mission. The brigade commander, Colonel James Rhea, readily approved the plan and expanded it to include more forces. Van Horn's 9th Regiment would lead the advance, followed by the 23rd Regiment. Behind them, the 2nd Battalion's 5th Marines would serve as the reserves of this brigade-level assault. Van Horn's lead battalion included a battery of 75mm guns from the 15th Artillery.[54]

The intent was not to draw any attention to this column, but rather to advance through the German lines using deception and stealth. If the column was compromised, flankers would sweep against the opposition and quickly overcome them. Van Horn placed at the head of the formation and along the flanks to the east and west soldiers who were fluent in German. These linguists would pretend to be German officers and respond to any challenges and then lure the German sentries out of their positions.[55] By the time the Germans realized that they had been deceived, they would be captured. Van Horn's audacious plan was helped by a heavy pouring rain that masked and covered his men's movements. The miserable weather also drove the Germans into their holes or shelters. The plan worked perfectly.[56] Van Horn had used a less ambitious version of this approach the night before with some effect.[57]

The brigade commander, Colonel Rhea, joined the fray, putting Van Horn at the vanguard. Van Horn's men advanced through and behind the German lines, covering some seven kilometers. They maneuvered past brightly lit German-occupied farmhouses, bypassed another with a general's car parked near it, and even crept past a battery of German artillery in action. This artillery unit was not assaulted because the objective was the ground north of the woods, and the battery would have to retreat on the only road in the area, the one now owned by the Americans. The rainy night served them well, making the night darker than usual.[58]

The men were ordered to march up the road as silently as possible. Commands were passed by a whisper, and cigarettes were forbidden. Only should action break out would weapons be used. The route of the advance was not an easy one. The near daily rain had turned the open areas into fields of mud, and the usually unimpressive streams were overflowing. Because of this, the brigade-size force of approximately four thousand men moved in a column of two up the road. The initial plan was for a shallow penetration that would stop north of Belval at the La Forge farm. However, Lejeune and Rhea decided to advance as far as Beaumont if possible. Securing the high ground near Beaumont would put the Americans well behind the Germans and unhinge their defensive line. Once there, the 9th and 23rd Regiments were to create a defensive perimeter, supported by the artillery battery and using the 5th Marine Regiment's 2nd Battalion as a reserve.[59]

Just as darkness settled in, the dauntless band began their advance. The tricky part was to quickly get through the German front line, where the enemy would surely be most vigilant. After that, the unit needed to pass through the village of Belval as quietly as possible, then on to Beaumont. The unit's German speakers advanced in front of the formation on the road and well in advance of the flanking units in the fields to the left and right. Occasionally a vigilant German machine gun opened fire on the Americans, which was quickly subdued by the flanking units. Most of the initial advance was uneventful, with the American German speakers confidently ordering any German sentinels encountered into the formation, which they dutifully obeyed, thereby capturing them without firing a shot. The Americans quickly advanced over the front and even through Belval without causing a general alarm by the Germans.

Thankfully, Van Horn had detailed maps of the area, as the route was difficult to follow, especially in the darkness. Up and down ridges, through forests, across fields, and onward they progressed. Once past Belval and the Bois de Belval (the forested ridgeline north of the village) the initiative was completely with the Americans as no German hearing the throng moving up the road so confidently would assume that this was a brigade of enemy troops. In the clearing after the Bois de Belval, the Americans seized the La Forge farm. A German detachment was using the farm to stay dry and was captured without incident. However, on the other side of the farm, a few hundred yards to the north, a German battalion was preparing defensive positions and opened fire. The American artillery battery had wisely paused at the La Forge farm while scouts went ahead. When firing commenced, the battery opened fire, and the lead battalion of infantry quickly scattered the German unit. Not knowing if the Germans would raise a general alarm, Van Horn conferred with Colonel Rhea and they decided to take the risk and continue on to Beaumont.

At 11:30 P.M., Van Horn's group arrived below the La Tuilerie farm. The first floor of the stone farmhouse was brightly lit, meaning that the Germans encountered earlier had failed to raise the alarm. Van Horn directed that the lead battalion seize the house. Once in position, the Americans kicked in the doors and captured most of the headquarters elements and officers of a German battalion, who were caught meticulously poring over maps and making plans for the next day's fight. One participant wrote, "This sort of warfare had a tang of New World daring that the disciples of von Clausewitz and Ludendorff could not comprehend." Colonel Rhea and Van Horn decided that this was far enough. Around midnight, Colonel Rhea decided to use the captured farm as the unit's headquarters and advance a battalion two hundred yards north to the La Petit Foret farm. The supporting Marine brigade deployed two hundred yards east of the La Tuilerie farm, while the 23rd Regiment covered the western and southern approaches. In all, 160 Germans were captured in this amazing operation.[60]

As the Marine brigade moved forward on the morning of 4 November to catch up with the army brigade, Van Horn began to advance his men on to Beaumont, but they were stopped by a large formation of German forces defending south of the town. This notwithstanding, the audacious night attack unhinged the German plan to blunt an American advance up the center of the Meuse Valley. This brilliant maneuver was followed by the rapid advance of the American 89th Division to the right of Van Horn's men. There was now no possibility of stopping the Americans south of the Meuse River.

Marwitz's forces had to withdraw as quickly as possible to the Meuse River to try to salvage the now overcome Fifth Army. This break in the line convinced Marwitz that there was now no possibility for the German Army to blunt the American advance. He visited the Army Group commander in person and explained to Gallwitz the dire situation, impressing upon him the need for the war to end before the army collapsed.[61] As they discussed the gravity of the situation, American artillery smashed into Gallwitz's headquarters, and a massive American air assault of 145 aircraft (100 pursuit and 45 bombers) bombed and strafed his men. It was like a scene out of a Hollywood movie. German aircraft tried to break up the attack but were driven back with heavy losses.[62]

Finally, on 4 November, Hindenburg issued orders calling for the withdrawal of the Fifth Army and the neighboring Third Army to the west across the Meuse. This order was three days too late and came at a great loss in men and material. Meanwhile, the Americans pressed the attack, of which Marwitz wrote, "The Americans' numerical superiority drives our line back. I have too few forces to plug the holes in my line. And now things with the Kaiser are becoming curious. The Imperial German government no longer exists and the princes need a scapegoat and shall require his head."[63]

For his leadership and daring, Van Horn was awarded the Distinguished Service Cross. The citation of his award captured the importance of this event: "Colonel Van Horn led his regiment of the 9th Infantry, 2d Division, against the enemy positions in the edge of the Bois de Belval. The regiment passed through the woods and the enemy lines and took up a position 6 kilometers in rear of the enemy, capturing many prisoners and much war material. . . . The effect of night penetration of the enemy lines caused the enemy on the right and left of the 2d Division sector to fall back to the east bank of the Meuse River."[64] As is the case in many battles and campaigns, small actions have strategic effects.

20

Mad Dash to Sedan

What momentous events had taken place . . . the Germans had
lost the initiative and had been driven steadily backward from
their . . . positions until now they faced certain defeat.
—General Pershing

As the Americans continued their pursuit of the Germans up the
Meuse Valley, Liggett ordered the III Corps to begin crossing the
Meuse River on the east flank of the advance. On 2 November,
the 5th "Red Diamond" Infantry Division received orders to push
patrols across the Meuse and prepare to execute river crossing
operations. This order was a result of reports from the U.S. Army
Air Service that the Germans east of the Meuse were withdrawing. The 88th Aviation Squadron reported, "The Boche are in full
retreat east of the Meuse. All the northbound roads are packed with
troops, artillery and trucks."[1] Eddie Rickenbacker, commander of
the 94th "Hat in the Ring" Aero Squadron, also reported, "All the
way up the Meuse as far as Stenay I found the same mad rush for
the rear. Every road was filled with retreating Heinies."[2] Liggett
intended to interdict this retreat by a river assault crossing at the
Meuse and then a vigorous advance toward Montmedy to prevent the German escape. The plan was to have the 5th Division
("Red Diamonds") cross near Brieulles and then the 90th Division
cross to the north of it. Crossing the river here would be no easy
endeavor.[3] The 5th's 10th Brigade would cross near Brieulles, and
its 9th Brigade would follow shortly thereafter with a crossing
near Clery le Petit.

The terrain, reinforced with German machine gun nests, posed
the biggest dilemma. The Meuse River was swollen from the incessant rains and proved a daunting obstacle to navigate when combined with the marshy ground that covered the western bank. In
addition to this, the river had a canal beyond its eastern shore,

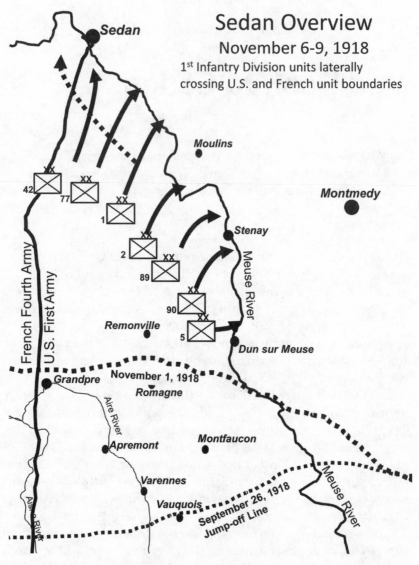

Map 20.1. Sedan Overview, 6–9 November 1918. (Josiah Mastriano)

making two water obstacles for the Americans to cross. Although the Meuse River was about five feet deep and not particularly rapid in movement, the canal had steep embankments, was deep, and had a strong current. Jutting up on the eastern side of the river and canal were the Meuse Heights, a series of hills and woods that dominated the area. This meant that any movement along the river below would be under the watchful eyes of the Germans.[4]

Using the cover of darkness, elements of the 7th Engineers laid a pontoon footbridge across the Meuse River south of Brieulles. The division's engineers relied on the expertise of Lieutenant Alfred Jacquin. Jacquin was a French engineer attached as a liaison officer to the Americans. Most of the soldiers in the division recognized him by his steel blue uniform and thick black beard. He was drawn to the sound of the guns and could be found involved in every battle. His heroism was so remarkable that the Americans awarded him the Distinguished Service Cross for "his fearless reconnaissance under heavy fire."[5]

Jacquin surveyed the ground to ascertain where the Americans could cross. The heavy rains limited their options, for in some areas there were marshy swamps several hundred meters wide. However, he found two locations near Brieulles and the engineers went to work. The darkness and heavy rain masked the work from German detection. During the construction, soldiers were rowed across to the far bank of the river (but not across the canal). Construction was completed on the pontoon footbridge by dawn on 3 November, and engineers with infantry support rushed across to begin work on crossing the canal. However, the Germans on the hills above saw this and unleashed a wall of fire from a group of machine guns defending the area. Dozens of soldiers were caught in the wide flat area between the river and canal. The only shelter was behind the canal embankment, which was just below the German machine guns. Although the embankment provided protection, the men were trapped and instantly killed if they exposed themselves from its relative safety. The order issued to the Germans here was, "The enemy's crossing of the Meuse is to be prevented absolutely."[6]

During the night of 3 November, two more footbridges were constructed near a destroyed bridge, and soldiers rushed across in the early morning darkness, only to be thrown back by a storm of lead. American artillery, mortars, and rifle grenades were fired by the thousands into the German machine gun emplacements without any effect. Dozens of men were still trapped behind the canal's embankment again on the 4th of November. Finally, as the sun set, a battalion of soldiers stormed across the shattered footbridges or waded across on the ruins of the destroyed bridge and secured the first American foothold across the Meuse River and canal at a

Captain Edward Allworth was awarded the Medal of Honor for heroically leading his men across the Meuse River in the face of German resistance in the waning days of the war. (U.S. Army Heritage and Education Center, Carlisle, Pennsylvania)

cost of twenty killed in action and another forty-eight wounded. The Americans cleared nine German machine guns and two minenwerfers, and captured twenty-one of the enemy.[7] They then pressed the attack and advanced two kilometers as more troops arrived to exploit this penetration. The 10th Brigade was poised to strike into the enemy flank.

Meanwhile, the 9th Brigade crossing near Clery le Petit was held up and driven back by the Germans. The unit's engineers managed to build a footbridge across the Meuse and the canal. However, German artillery and gunners put up a wall of lead that blunted progress of the lead company of the 60th Regiment endeavoring to cross to the eastern shore. Trapped on the narrow strip of land between the river and canal was company commander Captain Edward Allworth.

Hailing from Battle Ground, Washington, Allworth had studied agriculture, graduating from college in 1916. Less than a year later, he joined tens of thousands of other young men in volunteering for military service when the United States entered the war in April 1917. Now, trapped between the Meuse River and the Meuse Canal, Washington seemed like a different world altogether. Like the other men on the strip on land, he sought cover behind the canal embankment. Scanning the area, Allworth saw half of his company pinned down on the west side of the river, a group with him trapped between the river and canal, and a small portion of his men on the east bank, fearlessly advancing up the slope to assault the German machine gun positions. Upon seeing this, Allworth leapt into action.

Allworth fearlessly mounted the embankment behind which he and his men had sought safety. Standing in the open and fully exposed to the enemy, he called for the men to follow him across the canal. With German machine gun bullets spraying around him, Allworth jumped into the canal and swam across to the east bank. Seeing this, the remainder of the men followed his lead and likewise swam across the canal to join him and the lead elements of the company in the assault against the enemy machine guns. Allworth led the men forward, clearing a series of German machine gun nests, capturing one hundred prisoners, and advancing the unit a kilometer deep into the enemy lines. Thanks to his personal bravery and initiative, Allworth saved the unit's bridgehead and dislodged the enemy defenses in the area. For this action he was awarded the Medal of Honor.[8]

The 5th Division continued its northeasterly advance up and across the Meuse Heights in the face of determined German rearguard actions. The 90th Division attacked across the Meuse on 9 November in support of the 5th's left flank.[9] Meanwhile, the I Corps, far to the west, continued its pursuit of the withdrawing German Fifth Army. The 42nd Division was back in action late on 4 November and occupied the westernmost part of the U.S. First Army. The 42nd advanced brilliantly northward toward the Meuse River and the highly coveted city of Sedan. Major General Charles Dudley Rhodes had successfully commanded the division since December 1917. However, in early November Rhodes was injured in an airplane crash and delegated temporary command of the 42nd to Brigadier General Douglas MacArthur.

MacArthur had earned quite a reputation as the 84th Brigade commander. He was always at the front, readily identifiable to his men by the slouch cap that he wore in lieu of a helmet. He also

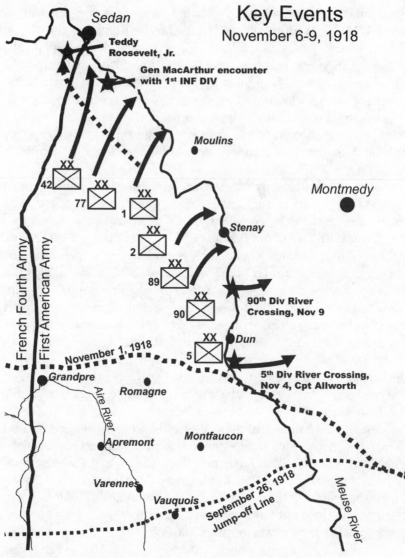

Map 20.2. Key Events, 6–9 November 1918. (Josiah Mastriano)

refused to wear a gas mask or a sidearm, and usually carried his characteristic riding crop. He reasoned that he did not require a weapon as it was his job to direct others in combat.[10] During the waning days of the war, the 42nd delivered results. The division kept effective liaison with the French 40th Division, of the French

Fourth Army, to its west as it advanced to the Meuse, anticipating an assault river crossing near Sedan. To the right of the 42nd was the veteran 77th Liberty Division, likewise advancing toward the Meuse in good form. It would arrive on the banks of that formidable river on 6 November. Major General Dickman, the I Corps commander, was satisfied with the progress his organization had made over the past week. However, this prevented any hopes of an American advance against Sedan.

Lieutenant General Hunter Liggett, the First Army commander, wrote of the hysteria surrounding Sedan:

> After Paris, Sedan was the best known, almost the only familiar geographical name in France to the average American officer. It happened too to be a division point on the all-important railroad for which we were driving. . . . Sedan became a sort of fetish. "On to Sedan" replaced "On to Berlin" as a shibboleth, and even the cooks talked knowingly of Sedan. . . . The magic name Sedan drove the First Corps faster and the night of the eighth, the Rainbow Division captured . . . [the] heights [commanding Sedan from the south], blasted the railroad apart with its artillery and caught the enemy with all four tracks blocked with long trains of supplies of every description.[11]

As the I Corps' 42nd and 77th Divisions advanced to the Meuse, General Pershing let it be known in his headquarters on 6 November to General Fox Conner, the AEF chief of operations, that it was his desire that the Americans should liberate Sedan.[12] Colonel George C. Marshall was a bit flabbergasted by this and said, "Am I expected to believe that this is General Pershing's order, when I know damn well you came to this conclusion during our conversation?" Conner answered, "That is the order of the Commander in Chief, which I am authorized to issue in his name. Now get it out as quickly as possible."[13] Upon hearing this, Colonel Marshall drafted up an order that triggered one of the greatest catastrophes of the war. To compound matters, Brigadier General Hugh Drum, the First Army chief of staff, added, "Boundaries will not be considered binding" to the memorandum. This would make a confusing order even more so. The memorandum was addressed to the I and V Corps and stated:

Memorandum for the Commanding Generals, I Corps, V Corps.
Subject: Message from the Commander-in-Chief.

1. General Pershing desires that the honor of entering Sedan should fall to the First American Army. He has every confidence that the troops of the I Corps, assisted by the 5th Corps, will enable him to realize this desire.
2. In transmitting the foregoing message, your attention is invited to the favorable opportunity now existing for pressing our advantage throughout the night. Boundaries will not be considered binding.

By command of Lieutenant General Liggett
Official:
G.C. Marshal
A.C. of S., G3[14]

With this memorandum in hand, Summerall, the V Corps commander, rushed to meet with the commander of the 1st Infantry Division, Brigadier General Frank Parker. Parker had recently taken command of the division. The Big Red One was making excellent progress toward the Meuse and would be on its southern bank by the next day. However, Summerall arrived and said to Parker, "I expect [you] to be in Sedan the next morning." Parker replied, "I understand Sir. I will now give my orders." With that Summerall departed Parker's headquarters, leaving him with the French liaison officer poring over maps of the region.[15] Summerall assumed that the 1st Infantry Division would cross the Meuse in its sector and then wheel toward Sedan north of the river. However, at that moment, the I Corps, together with the French Army, was better positioned to liberate Sedan. Summerall created an environment for disaster when he told Parker to be in Sedan the next morning but provided no further guidance on how it should be accomplished.

There was a strange partiality for the 1st Infantry Division in portions of the AEF. The unit was the first American force in France, the first to see combat in France, and naturally was one of the AEF's best divisions. There was a natural bias for the 1st Infantry Division. Pershing favored the Big Red One for its superb performance, and Summerall, as a former commander of the division, made his wishes known to Parker to advance the division into Sedan.

However, instead of crossing the Meuse River, as Summerall assumed would occur, Brigadier General Parker irrationally decided to move a brigade from his division laterally out of his V Corps zone of action and across the entire width of the I Corps. This meant that Parker's men would move across and through the 77th and 42nd Divisions. Parker planned then to continue this lateral western movement into the French Fourth Army's sector (in the French 40th Division's area of operations) and pivot north to attack Sedan from the south. This was an amateurish and dangerous move that led to a disaster for the U.S. First Army and embarrassment for the French.

Parker focused on the "Boundaries will not be considered binding" portion of the order and surmised that it would be easier and faster to move against Sedan by traversing across the I Corps and striking the city from the south. However, crossing unit boundaries is a labor-intensive effort and requires deconfliction, coordination, thorough planning, and liaison. Even one hundred years later, with sophisticated communications and a century of experience, crossing into another unit's area in the midst of combat operations with a large force is not an easy endeavor.

These unit boundaries are assigned to commanders and serve as control measures that define which part of the geography is their battlespace. Within the designated zones assigned to them, unit commanders literally own that area. They determine where, when, and how to synchronize the forces and fires assigned to them. These include both applying lethal kinetic fires against an adversary and maneuvering one's own forces. Unit boundaries also serve to prevent fratricide (friendly fire). The chances of "blue on blue" fighting are significantly reduced when soldiers know the limits of their area of operations. The boundaries also are designed to protect neighboring units. To engage enemy targets across boundaries requires clearance from the commander who owns that battlespace. This is designed to protect that commander's forces from mistakenly being fired upon by friendly units outside of the area of operations.

The situation on 6 November 1918 was intense for the AEF. Both the I and V Corps were directed to seize Sedan. This order circulated quickly through the units, with Father Duffy of the 42nd Division writing, "At 10:30 on the evening of the 6th, there came a most

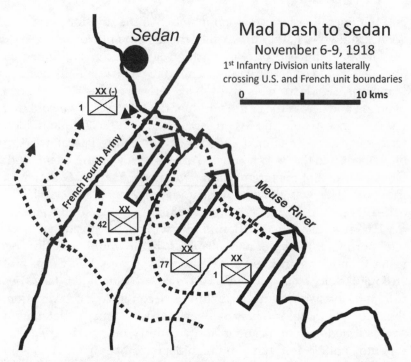

Map 20.3. Mad Dash to Sedan, 6–9 November 1918. (Josiah Mastriano)

extraordinary order . . . that it was imperative that Sedan should be captured before the end of the next day."[16]

General Dickman, commanding the I Corps, checked in with his two divisions in combat, the 42nd and 77th, and was satisfied with their plans to clear their zones of Germans and then to prepare for river crossing operations southeast of Sedan. The 77th Liberty Division was already on the banks of the Meuse on 6 November and planned on clearing the rest of its area of operations of Germans that day while making preparations to continue the attack across the river. Brigadier General Douglas MacArthur planned on finishing his division's advance to the Meuse on 7 November and likewise preparing for crossing.

As the 42nd and 77th Divisions advanced to the Meuse River, Father Duffy wrote, "Meanwhile events were happening which made the order to advance without ceasing seem more extraordinary. Elements of the 1st Division appeared on our flank and rear [claiming their right to occupy 42nd Division territory]."[17] Indeed,

This photograph shows soldiers from the 1st Infantry Division's 18th Infantry Regiment on their forced march to seize Sedan. The image was probably taken as the men crossed into the 42nd Division's sector. (U.S. Army Heritage and Education Center, Carlisle, Pennsylvania)

the 1st Infantry Division marched out of its V Corps sector and laterally across the entire front of the 77th Division. All forward moment of the 77th ground to a halt as the 1st Infantry seized the roads and blocked forward movement of the Liberty Division. To compound matters, officers of the 1st Infantry Division took command of groups of 77th Division soldiers, disrupting command and control and degrading the capacity of the division to complete its mission. The Big Red One seized the roads and intersections that the 77th needed to continue its attack. An eyewitness from the 77th wrote, "Mounted generals and staff officers, meeting platoons of [77th and 42nd Division] infantry on the march, would order them on new missions, of which their company or battalion commanders would never hear for days. . . . Everywhere there was haste, exhaustion and a growing disorganization."[18]

Captain W. Kerr Rainsford, a company commander in the 77th's 307th Infantry Regiment, watched as the 1st Infantry ground the 77th to a halt, but was horrified by what happened when it began crossing into the 42nd Division's sector. It took the 1st Infantry a greater part of the day to cut across the 77th's sector, and darkness was settling in when it reached the 42nd's area of operation. Soldiers guarding the flanks of the 42nd Division opened fire on this force, believing it to be a German counterattack. American soldiers were exchanging fire at points along the line. Rainsford wrote, "A part of the 1st Division . . . crossed the sector of the 77th Division, and in the darkness had become engaged with part of the 42nd."[19]

MacArthur could not believe what was happening and wrote that this "precipitated what narrowly missed being one of the great tragedies of American history. . . . the stage was set for tragic consequences." Early in the morning, reports arrived at MacArthur's headquarters that the 1st Infantry Division's 16th Brigade was moving across his front. He quickly rushed to the front to ascertain what was transpiring and to prevent his own troops from engaging the 1st Infantry. MacArthur found several 1st Infantry Division staff officers, who showed him their orders from Parker. MacArthur ordered them to turn their troops around before a catastrophe occurred, and then MacArthur rushed forward in his car with his aide to alert his units that the 1st Infantry Division was in the area and not to confuse them for Germans in the darkness.

During this episode a myth emerged that, upon seeing MacArthur with his nonregulation hat, 1st Infantry soldiers confused him for a German general and captured him. The morning of 7 November, MacArthur was at the front trying to prevent fratricide and to get the 1st Infantry out of his area of operations. While at the front, a 1st Infantry patrol appeared under Lieutenant Black. MacArthur said, "He recognized me at once and told me that the troops . . . were the leading battalion of the 16th Infantry under the command of Colonel W. E. Harrell." Harrell was a personal friend and West Point classmate of MacArthur's. MacArthur directed Lieutenant Black to stop the men, report directly to Harrell, and explain to him the danger of crossing his men in front of the 42nd Division. At this point, MacArthur noticed that one of the 1st Infantry Division soldiers was looking at him oddly and thought that the soldier envied the Camel cigarette that he was smoking. MacArthur offered him a pack of cigarettes, and as the soldier lit one to smoke, he said, "I was thinking, if you had just bin a Boche general, 'stead of an American one we would all of us got the D.S.C." MacArthur said that he laughed at that comment and replied, "If you don't get a medal in any event you do get a package of cigarettes." The soldier answered, "To tell the truth sir, I would rather have the cigarettes than a medal."[20] The general and soldier laughed and parted ways. He was never detained or molested by the 1st Infantry Division, and the long-perpetuated tale of his capture is a matter of not letting the facts gets in the way of a good story. Quite the contrary was true; MacArthur prevented a tragic outcome from the 1st Division's escapades. As an interesting aside, the commander of the 1st Infantry Division's 26th Regiment then advancing through MacArthur's divisional sector was Lieutenant Colonel Theodore Roosevelt Jr., the son of the famous president. Roosevelt was at the vanguard of the 1st Infantry Division and crossed the 42nd sector. He then advanced into the French Fourth Army's area of operations, crossed the Bar River, and advanced toward Sedan from the south. It looked like the Big Red One would indeed have the honor of liberating this symbolic city.[21] Roosevelt wrote of the dash to liberate Sedan:

All night long the men plowed like mud-caked specters through the dark, some staggering as they walked. . . . Everyone had reached the last stages of exhaustion. Captain [Eugene] Dye, a corking good officer, fainted on the march, lay unconscious in the mud for an hour, came to, and joined his company before the morning attack. Major [Lyman] Frazier, while riding at the head of his battalion, fell asleep on his horse and rolled off. As I rode up and down the column I watched the men. Most of them were so tired that they said but little. Occasionally, however, I would run into some of the old men, laughing and joking as usual. I remember hearing a sergeant. . . . "What is it, sergeant, aren't you getting enough exercise?" I said to him, "Exercise, is it, sir? It's not the exercise I'm worried with, but I do be afraid that them Germans are better runners than we are! Faith, to get them is like trying to catch a flea under your thumb."

In the morning we passed through a French unit at Omicourt and started our attack. By afternoon we were on the heights overlooking Sedan, where word reached us to halt our attack. Shortly after we were told to withdraw, turning over to the French. We found later that it was considered wise that the French should take Sedan on account of the large sentimental value attached to it because of the German victory there in the war of 1870.[22]

Meanwhile, the phones were ringing off of the hook at Liggett's army headquarters, at Dickman's I Corps, and at the AEF headquarters. Liggett said that the first he had heard of the 1st Infantry's march to glory was when the French Fourth Army called him to complain that the American Division was in its area of operations and impeding its progress toward Sedan. Liggett told the French that they must be mistaken and then mounted his car and traveled to the I and V Corps headquarters "as fast as I could travel." "This was the only occasion in the war when I lost my temper completely. . . . The movement had thrown the First Corps front and the adjoining French front into such confusion that had the enemy chosen to counter attack . . . a catastrophe might have resulted." The I Corps commander, General Dickman, was indignant and called the whole situation an "atrocity."[23]

Summerall, whose personal order to Parker the day before had created the crisis, did not learn of the details of it until the morning of 7 November. Only then did he try to stop the westward march, but it was too late to recall the troops, and it would take time to have messengers reach the lead elements. Instead of taking responsibility for the event, he instead placed blame on Marshal and others. Those in the First Army's headquarters who read Summerall's defense of his unit's actions said that it "was a lame affair, throwing the burden onto the memorandum."[24] Lieutenant Colonel Clarence Huebner, who commander the 1st Infantry Division's 28th Regiment, and who participated in this push across the I Corps to march upon Sedan, said, "Someone was glory hunting. An army officer is dangerous when he begins to be a glory hunter."[25] In this case, the glory hunting was largely by Parker, encouraged on by his corps commander, Summerall. Neither would pay the price for this folly, but those under their command suffered the consequences.

Summerall wrote that "in this operation, the division had lost 2 officers, and 127 men killed, 5 officers and 218 men wounded and 2 missing."[26] He did not specify how many of these casualties resulted from the clash with the 42nd during the early morning firefight of 7 November. Fratricide was rarely discussed by the U.S. Army and usually was covered up during and after the war. General officers' memoirs took considerable pains to avoid the subject. At least some of the 354 casualties suffered by the 1st Infantry's march to glory were a result of fratricide. Liggett's aide-de-camp confided in his diary that indeed "a clash had taken place between the 1st and

The French shared the glory of liberating Sedan by inviting a company of Americans to help take the city. Sedan was liberated after four years of German occupation by the French 40th Division and elements of the American 42nd Division on 9 November 1918. This photograph shows the first French and American officers to enter Sedan. Front row, left to right: Captain Boularron, Lieutenant Colonel Ludovic Abel de Ville, Captain Faivet (French officers of the 40th Division), and Captain Russell Baker, Lieutenant Alison Reppy, and Captain R. Gowdy (American officers of the 42nd Division). (U.S. Army Heritage and Education Center, Carlisle, Pennsylvania)

42nd."[27] There were simply not enough German forces on the south bank of the Meuse to have inflicted that many casualties, and the advance of the 42nd on the heights south of Sedan the day before had forced most German units in the area to withdraw completely from the south bank. The irony is that this episode stopped a U.S. Army corps-level advance and disrupted the right flank of the French Fourth Army. The 1st Infantry did far more damage than the Germans could have this late in the war. Had any other division committed such a blunder, there would have been hell to pay. But this was the 1st Division, Pershing's own, and he would not punish the men, saying, "Under normal circumstances the action of the officer or officers responsible for this movement of the 1st Division directly across the zones of action of two other divisions could not have been overlooked, but the splendid record of that unit and the approach of the end of hostilities suggested leniency."[28]

The French called the AEF headquarters to demand that the Americans withdraw from their front. Not only did Colonel Marshall have to answer questions from the French Fourth Army, but also the Group of Armies Center (Maistre) and Pétain's G3. The 1st Infantry's march single-handedly stopped the advance of an entire American corps and nearly triggered an international breach between the AEF and the French command. Teddy Roosevelt's men were literally advancing into the southern outskirts of Sedan when a messenger arrived ordering them to withdraw. Neither the 42nd nor the 77th would liberate Sedan, as the 1st Division broke up their preparation to conduct large unit river-crossing operations.

Although taken aback by the 1st Infantry's violation of their front, the French were magnanimous about the whole affair. Instead of rushing ahead and taking the glory for themselves, the French 40th Division asked MacArthur to detach a company of Americans to share the glory of liberating the city. MacArthur detached Company D, 166th Infantry Regiment, under the command of Captain Russell Baker to join the French in taking Sedan. Sedan was liberated the next day, 9 November, by both the French and American armies.

21

The End of the War

It was the astonishing display of American strength which
definitely decided the war against us.
                                  —General Max von Gallwitz,
                           commander of Army Group Gallwitz

Meanwhile, events were spinning out of control in Germany. The
new government in Berlin was putting pressure on the military
leadership to end the war. There was also growing hostility toward
the Kaiser and a movement speaking openly of his abdication. To
compound matters, a mutiny shook the German Imperial Navy.
On 24 October, the surface fleet was ordered by Admirals Franz
von Hipper and Reinhard Scheer to prepare to sail for a final battle
against the British fleet. The German Navy, aside from the U-boats
and smaller torpedo craft, had been largely stagnant since the 1916
Battle of Jutland.[1] The morale of the sailors was at an all-time low,
and they would not sally forth for one grand finish in battle. The
revolt commenced in earnest on 29 October, with the men refusing
to set sail, and spread across the Kiel Navy Yard on 4 November.
The governor (base commander) was held hostage, and the sailors
spread the revolution to other coastal towns and cities. By 7 November
ber it looked as if a Bolshevik sort of revolt would tear Germany
apart, as it had Russia a year before.[2]

Defeat was now just a matter of time, perhaps a few weeks at
best, and time was running out to achieve "peace with honor." The
crown prince rushed to the front after the meetings in Berlin to boost
the morale of his men. "When the troops caught sight of my car, I
was at once surrounded by a throng of waving and cheering men.
All of them betrayed only too clearly the effects of the heavy fighting
of the last few months. Their uniforms were tattered and their
stripes and badges scarcely visible; their faces were often shockingly
haggard; and yet their eyes flashed and their bearing was

proud and confident." But the crown prince knew that these soldiers would soon be influenced by the shocking news from home. The war had to be ended, and he rebuffed the fantasies from Hindenburg and General Wilhelm Groener (who had replaced Ludendorff as the new first quartermaster) that the army could defend the Antwerp–Meuse Line. This "line" did not exist, and the German High Command on the Western Front seemed detached from reality, continually issuing orders that were impossible to carry out.[3]

The strains of the war on the German Imperial Army began to manifest in early November when the entire line on the Western Front was being driven back by the Allies, from Verdun to the North Sea. Leaders experienced insubordination from junior soldiers, red flags of the revolution began appearing, and groups of soldiers refused to obey orders. In one situation, the crown prince was near a railway where German soldiers refused to obey orders given to them by the rail staff. The men began yelling out a phrase from the revolution, "Lights out! Knives out!" The crown prince approached the disgruntled throng and, through his charisma, rallied the men. He reminded the men of their duty and conduct as soldiers. He wrote of this: "In the end, a mere lad of perhaps seventeen, a Saxon, with a frank boyish face and decorated with the iron cross, stepped forward and said, 'Herr Kronprinz, don't take ill; they are only silly phrases; we mean nothing by them; we all like you and we know that you always look after your soldiers well. You see, we have been traveling now for three days and have had no food nor attention the whole time. No one troubles about us and there are no officers at all with us. Don't be angry with us.'"[4] Thus was the situation for much of the army in November 1918.

But the German Army fought on despite these occasional lapses in discipline. Marwitz's Fifth Army launched a series of counterattacks against the American penetrations across the Meuse, slamming into the U.S. 5th and 90th Divisions. On 5 November, the Germans blunted an American advance from their river crossings near Dun sur Meuse. The German 241st Division and the Saxon Chasseurs drove the Americans off of the high ground near the river and back to their positions along the east bank. The Germans blunted two further attacks there that day. The German army group commander, Gallwitz, was proud of his forces' performance and mentioned in particular the 228th Brandenburg Division for continually throwing back the Americans: "Although fighting for fully four weeks, the

228th Brandenburgian Division gave a wonderful account of itself."
Despite this good showing, Gallwitz confided: "The exhausted Fifth
Army had to fight on. Reinforcements arrived late and were inadequate. . . . All that was left for me under these circumstances was to
continue to hold out as long as I could."[5]

Meanwhile, a German delegation crossed the French lines to
negotiate an armistice. They began talks with Marshal Foch in the
Compiegne Forest on 7 November. Foch had the momentum and
was in a position of strength. He wanted the war to end on the best
terms for the Allies and feared that any slowing of the offensive
would give the German Army a respite and perhaps only drag the
war on. To avert such an eventuality, and to force the Germans to
quickly accept the armistice, Foch issued the following order:

> The enemy is disorganized by our repeated attacks, is giv-
> ing way all along the front.
>   It is urgent to hasten and intensify our efforts.
>   I appeal to the energy and initiative of commanders in
> chief and their armies to make the results achieved decisive.[6]

This order meant that the Allied armies' attacks would continue
until the end. There was to be no slackening or holding back. Pershing intended to carry out the letter and spirit of this order, especially
as his newly created U.S. Second Army began its offensive operations farther east of the Meuse-Argonne Offensive, advancing from
the St. Mihiel area toward Metz. The AEF now had 2 million men in
France and seemed unstoppable.

Although rumors circulated among the troops of an impending armistice, the offensive would continue until the end. The I
Corps did not completely untangle itself from the damage done by
1st Infantry's assault across its front until 10 November. Because of
this, large crossings of the Meuse River were delayed. The V Corps
finished clearing Germans from its front and prepared for an assault
across the Meuse as well. Meanwhile, the III Corps continued its
push across the eastern flank of the Meuse in the face of resolute
German resistance from the high ground there. These actions, combined with those of the Belgians, French, and British, drained all of
the German reserves. "Every division that they had was actually in
line."[7] This was precisely the effect that Foch had sought when he
planned the broad front attack in late July 1918.

324 THUNDER IN THE ARGONNE

The armistice was signed at 5:00 A.M. on 11 November, with the hostilities ending at 11:00 that morning. Ludendorff's replacement, General Karl Edward Wilhelm Groener, issued orders to the German armies to observe the cease-fire beginning at 10:55 A.M.[8] He did not want any allegations of German violations of the armistice. Yet, much to his surprise, the Americans fought to the last minute—and in some cases well after the cease-fire went into effect. The striking selection of this day and time to end the war would not be lost to commentators, who would say that indeed the war ended on the 11th hour of the 11th day of the 11th month of 1918. Word had to be passed to all the men, armies, and nationalities in the field on both sides of the line. Liggett received word of the cease-fire at 6:30, and his three commanders received their notification from him of the imminent armistice at 8:30 A.M.

However, Liggett had received orders from Pershing the night before to launch a general attack across the First Army front on 11 November. The announcement of the armistice's going into effect at 11:00 A.M. did not alter his plan. The Americans would attack until the end. It seemed that Liggett was glory hunting, saying, "Once our troops had crossed the Meuse south of Stenay and advanced in the direction of Montmedy, they would turn this position from the south, and it was apparent that such a maneuver . . . would develop excellent opportunities for the capture of a large mass of the enemy." On paper this read like a good plan. In reality, however, the Americans simply lacked the time to realize such a heroic ending of the war. Yet, like Sedan, Montmedy had an alluring pull to it. Located but seven kilometers northwest of Louppy, the fortress town of Montmedy had played an important role in history since 1221, and in 1918 it was the headquarters for Army Group Gallwitz. Regardless of the ability to actually accomplish this objective, the offensive would be pushed with vigor until the end.[9] The 5th Infantry Division, which at great cost in men had assaulted across the Meuse to clear the high ground on the eastern side of the river, was given the honor of pressing the attack toward Montmedy.

The fighting had not slackened for the 5th Division, and despite the mounting casualties the men pressed forward, even when rumors circulated of an impending end of the war. The Americans fought all morning to clear the town of Louppy, but the Germans showed no sign of breaking. The defense of the area fell to the German 10th Division. Composed of soldiers from the Posen region of

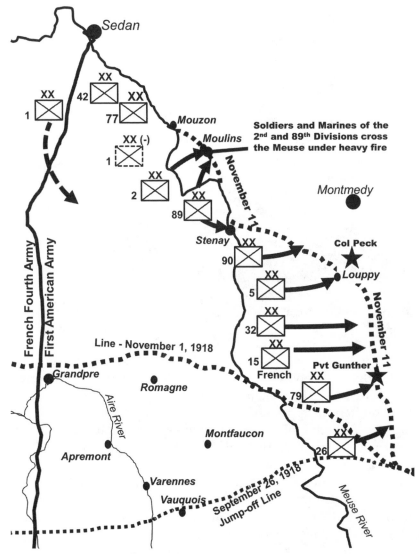

Map 21.1. Key Events, 10–11 November 1918. (Josiah Mastriano)

Prussia (modern day Poland), the division was rated first class and included the 6th Grenadier, 47th Regiment, and 398th Regiment. The 10th German Division made progress for the Americans difficult and costly.

The loss of Louppy compelled the Germans to fall back to the

Lieutenant Edward Lukert was dispatched to inform Colonel Robert Peck to cease further offensive actions, as the war was about to end. (U.S. Army Heritage and Education Center, Carlisle, Pennsylvania)

high ridges east and northeast of the town. The ridge was perfect for the defense. The Americans would have a long and open slope to climb from Louppy, while the Germans enjoyed both the advantages of the high ground and the concealment of a thick wood that crowned the summit. The U.S. 5th Division's 11th Infantry Regiment, under the command of Colonel Robert H. Peck, planned on assaulting the ridges in the morning of 11 November in the hope of breaking the German line and marching on to Montmedy. The German 10th Division left a regiment-size force to prevent the Americans from breaking the line. The order was to stop the Americans so as to give the German Army time to remove war material and supplies from Montmedy and Longuyon.

Meanwhile, at 9:00 A.M., word arrived at the headquarters of Brigadier General Paul Malone of the armistice's going into effect at 11:00. Malone knew that his two regiments planned on continuing their attacks that morning, and he was desperate to stop them before lives were lost needlessly. Malone tasked Lieutenant Edward Lukert with the solemn mission of stopping further attacks, especially by Peck's 11th Regiment. He told Lukert "to hurry for God's sake. . . . The Armistice was to be effective in two hours and the orders were to lay off and cancel all attacks; dig in and save as many men as we could. . . . no necessity for taking more territory and paying for it with good American lives."[10]

Lukert rushed to the front and found Colonel Peck in the Louppy church at 10:00. As Lukert climbed the steeple to pass the orders to Peck, a staff officer informed him that he already knew that the armistice was going into effect but that he intended to attack nonetheless. Peck was in the church steeple attempting to scan the ridge lines with his binoculars in anticipation of the 10:30 attack. A heavy fog filled the valley, and Peck was going to use this to his advantage. His men were going to slowly crawl up the hill through the fog to catch the Germans by surprise. The plan was moving ahead with or without an armistice.[11]

Lukert was astounded and at a loss for what to do. He wrote, "What the sense was—in launching another attack at this late hour no one knows. . . . In my opinion, no advance at such a stage . . . justified the loss of more lives." The men were saved by the sun and the Hun. As the Americans began their advance up the hill at 10:40, the sun broke through the clouds and burned off the fog, exposing the plan to the Germans above. With only twenty minutes remaining before the end of the war, the German commander on the ridge was appalled at what he saw. But instead of directing his men to open fire, which would have resulted in hundreds of American casualties, he came down the hill alone with a white flag and asked to speak with the American commander.[12] Colonel Peck was called for and met the German on the slope of the ridge. The advance and the shooting had ceased as the men on both sides waited to see the outcome of this meeting. The German officer greeted Peck with a salute and then said in perfect English:

We wish to cease firing and avoid further bloodshed. . . . Our Army is in retreat . . . I am ordered to cover that retreat and permit the removal of our material. This I must do and will. I know you will attack in a few minutes—one grand finish so to speak, and I am prepared to meet you on that crest. I have there (pointing), sixty five machine guns less the few you have captured in the last two hours back there [in Louppy]. They are laid and waiting to stop your advance up that hill. Will you come and cause more casualties, or

Colonel Robert H. Peck planned to have his men of the 11th Regiment, 5th Infantry, attack the Germans only minutes before the cease-fire went into effect. (U.S. Army Heritage and Education Center, Carlisle, Pennsylvania)

will you give us respite until eleven o'clock, when we can withdraw without further fighting?[13]

The official history records that Peck replied "No, is that so? Then that spoils all my scheme!" Lukert records that Peck scanned the hill and the locations that the German officer pointed out and replied that he "would act as he deemed fit." In truth, some of the men overheard this conversation, and no matter Peck's intentions or desires, there was no way he could pull off the attack with confirmation from the Germans of the end of the war. With a sigh of relief, Lukert wrote, "So the attack didn't come off . . . and I was darn glad of it." When the armistice went into effect, the Germans invited Lukert to see for himself their defensive position. He wrote, "It was true! He did have the guns so placed and they surely would have cleaned up on us in the event of further hostilities."[14]

Farther west, the 77th Division only managed to advance small patrols across the Meuse. Thanks to the 1st Infantry Division incident, any plans to force the Meuse had been delayed. But while waiting for the armistice to go into effect, the men found themselves in an artillery duel with the Germans. As the war drew to an end,

German artillery crashed into a dressing station, killing the unit's surgeon, and another shell killed the "driver, five horses, and rolling kitchen of the Machine-Gun Company." Orders were issued to avoid hitting the French villages across the Meuse and not cause civilian casualties.[15]

Upon hearing the news of the armistice, Father Duffy of the 42nd Division had an unexpected response to the end of the war. He expected to feel "delight," but instead sadness covered him. He said, "I could think of nothing except the fine lads who had come out with us to this war and who are not alive to enjoy the triumph. All day long I had a lonely and aching heart." Shortly after the armistice went into effect, Duffy's unit held a muster that beat home the cost of this war. He noted that barely half of the men for a full contingent were present and "far too few of the survivors were from the original group that shipped out a year ago from New York."[16]

Behind the 42nd Division lines, the 1st Infantry Division was trying to untangle itself from the mess it caused by marching across the I Corps' sector. Leading the last of the withdrawing Big Red One soldiers was Lieutenant Colonel Theodore Roosevelt Jr. As he busied himself with the tasks at hand, a soldier ran up to him, saluted, and said that his wife was waiting for him. Theodore's wife, Eleanor Butler Roosevelt, had volunteered in July 1917 to serve with the Young Men's Christian Association (YMCA) in Paris to support the deployed soldiers in France. Eleanor had been offered a chance to join several YMCA volunteers heading to the recently liberated village of Dun sur Meuse. Knowing that her husband's division was nearby, they thought she would have a chance to find him. As they were driving from Paris to the Meuse region, they providentially received word at one of their stops along the way that the war was about to end. After some effort, Eleanor surprised Ted, with him exclaiming, "How in the name of patience did you get here? Now I'm willing to believe the war's really over!"[17] A U.S. Army film crew captured part of her visit, with an elated Theodore Roosevelt walking through the damaged French village of Romagne, which would later become the location of the Meuse-Argonne American Cemetery.[18]

Meanwhile, at the AEF headquarters, the staff planned on a big breakfast to celebrate the impending end of the war. Among those attending was Colonel George C. Marshall. The breakfast was scheduled for 10:30 A.M. As the officers waxed on with emotion and eloquence about the war, suddenly there was a massive explosion near the breakfast area. Marshal and all of the others were blown off their chairs. Marshal said, "I thought I had been killed." A young aviator ran into the room a few minutes later to explain that a bomb had fallen off of his plane as he attempted to land in the field behind the headquarters.[19] A few feet closer and there would have been no future General George C. Marshall to lead the nation through the Second World War.

General Summerall ordered the 2nd Division to cross the Meuse late on 10 November. He did not alter this plan even upon hearing of the armistice. The 2nd Division commander, Major General Lejeune, selected the Marine brigade to lead the assault since the two army regiments had led the previous daring attack against Beaumont (the night attack). The plan was for the 5th and 6th Marine Regiments to cross the Meuse River once the pontoon foot bridges were completed by the engineer brigade. The crossing would take place north of Mouzon, and the objective was to seize two hills to the east. The 89th Division was ordered to cross the Meuse on 10 November at the same time as the Marines. Their crossing was to be near Bois de l'Hospice (with the Marines) with another crossing occurring north of Pouilly. Their objective once across was to take the high ground east of the river.[20] A 353rd Regiment, 89th Division, soldier mused on how little rest they had, saying, "Rest, did you say. Hell there ain't no such thing. We are shock troops. We'll get rest when we start to pushing up poppies." As the men crossed the Meuse River, seven German planes swooped down, dropping sixteen bombs, which killed eight men and wounded thirty. The regimental chaplain, Otis Gray, buried the dead men the next day.[21]

The 353rd Regiment crossed the Meuse with only hours remaining in the war. The lead men advanced into Stenay on the Meuse River and were relieved that the Germans had already abandoned the town. Once the town was secure, Second Lieutenant Edward Connors from Indianapolis reported the liberation of the town by sending a note to headquarters saying that one of his men, "Private [Ernest] Gielow defeated for mayor of Stenay by three votes." The action won the men a safe and warm place to stay at the end of the war.[22]

The river-crossing operation was a near disaster for the Marines. The Germans located several of the crossing points and laid down machine gun fire and artillery to destroy the bridges and to break up the crossing parties and engineers. The Mouzon crossing point had to be abandoned, with the Marines and soldiers then attempting to complete the pontoon at Bois de l'Hospice. One of the Marines' sister regiments, the U.S. Army 9th, advanced to help the engineers complete the bridge before morning. The 5th Marines crossed late on 10 November only to find that the 6th Marines had not crossed. Under heavy fire, the Marines and their army counterparts in the 89th Division completed their river-crossing operations and—at great cost in lives—advanced over a kilometer east to their designated objective. Men were cut down in droves as German machine gunners wildly laid down suppressive fire to prevent the Americans from crossing the river. Crossing in single file and then darting across a flat meadow made it a turkey shoot. The losses were staggering, with Private Mackin noting, "So many died that night, short hours away from Armistice."[23]

The Marines cleared the village of Moulins while the 89th likewise cleared Autreville and advanced forward to seize the high ground near Bois de Hache. The fighting here lasted well after the armistice, as it was difficult to get a messenger across the Meuse without the runner being mowed down by German machine gun fire.[24] The 2nd and 89th Divisions' lead elements across the Meuse did not get word of the end of the war until 11:00 was well past. Marine Private Mackin noticed around that time that the German machine gunners were no longer firing into the Americans. Instead, they fired between the lines of Americans, and the bursts seemed to no longer do harm. The Germans opposing the Marines knew that the war had ended and were trying to abide by the terms of the armistice and no longer wanted to shed blood. They were deliberately firing between the American formations simply to slow them down, hoping that they would soon learn of the war's end. About this time a runner arrived, out of breath, ordering the men to stop per the colonel's orders! Silence shrouded the fields of death.[25]

Summerall, still reeling from the folly of his Sedan order, learned that the "Marines resented my order to cross the Meuse River, as the armistice came immediately afterward and blamed me for their losses, which they said were unnecessary." Summerall shifted responsibility and said that he was obeying orders and that the selection of the Marine brigade to lead the attack was made by Major General Lejeune, a Marine. Inexplicably, Summerall added that Lejeune did this because "No doubt he wanted to gain credit for the Marines. There was no complaint from the Army brigade in the Second Division. From my experience with Marines, they should never be employed with the army or under army officers. They fight no better than the army and they complain, seek quick relief and try to gain publicity."[26]

Summerall's statement was unfair and did little to foster joint cooperation. The soldiers and Marines in the AEF fought superbly together, and these types of remarks from rising leaders in the U.S. military would create rifts between the services that would take another world war and decades to heal. By all accounts, the Marines were excellent warriors on the field of battle and were respected by friends and foes alike.

Meanwhile, farther to the south, the 79th Division, of Montfaucon fame, was back in the line and, like so many of the other AEF divisions, was ordered to attack on 11 November. Three of its regiments attacked the German line. This included elements of the 313th, 314th, and 315th Regiments. Their attack kicked off at 9:30 A.M., just as the transmission of the armistice was reaching the division. Despite this, the attack was not halted or called off. The Americans advanced with the French on the right flank and noticed an increased intensity of American artillery support, which was answered by the Germans. A wall of machine gun bullets likewise greeted the Americans. With only minutes remaining in the war, neither the Americans nor the Germans intended to relent. Large groups of Americans fell in the waning hours of the Great War, but up the long slope they went. The armistice message reached the attacking regiments at 10:44 A.M., just sixteen minutes before the end, and the men fought until the last minute. The 79th Division history captures what happened next, "On the right of the line at 10h 59, Private Henry Gunther . . . charging headlong upon an enemy weapon, was shot to death and almost as he fell the firing died away and appalling silence prevailed. The fighting was over. The roar of the guns had ceased as if by magic." Seemingly waxing philosophical to rationalize this last attack, the 79th Division history concluded:

> Armistice hour—11h, 11th day, 11th month and in the final thrust of the final day, the Seventy Ninth Division had gained a threefold distinction. The 313th Infantry had in the death of Private Gunther, the sad honor of losing perhaps the last

man killed in action on the Western Front. The 315th Infantry in the capture of the German field piece had secured likely the last large hostile trophy of the war. The 314th Infantry, as it halted on the slopes of the Cote de Romagne, had thrust the deepest salient into the German line on the entire front east of the Meuse.[27]

The ability of honest men to justify the one last dash to glory for ambiguous reasons was difficult for many to accept. In the last eleven hours of the war, nearly eleven thousand soldiers fell in combat. The preponderance of these casualties actually occurred in the morning when the sun arose. With astronomical twilight beginning at 5:52 A.M., this provided just five hours of light, an incredible loss in lives. The U.S. Congress held hearings on this in Washington, D.C., in 1919. Pershing was celebrated by the American public at large as a hero and therefore was too popular to reprimand, but the hearings provide a record of what some officers thought of the final attacks of 11 November. Colonel Conrad Babcock of the 89th Division's 354th Regiment saw firsthand the folly of the final attacks and testified under oath: "It was sickening and depressing to hear officers like Brigadier General Fox Conner . . . tell of the importance of gaining a certain ridge . . . before the armistice went into effect. What did these useless killings and injuries mean to officers who never commanded men in battle, whose entire war experience was a war on paper, where the expenditure of human life was necessary but with which they had no experience, no responsibly [sic] and apparently little sympathy."[28]

The war at last was over. Although no-fraternization orders were issued, some of the Doughboys wandered across the lines to meet their foes. There was shared respect between the adversaries, and whenever possible food was shared. The first night of peace greeted the men with colorful displays of flares being fired into the night sky. As the guns fell silent, Corporal Ellis Stewart with the 80th Division reflected on the war and his survival, writing home, "I got thru without a scratch but several times I wouldn't have given much for my chance of living. I thought that Jerry sure had my name and address."[29]

The foremost thought for soldiers, whether American or German, was home. News of the war's end spread across Europe like a wildfire. For the first time since August 1914, the bells rang across

Corporal Ellis Stewart of the 80th Division (dismounted soldier on right) was given the grim task of looking for wounded among the dead when the fighting neared its end. (U.S. Army Heritage and Education Center, Carlisle, Pennsylvania)

Great Britain in celebration. People poured into the streets of London, Paris, Rome, and elsewhere to rejoice at the end of this greatest of calamities. Meanwhile, in the old Roman spa town of Aix les Bains, France, recently promoted Sergeant Alvin C. York was on leave with his men. There, too, celebrations erupted. Music, wine, and dancing flowed. York, however, went to the town's church to pray. He reflected on the loss of so many friends in this terrible tragedy. Foremost in his thoughts was the death of his one true friend in the army, Corporal Murray Savage. The loss of such a true and good Christian man was difficult to rationalize or explain away. Such men fell on both sides of the lines.[30]

Leutnant Paul Vollmer, the German officer that York captured on 8 October 1918, likewise was relieved to hear that the war was at long last over. He lost many friends in the cataclysmic conflict. So many men in his unit had perished in the flames of war that it was increasingly difficult to remember them all. However, several stood out, such as the fearless and beloved Leutnant Mayer, who died leading the men in their first attack against the French at Eton in August 1914. His Christian faith was such that he was a humble and respected leader. His death so early in the war seemed to prophesy a long and costly struggle. And then there was Leutnant Fritz Endriss, the fearless officer and friend who led the bayonet attack against York to save Vollmer. In the end, it cost Endriss his life. And saving Endriss had been the reason Vollmer surrendered the battalion to York. What would Vollmer go home to? What would a defeated Germany be like, a Germany without an emperor or kings, all of whom would abdicate?

Many people truly believed that this was the war to end all wars. The magnitude of the bloodshed and the horrors were too great to imagine that a second and bloodier world war was only twenty years away. Eleanor Butler Roosevelt reflected this sentiment, writing, "Yes, the war was over. The world had been made safe for democracy and we could all go home and live happily ever after. At least we would never have to fight another war, nor would our children. People would have too much sense to fight wars. No doubt was in our minds."[31]

Over the next several months the American army slowly made its way back to North America, where soldiers carried on with life where they had left off. However, most of the Doughboys found simply carrying on was difficult to do. The adjustment was considerably more difficult for the German soldiers, going home to a defeated, bankrupt, and starving nation beset by gangs of socialists, Bolsheviks, and counterrevolutionaries.

The end of the First World War changed everything. Four empires collapsed and were replaced by new nations and new governments facing an uncertain future. The Romanov dynasty was gone, after having ruled Russia since 1613. It had fallen the year before to the Bolshevik Revolution that was still killing thousands of people in its wake. Likewise, the Ottoman Empire perished in the flames of World War One. Rising in 1299, the Ottomans had finished off the Eastern Roman Empire (Byzantines) in 1453 and conquered most of southeastern Europe in the name of Islam. The Ottomans laid waste to vast civilizations, committed genocide against the Armenians, Serbs, and others, and thrice in its colorful history besieged Vienna. Now this mighty empire was gone in the ashes of the First World War. The powerful Austrian Habsburg dynasty likewise fell, as did the once mighty Prussian Hohenzollerns. It was a new world,

After the debacle of the mad rush toward Sedan, Lieutenant Colonel Theodore Roosevelt Jr. was surprised when his wife, Eleanor Butler Roosevelt, appeared at the front within hours of the war ending. (U.S. Army Heritage and Education Center, Carlisle, Pennsylvania)

a world that the American soldier helped to shape, and a world in which the American army came of age and proved itself a force to be reckoned with. The rise of the modern American army was not easy and came at a great cost. It was forged in fire.

22

Aftermath and Commemoration

In great deeds, something abides. On great fields, something
stays. . . . And reverent men and women from afar, and
generations that know us not and that we know not of, heart-
drawn to see where and by whom great things were suffered
and done for them, shall come to this deathless field, to
ponder and dream.
> —Major General Joshua L. Chamberlain,
> American Civil War leader

The terms of the armistice that the Germans accepted on the morning of 11 November 1918 were neither generous nor magnanimous.
It included returning Alsace-Lorraine to France. Those were the
provinces that Germany had annexed after the 1870 Franco-Prussian
War. It also included the immediate withdrawal of German forces
from Luxembourg, France, and Belgium, the surrender of the lands
Germany seized in eastern, southern and northern Europe, the surrender of the Imperial Navy, and the return of prisoners of war. One
of the key aspects for the author of the armistice, Ferdinand Foch,
was the surrender of considerable war material and transport to the
Allies. This included most of Germany's steam engines, railcars, the
preponderance of its air force, 5,000 pieces of artillery, 3,000 mortars,
and some 25,000 machine guns. This was to deprive Germany of the
ability to resume hostilities. Another provision was the Allied occupation of the German Rhineland. American, Belgian, British, and
French forces deployed to the region in November, with the French
staying on until 1935. (The Americans withdrew in 1923.) The 11
November agreement was an armistice, not a treaty. The final resolution of the war would be negotiated in Versailles. The Treaty of
Versailles was signed on 28 June 1919.[1]

For the American soldiers in Europe, there was initially no slackening in their conditioning for war. If the Germans decided to renege on the armistice, Pershing wanted his army ready. The AEF was filled with combat-experienced officers and soldiers, and it performed well. One officer commented on the intense postwar training, saying, "In reality, we got some excellent training [here]. It is however, a matter of grave discussion, why, when at Camp Gordon, we were taught to sing, while after the armistice we were taught to fight."[2] The intensity and frequency of the training slackened by Christmas 1918, and the focus gradually shifted to bringing the army home.

The narrow nature of the defensive line in the Meuse-Argonne region compelled the German High Command to commit virtually all of its reserve divisions there, resulting in a weakening of the defense elsewhere in France. As Pershing wrote of the Meuse-Argonne campaign (as directed by Foch), the objective was "To draw the best German divisions to our front and to consume them." This is precisely what transpired, but at a great cost in men and material. By the time the guns fell silent, 1.2 million Americans were in the Meuse-Argonne region, making it America's largest ever offensive. In the vicious forty-seven days of fighting, the Americans suffered 122,093 casualties, of which 26,277 were killed in action. In every way, the Meuse-Argonne was a truly Franco-American operation, and nowhere is this more evident than in the blood spilled while serving side by side in this crusade to liberate France from the foreign invader. In addition to the American losses, the French suffered more than 70,000 casualties while fighting in, alongside, and in support of the offensive there.[3]

The combined Franco-American attack inflicted an estimated 126,000 casualties on the German forces, of which around 28,000 were killed in action. Roughly 150 French villages and towns were liberated in the forty-seven days of the Meuse campaign, and 840 planes, 324 tanks, and 2,417 pieces of artillery were employed in the operation.[4] The Meuse-Argonne campaign accomplished everything Foch had hoped that it would achieve. As part of the overall Allied broad front attack, the Franco-American advance drew off the precious and vital German reserve divisions, opening the door for an Allied penetration in the north of France.

The Versailles treaty was finally signed on 28 June 1919, forever changing the world and creating conflicts and fractures around the globe that still plague the nations today. Germany was compelled to accept full responsibility for the war and then subjected to war reparations that in the end (combined with an economic depression) set the conditions for the rise of Adolf Hitler. The aftermath of the war redrew the maps of both Europe and the Middle East.

Poland was reborn after 123 years since its last partition at the hands of the Austrians, Russians, and Prussians (Germans). The Baltic states emerged as fully independent in 1918. This was the first time Lithuania had enjoyed its independence since the 1721 Treaty of Nystad. Estonia and Latvia achieved their first ever independence as well. Czechoslovakia, a future Yugoslavia, and other nations emerged from the ashes of the Austro-Hungarian and Ottoman empires. The British and French agreed in 1916 on how to carve up the Ottoman Empire in the Middle East, resulting in new nations coming into existence, which would soon be called Syria, Iraq, and Jordan. More importantly, however, the promise of a rebirth of Israel came to life. The nation had ceased to exist in 70 A.D. when Roman legions besieged and sacked Jerusalem in the aftermath of the Jewish Revolt. Although this would not come to fruition until 1948, it was just a matter of time before the Jewish people would have a home of their own.

For the United States, General Dennis Nolan, a World War One hero and the father of American military intelligence, wrote, "The full flowering of the spirit of our Army did not, however, come until it had fought and won a series of battles known as the Meuse-Argonne Battle. It will be of this great victory, in which 1,200,000 Americans fought, and of which as yet so little is known, that this nation will in the future take the greatest pride."[5] For a time, Nolan's view was true, but today there is little collective memory of the Argonne.

A century later, the legacy of the First World War still casts a shadow on the world in which we live. Yet, sadly, few in the United States know anything about this war that forever changed our world. There were generations who knew about Pershing, the Lost Battalion, Cher Ami, Sergeant York, and Sam Woodfill. The word Argonne once sent chills down the spines of Americans, who instantly knew the price in blood that was paid to liberate that area. But as the United States passes through the centennial commemoration of the heroes of the Argonne, few seem to notice.

A veteran of the Meuse-Argonne Offensive wrote, "And after the war, I would like to see erected in Washington a shaft 100 feet high with panels about its base commemorative of the Military Service, and on its summit, I would want to see the proud, upstanding figure of an INFANTRYMAN. This monument would be erected 'To the Man Who Won the War.'"[6] Such a monument was not built. It took literally a century before the veterans of this war were finally recognized with a monument of their own in the nation's capital. Sadly, the nation has had little appetite for such commemorations and only after significant lobbying and time did this endeavor finally come to fruition. Sadly, there is not one veteran from the First World War remaining alive to enjoy the recognition that he so long deserved.

Private initiatives to preserve the legacy of those who fought in World War One were more successful. Although there have been several monuments or commemorations related to the Meuse-Argonne campaign, there are three in particular worth discussing as representations of the challenges that one faces when undertaking such an endeavor.

In discussing the selfless service of Americans in the Meuse-Argonne, General Pershing singled out only three soldiers for "typifying the spirit of . . . our great army." Pershing continued: "I would mention Lieutenant Samuel Woodfill, 5th Division, who attacked single-handed a series of German machine gun nests near Cunel and dispatched the crews of each in turn until reduced to the necessity of assaulting the last detachment with a pick; Sergeant Alvin C. York of the 82d Division, who stood off and captured 132 Germans after his patrol was literally surrounded and outnumbered ten to one; and Major Charles W. Whittlesey and his men of the 77th Division, who, when their battalion was cut off in the Argonne, refused to surrender and held out until finally relieved."

There is no marker or monument denoting the heroism of Lieutenant Sam Woodfill in the lonely French village of Cunel. Located but a few hundred yards from the Meuse-Argonne American Cemetery, Woodfill's actions are only known to those who take the time to study the topic. The village of Cunel has a declining population, and most of the buildings are unoccupied, with agriculture being the only work available in the area. I, with Jean Paul DeVries, the owner of the nearby 14–18 Museum, discussed Woodfill's heroism with Cunel's mayor and asked about the possibility of constructing a Woodfill historic trail. The mayor immediately gave his approval, but funds to construct it have been elusive and

Woodfill's action remains unavailable to the public until private funding is secured.

Robert Laplander, a historian from Wisconsin, dedicated some twenty years of his life to writing the most engaging and thorough book on the saga of the Lost Battalion. His research led to renewed interest in the leadership of Major Charles Whittlesey and the incredible sacrifice of the men with him. This led to the dedication of a monument to the Lost Battalion near the famous "pocket" in the Argonne Forest where Whittlesey and his men were encircled for five days. Laplander wrote of this endeavor, "My goal . . . was simply to give visitors a truer sense of what happened there. My work on the Lost Battalion has always been an exercise in remembrance— of the men, of the event and most especially of their sacrifice."[7]

At the same time that Robert Laplander expounded on his research related to the Lost Battalion, a team of people from across the United States and Europe endeavored to ascertain the location of the Sergeant York action. The exact location was lost to history, and this gave skeptics (even from York's home state of Tennessee) an opportunity to question the authenticity of his feat. I began research in earnest in the 1990s and field research in France starting in 2002 with my wife, Rebbie, and son, Josiah, and soon thereafter Kory and Beth O'Keefe, among many others. The goal was to find out exactly what happened that fateful morning on 8 October 1918. After spending more than a thousand hours in German and American archives, the site of the York action was easily narrowed down to a one-hundred-meter area in the Argonne. The mayor of nearby Chatel Chehery (first Roland Destenay and later Alain Rickal) granted permission for a dig using metal detectors. My approach was to combine archival research with military terrain analysis and archeology to find with 100 percent confidence the facts of the York fight. The artifacts would be ballistically analyzed for final authentication to remove any shadow of doubt of the findings. Soon historians, soldiers from eight NATO nations, Boy Scouts, and many others volunteered to support the endeavor.

Coming under the banner of the Sergeant York Discovery Expedition, my team spent more than one hundred days in the Argonne, where thousands of artifacts were recovered. This included the pistol and rifle casings fired by York on 8 October 1918. The details of this endeavor are recorded in *Alvin York: A New Biography of the Hero of the Argonne* and at the website www.sgtyorkdiscovery.com.

Left to right, Josiah, Rebecca, and Douglas Mastriano in the Argonne Forest following the dedication of the Sergeant York Historic Trail on the ninetieth anniversary in 2008. (Mastriano Collection)

Once the discoveries were authenticated and endorsed by American and French officials, money was raised to erect two monuments in the Argonne Forest in the exact location where York fought. This included cutting a three-kilometer historic trail in the Argonne Forest. Hundreds of Boy Scouts and their families dedicated thousands of hours to make this a reality. Working closely with French officials, the trail and monuments were completed in time for a large ninetieth anniversary commemoration. With the support and endorsement of Phil Rivers and Scott Desjardins, the director and deputy director of the Meuse-Argonne American Cemetery, more than eight hundred people attended. Three generations of Yorks were in attendance, including one of Alvin's sons, George Edward Buxton York, grandson Gerald, and great granddaughter Deborah. The trail follows York's steps, and now visitors to the Argonne can "walk where York walked." There are nine historic signs in French, German, and English to explain the events that occurred there on 8 October 1918. The monument park includes a stone table where York describes what occurred in the battle, and the other marker includes the names of all seventeen Americans who fought there.

Volunteers make World War One commemorations possible due to a lack of national will to honor the Doughboys of 1918. In this photograph from Josiah Mastriano's Eagle Scout Service Project, Boy Scouts and family members lay the last load of thirty tons of gravel along the Sergeant York Historic Trail in the Argonne Forest. Left to right, Rebbie Mastriano, Adam Jost, Josiah Mastriano, Nick Gallardo, and Peter Perkins. (Mastriano Collection)

Much space has been given to the commemoration of Pershing's three favorite Doughboys. The purpose of this is to highlight the immense work, time, and costs of such endeavors. Yet, any one of us can make such commemorations possible. The Sergeant York Historic Trail only came to reality thanks to the willingness of so many to be a part of it. All of the volunteers were important, but none more so than Phil Rivers, then the director of the nearby American Cemetery. Great men such as he are rare and make the seemingly impossible possible. He was able to cut through the bureaucracy to make this endeavor a success.

Despite the individual endeavors of so many to commemorate and remember the heroes of 1918, the Meuse-Argonne American Cemetery surpasses them all. This cemetery is the resting place for 14,246 Americans, most of whom gave the last full measure of devotion in the Meuse-Argonne campaign. It is the largest American cemetery in Europe and serves as a stark reminder of the cost of freedom. Their lives and legacy changed the course of history and affirms my belief that what a person does in life matters. It echoes across the generations and into eternity.

Conclusion

War is . . . a test of character: it makes bad men worse and good men better.

We know not of the future, and cannot plan for it much. But we can hold our spirits and our bodies so pure and high, we may cherish such thoughts and such ideals, and dream such dreams of lofty purpose, that we can determine and know what manner of men we will be whenever and wherever the hour strikes, that calls to noble action. This predestination God has given us in charge. No man becomes suddenly different from his habit and cherished thought.
—Major General Joshua L. Chamberlain,
American Civil War leader

While on a streetcar in Heidelberg, Germany, I was having a courteous conversation with a well-dressed German. He worked in the engineering world, where science and observable facts reign supreme. He politely asked what I studied in college, to which I replied, "History." He could not contain his response and comically blurted out, "Ha! What a waste! What can you do with that?" Having previously reflected on the utility of history, I had a ready response and answered, "There is considerable use of history. Consider your nation of Germany. Thank God that Allied leaders, such as George Marshall, learned the dangers of vanquishing a foe after the war. The French and British punished your nation for World War One with the harsh conditions of the Treaty of Versailles, creating conditions for the madman Adolf Hitler to rise here. Marshal Foch was there and witnessed the harsh terms of Versailles. However, after World War Two it was 180 degrees different. The Americans did not punish Germany as the Allies did after the First World War, but instead invested millions of dollars of American money to rebuild your nation, and hundreds of thousands of our young men stayed here to defend you. This turned Germany into a friend. The Marshal Plan was born in the ashes of World War One and our nations are no longer mortal enemies, but close friends, thanks to the application and understanding of history."

My German acquaintance just stared blankly at me, as he never had considered this. Just as he has a laboratory at work to measure his experiments, so do historians. Our lab is the past, and we can look to the past to observe human activity, decisions, actions, and see how they shaped the world in which we live. Many of the mistakes have already been made, and we are better off learning from the failures of others in the past than repeating them in our own lives, families, and nations. I would prefer to learn from the mistakes of those who have gone before us than to suffer the consequences of miscalculation and weakness.

Sadly, many of the valuable and hard-learned lessons of the Meuse-Argonne campaign are forgotten. To exacerbate this dilemma, the preponderance of historians either do not understand the value of this military campaign or are purists and choose not to see how the experience of the U.S. Army in 1918 can benefit people today. As Dr. John Lennox, a professor at Oxford University, astutely states, "New things are old things happening to new people."[1]

There is value to studying both the First World War and the Meuse-Argonne campaign. The subject is rich with historic examples and vignettes on the importance of having a coherent strategy, of having a viable and trained military force, of avoiding prevarication and clearly communicating your national policy and red lines, and then backing them up with force if they are violated. The root of the problem for the United States during the First World War was that it lacked a president who could see beyond his preconceived notions of the world. Wilson was focused on domestic policies and was ill-prepared for the world war that erupted around him. Hiding safely behind the oceans, Wilson imagined that the world was something that it was not. Even when the war began taking the lives of the citizens that he swore on a Bible to protect, Wilson's default setting was to give speeches and to send harsh letters. This weakness would be laughable if not for the lives it would later claim. When the nation finally entered the war, it had a smaller army than pre-war Belgium and was not ready for the realities of modern conflict.

There is a propensity for American national leaders to focus on domestic issues over international concerns. The luxury to do this is enabled by the two great oceans surrounding the United States.

However, the oceans, even in 1915, could not protect the nation from foreign aggression, and they are less likely to do so today.

Americans do not have a monopoly on such folly. History bears out that British foreign secretary Lord Edward Grey had an opportunity to perhaps prevent the German attack on Belgium by simply declaring that his nation would honor its treaty with Brussels. Instead, prevarication and doublespeak prevailed, convincing the Kaiser that Germany would not be opposed by the British. It seems that the pacifism and timidity of Wilson and Grey lingers. When confronted with daunting security challenges and flagrant acts of terror, leaders in North America and Europe tend to encourage vigils and benefit concerts, and give speeches defending the very people who attacked them. There is a decided lack of hard action to proactively respond to the attackers. The remarks from the mayor of London in the aftermath of the 2017 terror attacks against his people have a Wilsonian feel to them. Such a response, as experienced between 1915 through 1917, will only encourage further attacks and more loss of innocent lives. Mayor Khan is following the failed patterns of Prime Minister Chamberlain and President Wilson.

Sitting in the shadows of the powerful Soviet Union, Estonia, Latvia, and Lithuania surrendered their sovereignty to Stalin in 1940 to avoid a war and suffered unimaginable depravations and genocide at the hands of his atheistic thugs. They would have been better off fighting the Soviet hordes than enduring an ethnic cleansing and de facto national slavery. So too, in 1990, the Kuwaiti emir demobilized his army so as to reduce tensions with Iraq. Within days of doing this, Saddam Hussein invaded the emirate with virtually no opposition.

It was such weakness that encouraged Hitler in the 1930s to march on the Rhineland, to invade Austria, to barter away Czechoslovakian borderlands, and then to take the rest of the country in 1938, all with the de facto consent of Britain's Prime Minister Chamberlain. Not until the Nazis invaded Poland in 1939 did the Allies declare war, but after declaring war they did nothing and waited for the Germans to attack. The price for weak leaders, vague policies, and ill-prepared armies is too high to ponder.

Thus was the case for the United States in 1914, 1915, and 1916. Long speeches and fair words from a president increasingly detached from reality displayed weakness to Germany and encouraged it to take the risk of unrestricted submarine warfare and to negotiate with the Mexicans to invade the American Southwest. Wilson's high-minded commitment to pacifism veiled behind neutrality resulted in the nation having a weak, small, and ill-prepared army. When war was declared and the army expanded twenty-fold from 200,000 to 4 million, it was mostly an untrained and untested force. The test would come in the Meuse-Argonne campaign, and the price would be American blood.

The U.S. Army learned the hard way how to fight a modern war. The lessons from the Meuse-Argonne campaign are still relevant today. Fighting alongside, with, and even in multinational military formations was the norm in the Meuse-Argonne and remains more so even today. This has never been an easy endeavor, as each nation has distinct military traditions and differing political objectives. This is where the value of the North Atlantic Treaty Organization comes to prominence. In the Meuse-Argonne, there was no standardization of military equipment or fighting doctrine. It took a second world war before the United States, Canada, and Western Europe would come together in a military alliance to provide the basis for multinational operations. Indeed, NATO is the fruit of hard-learned lessons not just from the Meuse-Argonne and the First World War, but also the Second World War. Member nations take for granted the value of this Alliance and how it can serve as a basis to defend Europe or North America with a proven and exercised command and control system, a common military doctrine, and an understanding of each other's approach to war. The lessons of two world wars are harnessed in the form of the NATO Alliance.

The most glaring lesson from the American experience in the Meuse-Argonne campaign was the price of unpreparedness. This led to thousands of lives needlessly lost, as inexperienced leaders made tactical errors and ill-advised decisions that an experienced cadre would never have made. In this case, Pershing brought his experiences from the frontier, Cuba, Mexico, and the Philippines and believed that Americans with rifles and bayonets would simply brush aside the German Army once they broke through the trenches.

Bringing frontier and small war doctrines to the realities of a modern conventional war on the Western Front bordered on madness, especially since the folly of this doctrine had already been demonstrated in 1914 when the French tried to overcome German machine guns with similar frontal assaults. Pershing and the other American military leaders did not have far to look to adopt their tactics to the realities of modern warfare, especially after the French offered these lessons from the Great War to their allies. Yet, at great cost in lives and treasure, these valuable lessons were ignored or rejected out of hand. The Americans would employ the wrong tactics and doctrine to the Meuse-Argonne Offensive. As Premier Clemenceau warned, since the Americans did not permit the French to teach them, the Germans did.

But the most important lesson to emerge from the Meuse-Argonne Offensive is the difference that one person can make. In the midst of a crisis, or when all hope seemed lost, certain men stood in the gap to confront the enemy and change the course of history. It was Major James E. Rieger who led his men valiantly across the heavily defended hill of Vauquois on the first day of the Meuse-Argonne Offensive. This was no small matter and was an achievement that the French had failed to accomplish over the last four years. Rieger, a quiet lawyer from Kirksville, Missouri, was known for his work in organizing a very popular Sunday school program for the soldiers and was ridiculed by his commanding general as being "hopelessly useless." This officer would go on to lead the liberation of two French villages, fight off German counterattacks, and man the line that marked the furthest point of advance of his division.

Lieutenant John Wingate, a respected leader in the 35th Division, was in many ways like Major Rieger. His men said that he had "a gentle kindly heart of pure gold." He led his men confidently forward on the first day of the Meuse-Argonne campaign in the face of fierce German resistance and overcame each obstacle in their path. Among the men with Lieutenant Wingate was the son of Norwegian immigrants, Private Nels Wold. This young man endeavored to live out his beliefs in the face of the daily temptations facing him in France and proved faithful in these trials. On that one day in September 1918, Nels single-handedly attacked four German machine guns, in the end giving his life and being awarded the Medal of Honor in recognition of his selfless service. Wold's last words were "pray for me boys and write my folks and tell them I love them all." It is such men who changed the course of history.

Then there was the duo of the Irish Catholic "brawler" Captain George Mallon and his Jewish first sergeant Sydney Gumpertz, who, with their unit's chaplain, Father O'Donnell, led their men into a daring flanking maneuver that drove deep into the German flanks, breaking the enemy's hold on the west bank of the Meuse River on the first day of the Meuse-Argonne Offensive. The brilliant advance bagged one hundred German prisoners, a four-gun battery of German artillery, and eleven machine guns. Captain Mallon and First Sergeant Gumpertz were both awarded the Medal of Honor for their daring leadership.

And then there is Corporal Alvin York, a conscientious objector struggling to reconcile his Christian faith with military service. York's odyssey in the U.S. Army was not easy. He did not fit in with his platoon mates, who had recently immigrated to America or were from regions of the country that he could not relate to. To make matters worse, he was one of the few soldiers who would not journey downtown on weekends to get drunk and chase the ladies. Things took a turn for the worse for York when his platoon mates discovered that he was a conscientious objector. He was called a coward and a weakling for his moral struggle. Thankfully, York had sympathetic leaders, who spoke freely from the Bible with him on how to reconcile his faith with military service.

When that fateful day of 8 October 1918 came to fruition, York found himself making a decision between the life and death of his fellow soldiers. When that moment came and all hope was lost, York charged into the maelstrom, shot twenty-five of the enemy, captured another 132, and broke the German hold over the Argonne Forest, forever changing the outcome of the war. It was men like York, Rieger, Wold, and so many others who helped bring victory and enabled the U.S. Army to maintain forward momentum against a skilled and determined enemy. The common factor among these men was their moral courage.

The experience of the American soldier in the Meuse-Argonne demonstrates that a person does not suddenly become heroic in the heat of battle, but rather the response to the maelstrom is tied to personal character. Walking this path is not easy, especially these days. But when a person chooses daily to do the right thing, despite the pressure not to, there develops inside the person a sort of bravery, confidence, and courage that is almost impossible to describe. Colonel Joshua Lawrence Chamberlain captured the essence of character, writing: "We know not of the future, and cannot plan for it much. But we can hold our spirits and our bodies so pure and high, we may cherish such thoughts and such ideals, and dream such dreams of lofty purpose, that we can determine and know what manner of men we will be whenever the hour strikes that calls us to noble action. . . . No man becomes suddenly different from his habit and cherished thought."

These are uncertain times in which we live. The nation seems to have lost its way. It is heartbreaking to contemplate that I am giving the nation to my son less prosperous, less secure, and less good. We seem to have lost our way as a people as we collectively meander in the darkness of political correctness and moral collapse. It seems what is evil has become good and what is good has become evil in the eyes of many political and entertainment elites. Yet, hope remains. Average people rose up in the maelstrom of the Meuse-Argonne and stood in the gap. They confronted the evil around them and changed the course of history. It is this that gives us hope. It could be that good-for-nothing-drunk from Tennessee who people once thought would never amount to anything who changes the course of history. That is the Alvin York story, the man who went from an out-of-control drunk to a faithful Christian to an American hero.

Chamberlain was an American Civil War hero, and although outside the scope of this epoch, he is a grand example to finish this book. Chamberlain grew up in Maine to a devout Christian family. His one weakness, however, was a severe "stammering" (stuttering) problem. This impediment followed him into adulthood and seemed to be something that he would never overcome. He prayed for help, but none seemed to come. He was ridiculed and mocked for his terrible speech patterns, turning him into a severe introvert. Finally, in college, the curse was broken, and he went on to become the greatest orator of his generation.

Contemplate the irony of what happened next. In June 1863, the Confederate Army of Northern Virginia, under the leadership of General Robert E. Lee, invaded Pennsylvania with an eye on winning a decisive victory to achieve final southern independence. Meanwhile, 120 Union soldiers from the 2nd Maine Regiment had mutinied. It was up to Chamberlain to convince them to fight. This "stuttering fool" from Maine stood before the men and gave such a moving speech that all 120 joined his men in saving the Union during the Battle of Little Round Top on 2 July 1863. A favorite verse of Chamberlain's was I Corinthians 1:27, which states, "But God hath chosen the foolish things of the world to confound the wise; and God hath chosen the weak things of the world to confound the things which are mighty." This is Chamberlain's story, this is York's story, and perhaps it is your story.

Although confronted by a determined foe and an uncertain future, the Doughboys of 1918 faced the tempest and turned the tide. The reality is that few of us will be the next Sergeant York, and perhaps fewer still the next Joshua Chamberlain, but we have an opportunity to pass on a legacy like them and perhaps raise or influence the next generation of heroes that will stand in the gap in that hour when the nation needs them most. Or perhaps we are the ones called "for such a time as this." If that is the case, then we should endeavor to daily build our character muscles so that "we can determine and know what manner of men [or women] we will be whenever the hour strikes that calls us to noble action." Indeed, as Chamberlain added, "This predestination God has given us in charge. No man becomes suddenly different from his habit and cherished thought."

The fate of the world rests in the hands of everyday people. Although confronted with seemingly overwhelming odds, we have the opportunity to determine how we will respond "on that day that calls us to noble action," by living life with honor and integrity. The lesson to take away from the American experience in the Meuse-Argonne campaign is that average people changed the course of history. That is their story. This can be our story. Indeed, your life matters, and what you do in life echoes across the generations and into eternity.

Acknowledgments

Thunder in the Argonne was only possible with the love and support of my wife, Rebecca, and son, Josiah. They are part of the story, which included more than one hundred days of exploring or working in the Meuse-Argonne region of France. The odyssey for this adventure began with finding the location where Alvin York charged a German machine gun, fought off a bayonet attack, and captured 132 Germans. My wife, with my son, was the first to locate the position of the German machine gun. This was just the beginning, and *Thunder in the Argonne* tells the rest of the story. What we discovered is that even one hundred years later, the events and people of the Great War reverberate across the generations to us today. I am blessed to have a family that was part of the journey. Rebbie, thank you for helping me get this book done with your advice, suggestions, and encouragement. Josiah, thank you for your amazing work on creating the thirty-plus maps in this book!

Thanks go to Roger Cirillo for his support and leadership in completing this book. Roger has led the endeavor to tell the soldiers' story and has made a lasting contribution in keeping their memory alive. Sincere thanks to Major General David T. Zabecki, America's premier military historian. He has been a mentor to me for more than a decade and is a true patriot. General Zabecki's wisdom, guidance, and expertise really made the difference. Thanks also to Professor Marc Milner for his words of wisdom on how to tell the Meuse-Argonne story. Heartfelt thanks to Kory and Beth O'Keefe, who poured their energy into keeping the memory of the Doughboys alive and for their leadership in maintaining the Sergeant York Historic Trail in the Argonne Forest.

Thank you also to Bill and Karen Rudge of Bill Rudge Ministry of Living Truth. Bill and Karen provided essential support and encouragement to me while endeavoring to complete this book. Thank you to Lieutenant Colonel Jeff Parmer (U.S. Army), who sadly recently passed away. Jeff was a great American who captivated me with his tales of Vauquois, and the other Meuse-Argonne sites.

A salute to our many valuable French friends who made the work in the Argonne possible, especially Mayor Roland Destenay and mon ami Mayor Alain Rickal. Merci beaucoup to Richard Steffan of the Grandpré Development Department, Frederic Chopin, and French senator Jean-Luc Warsmann and the Arnould family of Montflix in Grandpré. Thank you to Dominique Lacorde for sharing his photos of the Württembergers in the Meuse-Argonne. Merci to Henri Autret for his assistance on discovering the truth of the Sam Woodfill saga.

Great respect to John "Phil" Rivers, the best director of the Meuse-Argonne American Cemetery. The United States was blessed to have Mr. Rivers serve in the Meuse-Argonne, as he went above and beyond the call of duty to pass the memory of the Doughboys to the next generation. Thank you also to Scott Desjardins, who has the same professionalism and passion for American history. Thanks to Jean-Paul DeVries of the Romagne 14–18 Museum for his expert advice and assistance in tracing the steps of so many American Doughboys. His museum is the best on the Western Front and the fruit of thirty-plus years of fieldwork. A hearty thanks to Lieutenant General Theodore and Mrs. Harriet Stroup for their generous help with telling the amazing story of Captain Harris.

Thanks to the many outstanding archivists across North America and Europe. I especially thank Mitch Yockelson of the U.S. National Archives for his excellent help and his friendship. Mitch, who recently published his own excellent book on the Meuse-Argonne called *Forty-Seven Days*, generously shared many important archival records that he had uncovered. A true gentleman! Sincere appreciation also to my friend and fellow U.S. Army War College colleague, Dr. Mike Neiburg. Mike provided expert and helpful advice on writing this book and answered my questions, even while overseas on speaking engagements.

Danke Colonel Gerhard Gross, and Major Peter Popp, German Bundeswehr, and their staff at the Militärgeschichtliches Forschungsamt, Potsdam, and the Militärarchiv, Freiburg im Breisgau. Danke also to Bundeswehr Oberst (Colonel) Thorsten Alme, Sven Lange, and Markus Kreitmayr for their help translating German documents and for answering questions on German tactics. Gratitude to the Boy Scouts who focused their Eagle Scout Service Projects on the Sergeant York Historic Trail over the years. These Eagle Scouts are Nate Eggert (2007–2008), Jeffrey Perkins (2009), John Gerber (2010), Drew Burns (2011), Josiah Mastriano (2011), and Jeremiah Gerber (2015). Thank you to the Alvin York family, Colonel Gerald

York (U.S. Army Retired), and his children, Gerald Jr. and Deb. My gratitude also extends to Alvin's three surviving children, George Edward, Betsy Ross, and Andrew Jackson York and to Travis Stover of the Alvin C. York State Historic Park.

Thank you Rob Laplander, the leading historian of the Lost Battalion, for your amazing research, extensive help, and advice. Thank you Jodi Engebrecht for the photo of Corporal Murray Savage. Thank you Debbie Hanagan for the help with French translations early on in this project. Danke to Family Breusch, especially Friedrich and Alexander, for sharing photos and the life story of Leutnant Fritz Endriss, who died trying to save his friends. Semper Fi to my good friend Professor G. K. Cunningham (Colonel, USMC Retired) for co-leading the U.S. Army War College World War One elective with me for four years and bringing many brilliant observations of the Great War to the forefront. A thank you also to Professors Paul Jussel, Mike Marre, and Jim Scudieri as well at Carlisle Barracks for their mentorship and support. Thanks to Lieutenant Colonel Joe Buccino of the 82nd Division, and thank you to the Pritzker Military Museum and Library.

My appreciation goes to Nancy Schaff, Paul Cora, and all of the supporters of the Log Cabin Memorial for preserving the legacy of the 314th Regiment of the 79th Division. Thank you to George and Joy Hammar for generously sharing your extensive Great War photo archive with me. Thank you also to Joe Ogile, Stan Crader, and Wayne Bowen for providing an excellent forum to pass on the legacy of great men to the next generation.

A heartfelt thank you to my many friends at the Army Heritage Education Center (AHEC) in Carlisle, Pennsylvania. Special recognition and an extra thank you go to Melissa Wiford, DiAnne Evans, Tom Buffenbarger, Steve Bye, and Rodney Foytik. Also, thanks to Richard Baker, Karl Warner, Steve Johnson, Mary Gasper, John and Emily Heckman, John Giblin, Louisa Arnold-Friend, Kaleb Dissinger, Jessica Sheets, Mary Gaspar, Jessie Faller-Parett, Jeff Hawks, Mike Perry, and so many others. Thank you to the AHEC director, Colonel Pete Crean, for his vision in sharing the American story during the centennial. Thanks also to Theo Mayer, Chris Christopher, and Chris Isleib of the World War One Centennial Commission, and to Dane Coffman, Matt Davenport, and Gary Andrejak for their passion in preserving the legacy of the Great War.

Sincere appreciation to my many friends at Pond Bank

Community Church and Pastor Jeremy Lehman for their support during this daunting process. Above all, a soldier's salute to the men of 1918, who performed superbly on the fields of honor in France and accomplished the impossible. Their story must not be forgotten. What these men did made the difference, and echoes across the generations . . . and into eternity.

Notes

1. The War That Changed the World

Epigraph: Lodge and Roosevelt, *Hero Tales from American History,* ix.

1. Sheffield, *Forgotten Victory,* 207–210.

2. American divisions were 2 to 2.5 times the size of their European counterparts in men. The American forces' strength equaled about fifty-five French, British, or German divisions.

3. Horne, ed., *Source Records of the Great War,* 6: 401–402. These figures are taken by a joint report published by Field Marshal Ferdinand Foch and General John J. Pershing.

4. Sheffield, *Forgotten Victory,* 218–219.

5. Terraine, *To Win a War,* 68.

6. Ibid., 18–20. What is often overlooked with America's entry into the Great War is that all of South America either followed the United States in its declaration of war or severed relations with Imperial Germany. China also entered the war, as did several other nations. This means that the geopolitical initiative was now firmly in the Allies' (Entente's) favor. The last advantage that the Central Powers experienced was in 1915 when Bulgaria joined the war. After that, there was geopolitical stalemate among the global powers (although the capitulation of Russia was a major event for Germany and Austria-Hungary). The point is that with more of the world's powers arrayed against Germany, most agree that Germany's fate for an ultimate defeat was just a matter of time. The challenge that the leaders had was how to achieve that final victory and under what conditions and terms. See Strachan, *The First World War* (1:300–313), for some discussion of this.

7. Herwig, *The First World War,* 394.

8. Trask, *The AEF and Coalition War Making,* 30, 43.

9. Ibid., 30, 75; Terraine, *To Win a War,* 69.

10. Pershing, *My Experiences in the World War,* 2:207–211.

11. Liggett, *A.E.F.,* 172–174.

12. Grotelueschen, *The AEF Way of War,* 125–128. The distances between no-man's-land and the third line of German defenses across the Western Front varied greatly. At Cambrai it was thirty kilometers deep. At Arras it was forty kilometers, and sixty at Laon. In the Argonne it was only eighteen kilometers. With this shallow sector the Germans had very little space to give up in the defense, and thus they were compelled to defend every line tenaciously. There was little room

for German error in the Meuse-Argonne, and here they could not trade space for time as they could in the other portions of the front.

13. Grotelueschen, *The AEF Way of War*, 127. However, the French and Germans continued to conduct attacks in the area in 1916 and 1917, even though the area did generally become a "quiet" sector of the front after the Battle of Verdun ended in November 1916. In particular, mine warfare for control of several hills continued during this epoch, which included Vauquois, a dominant hill just east of the Argonne Forest, and Hill 285 in the midst of the Argonne proper.

14. Terraine, *To Win a War*, 153.

15. This does not include the battles of the American Civil War. Pershing, *My Experiences in the World War*, 2:388–390.

2. The German Attack of 1914 to the Crisis of 1918

Epigraph: Erich Ludendorff, in Viereck, ed., *As They Saw Us*, 27.

1. Geiss, *German Foreign Policy*, 161–174.

2. Ibid., 35–59.

3. Langer, "The Franco-Russian Alliance (1890–1894)," 554–575; Langer, "The Dual Alliance," 23 September 1918.

4. Foley, "The Schlieffen Plan-A War Plan," 69–74.

5. Neiberg, *The Western Front 1914–1916*.

6. Mead, *The Eye in the Air: History of Air Observation and Reconnaissance for the Army 1785–1945*, 54–59.

7. Strachan, *The First World War*, 1:242–260.

8. Shuddekopf, *Der Erste Weltkrieg*, 16–19.

9. Broadbent, *Gallipoli: The Fatal Shore*.

10. The distinction between an alliance and a coalition is significant. An alliance is a long-term binding agreement, is consensus driven, and is composed of members who are equal in making strategic decisions. For instance, in NATO all twenty-nine members must agree to a plan, policy, or approach for it to be implemented. This means that a "no" vote from even the smallest member can prevent decision or action. A coalition, however, is composed of voluntary contributions under a lead nation, where consensus is not the norm. A coalition is usually short-term and built around a crisis.

3. Dithering, Dreaming, and Speechmaking

Epigraph: Roosevelt, *Day before Yesterday*, 67.

1. Ikenberry, *The Crisis of American Foreign Policy*, 10.

2. Woodrow Wilson, *Message to Congress*, 63rd Cong., 2d sess., Senate Doc. No. 566 (Washington, D.C.: Government Printing Office, 1914), 3–4.

3. Letter from Sir Cecil Spring-Rice to Sir Arthur Nicolson, concerning William Jennings Bryan's Opinion of the Great War, 13 November 1914, available online at http://wwi.lib.byu.edu/index.php/Letter_Concerning_William_Jennings_Bryan's_Opinion_of_the_Great_War (accessed 25 March 2016).

4. Roosevelt, *Day before Yesterday*, 68.

5. Striner, *Woodrow Wilson and World War I*, 16–17.

6. Quoted in ibid., 12.

7. Görlitz, ed., *The Kaiser and His Court*, 70–72. This book is a compilation of the eyewitness accounts of Admiral Georg Alexander von Müller, chief of the German Imperial Navy Cabinet during the First World War.

8. Compton-Hall, *Submarines at War 1914–1918*, 195–197, 343.

9. Ramsey, *Lusitania*, 59–63; and Bailey, *The Lusitania Disaster*.

10. Woodrow Wilson, "First Lusitania Note," 13 May 1915, available online at http://wwi.lib.byu.edu/index.php/Wilson's_First_Lusitania_Note_to_Germany (accessed 25 March 2016); also see the following webpage dedicated to research on the RMS *Lusitania*: http://www.rmslusitania.info/primary-docs/wilson-notes/ (accessed 25 March 2016).

11. William Jennings Bryan wanted an even-handed American approach to the dilemma it faced. Contemplating the starvation of portions of the German populace due to the British naval blockade, he retorted, "why be so shocked by the drowning of a few people, if there is to be no objection to starving a nation." See Schmidt, *The Folly of War*, 78–79.

12. Woodrow Wilson, "Americanism and the Foreign Born," 10 May 1915.

13. Cramer, *Newton D. Baker*, 80–82.

14. Striner, *Woodrow Wilson and World War I*, 35.

15. Knock, *To End All Wars*, 106.

16. Striner, *Woodrow Wilson and World War I*, 74–77.

17. Woodrow Wilson, "Speech of Acceptance," 2 September 1916, available online at http://millercenter.org/president/wilson/speeches/speech-3795 (accessed 25 March 2016).

18. Woodrow Wilson, "American Principles," address delivered at the first annual League to Enforce Peace assembly, 27 May 1916, available online at http://www.presidency.ucsb.edu/ws/?pid=65391 (accessed 25 March 2016).

19. An excellent description of this in the introduction to Ikenberry, *The Crisis of American Foreign Policy*, 11–24.

20. Woodrow Wilson, "Peace without Victory," 22 January 1917, available online at http://www.firstworldwar.com/source/peacewithoutvictory.htm (accessed 25 March 2016).

21. Ibid.

22. Morrow, *The Great War*, 200–205.

23. Zimmermann confessed that the telegram was true when asked by an American reporter.

24. Woodrow Wilson, "Wilson's War Message to Congress," 2 April 1917, available online at http://wwi.lib.byu.edu/index.php/Wilson's_War_Message_to_Congress (accessed 25 March 2016).

25. Ibid.

26. Ludendorff, *Meine Kriegserinnerungen*, 473–499.

27. Pershing, *My Experiences in the World War*, 1:36–38.

28. Woodrow Wilson, "The Fourteen Points," 8 January 1918, available online at http://avalon.law.yale.edu/20th_century/wilson14.asp (accessed 25 March 2016).

29. Adapted from Ikenberry, *The Crisis of American Foreign Policy*, 11–13.

30. Adapted from ibid., 11–13.

31. Clemenceau, *Grandeur and Misery of Victory*, 74–76.

32. Foch, *The Memoirs of Marshal Foch*, 398.

33. U.S. Army, History Division, *United States Army in the World War, 1917–1919*, 3–21.

34. Mouravieff, "A History of the Church in Russia," 265.

4. The Plan for Victory

Epigraph: Foch, *The Memoirs of Marshal Foch*, 370.

1. Portions of this chapter appeared previously in Mastriano, "The Meuse Argonne Offensive," 130–135.

2. Clausewitz, *On War*, 100, 136.

3. Neiberg, *Foch*, 45–52, and correspondence with Michael Neiberg on 1 March 2016.

4. Neiberg, *Foch*, 75–76.

5. Foch, *The Memoirs of Marshal Foch*, 369.

6. Ibid., 398.

7. Ibid., 371–373.

8. Fuller, *A Military History of the Western World*, 3:282–283, 318–341; Fuller, *Memoirs of an Unconventional Soldier*, 280–333.

9. Foch, *The Memoirs of Marshal Foch*, 371.

10. Ibid., 371–373.

11. Ibid., 389–400.

12. U.S. Army, *Final Report of Gen. John J. Pershing*, 38–43. Pershing says that neither Foch nor any of his counterparts envisioned the war ending in 1918. Although Foch did not explicitly say he expected to win in 1918, his Memorandum of 24 July and his subsequent statements in

August and September suggest that such an outcome was in the realm of the possible, explaining why he was willing to take considerable strategic risk to order the Grand Offensive.

13. Foch, *The Memoirs of Marshal Foch*, 408–409.
14. Mastriano, "The Meuse Argonne Offensive," 130–135.
15. Sheffield, *Forgotten Victory*, 207–210.
16. Clausewitz defined the center of gravity in this manner: "Out of these characteristics a certain center of gravity develops, the hub of all power and movement on which everything depends. That is the point against which all our energies should be directed." Clausewitz, *On War*, 486.
17. Mastriano, "The Meuse Argonne Offensive," 130–135.
18. Grotelueschen, *The AEF Way of War*, 125–128.
19. Pershing, *My Experiences in the World War*, 2:240–246.
20. Ibid., 2:250–260.
21. Clemenceau, *Grandeur and Misery of Victory*, 73–77.
22. Foch, *The Memoirs of Marshal Foch*, 394–397.
23. Ibid., 395–396.
24. American Battle Monuments Commission, *American Armies and Battlefields in Europe*, 105–107.
25. Pershing, *My Experiences in the World War*, 2:249–259.
26. Mastriano, *Alvin York*, 60–61.

5. St. Mihiel

Epigraph: D'Este, *Patton: A Genius for War*, 233.
1. American Battle Monuments Commission, *American Armies and Battlefields in Europe*, 105–107.
2. Gallwitz, "Retreat to the Rhein," in Viereck, ed., *As They Saw Us*, 230–235.
3. U.S. Army, *Final Report of Gen. John J. Pershing*, 38–43.
4. American Battle Monuments Commission, *American Armies and Battlefields in Europe*, 110.
5. Ludendorff, *Meine Kriegserinnerungen*, 572–573; Hindenburg, *Aus Meinem Leben*, 364–366.
6. Harris, *The War as I Saw It*, 84–88.
7. Meilinger, "Mitchell Biography," available online at http://www.airpower.maxwell.af.mil/airchronicles/cc/biograph.html (accessed 15 March 2011); also see Michael Hanlon, "The St. Mihiel Offensive," available online at http://www.worldwar1.com/dbc/stmihiel.htm (accessed 15 March 2011). Michael Hanlon is an expert on the St. Mihiel fight and is both well published on this subject and a frequent battlefield tour guide of the area.

8. York, *Sergeant York*, 207–208.
9. Blumenson, *The Patton Papers*, 582.
10. James, *The Years of MacArthur*, 1:203–205.
11. Blumenson, *The Patton Papers*, 590.
12. U.S. Army, *Final Report of Gen. John J. Pershing*, 38–43; Pershing, *My Experiences in the World War*, 2:269–273.
13. Pershing, *My Experiences in the World War*, 2:266–2673.
14. Grotelueschen, *The AEF Way of War*, 30–43.
15. Gorce, *Charles de Gaulle: 1890–1945*, vol. 1; Gorce, *The French Army*, 102.
16. See an excellent article on this topic by Damien Fenton, "Unjustly Accused: Marshal Ferdinand Foch and the French 'Cult of the Offensive,'" August 2009, http://www.firstworldwar.com/features/foch.htm (accessed on 22 December 2010).
17. Clemenceau, *Grandeur and Misery of Victory*, 77.
18. Hart, *Reputations, Ten Years After*, 145, 270–275, 278–284, 306–313; Clemenceau, *Grandeur and Misery of Victory*, 76.
19. American Battle Monuments Commission, *82d Division: Summary of Operations*, 12–13; Cooke, *The All-Americans at War*, 77.
20. York, *Sergeant York*, 210.

6. Meuse-Argonne

Epigraph: Lapple, *Das Württembergishche Landwehr Infanterie Regiment nr. 125 im Weltkrieg 1914–1918*, Band 38, 157.

1. The L'Aire River meanders below the eastern slope of the Argonne Forest. American sources and maps call this the Aire River, while French sources label it L'Aire. Both Aire and L'Aire are used in this book to denote the same river.
2. Doyle, *A Visit to Three Fronts*, 18.
3. Buchner and Hoppe, *In Stellund nach Vauquois*, 90–160.
4. During the 1918 Meuse-Argonne campaign, only the first three lines of German defense were actually complete.
5. Braim, *The Test of Battle*, 76–77.
6. Pershing, *My Experiences in the World War*, 2:282–283.
7. General Anton Franke, section 8/III, 2nd Württemberg Landwehr Division Reports, Stuttgart Landesarchiv, Germany, pages 1–22.
8. U.S. Army, History Division, *United States Army in the World War, 1917–1919*, 9:508.
9. General Anton Franke, section 8/III, 2nd Württemberg Landwehr Division Reports, Stuttgart Landesarchiv, Germany, pages 1–22.
10. U.S. Army, History Division, *United States Army in the World War 1917–1919*, 9:508.

11. Pershing, *My Experiences in the World War,* 2:282–283.

12. General Anton Franke, section 8/III, 2nd Württemberg Landwehr Division Reports, Stuttgart Landesarchiv, Germany, pages 1–22.

13. Braim, *The Test of Battle,* 76–77.

14. Pershing, *My Experiences in the World War,* 2:282–283.

15. General Hunter Liggett recommended on 22 September that an American division occupy the part of the valley west of the Argonne to establish unified command under the AEF to pinch off the Argonne. However, Pershing's headquarters declined the recommendation, forcing the cooperation under divided command of the pincher attack of the Argonne under separate American and French commands. Liggett, *A.E.F.,* 168–172.

16. Pershing, *My Experiences in the World War,* 2:290–293.

17. "Final Report of Gen. John J. Pershing," in Horne, ed., *Source Records of the Great War,* 6:346–348.

18. Clausewitz, *On War,* 595.

19. "Final Report of Gen. John J. Pershing," in Horne, ed., *Source Records of the Great War,* 6:346–348.

20. "General Ludendorff," in Horne, ed., *Source Records of the Great War,* 6:355–356.

21. "Final Report of Gen. John J. Pershing," in Horne, ed., *Source Records of the Great War,* 6:346–348.

22. "General Ludendorff," in Horne, ed., *Source Records of the Great War,* 6:355–356.

23. Pershing, *My Experiences in the World War,* 2:290–293.

24. "Final Report of Gen. John J. Pershing," in Horne, ed., *Source Records of the Great War,* 6:346–348.

25. *Joint Operational Planning* (JP) 5-0, xii.

26. "General Ludendorff," in Horne, ed., *Source Records of the Great War,* 6:355–356.

27. Pershing, *My Experiences in the World War,* 2:290–293.

28. Ibid.

29. "Final Report of Gen. John J. Pershing," in Horne, ed., *Source Records of the Great War,* 6:346–348.

30. U.S. Army, History Division, *United States Army in the World War, 1917–1919,* 1:xx.

31. "General Max von Gallwitz," in Horne, ed., *Source Records of the Great War,* 6:235–238.

32. Pershing, *My Experiences in the World War,* 2:284.

33. "Final Report of Gen. John J. Pershing," in Horne, ed., *Source Records of the Great War,* 6:349.

34. Pershing, *My Experiences in the World War,* 2:287.

35. Coffman, *The War to End All Wars,* 304–306.

366 Notes to Pages 50–59

36. Lengel, *To Conquer Hell*, 62.

37. "General Max von Gallwitz," in Horne, ed., *Source Records of the Great War*, 6:235–238.

38. Ibid.

39. Strohm, *Die Württembergishchen Regimenter im Weltkrieg 1914–1918*, Band 25, *Das Württembergishche Landwehr Infanterie Regiment nr. 120*, 140–145.

40. Ibid., 140–145.

41. Baden-Württemberg Hauptstaatsarchiv, Stuttgart, Kriegsrange-liste, M430/3, 11828 OberLeutnant Paul "Kuno" Vollmer.

42. Lapple, *Das Württembergishche Landwehr Infanterie Regiment nr. 125 im Weltkrieg 1914–1918*, Band 38, 154–157.

43. Baden-Württemberg Hauptstaatsarchiv, Stuttgart, Kriegsrange-liste, M430/3, 11828 OberLeutnant Paul "Kuno" Vollmer.

44. Baden-Württemberg Hauptstaatsarchiv Stuttgart, Kriegsrange-liste, M430/3, 6907—Paul Adolf August Lipp.

45. Lapple, *Das Württembergishche Landwehr Infanterie Regiment nr. 125 im Weltkrieg 1914–1918*, Band 38, 154–157.

46. Ibid.

47. Ibid.

48. "General Max von Gallwitz," in Horne, ed., *Source Records of the Great War*, 6:235–238.

49. Etzel, *Das Königlich Bayerisches Reserve Infanterie Regiment Nr. 10*, 128–131.

50. Gallwitz, "Retreat to the Rhein," in Viereck, ed., *As They Saw Us*, 239–245.

51. Ibid., 240–244.

52. Bürkner, *Infanterie Regiment Nr. 150* (1. ermländisches), Book 2, 188–192.

7. The Americans Attack!

Epigraph: Lapple, *Das Württembergishche Landwehr Infanterie Regiment nr. 125 im Weltkrieg 1914–1918*, Band 38, 159.

1. Additional artillery from the St. Mihiel Offensive soon arrived, meaning that 3,980 artillery pieces (2,516 manned by Americans crews and 1,464 manned by French crews) would support the first several days of the Meuse-Argonne campaign (see "Final Report of Gen. John J. Pershing," in Horne, ed., *Source Records of the Great War*, 6:349). Pershing, *My Experiences in the World War*, 2:285.

2. "General Max von Gallwitz," in Horne, ed., *Source Records of the Great War*, 6:239.

3. Baker, *Doughboy's Diary*, 94.

4. Lapple, *Das Württembergishche Landwehr Infanterie Regiment nr. 125 im Weltkrieg 1914–1918*, Band 38, 154–157.

5. Strohm, *Die Württembergishchen Regimenter im Weltkrieg 1914–1918*, Band 25, *Das Württembergishche Landwehr Infanterie Regiment nr. 120*, 148–149.

6. Friedrich, *1st Guards Regiment (Foot)*, 205–206.

7. Donald, *Citizen Soldier.*

8. Zabecki, "America's Top World War I Ace," 26.

9. Rickenbacker, *Fighting the Flying Circus*, 269.

10. Lapple, *Das Württembergishche Landwehr Infanterie Regiment nr. 125 im Weltkrieg 1914–1918*, Band 38, 158.

11. Baker, *Doughboy's Diary*, 95.

12. Lapple, *Das Württembergishche Landwehr Infanterie Regiment nr. 125 im Weltkrieg 1914–1918*, Band 38, 158–159.

13. Blumenson, *The Patton Papers*, 608–612.

14. Coulter, *History of the 110th Infantry*, 93–95.

15. Friedrich, *1st Guards Regiment (Foot)*, 205–206.

16. Proctor, *The Iron Division*, 258–260.

17. Ibid., 260.

18. "Where Are the Heroes of the Great War?" 49.

19. Friedrich, *Das Erste Garderegiment zu Fuss im Weltkreig 1914–1918*, 266–269.

20. Friedrich, *1st Guards Regiment (Foot)*, 205–209.

21. Fuller, *Tanks in the Great War*, 262–268; Ball, *Mauser Military Rifles of the World*, 193.

22. Friedrich, *Das Erste Garderegiment zu Fuss im Weltkreig 1914–1918*, 266–269.

23. Friedrich, *1st Guards Regiment (Foot)*, 205–206.

24. Coulter, *History of the 110th Infantry*, 93–94.

25. Proctor, *The Iron Division*, 260–261.

26. Triplet, *A Youth in the Meuse-Argonne*, 165–169.

27. Ibid.

28. Clair Kenamore, *The Story of the 139th* (St. Louis, Mo.: Guard Publishing, 1920), 28.

29. Blumenson, *The Patton Papers*, 609–612.

30. Ibid., 609–617.

31. "'Bravest Man in the American Army.'"

32. Blumenson, *The Patton Papers*, 614–617.

33. "'Bravest Man in the American Army.'"

34. Ibid.

35. Kenamore, *From Vauquois Hill to Exermont*, 102.

36. Ibid., 102.

37. Turlock, *In the Hands of Providence*, 241.

368 Notes to Pages 73–81

38. Kenamore, *From Vauquois Hill to Exermont*, 102.

39. Ibid., 102–105.

40. Gray, "Nels T. Wold's Story."

41. Kenamore, *From Vauquois Hill to Exermont*, 102–105.

42. Gray, "Nels T. Wold's Story."

43. Ibid.

44. *World War I Medal of Honor Recipients* (Washington, D.C.: Center of Military History, 2009), available online at http://www.history.army.mil/html/moh/worldwari.html (accessed 14 July 2016).

45. Lapple, *Das Württembergishche Landwehr Infanterie Regiment nr. 125 im Weltkrieg 1914–1918*, Band 38, 159.

46. Rosenberg-Lipinsky, *Das Konigen Elisabeth Garde-Grenadier Regiment Nr. 3 im Weltkrieg 1914–1918*, 662–667.

47. Gallwitz, "Retreat to the Rhein," in Viereck, ed., *As They Saw Us*, 241–244.

48. Liggett, *A.E.F.*, 159.

49. Horne, *The Price of Glory*, 161–190.

50. Pershing, *My Experiences in the World War*, 2:290–293.

51. Hadley, "The Battle of Montfaucon."

52. Ibid.

53. Thorn, *History of the 313th Infantry Regiment*, 25–30.

54. Ibid.

55. Hadley, "The Battle of Montfaucon."

56. Thorn, *History of the 313th Infantry Regiment*, 25–30.

57. Hadley, "The Battle of Montfaucon."

58. See Walker, *Betrayal at Little Gibraltar*.

59. *Handbuch der Provinz Sachsen*.

60. U.S. Army, American Expeditionary Forces, Intelligence section of the General Staff, *Histories of Two Hundred and Fifty-One Divisions of the German Army*, 149–152.

61. Machesney, "Court Martial in Europe: Report on Disciplinary System and Courts Martial in the 33rd Ill. Division AEF," 552.

62. Huidekoper, *Illinois in the War*, 1:60–70.

63. Ibid., 1:69.

64. Although the French were the first to innovate with small unit tactics, there is debate on whether it was indeed a French or German adaptation. One esteemed historian of this topic, Major General David Zabecki, wrote to the author of this book, "Storm troop tactics were far more a German innovation than a French one. Wilhelm Rohr's storm troop battalion started experimenting with such tactics as early as August 1915. The system was pretty much fully developed by the time Rohr's battalion was committed at Verdun in 1916. Thereafter, Rohr's battalion became the storm troop training cadre for the entire Fifth

Army. The French never really started to adopt such tactics until after Pétain assumed command in mid-1917."

65. Huidekoper, *Illinois in the War*, 1:320–330.

66. Army Doctrine Reference Publication 6-0, Mission Command (Headquarters, Department of the Army, Washington, D.C.: Government Printing Office, 2012), 1–5.

67. Huidekoper, *Illinois in the War*, 1:324–327.

68. Hopper, *Medals of Honor*, 46–48.

69. Ibid., 50–52.

70. Ibid.

71. Ibid., 55–59.

72. "Jewish Medal of Honor Men," 598–600. The other recipients included Sergeant Benjamin Kaufman of the 308th Infantry Regiment, 77th Division, and Corporal Harry Weiner for heroism in the Argonne Forest on 4 October 1918 and Sergeant William Sawelson for incredible courage under fire during the Battle for Grandpré, just north of the Argonne on 26 October 1918 while serving in the 78th Division. Sergeant Sawelson received his Medal of Honor posthumously.

73. Huidekoper, *Illinois in the War*, 1:328.

74. Broecker, *Das 5. Lotharingen Infanterie Regiment Nr. 144 im Weltkrieg*, 315–318.

75. Yockelson, *Forty-Seven Days*, 136–137.

76. Mastriano, *Alvin York*, 51–52.

77. Lengel, *To Conquer Hell*, 120–123.

78. Johnson, *Without Censor*, 165.

8. Grinding to a Halt in the Argonne

Epigraph: Lengel, *To Conquer Hell*, 124.

1. Gallwitz, "Retreat to the Rhein," in Viereck, ed., *As They Saw Us*, 242.

2. Junker was an honorific titled given to the "landed" nobility. Although they lacked noble blood, they were affluent and owned land. They included wealthy merchants and others who acquired wealth through business and investment ventures.

3. Sheffield, *Forgotten Victory*, 218–219.

4. Ibid., 207–210.

5. Hindenburg, *Aus Meinem Leben*, 366.

6. Johnson, *Without Censor*, 173–175.

7. Gallwitz, "Retreat to the Rhein," in Viereck, ed., *As They Saw Us*, 238–245.

8. Ibid., 238–245.

9. Johnson, *Without Censor*, 173–175.

10. Ibid.

11. Gallwitz, "Retreat to the Rhein," in Viereck, ed., *As They Saw Us*, 238–245.

12. Johnson, *Without Censor*, 168.

13. Ibid.

14. Diary of Lieutenant Colonel P. L. Stackpole, aide-de-camp to General Liggett, 25 January 1918–2 August 1919, Library of Congress, graciously provided by Mitch Yockelson.

15. Herman von Giehrl, "The Battle of the Argonne and the Meuse in the Autumn of 1918," Library of Congress, RG165–E320 (Box 3).

16. Field Message from Major Norris, 27 September 1918, W. E. B. Du Bois Papers, University of Massachusetts.

17. Liggett, *A.E.F.*, 177–180.

18. Lapple, *Das Württembergishche Landwehr Infanterie Regiment nr. 125 im Weltkrieg 1914–1918*, Band 38, 160.

19. Diary of Lieutenant Colonel P. L. Stackpole, aide-de-camp to General Liggett, 25 January 1918–2 August 1919, Library of Congress.

20. Strohm, *Die Württembergishchen Regimenter im Weltkrieg 1914–1918*, Band 25, *Das Württembergishche Landwehr Infanterie Regiment nr. 120*, 150–155.

21. Ibid.

22. Ibid.

23. Ibid.

24. *Pennsylvania in the Great War*, 2:543.

25. Coulter, *History of the 110th Infantry*, 95–98.

26. Rosenberg-Lipinsky, *Das Konigen Elisabeth Garde-Grenadier Regiment Nr. 3 im Weltkrieg 1914–1918*, 665–670.

27. Ibid., 668.

28. Ibid., 665–670.

29. Ibid.

30. Coulter, *History of the 110th Infantry*, 95–98.

31. Lapple, *Das Württembergishche Landwehr Infanterie Regiment nr. 125 im Weltkrieg 1914–1918*, Band 38, 159–160.

32. Coulter, *History of the 110th Infantry*, 95–98.

33. Strohm, *Die Württembergishchen Regimenter im Weltkrieg 1914–1918*, Band 25, *Das Württembergishche Landwehr Infanterie Regiment nr. 120*, 152.

34. Lapple, *Das Württembergishche Landwehr Infanterie Regiment nr. 125 im Weltkrieg 1914–1918*, Band 38, 160.

35. Ibid., 160–161.

36. Strohm, *Die Württembergishchen Regimenter im Weltkrieg 1914–1918*, Band 25, *Das Württembergishche Landwehr Infanterie Regiment nr. 120*, 153.

37. Lapple, *Das Württembergishche Landwehr Infanterie Regiment nr. 125 im Weltkrieg 1914–1918*, Band 38, 160.
38. Coulter, *History of the 110th Infantry*, 98–99.
39. Ibid., 98–99, 102.
40. Lapple, *Das Württembergishche Landwehr Infanterie Regiment nr. 125 im Weltkrieg 1914–1918*, Band 38, 160–170; Strohm, *Die Württembergishchen Regimenter im Weltkrieg 1914–1918*, Band 25, *Das Württembergishche Landwehr Infanterie Regiment nr. 120*, 153–160.
41. Lapple, *Das Württembergishche Landwehr Infanterie Regiment nr. 125 im Weltkrieg 1914–1918*, Band 38, 160–170; Strohm, *Die Württembergishchen Regimenter im Weltkrieg 1914–1918*, Band 25, *Das Württembergishche Landwehr Infanterie Regiment nr. 120*, 153–160.
42. Proctor, *The Iron Division*, 280–285.
43. Ibid.
44. Ibid.

9. Stalling in the Meuse Valley

Epigraph: Rosenberg-Lipinsky, *Das Konigen Elisabeth Garde-Grenadier Regiment Nr. 3 im Weltkrieg 1914–1918*, 731.
1. Diary of Lieutenant Colonel P. L. Stackpole, aide-de-camp to General Liggett, 25 January 1918–2 August 1919, Library of Congress.
2. Kenamore, *From Vauquois Hill to Exermont*, 131–133; Center of Military History, *35th Division: Summary of Operations in the World War*, 138.
3. Kenamore, *From Vauquois Hill to Exermont*, 131–133; Center of Military History, *35th Division: Summary of Operations in the World War*, 16–18.
4. Kenamore, *From Vauquois Hill to Exermont*, 131–133; Center of Military History, *35th Division: Summary of Operations in the World War*, 133–135, 142.
5. Ferrell, *America's Deadliest Battle*, 60.
6. Kenamore, *From Vauquois Hill to Exermont*, 131–133; Center of Military History, *35th Division: Summary of Operations in the World War*, 147.
7. Edwards, *From Doniphan to Verdun*, 59.
8. Kenamore, *The Story of the 139th*, 26–30.
9. Kenamore, *From Vauquois Hill to Exermont*, 153.
10. Ibid., 154.
11. Rosenberg-Lipinsky, *Das Konigen Elisabeth Garde-Grenadier Regiment Nr. 3 im Weltkrieg 1914–1918*, 667.
12. Ibid., 731–735.
13. Ibid., 731.

14. Kenamore, *The Story of the 139th*, 26–30.

15. Rosenberg-Lipinsky, *Das Konigen Elisabeth Garde-Grenadier Regiment Nr. 3 im Weltkrieg 1914–1918*, 669.

16. Kenamore, *The Story of the 139th*, 26–30.

17. Ferrell, *America's Deadliest Battle*, 61.

18. Rosenberg-Lipinsky, *Das Konigen Elisabeth Garde-Grenadier Regiment Nr. 3 im Weltkrieg 1914–1918*, 669.

19. Kenamore, *The Story of the 139th*, 26–39.

20. Ibid., 41.

21. Edwards, *From Doniphan to Verdun*, 97.

22. Kenamore, *The Story of the 139th*, 42.

23. Kenamore, *From Vauquois Hill to Exermont*, 205–207.

24. Ibid.

25. Ibid., 209.

26. Some accounts credit Rieger with leading the first successful assault of Exermont, while the 140th history suggests he arrived after the village was secured. This discrepancy is most likely due to the fact that Exermont was a 140th Regiment objective, and some slight embarrassment that a 139th battalion led the successful assault to take it. The most likely history is described in this chapter—that he indeed was part of the sweep that liberated the town, being among the first Americans to enter it. Edwards, *From Doniphan to Verdun*, 59.

27. Kenamore, *From Vauquois Hill to Exermont*, 21–23, 207–209.

28. Full Text Citations For Award of the Distinguished Service Cross, World War I, available at http://www.homeofheroes.com/members/02_DSC/citatons/01_wwi_dsc/dsc_05wwi_Army_QR.html (accessed on 18 June 2017).

29. General John J. Pershing, War Diary, 28 September 1918, Library of Congress.

30. Kenamore, *From Vauquois Hill to Exermont*, 21–23, 201, 252.

31. Rosenberg-Lipinsky, *Das Konigen Elisabeth Garde-Grenadier Regiment Nr. 3 im Weltkrieg 1914–1918*, 675.

32. Friedrich, *1st Guards Regiment (Foot)*, 205–207.

33. Rosenberg-Lipinsky, *Das Konigen Elisabeth Garde-Grenadier Regiment Nr. 3 im Weltkrieg 1914–1918*, 675.

34. Kenamore, *From Vauquois Hill to Exermont*, 155–169.

35. These remarks are adapted from comments provided by Major General David Zabecki.

36. Edwards, *From Doniphan to Verdun*, 97–99.

37. Kenamore, *From Vauquois Hill to Exermont*, 220–224.

38. Ibid., 226.

39. Edwards, *From Doniphan to Verdun*, 87.

40. Kenamore, *From Vauquois Hill to Exermont*, 125.

41. Diary of General Pershing, 28 September 1918, Library of Congress; Kenamore, *From Vauquois Hill to Exermont*, 229.

10. Securing Montfaucon and the Center of the Meuse Valley

Epigraph: Diary of General Pershing, 27 September 1918, Library of Congress.

1. Center of Military History, *4th Division: Summary of Operations in the World War*, 53.
2. Coffman, *The War to End All Wars*, 309.
3. Barber, *History of the 79th Division*, 106–108.
4. Ibid., 115.
5. Center of Military History, *79th Division: Summary of Operations in the World War*, 16–18.
6. Laffargue, *Étude sur l'attaque dans la période actuelle de la guerre Impressions et réflexions d'un Commandant de Compagnie* [U.S. Army translation: *The Attack in Trench Warfare Impressions and Reflections of a Company Commander, Translated for the Infantry Journal by an Officer of Infantry*].
7. Lanza, "Artillery in Support of the Infantry in the AEF," 70.
8. Diary of Lieutenant Colonel P. L. Stackpole, aide-de-camp to General Liggett, 25 January 1918–2 August 1919, Library of Congress.
9. Fax, *With Their Bare Hands*, 250–255.
10. Center of Military History, *79th Division: Summary of Operations in the World War*, 15–18.
11. Ibid., 16–18.
12. Grotelueschen, *The AEF Way of War*, 23–25.
13. Barber, *History of the 79th Division*, 108.
14. Plickert, *Infanterie Regiment Nr. 151* (2. ermländisches), Book 2, 297–300.
15. Ibid., 303.
16. Ibid.
17. Ibid.
18. Ibid.
19. Barber, *History of the 79th Division*, 111.
20. Ibid., 116.
21. Memorial to Colonel Sweezey, http://apps.westpointaog.org/Memorials/Article/3474/ (accessed 28 March 2017).
22. Barber, *History of the 79th Division*, 112.
23. Ibid.
24. Ibid., 134–140.
25. Bürkner, *Infanterie Regiment Nr. 150* (1. ermländisches), Book 2, 196.

26. Ibid.

27. Barber, *History of the 79th Division*, 118.

28. Ibid., 129.

29. Ibid., 134–140.

30. Ibid., 134.

31. Ibid.

32. *History of the 315th U.S. Infantry*, 60–75.

33. Ibid.

34. Ibid.

35. Barber, *History of the 79th Division*, 134–140.

36. *History of the 315th U.S. Infantry*, 60–75.

37. Siebert, *Geschichte des Infanterie Regiments Generalfeldmarschall von Hindenburg (2. Masurisches) Nr. 147 im Weltkrieg*, 280–282.

38. Barber, *History of the 79th Division*, 168.

39. *History of the 315th U.S. Infantry*, 60–75.

40. Siebert, *Geschichte des Infanterie Regiments Generalfeldmarschall von Hindenburg (2. Masurisches) Nr. 147 im Weltkrieg*, 280–282.

41. Plickert, *Infanterie Regiment Nr. 151 (2. ermländisches)*, Book 2, 303–305.

42. Siebert, *Geschichte des Infanterie Regiments Generalfeldmarschall von Hindenburg (2. Masurisches) Nr. 147 im Weltkrieg*, 280–282.

43. Ibid..

44. Ibid., 285–322.

45. Etzel, *Das K.B. Reserve Infanterie Regiment Nr. 10*, 134–140.

46. Thorn, *History of the 313th Infantry Regiment*, 13–17.

47. Barber, *History of the 79th Division*, 168.

48. Adapted from Ikenberry, *The Crisis of American Foreign Policy*, 11–13.

49. Adapted from ibid.

11. Stagnation and Stalemate

Epigraph: Liggett, *A.E.F.*, 159.

1. The unit was dubbed the "Flying Circus" not only due to the colorful aircraft, but for the ability of the unit to move and deploy anywhere it was needed on the Western Front. Such units would move like a circus with tents, trucks, etc. to where they were most needed to surge air assets in a particular area.

2. Rickenbacker, *Fighting the Flying Circus*, 312–315.

3. Ibid., 312–315.

4. Ludendorff, orders to Group of Armies German Crown Prince, in U.S. Army, History Division, *United States Army in the World War, 1917–1919*, vol. 9, *Military Operations of the American Expeditionary Forces*, 533.

5. General Karl von Einem, Third Army War Diary, 4 October 1918, in U.S. Army, History Division, *United States Army in the World War, 1917–1919,* 536–537.

6. General Max von Gallwitz, Army Group Gallwitz War Diary, 5 October 1918, in U.S. Army, History Division, *United States Army in the World War, 1917–1919,* 2:536–537.

7. Barkley, *Scarlet Fields,* 151–170.

8. Ibid.

9. Pershing, *My Experiences in the World War,* 2:392.

10. The National Army would later include elements of the Regular Army and National Guard. However, the term was first coined to denote the force put together by the volunteers who joined the U.S. Army in 1917 as well as those drafted to fill the ranks. By the end of the war, the "three armies" would really be one powerful lethal force, forged by fire in the forests of the Argonne and along the Meuse Valley. However, after each war a wedge tends to grow between the Regular Army and the National Guard. This is something that America's army should endeavor to prevent from transpiring again in the future.

12. The Siege of the Lost Battalion

Epigraph: *History of the Seventy Seventh Division,* 59.

1. *History of the Seventy Seventh Division,* 59.

2. Foch, *The Memoirs of Marshal Foch,* 412.

3. Ibid., 410–415.

4. Ibid., 412.

5. Pershing, War Diary, 700.

6. Foch, *The Memoirs of Marshal Foch,* 412–413.

7. Ibid.

8. Pershing, War Diary, 704.

9. Diary of Lieutenant Colonel P. L. Stackpole, aide-de-camp to General Liggett, 25 January 1918–2 August 1919, Library of Congress, 235–237.

10. Laplander, *Finding the Lost Battalion,* 116–117.

11. Ibid., 61.

12. Center of Military History, *77th Division: Summary of Operations in the World War,* 46–47.

13. Lengel, *To Conquer Hell,* 224.

14. Yockelson, *Forty-Seven Days,* 185–186.

15. McKeogh, *The Victorious 77th Division,* 22–24.

16. Ibid.

17. Center of Military History, *77th Division: Summary of Operations in the World War,* 46–48.

18. McKeogh, *The Victorious 77th Division*, 22–24.

19. Center of Military History, *77th Division: Summary of Operations in the World War*, 46–49.

20. McKeogh, *The Victorious 77th Division*, 22–24.

21. Rainsford, *From Upton to the Meuse with the 307th*, 180–185.

22. Ibid.

23. Ibid.

24. *History of the Seventy Seventh Division*, 72–74.

25. Laplander, *Finding the Lost Battalion*, 238–239.

26. *History of the Seventy Seventh Division*, 72–74.

27. Lengel, *To Conquer Hell*, 226.

28. Center of Military History, *77th Division: Summary of Operations in the World War*, 48.

29. Ibid.

30. Laplander, *Finding the Lost Battalion*, 575.

31. Hünicken, *Reserve Infanterie Regiment Nr. 254*, 367–377.

32. Ibid.

33. Center of Military History, *77th Division: Summary of Operations in the World War*, 48–50.

34. The number 694 is based on the comprehensive research of Robert Laplander. See Laplander, *Finding the Lost Battalion*, 575.

35. Hünicken, *Reserve Infanterie Regiment Nr. 254*, 367.

36. Laplander, *Finding the Lost Battalion*, 281–283.

37. From Laplander, "Enemy in All Directions," provided to the author by Robert Laplander.

38. Hünicken, *Reserve Infanterie Regiment Nr. 254*, 368.

39. Johnson, *The Lost Battalion*, 58–61.

40. *History of the Seventy Seventh Division*, 73.

41. Kling, *Die Württembergishchen Regimenter im Weltkrieg 1914–1918*, Band 27, *Das Württembergishche Landwehr Infanterie Regiment nr. 122*, 152–196; Das Württembergishche Landwehr Infanterie Regiment nr. 122 Kriegstagebuch, REP M, 396, Baden-Württemberg Hauptstaatsarchiv Stuttgart; Hünicken, *Reserve Infanterie Regiment Nr. 254*, 368.

42. Kling, *Die Württembergishchen Regimenter im Weltkrieg 1914–1918*, Band 27, *Das Württembergishche Landwehr Infanterie Regiment nr. 122*, 152–196; Das Württembergishche Landwehr Infanterie Regiment nr. 122 Kriegstagebuch, REP M, 396, Baden-Württemberg Hauptstaatsarchiv Stuttgart; Hünicken, *Reserve Infanterie Regiment Nr. 254*, 368; Johnson, *The Lost Battalion*, 60–63.

43. McKeogh, *The Victorious 77th Division*, 23.

44. Ibid.

45. From Laplander, "Enemy in All Directions."

46. McKeogh, *The Victorious 77th Division*, 25.

47. Hünicken, *Reserve Infanterie Regiment Nr. 254*, 369.

48. Ibid.

49. Ibid., 367–377.

50. Center of Military History, *77th Division: Summary of Operations in the World War*, 52.

51. Laplander, *Finding the Lost Battalion*, 350–380.

52. Hart, *Reputations, Ten Years After*, 280–281.

53. Diary of Lieutenant Colonel P. L. Stackpole, aide-de-camp to General Liggett, 25 January 1918–2 August 1919, Library of Congress, 3 October 1918.

54. Ibid.

55. Laplander, *Finding the Lost Battalion*, 352.

56. Ibid., 352–355.

57. Ibid., 354.

58. From Laplander, "Enemy in All Directions"; Laplander, *Finding the Lost Battalion*, 352–355.

59. From Laplander, "Enemy in All Directions"; Laplander, *Finding the Lost Battalion*, 358–367.

60. Hünicken, *Reserve Infanterie Regiment Nr. 254*, 369.

61. Ibid.

62. Laplander, *Finding the Lost Battalion*, 366.

63. Hünicken, *Reserve Infanterie Regiment Nr. 254*, 370.

64. Johnson, *The Lost Battalion*, 127.

65. Laplander, "Enemy in All Directions"; Laplander, *Finding the Lost Battalion*, 358–367.

66. Hünicken, *Reserve Infanterie Regiment Nr. 254*, 370.

67. Zabecki, "Finding the Lost Battalion," 15.

68. Diary of Lieutenant Colonel P. L. Stackpole, aide-de-camp to General Liggett, 25 January 1918–2 August 1919, Library of Congress, 4–7 October 1918.

69. Ibid.

70. Hünicken, *Reserve Infanterie Regiment Nr. 254*, 370–373.

71. Laplander, *Finding the Lost Battalion*, 366.

72. Johnson, *The Lost Battalion*, 245.

73. Laplander, "Enemy in All Directions."

74. Rainsford, *From Upton to the Meuse with the 307th*, 199–223.

75. McKeogh, *The Victorious 77th Division*, 25.

76. Hünicken, *Reserve Infanterie Regiment Nr. 254*, 370–373.

13. Alvin York

Epigraph: Mastriano, *Alvin York*, 141. The Foch quotation translates as "The greatest exploit by an individual soldier in all the armies of Europe."

1. Strohm, *Die Württembergishchen Regimenter im Weltkrieg 1914–1918*, Band 25, *Das Württembergishche Landwehr Infanterie Regiment nr. 120*, 161–173.

2. Ibid., 161–173.

3. John J. Pershing, "In the Matter of MG William P. Burnham, 82nd Division," Pershing Papers, on Relief of Officers, August–October 1918, Box 8, National Archives; Duncan, "Reminiscences," 117–118.

4. H. A. Drum, Field Order number 44, 6 October 1918, in U.S. Army, History Division, *United States Army in the World War, 1917–1919*, vol. 16, *General Orders, GHQ, AEF*, 215.

5. Ibid.

6. Duncan, "Reminiscences," 145–146.

7. Ibid., 148.

8. II Timothy 4:1–8 (KJV).

9. Day, "The B That Stung," 10–13; Franke, *Die 2. Württemberg Landwehr Division Im Weltkrieg 1914–1918*, 48–58.

10. Strohm, *Die Württembergishchen Regimenter im Weltkrieg 1914–1918*, Band 25, *Das Württembergishche Landwehr Infanterie Regiment nr. 120*, 161–173.

11. German Archives, Potsdam, "Testimony of German Officers and Men about Sergeant York," translated by U.S. Army War College, Carlisle, Pennsylvania, June 1936.

12. 5th Guards Prussian Division Kriegstagebuch, 5 October 1918–9 October 1918.

13. York, *Sergeant York*, 128–129.

14. Ibid., 142–143.

15. Interview with George Edward Buxton York in Montfaucon, France, 4 October 2008, during the ninetieth anniversary commemoration of his father's actions in the Great War; York, *The Reminisces of Mrs. Alvin 'Sergeant' York*, 3.

16. York, *Sergeant York*, 146.

17. Ibid., 145.

18. Buxton, *Official History of 82nd Division, American Expeditionary Forces*, 54–58; 82nd Division, entry 1241, RG 120, National Archives; 328th Infantry Regiment, entry 2133, RG 391, National Archives; American Battle Monuments Commission, Division files, 82nd Division, RG 117, National Archives; American Battle Monuments Commission, *82d Division: Summary of Operations in the World War*, 22.

19. 82nd Division, entry 1241, RG 120, National Archives; 328th Infantry Regiment, entry 2133, RG 391, National Archives; American Battle Monuments Commission, Division files, 82nd Division, RG 117, National Archives; Buxton, *Official History of 82nd Division, American Expeditionary Forces*, 59; York, *Sergeant York*, 220–222.

20. Duncan, "Reminiscences," 151.

21. 82nd Division, entry 1241, RG 120, National Archives; 328th Infantry Regiment, entry 2133, RG 391, National Archives; American Battle Monuments Commission, Division files, 82nd Division, RG 117, National Archives; "Americans in the Meuse-Argonne Region," in U.S. Army, History Division, *United States Army in the World War, 1917–1919*, vol. 9, *Military Operations of the American Expeditionary Forces*, 229; York, *Sergeant York*, 223–224; Pattullo, "The Second Elder Gives Battle," 3–4, 71–74.

22. York, *Sergeant York*, 223–224; Cahill, "America Needed a Hero," 30–39.

23. Württembergische Landwehr-Infanterie-Regiment Nr. 120, File M 115: regimental operations 1914–1918, File M 411: Kriegstagebuch, File M433/2: Personnel Lists 1914–1921, File M 484: Kriegsstammrollen 1914–1918, all in Baden-Württemberg Hauptstaatsarchiv, Stuttgart, Germany; German Archives, Potsdam, "Testimony of German Officers and Men about Sergeant York," translated by U.S. Army War College, Carlisle, Pennsylvania, June 1936.

24. German Archives, Potsdam, "Testimony of German Officers and Men about Sergeant York," translated by U.S. Army War College, Carlisle, Pennsylvania, June 1936.

25. 82nd Division, entry 1241, RG 120, National Archives; 328th Infantry Regiment, entry 2133, RG 391, National Archives; American Battle Monuments Commission, Division files, 82nd Division, RG 117, National Archives; Michael Sacina, affidavit of 8 October 1918 battle near Châtel Chéhéry, given at Frettes, France, 6 February 1919, National Personnel Records Center; Buxton, *Official History of 82nd Division, American Expeditionary Forces*, 60–61; German Archives, Potsdam, "Testimony of German Officers and Men about Sergeant York," translated by U.S. Army War College, Carlisle, Pennsylvania, June 1936.

26. Buxton, *Official History of 82nd Division, American Expeditionary Forces*, 60–61; Pattullo, "The Second Elder Gives Battle," 3–4, 71–74.

27. Swindler, "Turkey Match," 349–350; Captain Bertrand Cox, affidavit given on 21 February 1919 in Frettes, France, filed by the 328th Infantry Regiment Advocate General (actual swearing of the affidavit was on 26 February 1919), National Personnel Records Center; Strom, *Das Württembergishche Landwehr Infanterie Regiment nr. 120 im Weltkrieg 1914–1918*, Band 4; Lapple, *Das Württembergishche Landwehr Infanterie Regiment nr. 125 im Weltkrieg 1914–1918*, Band 38. Also see the following unit reports: 1st Battalion, 125 Landwehr Regiment Kriegstagebuch; 2nd Battalion, 125 Landwehr Regiment Kriegstagebuch; 3rd Battalion, 125 Landwehr Regiment Kriegstagebuch, all in the Stadt Archiv Baden-Württemberg, Stuttgart, Germany.

28. Patrick Donohue, affidavit of 8 October 1918 battle near Châtel

Chéhéry, given at Frettes, France, 6 February 1919, National Personnel Records Center; Captain Bertrand Cox, affidavit given on 21 February 1919 in Frettes, France, filed by the 328th Infantry Regiment Advocate General (actual swearing of the affidavit was on 26 February 1919), National Personnel Records Center; Pattullo, "The Second Elder Gives Battle," 3–4, 71–74.

29. York, *Sergeant York*, 229.

30. Strohm, *Die Württembergishchen Regimenter im Weltkrieg 1914–1918*, Band 25, *Das Württembergishche Landwehr Infanterie Regiment nr. 120*, 161–173.

14. Cracking the Siegfried Line

Epigraph: Pirscher, *Das (Rheinisch-Westfalische) Infanterie Regiment Nr. 459*, 242.

1. Boraston, ed., *Sir Douglas Haig's Dispatches*, 280–292.

2. Pershing, *My Experiences in the World War*, 2:336–340.

3. Mastriano, *Alvin York*, 121–127.

4. Center of Military History, *32nd Division: Summary of Operations in the World War*, 55–60.

5. Liggett, *A.E.F.*, 205.

6. Pershing, *My Experiences in the World War*, 2:341.

7. MacArthur, *Reminiscences*, 51–52.

8. Ibid.

9. See Young, *The General's General*, 1994.

10. Yockelson, *Forty-Seven Days*, 257.

11. The other father/son Medal of Honor recipients were Theodore Roosevelt for his leadership during the Spanish-American War and his son, Theodore Roosevelt Jr, for his leadership during the Normandy landings in 1944.

12. Summerall, *Duty, Honor, Country*, 143–146.

13. MacArthur, *Reminiscences*, 51–52.

14. Reilly, *Americans All*, 677.

15. Summerall, *Duty, Honor, Country*, 143–146.

16. Reilly, *Americans All*, 677.

17. Ibid., 684.

18. Ibid., 677–679.

19. Ibid., 679.

20. Ibid., 686.

15. The Battle for the Siegfried Line Continues

Epigraph: MacArthur, *Reminiscences*, 51–52.

1. Miller, "The Outstanding Soldier of the A.E.F.," 15–20.
2. Ibid., 17.
3. Jacobs, *Heroes of the Army*, 72–75.
4. Stine, *Samuel Woodfill, Hero*, 1–5.
5. Thomas, *Woodfill of the Regulars*, 279.
6. Ibid., 280–281.
7. Stine, *Samuel Woodfill, Hero*, 3–9.
8. Jacobs, *Heroes of the Army*, 76–77.
9. Thomas, *Woodfill of the Regulars*, 280–284.
10. Ibid., 283–285.
11. Caldwell, "Above and Beyond the Call of Duty," 9–12.
12. Ibid.; Thomas, *Woodfill of the Regulars*, 283–288.
13. Caldwell, "Above and Beyond the Call of Duty," 9–12; Thomas, *Woodfill of the Regulars*, 283–289.
14. Thomas, *Woodfill of the Regulars*, 283–305; Caldwell, "Above and Beyond the Call of Duty," 9–12.
15. Liggett, *A.E.F.*, 200–208.
16. Pershing, *My Experiences in the World War*, 2:338–339.
17. Center of Military History, *5th Division: Summary of Operations in the World War*, 30.
18. Trott, *The Fifth U.S. Division in the World War*, 140–149.
19. Hammer, *Das Buch der 236. Infanterie Division*, 232–242.
20. U.S. Army, American Expeditionary Forces, Intelligence Section of the General Staff, *Histories of Two Hundred and Fifty-One Divisions of the German Army*, 727.
21. Pirscher, *Das (Rheinisch-Westfalische) Infanterie Regiment Nr. 459*, vii–x, 242–270.
22. Ibid., 242–270.
23. Trott, *The Fifth U.S. Division in the World War*, 149–160.
24. Ibid., 145.
25. Ibid.
26. Haan, *The 32nd Division in the World War, 1917–1919*, 115–117.
27. Trott, *The Fifth U.S. Division in the World War*, 149–160.
28. Ibid.

16. Falling Short of Glory

Epigraph: Liggett, *A.E.F.*, 206.
1. Liggett, *A.E.F.*, 198–209.
2. Ibid., 198–209.
3. Foch, *The Memoirs of Marshal Foch*, 433–440.
4. Yockelson, *Forty-Seven Days*, 160–161.
5. Clemenceau, *Grandeur and Misery of Victory*, 79–86.

6. Foch, *The Memoirs of Marshal Foch*, 433–440.
7. Clemenceau, *Grandeur and Misery of Victory*, 79–86; Foch, *The Memoirs of Marshal Foch*, 433–440.
8. Liggett, *A.E.F.*, 198–220.

17. Maintaining the Initiative

Epigraph: Horne, ed. *Source Records of the Great War*, 6:312.
1. Center of Military History, *3rd Division: Summary of Operations in the World War*, 85–89.
2. *Records of the World War: Field Orders 5th Division, 1918* (Washington, D.C.: Government Printing Office, 1921), 133–134.
3. Crane, "The Sixth Engineers in the Meuse-Argonne," 124–127.
4. "Captain Charles Dashiell Harris, Sixth United States Engineers," reprint from the Fiftieth Annual Report of the Association of Graduates of the United States Military Academy.
5. Pershing, *My Experiences in the World War*, 352; Trott, *The Fifth U.S. Division in the World War*, 166–170.
6. "Captain Charles Dashiell Harris, Sixth United States Engineers," reprint from the Fiftieth Annual Report of the Association of Graduates of the United States Military Academy.
7. Ibid.
8. Special thanks to Lieutenant General Theodore Stroup and Harriet Stroup for their help in telling the Captain Harris story. Harriet Stroup is a descendant of Captain Harris. They provided invaluable assistance, primary sources, and comments to make the telling of this story possible.
9. Buxton, *Official History of 82nd Division, American Expeditionary Forces*, 87, 122; 82nd Division, entry 1241, RG 120, National Archives; 328th Infantry Regiment, entry 2133, 391; 82nd Division, RG 117, National Archives.
10. Holden, *War Memories*, 143–145.
11. John 15:13 (KJV).
12. II Timothy 4:1–8 (KJV).
13. "82d Division: Record of Events," in Department of the Army, *American Expeditionary Forces Divisions*, 2:355; 82nd Division, entry 1241, RG 120, National Archives; 328th Infantry Regiment, entry 2133, RG 391, National Archives; American Battle Monuments Commission, Division files, 82nd Division, RG 117, National Archives.
14. Buxton, *Official History of 82nd Division, American Expeditionary Forces*, 134–136.
15. Center of Military History, *77th Division: Summary of Operations in the World War*, 70.

16. York, *Sergeant York,* 281.

17. Duffy, *Father Duffy's Story,* viii.

18. Ibid., 109.

19. Major W. L. D. O'Grady wrote this of Father Corby after the Civil War. It is available online at https://civilwarstoriesofinspiration .wordpress.com/2008/08/30/father-william-corby-of-the-irish-brigade/ (accessed on 17 June 2017).

20. Absolution is a sacrament in the Roman Catholic Church where a priest prays for the forgiveness of one's sins, saying, "May our Lord Jesus Christ absolve you; and by His authority I absolve you from every bond of excommunication (suspension) and interdict, so far as my power allows and your needs require. [*Making the Sign of the Cross:*] Thereupon, I absolve you from your sins in the name of the Father, and of the Son, and of the Holy Spirit. Amen."

21. Corby, *Memoirs of Chaplain Life,* 179–186.

22. Duffy, *Father Duffy's Story,* 108–111.

23. Thomas, "Spymaster General."

24. Duffy, *Father Duffy's Story,* 271.

25. Ibid., 270–280.

26. Ibid., 276–279.

27. Ibid., 276.

28. Army Group Gallwitz Report, 15 October 1918, in U.S. Army, History Division, *United States Army in the World War, 1917–1919,* vol. 9, *Military Operations of the American Expeditionary Forces,* 557; Buxton, *Official History of 82nd Division, American Expeditionary Forces,* 144–159.

29. American Battle Monuments Commission, *82d Division: Summary of Operations in the World War,* 42–44; Buxton, *Official History of 82nd Division, American Expeditionary Forces,* 159.

30. Center of Military History, *77th Division: Summary of Operations in the World War,* 70–71; Clifford, *The World War One Memoirs of Robert P. Patterson,* 30–33, 65–67.

31. Clifford, *The World War One Memoirs of Robert P. Patterson,* 30–33, 65–67.

32. Ibid.

33. Ibid.

34. Gieraths, *Geschichte des Reserve Infanterie Regiments Nr. 210,* 505–508.

35. American Battle Monuments Commission, *82d Division: Summary of Operations in the World War,* 42–44; Buxton, *Official History of 82nd Division, American Expeditionary Forces,* 159.

36. Gieraths, *Geschichte des Reserve Infanterie Regiments Nr. 210,* 505–508.

37. Ibid., 507.

38. Buxton, *Official History of 82nd Division, American Expeditionary Forces,* 159–166.

39. Gieraths, *Geschichte des Reserve Infanterie Regiments Nr. 210*, 505–508.

40. 82nd Division, entry 1241, RG 120, National Archives; 328th Infantry Regiment, entry 2133, RG 391, National Archives; American Battle Monuments Commission, Division files, 82nd Division, RG 117, National Archives; American Battle Monuments Commission, *82d Division: Summary of Operations in the World War*, 42–44; Buxton, *Official History of 82nd Division, American Expeditionary Forces*, 161–166.

41. Buxton, *Official History of 82nd Division, American Expeditionary Forces*, 160–161; Day, "The B That Stung," 14–15.

42. Day, "The B That Stung," 13–15; Jones, *History of C. Company, 328th Infantry*, 22–24; Buxton, *Official History of 82nd Division, American Expeditionary Forces*, 165–166.

43. 82nd Division, entry 1241, RG 120, National Archives; 328th Infantry Regiment, entry 2133, RG 391, National Archives; American Battle Monuments Commission, Division Files, 82nd Division, RG 117, National Archives; Buxton, *Official History of 82nd Division, American Expeditionary Forces*, 160–161; Day, "The B That Stung," 14–15; American Battle Monuments Commission, *82d Division: Summary of Operations in the World War*, 46–48.

44. 82nd Division, entry 1241, RG 120, National Archives; 328th Infantry Regiment, entry 2133, RG 391, National Archives; American Battle Monuments Commission, Division Files, 82nd Division, RG 117, National Archives; "Americans in the Meuse-Argonne Region," in U.S. Army, History Division, *United States Army in the World War, 1917–1919*, vol. 9, *Military Operations of the American Expeditionary Forces*, 252.

45. Patrick Donohue, affidavit of 8 October 1918 battle near Châtel Chéhéry, given at Frettes, France, 6 February 1919, National Personnel Records Center; approval of Medal of Honor, letter from General John Pershing to Major General Duncan, 1 April 1919, Alvin C. York US Army Service Record, Military Record, Army Service File, 1917–1919, under awards, 1919, National Personnel Records Center.

46. American Battle Monuments Commission, *82d Division: Summary of Operations in the World War*, 54.

47. York, *Sergeant York*, 272.

48. Ibid., 215.

18. Planning for the Last Grand Push

Epigraph: von Tschischwitz, *General von der Marwitz*, 240–242.

1. Liggett, *A.E.F.*, 224.

2. Order of Crown Prince Wilhelm, 19 October 1918, in U.S. Army, History Division, *United States Army in the World War, 1917–1919*, 561.

3. von Tschischwitz, *General von der Marwitz*, 337–341.

4. Ludendorff, *My War Memories 1914–1918*, 2:418–422.

5. Ibid., 2:422–430.

6. Ludendorff said this during a meeting at the Ministry of the Interior (ibid., 2:424–425).

7. Crown Prince Wilhelm, *The Memoirs of the Crown Prince of Germany*, 274.

8. Gallwitz, "Retreat to the Rhein," in Viereck, ed., *As They Saw Us*, 272–277.

9. Foch, *The Memoirs of Marshal Foch*, 447–448.

10. Pershing, War Diary, 25 September 1918; Pershing, *My Experiences in the World War*, 2:360–366; Foch, *The Memoirs of Marshal Foch*, 438–468; Robert Blake, ed., *Private Papers of Marshal Haig* (London: Eyre, 1952), 336.

11. Liggett, *A.E.F.*, 198–220.

12. Ibid., 207.

13. Ibid., 207–213.

14. Grotelueschen, *The AEF Way of War*, 332–335.

15. Summerall, *Duty, Honor, Country*, 148–150.

16. First Army AEF, G3 Operations Report, 1 November 1918, U.S. Army Heritage and Education Center; Colonel Marshall, Report of the First Army, Second Operation, in U.S. Army, History Division, *United States Army in the World War, 1917–1919*, vol. 9, *Military Operations of the American Expeditionary Forces*, 365–370.

17. Grotelueschen, *The AEF Way of War*, 266–268.

18. Diary of Lieutenant Colonel P. L. Stackpole, aide-de-camp to General Liggett, 25 January 1918–2 August 1919, Library of Congress, 278; Liggett, *A.E.F.*, 222–225; Summerall, *Duty, Honor, Country*, 151.

19. Diary of Lieutenant Colonel P. L. Stackpole, aide-de-camp to General Liggett, 25 January 1918–2 August 1919, Library of Congress, 277.

20. First Army AEF, G3 Operations Report, 1 November 1918, U.S. Army Heritage and Education Center.

21. Liggett, *A.E.F.*, 212–219; First Army AEF, G3 Operations Report, 1 November 1918, U.S. Army Heritage and Education Center.

22. Summerall, *Duty, Honor, Country*, 151.

23. Foch, *The Memoirs of Marshal Foch*, 434.

24. Ibid., 434–440.

25. Ibid.

26. Diary of Lieutenant Colonel P. L. Stackpole, aide-de-camp to General Liggett, 25 January 1918–2 August 1919, Library of Congress, 277.

27. Summerall, *Duty, Honor, Country*, 150.

19. Heaven, Hell or Hoboken

Epigraph: Personal letters of Ellis James Stewart, written in 1918–1918, private collection of Rebecca (Stewart) Mastriano.

1. Gallwitz, "Retreat to the Rhein," in Viereck, ed., *As They Saw Us*, 272–277.

2. Haswell, *A History of Company A—314th Engineers, 89th Division*, 66.

3. von Tschischwitz, *General von der Marwitz*, 339.

4. Ibid.

5. Grotelueschen, *The AEF Way of War*, 267–270.

6. Mackin, *Suddenly We Didn't Want to Die*, 225–227.

7. Coffman, *The War to End All Wars*, 344–346.

8. Summerall, *Duty, Honor, Country*, 150.

9. Grotelueschen, *The AEF Way of War*, 267–270.

10. Summerall, *Duty, Honor, Country*, 150–152.

11. Colonna, *The History of Company B, 311th Infantry*, 70–71.

12. McGrath, *War Diary of the 354th Infantry*, 29.

13. Mackin, *Suddenly We Didn't Want to Die*, 235.

14. Dienst, *History of the 353rd Infantry Regiment, 89th Division*, 219–225.

15. Ibid.

16. Haswell, *A History of Company A—314th Engineers, 89th Division*, 67.

17. McGrath, *War Diary of the 354th Infantry*, 13.

18. *World War I Medal of Honor Recipients* (Washington, D.C.: Center of Military History, 2009).

19. Dienst, *History of the 353rd Infantry Regiment, 89th Division*, 219–225 and 262–266, as reported by the regimental commander, Colonel James Reeves.

20. Ibid.

21. Ibid.

22. McGrath, *War Diary of the 354th Infantry*, 29.

23. Ibid., 55–57.

24. Shoemaker, "Missouri and the War," 356–360.

25. "Arthur Forrest, World War Hero, Now Catching in Piedmont League," *Tampa Tribune*, 25 May 1930, 32.

26. Shoemaker, "Missouri and the War," 356–360.

27. *World War I Medal of Honor Recipients* (Washington, D.C.: Center of Military History, 2009).

28. Yockelson, *Forty-Seven Days*, 299–300.

29. *A Brief History of the 5th Marines* (Washington, D.C.: Headquarters, U.S. Marine Corps, 1963).

30. Eggleston, *The 5th Marine Regiment Devil Dogs in World War I,* 99–101.

31. Gallwitz actually was wrong in his assessment. Phosgene was a nonpersistent agent similar to the German Green Cross gas. The German Yellow Cross was a mustard agent. Gallwitz, "Retreat to the Rhein," in Viereck, ed., *As They Saw Us,* 272–277.

32. Ferrell, *America's Deadliest Battle,* 132.

33. von Tschischwitz, *General von der Marwitz,* 339–341.

34. Ibid.

35. Gallwitz, "Retreat to the Rhein," in Viereck, ed., *As They Saw Us,* 272–277.

36. Ibid.

37. Ibid.

38. Ibid.; von Tschischwitz, *General von der Marwitz,* 339–341.

39. Gallwitz, "Retreat to the Rhein," in Viereck, ed., *As They Saw Us,* 272–277.

40. Diary of Lieutenant Colonel P. L. Stackpole, aide-de-camp to General Liggett, 25 January 1918–2 August 1919, Library of Congress, Friday, 1 November 1918, 278.

41. Personal letters of Ellis James Stewart, written in 1918–1918, private collection of Rebecca (Stewart) Mastriano.

42. Ibid.

43. Liggett, *A.E.F.,* 220–226.

44. Pershing, *My Experiences in the World War,* 374–377.

45. Liggett, *A.E.F.,* 223.

46. Ibid., 223–225.

47. Personal letters of Ellis James Stewart, written in 1918–1918, private collection of Rebecca (Stewart) Mastriano.

48. Late on 2 November, German High Command (OHL) attached the Fifth Army to Army Group Crown Prince.

49. Colonna, *The History of Company B, 311th Infantry,* 70–77.

50. Gallwitz, "Retreat to the Rhein," in Viereck, ed., *As They Saw Us,* 272–277.

51. Center of Military History, *2nd Division: Summary of Operations in the World War,* 78–85.

52. *Michigan Alumnus,* 16 May 1942, 385.

53. Center of Military History, *2nd Division: Summary of Operations in the World War,* 78–85; *Michigan Alumnus,* 16 May 1942, 385.

54. Clark, *The Second Infantry Division in World War One,* 164–170.

55. Yockelson, *Forty-Seven Days,* 302–303.

56. Ferrell, *America's Deadliest Battle,* 134.

57. Hanson, "The Night March on Beaumont," 2–6; *Trench Journals and Unit Magazines of the First World War,* 14.

58. Hanson, "The Night March on Beaumont," 2–6; *Trench Journals and Unit Magazines of the First World War*, 14.

59. Center of Military History, *2nd Division: Summary of Operations in the World War*, 78–85.

60. Ibid.

61. von Tschischwitz, *General von der Marwitz*, 341–345.

62. Gallwitz, "Retreat to the Rhein," in Viereck, ed., *As They Saw Us*, 279–285.

63. von Tschischwitz, *General von der Marwitz*, 341–345.

64. War Department, General Orders No. 38, U.S. Army Heritage and Education Center, 1921.

20. Mad Dash to Sedan

Epigraph: Pershing, *My Experiences in the World War*, 2:359.

1. Trott, *The Fifth U.S. Division in the World War*, 199–222.

2. Rickenbacker, *Fighting the Flying Circus*, 352.

3. Center of Military History, *32nd Division: Summary of Operations in the World War*, 42–55.

4. Trott, *The Fifth U.S. Division in the World War*, 199–222.

5. Ibid.

6. Ibid.

7. Ibid.

8. Ibid.

9. Center of Military History, *90th Division: Summary of Operations in the World War*, 40–44.

10. MacArthur, *Reminisces*, 69–72.

11. Liggett, *A.E.F.*, 226–228.

12. Pershing, *My Experiences in the World War*, 2:381.

13. Marshal, *Memoirs of My Services in the World War*, 188–192.

14. MacArthur, *Reminisces*, 68; Summerall, *Duty, Honor, Country*, 152. Marshal states that General Drum added "Boundaries will not be considered binding." See Marshal, *Memoirs of My Services in the World War*, 189.

15. Summerall, *Duty, Honor, Country*, 152–155.

16. Duffy, *Father Duffy's Story*, 301.

17. Ibid., 302–303.

18. Rainsford, *From Upton to the Meuse with the 307th*, 260.

19. Ibid.

20. MacArthur, *Reminiscences*, 68–70.

21. Liggett, *A.E.F.*, 228–330.

22. Roosevelt, *Average Americans*, 209–210.

23. Liggett, *A.E.F.*, 229–331.

24. Diary of Lieutenant Colonel P. L. Stackpole, aide-de-camp to General Liggett, 25 January 1918–2 August 1919, Library of Congress, 281.
25. Coffmann, *The War to End All Wars*, 352–253.
26. Summerall, *Duty, Honor, Country*, 153.
27. Diary of Lieutenant Colonel P. L. Stackpole, aide-de-camp to General Liggett, 25 January 1918–2 August 1919, Library of Congress, 280.
28. Pershing, *My Experiences in the World War*, 2:381.

21. The End of the War

Epigraph: Gallwitz, "Retreat to the Rhein," in Viereck, ed., *As They Saw Us*, 286–287.
1. Crown Prince Wilhelm, *The Memoirs of the Crown Prince of Germany*, 224.
2. Görlitz, ed., *The Kaiser and His Court*, 114–422.
3. Crown Prince Wilhelm, *The Memoirs of the Crown Prince of Germany*, 224.
4. Ibid., 226–227.
5. Gallwitz, "Retreat to the Rhein," in Viereck, ed., *As They Saw Us*, 279–285.
6. Foch, *The Memoirs of Marshal Foch*, 464–450.
7. Pershing, *My Experiences in the World War*, 7:388–396.
8. Armistice Orders from German Supreme Headquarters, 11 November 1918, issued by General Groener, in U.S. Army, History Division, *United States Army in the World War, 1917–1919*, 597–598.
9. Liggett, *A.E.F.*, 230–238.
10. Edward P. Lukert, "Stand Fast!" in *Vignettes of Military History*, ed. Richard Sommers (Carlisle, Pa.: AHEC, 1976), 43.
11. Center of Military History, *5th Division: Summary of Operations in the World War*, 251.
12. Lukert, "Stand Fast!" in Sommers, ed., *Vignettes of Military History*, 43.
13. Ibid.
14. Ibid.; Center of Military History, *5th Division: Summary of Operations in the World War*, 251.
15. Rainsford, *From Upton to the Meuse with the 307th*, 271.
16. Duffy, *Father Duffy's Story*, 304.
17. Roosevelt, *Day before Yesterday*, 112–115.
18. Ibid., 214–215.
19. Marshal, *Memoirs of My Services in the World War*, 199.
20. Center of Military History, *2nd Division: Summary of Operations in the World War*, 91–96.

21. Dienst, *History of the 353rd Infantry Regiment, 89th Division*, 141–142.

22. Ibid., 145.

23. Mackin, *Suddenly We Didn't Want to Die*, 261.

24. Center of Military History, *2nd Division: Summary of Operations in the World War*, 91–96.

25. Mackin, *Suddenly We Didn't Want to Die*, 263.

26. Summerall, *Duty, Honor, Country*, 155.

27. Barber, *History of the 79th Division*, 315–317.

28. As quoted in Ferrell, *America's Bloodiest Battle*, 147. It is derived in Ferrell's book from Babcock's memoirs and Persico's book on the last day of the war.

29. Personal letters of Ellis James Stewart, written in 1918–1918, private collection of Rebecca (Stewart) Mastriano.

30. Mastriano, *Alvin York*, 127.

31. Roosevelt, *Day before Yesterday*, 114.

22. Aftermath and Commemoration

Epigraph: Chamberlain, *Bayonet! Forward*, 202.

1. Foch, *The Memoirs of Marshal Foch*, 476–490.

2. Day, "The B That Stung," 16.

3. Ayres, *The War with Germany*, 2nd ed., 13–101.

4. Ibid.

5. Major General Dennis E. Nolan, 8 October 1935, joint meeting of the International Association of Casualty and Surety, Library of Congress.

6. McGrath, *War Diary of the 354th Infantry*.

7. Correspondence between Robert Laplander and Douglas Mastriano, 12 June 2017.

Conclusion

Epigraph: Chamberlain, *The Passing of the Armies*, 386–388.

1. Mastriano, "Project 1721: Assessment on Russia," xv–xviii, available online at https://ssi.armywarcollege.edu/pubs/display.cfm?pubID=1342 (accessed on 29 August 2017).

Bibliography

Archives

Army Historical and Education Center (AHEC), Carlisle Barracks, Pennsylvania
Baden-Württemberg Stadtsarchive, Stuttgart, Federal Republic of Germany
Bayerisches Hautpstaatarchiv, München, Federal Republic of Germany
Bundesarchiv-Militärarchiv, Freiburg, Federal Republic of Germany
Joint Forces Staff College Library, Norfolk, Virginia
Ludwigsburg Stadtsarchive, Baden-Württemberg, Federal Republic of Germany
Militärgeschichtliches Forschungsamt, Potsdam, Federal Republic of Germany
National Archives and Records Administration, College Park, Maryland
National Archives (Southeast Region), Morrow, Georgia
National Personnel Records Center, Military Personnel Records (NPRC-MPR), St. Louis, Missouri
Rottweil Stadtsarchive, Baden-Württemberg, Federal Republic of Germany
Ulm Stadtsarchive, Baden-Württemberg, Federal Republic of Germany
University of Kentucky, Special Collections, Lexington, Kentucky
U.S. Library of Congress, Washington, D.C.

Primary Sources

1st Foot Guards Regiment, written by Major-General Eitel Friedrich, Prince of Prussia. Defense of the Tiefland Sector of Group Argonne, September–October 1918. National Archives.
1st Guards Field Artillery Regiment, written by Herrmann Kohn. Defense of the Tiefland Sector of Group Argonne, September–October 1918. Bundesarchiv.
2nd Guards (Foot) Regiment, written by Major-General von Brauchtisch. Defense of the Tiefland Sector of Group Argonne, September–October 1918. National Archives.
2nd Landwehr Division. Divisional Situation Report, 6–9 October 1918 (Generalkommando z.b.v. 58, Fifth German Army, German Imperial Army notebooks 4, 5). Landesarchiv Stuttgart.
2nd Machine Company, 2nd Landwehr Division. Kriegstagebuch, October 1918, Baden-Württemberg Hauptstaatsarchiv Stuttgart.

2nd Württemberg Landwehr Division. Argonne Defensive Line, Ia 5608, 31 August 1918. Landesarchiv Stuttgart.

2nd Württemberg Landwehr Division. Divisional Situation Map, 4 October 1918, 1:25,000. Landesarchiv Stuttgart.

2nd Württemberg Landwehr Division. Divisional Situation Map, 5 October 1918, 1:25,000. Landesarchiv Stuttgart.

2nd Württemberg Landwehr Division. Divisional Situation Map/Overlay, 6 October 1918, 1:25,000 (Generalkommando z.b.v. 58, Fifth German Army, German Imperial Army). Landesarchiv Stuttgart.

2nd Württemberg Landwehr Division, Divisional Situation Map/Overlay, Ia 6503, 7 October 1918, 1:25,000 (Generalkommando z.b.v. 58, Fifth German Army, German Imperial Army). Landesarchiv Stuttgart.

2nd Württemberg Landwehr Division. Divisional Situation Map/Overlay, 9 October 1918, 1:25,000 (Generalkommando z.b.v. 58, Fifth German Army, German Imperial Army). Landesarchiv Stuttgart.

2nd Württemberg Landwehr Division. Divisional Situation Map/Overlay, 10 October 1918, 1:25,000 (Generalkommando z.b.v. 58, Fifth German Army, German Imperial Army). Landesarchiv Stuttgart.

3rd Guards (Foot) Regiment, vol. 2, written by Lieutenant Michaelis. Defense of the Tiefland Sector of Group Argonne, September–October 1918. National Archives.

4th Guards (Foot) Artillery Regiment, written by Lieutenant Colonel Freiherr von Braun. Defense of the Tiefland Sector of Group Argonne, September–October 1918. National Archives.

4th Guards (Foot) Regiment, written by Colonel Wilhelm Reinhard. Defense of the Tiefland Sector of Group Argonne, September–October 1918. Freiburg-Bundesarchiv.

270th Field Artillery Regiment, written by Dr. (Lieutenant) Hans Wiglow. Defense of the Tiefland Sector of Group Argonne, September–October 1918. Bundesarchiv.

American Battle Monuments Commission. *82d Division: Summary of Operations in the World War.* Washington, D.C.: Government Printing Office, 1944.

———. *American Armies and Battlefields in Europe: A History, Guide, and Reference Book.* Washington, D.C.: Government Printing Office, 1938.

———. *Terrain Photographs, American World War.* 69 vols. Photo Arch. U.S. Army Heritage and Education Center.

Artillery Kdr. No. 148, ktb. Kriegstagebuch, 01 September 1918 through 18 October 1918. Bundesarchiv.

Ayres, Leonard P. *The War with Germany: A Statistical Summary,* 2nd ed. Washington, D.C.: Government Printing Office, 1919.

Baker, Chester E. *Doughboy's Diary.* Shippensburg, Pa.: Burd Street Press, 1998.

Baker, Newton. *America at War.* New York: Dodd and Mead, 1931.

Barber, J. Frank. *History of the 79th Division.* Lancaster, Pa.: Steinman, 1922.

Barker, Bryon W. *History of the Machine Gun Company 328 Infantry, 82nd Division.* Worcester, Mass.: Belisle Printing and Publishing Company, 1919.

Barkley, John. *Scarlet Fields.* Lawrence: Univ. Press of Kansas, 2012.

Beery, Henry. *Make the Kaiser Dance.* New York: Arbor House, 1978.

Biddle, John. *Soldier's Handbook of the Rifle; United States Rifle Model of 1917.* Washington, D.C.: Government Printing Office, November 1917.

Bloch, Marc. *Memoirs of War.* New York: Cambridge Univ. Press, 1988.

Blumenson, Martin. *The Patton Papers: 1885–1940.* Boston: Houghton Mifflin, 1972.

Booth, Evangeline. *The War Romance of the Salvation Army.* Philadelphia, Pa.: J. B. Lippincott, 1919.

Boraston, J. H., ed. *Sir Douglas Haig's Dispatches.* London: Dent Publishing, 1919.

Brittain, Vera. *Testament of Youth.* New York: Penguin Books, 1993.

Broecker, Paul von. *Das 5. Lotharingen Infanterie Regiment Nr. 144 im Weltkrieg.* Berlin: Oldenburg, 1928.

Buchner, Adolf, and Hermann Hoppe. *In Stellung nach Vauquois.* Nordlingen, Germany: Steinmeier, 1986.

Burg, Maclyn, ed. *The Great War at Home and Abroad: WW I Diaries and Letters of W. Stull Holt.* Manhattan, Kans.: Sunflower Univ. Press, 1999.

Bürkner, Generalmajor a. D. *Infanterie Regiment Nr. 150* (1. ermländisches). Zeulenroda, Thuringia, Germany: Bernhard Sporn, 1932.

Burtt, Wilson B. "Explanation and Execution of Plans of Operation—5th Army Corps—Argonne-Meuse Operation." Allied Expeditionary Force, 1919. U.S. Army Heritage and Education Center.

Butler, Alan B. *Happy Days!* New York: Osprey, 2011.

Buxton, G. Edward, Jr., et al. *Official History of 82nd Division, American Expeditionary Forces, 1917–1919.* Indianapolis, Ind.: Bobbs-Merrill, 1920.

Byerly, Betty. *Dad's Diary—1918.* N.p.: 1st Books Library, 2002.

Center of Military History. *1st Division: Summary of Operations in the World War.* Washington, D.C.: Government Printing Office, 1944.

———. *2nd Division: Summary of Operations in the World War.* Washington, D.C.: Government Printing Office, 1944.

———. *3rd Division: Summary of Operations in the World War.* Washington, D.C.: Government Printing Office, 1944.

———. *4th Division: Summary of Operations in the World War.* Washington, D.C.: Government Printing Office, 1944.

————. *5th Division: Summary of Operations in the World War.* Washington, D.C.: Government Printing Office, 1944.

————. *7th Division: Summary of Operations in the World War.* Washington, D.C.: Government Printing Office, 1944.

————. *26th Division: Summary of Operations in the World War.* Washington, D.C.: Government Printing Office, 1944.

————. *27th Division: Summary of Operations in the World War.* Washington, D.C.: Government Printing Office, 1944.

————. *28th Division: Summary of Operations in the World War.* Washington, D.C.: Government Printing Office, 1944.

————. *29th Division: Summary of Operations in the World War.* Washington, D.C.: Government Printing Office, 1944.

————. *30th Division: Summary of Operations in the World War.* Washington, D.C.: Government Printing Office, 1944.

————. *32nd Division: Summary of Operations in the World War.* Washington, D.C.: Government Printing Office, 1944.

————. *33rd Division: Summary of Operations in the World War.* Washington, D.C.: Government Printing Office, 1944.

————. *35th Division: Summary of Operations in the World War.* Washington, D.C.: Government Printing Office, 1944.

————. *36th Division: Summary of Operations in the World War.* Washington, D.C.: Government Printing Office, 1944.

————. *37th Division: Summary of Operations in the World War.* Washington, D.C.: Government Printing Office, 1944.

————. *42nd Division: Summary of Operations in the World War.* Washington, D.C.: Government Printing Office, 1944.

————. *77th Division: Summary of Operations in the World War.* Washington, D.C.: Government Printing Office, 1944.

————. *78th Division: Summary of Operations in the World War.* Washington, D.C.: Government Printing Office, 1944.

————. *79th Division: Summary of Operations in the World War.* Washington, D.C.: Government Printing Office, 1944.

————. *80th Division: Summary of Operations in the World War.* Washington, D.C.: Government Printing Office, 1944.

————. *81st Division: Summary of Operations in the World War.* Washington, D.C.: Government Printing Office, 1944.

————. *82nd Division: Summary of Operations in the World War.* Washington, D.C.: Government Printing Office, 1944.

————. *89th Division: Summary of Operations in the World War.* Washington, D.C.: Government Printing Office, 1944.

————. *90th Division: Summary of Operations in the World War.* Washington, D.C.: Government Printing Office, 1944.

———. *91st Division: Summary of Operations in the World War.* Washington, D.C.: Government Printing Office, 1944.

———. *92nd Division: Summary of Operations in the World War.* Washington, D.C.: Government Printing Office, 1944.

———. *93rd Division: Summary of Operations in the World War.* Washington, D.C.: Government Printing Office, 1944.

———. *American Armies and Battlefields in Europe.* CMH Pub 23-24, GPO S/N 008-029-00265-5, 1995.

———. *Order of Battle of the United States Land Forces in the World War,* vol. 1 (CMH Pub 23-1), *American Expeditionary Forces: General Headquarters, Armies, Army Corps, Services of Supply, and Separate Forces.* 1931–49; reprint, 1988.

———. *Order of Battle of the United States Land Forces in the World War,* vol. 2 (CMH Pub 23-2), *American Expeditionary Forces: Division.* 1931–49; reprint, 1988.

———. *Order of Battle of the United States Land Forces in the World War,* vol. 3, part 1 (CMH Pub 23-3), *Zone of the Interior: Organizations and Activities of the War.* 1931–49; reprint, 1988.

———. *Order of Battle of the United States Land Forces in the World War,* vol. 3, part 2 (CMH Pub 23-4), *Zone of the Interior: Territorial Departments, Tactical Divisions Organized in 1918, and Posts, Camps, and Stations.* 1931–49; reprint, 1988.

———. *Order of Battle of the United States Land Forces in the World War,* vol. 3, part 3 (CMH Pub 23-5), *Zone of the Interior: Directory of Troops.* 1931–49; reprint, 1988.

Chamberlain, Joshua Lawrence. *Bayonet! Forward: My Civil War Reminiscences.* Gettysburg, Pa.: Stan Clark, 1994.

———. *The Passing of the Armies.* New York: Skyhorse Publishing, 2013.

Chandler, Scott. *Roster of the Regiment 328th American Expeditionary Forces.* France: A.E.F., 1918.

Churchill, Winston S. *Memoirs of the Second World War.* New York: Houghton-Mifflin, 1991.

Clemenceau, Georges. *Grandeur and Misery of Victory.* New York: Harcourt, Brace, 1930.

Clifford, Garry. *The World War One Memoirs of Robert P. Patterson.* Knoxville: Univ. of Tennessee Press, 2012.

Colonna, D. A. *The History of Company B, 311th Infantry.* Freehold, N.J.: Transcript Printing House, 1922.

Corby, William. *Memoirs of Chaplain Life.* Chicago: La Monte, 1893.

Cramer, C. H. *Newton D. Baker: A Biography.* New York: World Publishing Company, 1961.

Crane, A. E. "The Sixth Engineers in the Meuse-Argonne." *Military Engineer* 23, no. 128 (March–April 1931): 124–127.

Das Württembergishche Landwehr Infanterie Regiment nr. 122 im Weltkrieg 1914–1918, Band 27. Stuttgart, Germany: Belser, 1923.

Day, Charles M. "The B That Stung. B Company, 328th Regiment, on the War Path" (pamphlet).

Delbrück, Hans. *Modern Military History*. Lincoln: Univ. of Nebraska Press, 1997.

Dem Gedächtnis Unserer Gefallen Kameraden Das Offizierkorps des Infanterie Regiments Kaiser Wilhelm König von Preussen (2. Württ) Nr. 120. Ulm, Germany: Bearb. Von Herbert Maisch, 1923.

Dienst, Charles Franklin. *History of the 353rd Infantry Regiment, 89th Division*. Wichita, Kans.: 353rd Infantry Society, 1921.

Divisionstab. *Die 26 Infanterie Division (1 Kgl.Württ) im Krieg 1914–1918*. Stuttgart, Germany: Stable and Friedel, 1920.

Doyle, Arthur Conan. *A Visit to Three Fronts*. London: Hodder and Soughton, 1916.

Duffy, Francis. *Father Duffy's Story*. New York: Doran, 1919.

Duncan, George Brand. "Reminiscences, 1886–1919." Typescript. 2 vols. University of Kentucky, Special Collections, Lexington, Kentucky.

Durlewanger, A. *Das Drama des Lingenkopfes*. Colmar, Germany: S.A.E.P., Ingersheim, 1988.

Edwards, Evan Alexander. *From Doniphan to Verdun: The Official History of the 140th Infantry*. Kansas City, Mo.: World Company, 1920.

Etzel, Generalmajor a. D. Hans. *Das Königlich Bayerisches Reserve Infanterie Regiment Nr. 10*. Munich, Germany: Mar Schick, 1930.

Etzel, Hans. *Das K.B. Reserve Infanterie Regiment Nr. 10*. Munich, Germany: Schick, 1930.

The European War, vol. 17, October–November–December 1918. New York: New York Times Company, 1919.

Foch, Ferdinand. *The Memoirs of Marshal Foch*, translated by Colonel T. Bentley Mott. Garden City, N.Y.: Doubleday, Duran, 1931.

Franke, Anton. *Die 2. Württemberg Landwehr Division Im Weltkrieg 1914–1918*. Stuttgart, Germany: Verlag Bergers Literarchives, 1921.

Frasier, Lyman S. "Operations of the Third Battalion, 26th Infantry, First Division, Second and Third Phases of the Meuse-Argonne Offensive." Typescript, 1926. U.S. Army Heritage and Education Center.

Friedrich, Eitel, Prinz von Preussen. *1st Guards Regiment (Foot)*. Oldenburg, Germany: Berline, 1922.

———. *Das Erste Garderegiment zu Fuss im Weltkreig 1914–1918*. Berlin: Junker und Dunnhaupt, 1934.

Fuller, J. F. C. *Memoirs of an Unconventional Soldier*. London: Nicholson and Watson, 1936.

———. *Tanks in the Great War*. New York: Dutton, 1920.

Gallwitz, Max von. "Retreat to the Rhein." In *As They Saw Us,* edited by George Sylvester Viereck. New York: Doubleday-Doran, 1929.

Generalkommando z.b.v. 58, Fifth German Army. Battle Logs, 25 September 1918 through 4 October 1918. Bundesarchiv.

German General Staff. *The German Forces in the Field.* London: Imperial War Museum, 1995.

Gieraths, Günter. *Geschichte des Reserve Infanterie Regiments Nr. 210.* Berlin: Gerhard Stalling, 1928.

Görlitz, Walter, ed. *The Kaiser and His Court.* London: Macdonald, 1961.

Gruppe Argonne and Gruppe Aisne unit deployment locations, 8 October 1918, 1:25,000 (Nr. 50, Nr. 51) (Generalkommando z.b.v. 58, Fifth German Army, German Imperial Army). National Archives.

Gruppe Argonne attack plan/objectives between Fleville and Gesnes, Ia 6512, 7 October 1918 (Nr. 47a) (Generalkommando z.b.v. 58, Fifth German Army, German Imperial Army). National Archives.

Gruppe Argonne Battle Log Book (Generalkommando z.b.v. 58, Fifth German Army). National Archives.

Gruppe Argonne unit deployment locations/unit situations/front line trace of German forces, 6 October 1918 (Nr. 46) (Generalkommando z.b.v. 58, Fifth German Army, German Imperial Army). National Archives.

Gruppe Argonne unit deployment locations, 7 October 1918 (Nr. 47) (Generalkommando z.b.v. 58, Fifth German Army, German Imperial Army). National Archives.

Gruppe Argonne unit order of battle, 7 October 1918 (Generalkommando z.b.v. 58, Fifth German Army, German Imperial Army). National Archives.

Haan, W. G. *The 32nd Division in the World War, 1917–1919.* Madison: Wisconsin War History Commission, 1920.

Hammer, Walter. *Das Buch der 236. Infanterie Division.* Elberfeld, Germany: Baedecker, 1919.

Hanson, Joseph Mills. "The Night March on Beaumont." *Home Sector: A Weekly for the New Civilian,* 7 February 1920, 2–6.

Harris, Harvey L. *The War as I Saw It.* St. Paul, Minn.: Pogo Press, 1998.

Haswell, William. *A History of Company A—314th Engineers, 89th Division.* N.p.: 314th Engineers, AEF, 1919.

Hay, Donald. "Machine Guns, 35th Division, Meuse-Argonne, 26 Sep–1 Oct 1918." *Infantry Journal* (May/June 1933). U.S. Army Heritage and Education Center.

Hindenburg, Generalfeldmarshall Paul von. *Aus Meinem Leben.* Leipzig, Germany: Hirzel, 1920.

"History of C Company, 328th Infantry." 58-page published history with an honor roll and a complete company roster containing brief individual service biographies, including information on wounds and awards.

"History of Company 'B,' 328th Infantry, 82nd Division." U.S. Army 24-page typescript history containing an honor roll and a roster of all soldiers serving in the company. National Archives.

History of the Seventy Seventh Division. New York: Hynkoop, Hallenbeck and Crawford, 1919.

History of the 315th U.S. Infantry. N.p.: Historical Board of the 315 Infantry, 1920.

History of the Three Hundred and Twenty-Eighth Regiment of Infantry, Eighty-Second Division, American Expeditionary Forces, United States Army. Atlanta, Ga.: Foote and Davies, 1920.

Holden, Frank A. *War Memories.* Athens, Ga.: Athens Book Company, 1922.

Hopper, James. *Medals of Honor.* Rahway, N.J.: Quinn and Boden, 1929.

Horne, Charles F., ed. *Source Records of the Great War,* vol. 6, *1918.* New York: National Alumni, 1923.

Huidekoper, Frederick Louis. *Illinois in the War,* vol. 1. Springfield, Ill.: State Historic Library, 1921.

Hull, Cordell. *The Memoirs of Cordell Hull.* New York: Macmillan, 1948.

Hünicken, Emil. *Reserve Infanterie Regiment Nr. 254 (Grossherzoglich Hessisches).* Zeulenroda, Germany: Sporn, 1934.

Huston, John. *An Open Book.* New York: Knopf, 1980.

Ickes, Harold. *The Lowering Clouds, 1939–1941.* New York: Simon and Schuster, 1954.

Jones, Herbert D. N. *History of C. Company, 328th Infantry.* Brooklyn, N.Y.: Hunter Collins, 1919.

Jünger, Ernst. *The Storm of Steel.* New York: Howard Fertig, 1996.

Kellermann, Bernhard. *Der Krieg im Argonnewald.* Berlin, Germany, 1916.

Kenamore, Clair. *From Vauquois Hill to Exermont.* St. Louis, Mo.: Guard Publishers, 1919.

Kirchbach, Arndt. *Kampfe im Champagne.* Oldenburg, Germany: Gerhard Stalling, 1919.

Kling, Rektor. *Die Württembergishchen Regimenter im Weltkrieg 1914–1918,* Band 27, *Das Württembergishche Landwehr Infanterie Regiment nr. 122.* Stuttgart, Germany: Belser Verlasbuchhandklung, 1923.

Kniptash, Vernon E. *On the Western Front with the Rainbow Division: A World War I Diary.* Norman: Univ. of Oklahoma Press, 2009.

Koch, Howard. *As Time Goes By: Memoirs of a Writer.* New York: Harcourt Brace Jovanovich, 1979.

Kohn, Herrmann. "Notes and Translations of Texts of the Histories of the Following German Regiment, which took part in the Defense of Tiefland Sector of Group Argonne: Meuse-Argonne Offensive, September–October, 1918." Typescript, 1930. National Archives.

Laffargue, André. *Étude sur l'attaque dans la période actuelle de la guerre Impressions et réflexions d'un Commandant de Compagnie.* Paris: Service geographique de l'armee, 1915.

Landwehr-Infanterie-Regiment Nr. 120. *Regimental Structures and All Operations 1914–1918.* 120 Landwehr Regiment Kriegstagebuch. Landesarchiv Stuttgart.

Langille, Leslie. *42: Men of the Rainbow.* Chicago: O'Sullivan, 1933.

Lapple, Viktor-Karl. *Das Württembergishche Landwehr Infanterie Regiment nr. 125 im Weltkrieg 1914–1918,* Band 38. Stuttgart, Germany: Belser, 1926.

Lasky, Jesse L., with Don Weldon. *I Blow My Own Horn.* Garden City, N.Y.: Doubleday, 1957.

Lasky, Jesse L., Jr. *What Ever Happened to Hollywood?* New York: Funk and Wagnalls, 1975.

Leatherman, Noah H. *Diary.* Rosenort, Canada: Prairie View Press, 1973.

Ledebur, Otto von. "Rushing the St. Mihiel Salient." In *As They Saw Us,* edited by George Sylvester Viereck, 172–212. New York: Doubleday, Doran, 1929.

Legge, Barnwell R. *The First Division in the Meuse-Argonne September 26– October 12, 1918.* Fort Benning, Ga.: Infantry School, 1925.

Liggett, Hunter. *A.E.F.: Ten Years Ago in France.* New York: Dodd, Mead, 1928.

———. *Commanding an American Army: Recollections of the World War.* Boston: Houghton-Mifflin, 1925.

Lindbergh, Charles. *The Wartime Journals of Charles A. Lindbergh.* New York: Harcourt Books, 1970.

Ludendorff, Erich. *Meine Kriegserinnerungen.* Berlin: Ernst Siegfried Mittler und Sohn, 1919.

———. *My War Memories 1914–1918.* London: Hutchinson, 1919.

MacArthur, Douglas. *Reminiscences.* Pennington, N.J.: Time, 1964.

Machesney, Nathan William. "Court Martial in Europe: Report on Disciplinary System and Courts Martial in the 33rd Ill. Division AEF." *American Institute of Criminology* (May 1919 to February 1920): 552.

Mackin, Elton. *Suddenly We Didn't Want to Die.* Novato, Calif.: Presidio, 1993.

Marshal, George C. *Memoirs of My Services in the World War: 1917–1918.* Boston: Houghton-Mifflin, 1976.

McGrath, John. *War Diary of the 354th Infantry.* Trier, Germany: Lintz, 1919.

McKeogh, Arthur. *The Victorious 77th Division.* New York: John Eggers, 1919.

Merkatz, Freidrich von. *Unterrictsbuch fur die Maschinengewehr= Koampagnien.* Berlin: Eisenschmidt, 1917.

Mitchell, William. *Memoirs of World War I: "From Start to Finish of Our Greatest War."* New York: Random House, 1928.

Moser, Otto von. *Die Württemberger im Weltkrieg.* Stuttgart, Germany: Christian-Belser, 1928.

Niethammer, Herman. *Erinnerungsblätter aus der Geschichte des Regiments Kaiser Friedrich König von Preussen (7. Württ) Nr. 125.* Stuttgart, Germany: Christian Belser, 1934.

Nye, Gerald. "Report of the Special Committee on Investigation of the Munitions Industry" (also called "The Nye Report"). U.S. Congress, Senate, 74th Congress, 2nd sess., 24 February 1936. Washington, D.C., Government Printing Office, 1936.

Official History of Australia in the War of 1914–1918, vol. 1, *The Story of ANZAC from the Outbreak of War to the End of the First Phase of the Gallipoli Campaign, 4 May 1915.* Brisbane, Australia: Univ. of Queensland Press, 1980.

Pennsylvania in the Great War, vol. 2. Pittsburgh, Pa.: States Publications Society, 1921.

Pershing, John J. *My Experiences in the World War.* 2 vols. New York: Stokes, 1931.

———. War Diary. Library of Congress, Washington, D.C.

Pershing, John J., and Major General Hunter Liggett. *American Armies and Battlefields in Europe.* Washington, D.C.: Government Printing Office, 1938.

———. *Report of the First Army, American Expeditionary Forces.* Fort Leavenworth, Kans.: General Service School Press, 1923.

———. *Report of the First Army, American Expeditionary Forces, 10 August 1918–20 April 1920.* Fort Leavenworth, Kans.: General Service School Press, 1923.

Pirscher, Friedrich von. *Das (Rheinisch-Westfälische) Infanterie Regiment Nr. 459.* Berlin: Gerhard Stalling, 1926.

Pistorius, Theodor. *Die Letzen Tage des Königreichs Württemberg.* Stuttgart, Germany: Kohlhammer, 1935.

Plickert, Heinrich. *Infanterie Regiment Nr. 151* (2. ermländisches), Book 2. Berlin: Oldenburg, 1929.

Rainsford, W. Kerr. *From Upton to the Meuse with the 307th.* New York: Appleton, 1920.

Ralphson, George. *Over There with the Yanks in the Argonne Forest.* Chicago: Donohue, 1920.

Reilly, Henry J. *Americans All: The Rainbow at War: Official History of the 42nd Rainbow Division in the World War.* Columbus, Ohio: Heer Publishing, 1936.

Rickenbacker, Edward V. *Fighting the Flying Circus*. New York: Stokes, 1919.

Roosevelt, Eleanor Butler. *Day before Yesterday*. Garden City, N.Y.: Doubleday, 1959.

Roosevelt, Elliott (editor of FDR's papers). *His Personal Letters, 1928–1945*. New York: Duell, Sloan and Pierce, 1950.

Roosevelt, Theodore. *Average Americans*. New York: Putnam, 1919.

Rosenberg-Lipinsky, Hans Oskar von. *Das Konigen Elisabeth Garde-Grenadier Regiment Nr. 3 im Weltkrieg 1914–1918*. Zeulenroda, Thuringen, Germany: Bernhard Sporn, 1935.

Schmidt, Ernst. *Argonnen*. Schlacten des Weltkrieges, Band 18. Berlin: Gerhard Stalling, 1927.

Scott, Major General H. L., Army Chief of Staff. *Manual for Infantry*. Menasha, Wisc.: George Banta Publishing, 1917.

———. *Manual for Noncommissioned Officers and Privates of Infantry of the Army of the United States 1917*. Menasha, Wisc.: George Banta Publishing, 1917.

Seldte, Franz. *M.G.K. Maschinen Gewehr Kompanie*. Leipzig, Germany: Köhler, 1929.

Seymore, Charles. *The Intimate Papers of Colonel House*, vols. 1–3. New York: Houghton-Miffin, 1926.

Shipley, Thomas. *The History of the A.E.F.* New York: Doran, 1920.

Siebert, Heinrich. *Geschichte des Infanterie Regiments Generalfeldmarschall von Hindenburg (2. Masurisches) Nr. 147 im Weltkrieg*. Berlin: Oldenburg, 1927.

Silberreisen, Leutnant der Reserve. *Schwäbische Kunde aus dem Grossen Krieg*. Stuttgart, Germany: Deutschen Verlags Anstalt, 1918.

Simon, A. D. *Das Infanterie Regiment "Kaiser Wilhelm, König von Preussen" (2. Württ) Nr. 120. im Weltkrieg 1914–1918*. Berlin: Christian Belshersche, 1922.

Smythe, Donald. "St.-Mihiel: The Birth of an American Army." In *In Defense of the Republic: Readings in American Military History*, edited by David Curtis Skaggs and Robert Browning. Belmont, Calif.: Wadsworth, 1991.

Sotheby, Lionel. *Great War: Diaries and Letters from the Western Front*. Athens: Ohio Univ. Press, 1997.

Souvenir of Camp Gordon. Atlanta, Ga.: Byrd Printing, 1918.

Stackpole, Robert. Diary. Library of Congress, Washington, D.C.

Stein, Kurt. *Das Württembergishche Landwehr Infanterie Regiment nr. 121 im Weltkrieg 1914–1918*, Band 4. Stuttgart, Germany: Belser, 1925.

Straub, Elmer Frank. *A Sergeant's Diary in the World War: The Diary of an Enlisted Member of the 150th Field Artillery, Rainbow Division*. Indianapolis: Indiana Historical Commission, 1923.

Strohm, Gustav. *Das Württembergishche Landwehr Infanterie Regiment nr. 120 im Weltkrieg 1914–1918*. Band 4. Stuttgart, Germany: Belser, 1920.

———. *Die Württembergishchen Regimenter im Weltkrieg 1914–1918*, Band 25, *Das Württembergishche Landwehr Infanterie Regiment nr. 120*. Stuttgart, Germany: Belser Verlasbuchhandklung, 1922.

Summerall, Charles Pelot. *Duty, Honor, Country*. Lexington: Univ. Press of Kentucky, 2010.

Swindler, H. O. "Turkey Match." *Infantry Journal* 37, no. 4 (October 1930).

Terrain, John. *General Jack's Diary 1914–1918: The Trench Diary of Brigadier-General J. L. Jack*. London: Eyre and Spottiswoode, 1964.

Thorn, Henry C. *History of the 313th Infantry Regiment*. New York: Wynkoop, Hallenback and Crawford, 1920.

Triplet, William S. *A Youth in the Meuse-Argonne: A Memoir, 1917–1918*. Columbia: Univ. of Missouri Press, 2000.

Trott, C. A. *The Fifth U.S. Division in the World War, 1917–1919*. Washington, D.C.: Society of the Fifth Division, 1919.

Uncle Sam's Boys. Chicago: Black, 1918.

U.S. Army. *History of Three Hundred and Twenty-Eighth Regiment of Infantry*. Atlanta, Ga.: Foote and Davis, 1922.

———. *Military Exposition and Carnival*. Washington, D.C.: Government Printing Office, 1929.

U.S. Army. A.E.F. GHQ. *American Official Communiqués*. Bulletin No. 4, April 1920. Issued daily, 15 May–13 December 1918.

———. *Final Report of Gen. John J. Pershing*. Washington, D.C.: Government Printing Office, 1919. U.S. Army Heritage and Education Center.

U.S. Army, American Expeditionary Forces, General Staff College. *Staff Ride: Meuse-Argonne Operations*. France, January 1919. U.S. Army Heritage and Education Center.

U.S. Army, American Expeditionary Forces, G2. *The German and American Combined Daily Order of Battle, 25 Sep to 11 Nov 1918*. France, 1919.

U.S. Army, American Expeditionary Forces, Intelligence section of the General Staff. *Histories of Two Hundred and Fifty-One Divisions of the German Army*. Washington, D.C.: Center of Military History, 1920.

U.S. Army, First Army. "First Army Lecture Courses: St. Mihiel and Argonne-Meuse." France, 1919.

U.S. Army, History Division. *United States Army in the World War, 1917–1919*, vol. 1, *Organization of the American Expeditionary Forces* (Washington, D.C.: Government Printing Office, 1948; first CMH ed. 1988). CMH Pub 23-6, GPO S/N 008-029-00176-4.

———. *United States Army in the World War, 1917–1919*, vol. 2, *Policy-Forming Documents of the American Expeditionary Forces* (Washington,

D.C.: Government Printing Office, 1948; first CMH ed. 1989). CMH Pub 23-7.

———. *United States Army in the World War, 1917–1919*, vol. 3, *Training and Use of American Units with the British and French* (Washington, D.C.: Government Printing Office, 1948; first CMH ed. 1989). CMH Pub 23-8.

———. *United States Army in the World War, 1917–1919*, vol. 4, *Early Military Operations of the American Expeditionary Forces* (Washington, D.C.: Government Printing Office, 1948; first CMH ed. 1989). CMH Pub 23-9.

———. *United States Army in the World War, 1917–1919*, vol. 5, *Military Operations of the American Expeditionary Forces* (Washington, D.C.: Government Printing Office, 1948; first CMH ed. 1989). CMH Pub 23-10.

———. *United States Army in the World War, 1917–1919*, vol. 6, *Military Operations of the American Expeditionary Forces* (Washington, D.C.: Government Printing Office, 1948; first CMH ed. 1990). CMH Pub 23-11.

———. *United States Army in the World War, 1917–1919*, vol. 7, *Military Operations of the American Expeditionary Forces* (Washington, D.C.: Government Printing Office, 1948; first CMH ed. 1990). CMH Pub 23-12.

———. *United States Army in the World War, 1917–1919*, vol. 8, *Military Operations of the American Expeditionary Forces* (Washington, D.C.: Government Printing Office, 1948; first CMH ed. 1990). CMH Pub 23-13.

———. *United States Army in the World War, 1917–1919*, vol. 9, *Military Operations of the American Expeditionary Forces* (Washington, D.C.: Government Printing Office, 1948; first CMH ed. 1990). CMH Pub 23-14.

———. *United States Army in the World War, 1917–1919*, vol. 10-1, *The Armistice Agreement and Related Documents* (Washington, D.C.: Government Printing Office, 1948; first CMH ed. 1991). CMH Pub 23-15.

———. *United States Army in the World War, 1917–1919*, vol. 10-2, *The Armistice Agreement and Related Documents* (Washington, D.C.: Government Printing Office, 1948; first CMH ed. 1991). CMH Pub 23-16.

———. *United States Army in the World War, 1917–1919*, vol. 11, *American Occupation of Germany* (Washington, D.C.: Government Printing Office, 1948; first CMH ed. 1991). CMH Pub 23-17.

———. *United States Army in the World War, 1917–1919*, vol. 12, *Reports of the Commander-in-Chief, AEF, Staff Sections and Services* (Washington, D.C.: Government Printing Office, 1948; first CMH ed. 1991). CMH Pub 23-18.

————. *United States Army in the World War, 1917–1919,* vol. 13, *Reports of the Commander-in-Chief, AEF, Staff Sections and Services* (Washington, D.C.: Government Printing Office, 1948; first CMH ed. 1991). CMH Pub 23-19.

————. *United States Army in the World War, 1917–1919,* vol. 14, *Reports of the Commander-in-Chief, AEF, Staff Sections and Services* (Washington, D.C.: Government Printing Office, 1948; first CMH ed. 1991). CMH Pub 23-20.

————. *United States Army in the World War, 1917–1919,* vol. 15, *Reports of the Commander-in-Chief, AEF, Staff Sections and Services* (Washington, D.C.: Government Printing Office, 1948; first CMH ed. 1991). CMH Pub 23-21.

————. *United States Army in the World War, 1917–1919,* vol. 16, *General Orders, GHQ, AEF* (Washington, D.C.: Government Printing Office, 1948; first CMH ed. 1992). CMH Pub 23-22.

————. *United States Army in the World War, 1917–1919,* vol. 17, *Bulletins, GHQ, AEF* (Washington, D.C.: Government Printing Office, 1948; first CMH ed. 1992). CMH Pub 23-23.

U.S. Congress. "Propaganda in Motion Pictures: Hearings before a Subcommittee of the Committee on Interstate Commerce, United States Senate, Seventy-Seventh Congress First Session on S. Res. 152, a Resolution Authorizing an Investigation of War Propaganda Disseminated by the Motion-Picture Industry and of Any Monopoly in the Production, Distribution, or Exhibition of Motion Pictures. September 9 to 26, 1941." Washington, D.C.: Government Printing Office, 1942.

U.S. War Department. *AEF Field Intelligence Reports, 26 September– 11 November 1918.* First U.S. Army, 1918.

U.S. War Department, Office. *Report of the Chief Engineer, First Army American Expeditionary Forces, on the Engineer Operations in the St. Mihiel and Meuse-Argonne Offensives, 1918.* Washington, D.C.: Government Printing Office, 1929.

Viereck, George Sylvester, ed. *As They Saw Us: Foch, Ludendorff, and Other Leaders Write Our War History.* Cranbury, N.J.: Scholar's Bookshelf, 2005.

von Tschischwitz, General der Infanterie. *General von der Marwitz Weltkriegsbriefe.* Berlin: Steiniger Verlag, 1940.

Walsh, Milly. *We're Not Dead Yet: First World War Diary of Private Bert Cooke.* St. Catharines, Ontario: Vanwell Publishing, 2004.

Wanamaker, John. *The Wanamaker Diary: 1918.* Philadelphia, 1917.

Warner, Jack. *Hollywood Be Thy Name: The Warner Brothers Story.* Rocklin, Calif.: Prima, 1994.

Warner, Jack, with Dean Jennings. *My First Hundred Years in Hollywood.* New York: Random House, 1965.

Wilhelm, Crown Prince. *The Memoirs of the Crown Prince of Germany.* London: Thornton-Butterworth, 1923.
Wilhelm, Crown Prince of Prussia (Frederick William Victor Augustus Ernest). *Memoirs of the Crown Prince of Germany.* Uckfield, East Sussex, UK: Naval and Military Press, 2005.
Wilhelm, Kronprinzen. *Erinnerungen des Kronprinzen Wilhelm.* Stuttgart, Germany: Gotta'sche Buchhandlung Nachfolger, 1923.
York, Alvin C. "The Diary of Sergeant York: A Famous Hero's Own Story of His Great Adventure." *Liberty Magazine* (14 July 1928, 21 July 1928, 28 July 1928, 4 August 1928).
———. *Sergeant York: His Own Life Story and War Diary.* Garden City, N.Y.: Doubleday, Doran, 1928.
York, Gracie Williams. *The Reminisces of Mrs. Alvin "Sergeant" York.* Tennessee Regional Oral History Collection, part 1, number 8 (1976).

Secondary Sources

Allen, H. Warner. "The American Achievement." *National Review* (June 1919).
Andriessen, J. H. J. *World War I.* Lisse, Netherlands: Rebo Publishers, 2006.
Andrews, Peter. *Sergeant York: Reluctant Hero.* New York: Putnam, 1969.
Arce, Hector. *Gary Cooper: An Intimate Biography.* New York: William Morrow, 1979.
Asprey, Robert B. *The German High Command at War.* New York: Morrow, 1959.
Audoin-Rouzeau, Stephane, and Annette Becker. *14–18: Understanding the Great War.* New York: Hill and Wang, 2002.
Bachman, Senator Nathan. "Alvin C. York, U.S. Congress. Senate Committee on Military Affairs," Report No. 120, 24 February 1937. Washington, D.C.: Government Printing Office, 1937.
Bailey, Thomas. *The Lusitania Disaster: An Episode in Modern Warfare and Diplomacy.* New York: Free Press, 1975.
Beattie, Taylor V. "Continuing the Search for York." *Army History* 66 (winter 2008): 20–27.
———. "In Search of Sergeant York: The Man, the Myth, and the Legend." *Army Heritage* 50 (summer–fall 2000), 1–5.
Borchard, Edwin M., and William P. Lange. *Neutrality for the United States,* 2nd ed. New Haven, Conn.: Yale Univ. Press, 1940.
Braim, Paul F. *The Test of Battle.* Shippensburg, Pa.: White Mane Books, 1998.
"'Bravest Man in the American Army' Is Compliment Bestowed on

New Jersey Boy by Tank Commander." *Indiana Evening Gazette,* 4 April 1919.

Brisbane, Arthur. *U.S. Official Pictures of the World War.* Washington, D.C.: Pictorial Bureau, 1920.

Broadbent, Harvey. *Gallipoli: The Fatal Shore.* Camberwell, Victoria, Australia: Viking/Penguin, 2005.

Budreau, Lisa M. *Bodies of War: World War One and the Politics of Commemoration in America, 1919–1933.* New York: New York Univ. Press, 2010.

Bull, Stephen. *World War I Trench Warfare,* vols. 1–2. Oxford, UK: Osprey, 2002.

Caldwell, Fred. "Above and Beyond the Call of Duty." *Register of Kentucky State Historical Society* 18, no. 53 (May 1920): 9–12.

Canfield, Bruce. *U.S. Infantry Weapons of the First World War.* Lincoln, R.I.: Mowbray, 2000.

Chase, Joseph Cummings. *Soldiers All.* New York: Scribner's, 1920.

Clark, George. *The Second Infantry Division in World War One.* Jefferson, N.C.: McFarland, 2007.

Clausewitz, Carl von. *On War.* Princeton, N.J.: Princeton Univ. Press, 1984.

Coffmann, Edward M. *The War to End All Wars.* Lexington: Univ. Press of Kentucky, 1998.

Compton-Hall, Richard. *Submarines at War 1914–1918.* Cornwall, UK: Periscope Publishing, 2004.

Cooke, James J. *The All-Americans at War: The 82nd Division in the Great War, 1917–1918.* West Port, Conn.: Praeger, 1999.

Coulter, Henry W. *History of the 110th Infantry.* Pittsburgh, Pa.: Pittsburgh Printing Company, 1920.

D'Este, Carlo. *Patton: A Genius for War.* New York: Harper, 1995.

Devlin, Patrick. *Too Proud to Fight: Woodrow Wilson's Neutrality.* New York: Oxford Univ. Press, 1975.

Divine, Robert A. *The Illusion of Neutrality.* Chicago: Univ. of Chicago Press, 1962.

Donald, Aida. *Citizen Soldier: A Life of Harry S. Truman.* New York: Basic Books, 2012.

Donecke, Justus D. *Storm on the Horizon.* New York: Rowman and Littlefield, 2000.

Duffy, Christopher. *The Military Life of Frederick the Great.* New York: Atheneum Books, 1986.

Ebel, Jonathan H. *Faith in the Fight: Religion and the American Soldier in the Great War.* Princeton, N.J.: Princeton Univ. Press, 2010.

Edwards, Jerome E. *The Foreign Policy of Col. McCormick's Tribune, 1929–1941.* Reno: Univ. of Nevada Press, 1971.

Eggleston, Michael. *The 5th Marine Regiment Devil Dogs in World War I: A History and Roster.* Jefferson, N.C.: McFarland, 2016.

"82d Division: Record of Events." In Department of the Army, *American Expeditionary Forces Divisions,* vol. 2. Washington, D.C.: CMH, 1988.

Eisenhower, John, S.D. *Yanks.* New York: Simon and Schuster, 2001.

Fax, Gene. *With Their Bare Hands.* New York: Osprey, 2016.

Ferrell, Robert H. *America's Deadliest Battle: Meuse-Argonne, 1918.* Lawrence: Univ. Press of Kansas, 2007.

Foley, Robert T. "The Schlieffen Plan-A War Plan." In *The Schlieffen Plan,* edited by Gerhardt Gross, Hans Ehlert, and Michael Epkenhas, translated by Major General David T. Zabecki, 69–74. Lexington: Univ. Press of Kentucky, 2014.

Ford, Nancy. *Americans All! Foreign-Born Soldiers in World War I.* College Station, Tex.: Texas A&M Univ. Press, 2001.

Fosten, D. S. V. *The German Army 1914–1918.* Oxford, UK: Osprey, 1978.

Fuller, J. F. C. *A Military History of the Western World,* vol. 3. New York: Funk and Wagnalls, 1956.

Gawne, Jonathan. *Over There! The American Soldier in World War I.* Mechanicsburg, Pa.: Stackpole Books, 1997.

Geiss, Imanuel. *German Foreign Policy 1871–1914.* New York: Routledge, Taylor and Francis, 1976.

Gillette, A. Ward. *The Meuse-Argonne Offensive, First Phase.* Fort Benning, Ga.: Infantry School, 1937.

Gorce, Paul-Marie de La. *Charles de Gaulle: 1890–1945,* vol. 1. Paris: Nouveau Monde, 2008.

———. *The French Army: A Military-Political History,* translated by Kenneth Douglas. New York: George Braziller, 1963.

Graevenitz, Fritz von. *Die deutsche Oberste Fuhrung im Weltkrieg in ihnen Bedeutung fur die Württembergishchen Steitkrafte.* Stuttgart, Germany: Bergers, 1921.

———. *Die Entwicklung des Württembergishche Heerwesens im Rahmen des deutschen Reichheerews.* Stuttgart, Germany: Bergers, 1921.

Gray, Kristina. "Nels T. Wold's Story." *Crooksten Times,* 25 July 2013.

Gregory, Barry. *Argonne.* New York: Ballantine, 1972.

Grieves, Keith. *The Politics of Manpower, 1914–1918.* Manchester, UK: Manchester Univ. Press, 1988.

Grotelueschen, Mark Ethan. *The AEF Way of War: The American Army and Combat in World War One.* Cambridge, UK: Cambridge Univ. Press, 2007.

Gruppo, Giunti. *Der Erste Weltkrieg.* Florenz, Italy: Gruppo Editoriale, 1999.

Gudmundsson, Bruce I. *Stormtroop Tactics: Innovation in the German Army, 1914–1918.* New York: Praeger, 1989.

Guerard, von. *Von Reims bis zu den Argonnen.* Leipzig, Germany: Greth-lein, 1918.

Hadley, Lieutenant Colonel A. "The Battle of Montfaucon." Defense Technical Information Center, Fort Leavenworth, Kans., May 1984.

Handbuch der Provinz Sachsen. Magdeburg: Baensch, 1900.

Harder, Hans-Joachim. *Militäreschichtliches Handbuch Baden-Württemberg.* Stuttgart, Germany: Kohlhammer, 1987.

Hart, B. H. Liddell. *Reputations, Ten Years After.* Boston: Little, Brown, 1928.

"Hearings before the Committee on Military Affairs." House of Representatives. 74th Congress, 1st sess. Washington, D.C.: Government Printing Office, 1935.

Henry, Mark. *US Army of World War I.* Oxford, UK: Osprey, 2003.

Herwig, Holger, H. *The First World War: Germany and Austria-Hungary 1914–1918.* London: Arnold Publishing, 1997.

Higham, Charles. *Warner Bros.* New York: Scribner's, 1975.

Hirschorn, Clive. *The Warner Bros. Story.* New York: Crown, 1979.

Hoff, Thomas. *US Doughboy 1916–1919.* Oxford, UK: Osprey, 2005.

Holt, Toni, and Valmai Holt. *The Western Front-South.* South Yorkshire, UK: Pen and Sword, 2005.

Horne, Alistair. *The Price of Glory.* New York: Penguin, 1993.

Howard, Michael. *War in European History.* Oxford, UK: Oxford Univ. Press, 1976.

Hull Cordell. "Hearing before the Committee on Military Affairs—House Resolution 8599 to Appoint Alvin C. York to Second Lieutenant, with Pay and Benefits of a Retired Officer." 66th Congress, 1st sess. Washington, D.C.: Government Printing Office, 1919.

Ikenberry, G. John. *The Crisis of American Foreign Policy: Wilsonianism in the Twenty-First Century.* Princeton, N.J.: Princeton Univ. Press, 2009.

Innes, T. A. *Covenants with Death.* London: Daily Express, 1934.

Jacobs, Bruce. *Heroes of the Army.* New York: Norton, 1956.

James, D. Clayton. *The Years of MacArthur,* vol. 1, *1880–1941.* Boston: Houghton Mifflin, 1970.

"Jewish Medal of Honor Men." *American Hebrew and Messenger* 107, nos. 14–26 (1 October 1920), 598–600.

Johnson, Thomas. *Without Censor.* Indianapolis, Ind.: Bobbs-Merrill, 1927.

Johnson, Thomas M. *The Lost Battalion.* Lincoln: Univ. of Nebraska Press, 2000.

Joint Operational Planning (JP) 5-0. Washington, D.C.: Joint Publication, 2011.

Jomini, Henri. *The Art of War.* Westport, Conn.: Greenwood, 1971.

Katcher, Philip. *The American Soldier.* New York: Military Press, 1990.

Kauffman, Bill. *America First! Its History, Culture and Politics*. New York: Prometheus Books, 1995.

Keegan, John. *The First World War*. New York: Knopf, 2001.

Kenamore, Clair. *The Story of the 139th*. St. Louis, Mo.: Guard Publishing, 1920.

Kennedy, Paul. *Grand Strategies in War and Peace*. New Haven, Conn.: Yale Univ. Press, 1991.

Kent, Daniel W. *German 7.9 mm Military Ammunition: 1888–1945*. Ann Arbor, Mich.: Edwards Brothers, 1973.

Kitchen, Martin. *The German Offensives of 1918*. Gloucestershire, UK: Tempus Printing, 2005.

Knock, Thomas J. *To End All Wars*. New York: Oxford Univ. Press, 1992.

Kuhnhausen, Jerry. *The Colt .45 Automatic, A Shop Manual*. McCall, Idaho: Hertiage-VSP Shop Manual, 1990.

Lacorde, Dominique. *Gesnes en-Argonne*. Fort Moselle, France: L'imprierie, 2005.

LaFeber, Walter. *The American Age: United States Foreign Policy at Home and Abroad*. New York: Norton, 1994.

Laffargue, André. *Étude sur l'attaque dans la période actuelle de la guerre Impressions et réflexions d'un Commandant de Compagnie*. Paris: Service geographique de l'armee, 1915.

Langer, William L. "The Dual Alliance." *New York Times*, 23 September 1918.

———. "The Franco-Russian Alliance (1890–1894)." *Slavonic Review* vol. 3, no. 9 (March 1925): 554–575.

Lanza, Conrad H. "Artillery in Support of the Infantry in the AEF." *Field Artillery Journal* 36, no. 1 (January–February 1936): 70.

Laparra, Jean-Claude. *The German Infantryman 1914–1918*. Paris: Histories and Collections, 2008.

Laplander, Robert J. "Enemy in All Directions: A Brief History of the Lost Battalion." Unpublished manuscript provided to the author by Robert Laplander.

———. *Finding the Lost Battalion*. Waterford, Wisc.: Lulu Press, 2006.

Lengel, Edward G. *To Conquer Hell*. New York: Holt, 2008.

Lindbergh, Anne Morrow. *The Flower and the Nettle: Diaries and Letters, 1936–1939*. New York: Harcourt Brace Jovanovitch, 1976.

Lodge, Henry Cabot, and Theodore Roosevelt. *Hero Tales from American History*. New York: New York Century Company, 1895.

Lupfer, Timothy. *The Dynamics of Doctrine: Changes in Tactical Doctrine during the First World War*. Fort Leavenworth, Kans.: Combat Studies Institutes, 1981.

Luther, Dr. Rev. Martin. *Smalcald Articles*. 1537. Translated by F. Bente. St. Louis, Mo.: Concordia Publishing House, 1921.

Lynn, John. *Battle: A History of Combat and Culture.* Cambridge, Mass.: Westview Press, 2003.

MacDonald, S. C. *Machine Gun Operations during 28th Division Attack, 26 September–8 October 1918.* Fort Leavenworth, Kans.: Command and General Staff College, 1936.

Mastriano, Douglas. *Alvin York: A New Biography of the Hero of the Argonne.* Lexington: Univ. Press of Kentucky, 2014.

———. "The Meuse Argonne Offensive." In *The First World War Battlefield Guide: The Western Front*, edited by Major General Mungo Melvin, 171–177. Andover, UK: Royal United Services Institute, 2014.

———. "Project 1721: Assessment on Russia." Carlisle, Pa.: U.S. Army War College, 2017.

Mattox, John Mark. *Saint Augustine and the Theory of Just War.* New York: Continuum, 2006.

McCollum, Lee Charles. *History and Rhymes of the Lost Battalion.* Chicago: Foley, 1919.

McPhail, Helen. *The Long Silence.* London: Tauris, 2001.

Mead, Peter. *The Eye in the Air: History of Air Observation and Reconnaissance for the Army 1785–1945.* London: Her Majesty's Stationery Office, 1983.

Meilinger, Phillip S. "Mitchell Biography." *American Airpower Biography: A Survey of the Field.* Montgomery, Ala.: Maxwell Air Force Base, 1997.

Michelin. *The Americans in the Great War*, vols. 1–3. Milltown, N.J.: Michelin Tire Company, 1920.

Miller, Tony. "The Outstanding Soldier of the A.E.F." *Traces* (fall 2000), 15–20.

Morrow, John H. *The Great War: An Imperial History.* New York: Routledge, 2004.

Murray, Williams, ed. *The Making of Strategy: Rulers, States, and War.* Cambridge, UK: Cambridge Univ. Press, 1997.

Nash, David. *German Army Handbook April 1918.* London: Arms and Armour Press, 1977.

Nathusius, Martin. *Polte Armaturen-und Maschinenfabrik: 1885–1935, 50 Jahre Armaturen.* Magdeburg, Germany: Polte, 1935.

———. "Vor 50 Jahren wurde Polte gegründet. Jubiläum der angesehenen Magdeburger Maschinenfabrik." *Magdeburgische Zeitung* (6–7 April 1925).

Neiberg, Michael S., ed. *Finding Common Ground.* Boston: Leiden, 2011.

———. *Foch.* Washington, D.C.: Brassey's, 2003.

———. *The Western Front 1914–1916.* London: Amber Books, 2011.

Oertel, Walter. *Die Waffentaten Württemberger im Bewegungskrieg.* Stuttgart, Germany: Stuttgarter Neues Tagblatt, 1934.

O'Grady, Joseph P., ed. *The Immigrants' Influence on Wilson's Peace Policies*. Lexington: Univ. of Kentucky Press, 1967.

O'Leary, Jeff. *Brave Hearts under Red Skies*. Colorado Springs, Colo.: Cook Publishers, 2003.

Olmsted, Kathryn S. *Real Enemies*. New York: Oxford Univ. Press, 2009.

Palmer, Frederick. *Newton D. Baker*. New York: Dodd, Mead, 1931.

———. *Our Greatest Battle: The Meuse-Argonne*. New York: Dodd, Mead, 1919.

Passingham, Ian. *All the Kaiser's Men*. Gloucestershire, UK: Sutton Mill, 2003.

Pattullo, George. "The Second Elder Gives Battle." *Saturday Evening Post*, 26 April 1919.

Proctor, H. G. *The Iron Division*. Philadelphia, Pa.: Winston, 1919.

Ramsey, David. *Lusitania: Saga and Myth*. New York: Norton, 2001.

Reilly, Henry J. *America's Part*. New York: Cosmopolitan Books, 1938.

Remak, Joachim. *Sarajevo*. New York: Criterion Books, 1959.

Remarque, Erich Marie. *All Quiet on the Western Front*. New York: Little, Brown, 1929.

Ridout, G. W. *The Greatest Soldier of the War*. Louisville, Ky.: Pentecostal Publishing Company, 1929.

Roosevelt, Theodore, Jr. *Rank and File: True Stories of the Great War*. New York: Charles Scribner and Sons, 1928.

Rumer, Thomas A. *The American Legion: An Official History, 1919–1989*. New York: Evans, 1990.

Santayana, George. *The Life of Reason*. New York: Charles Scribner and Sons, 1920.

Schmidt, Donald. *The Folly of War: American Foreign Policy 1898–2005*. New York: Algora, 2005.

Schreiber, Shane B. *Shock Army of the British Empire*. St. Catharines, Ontario: Vanwell Publishing, 2004.

Sheffield, Gary. *Forgotten Victory*. London: Headline Book Publishing, 2001.

Shoemaker, Floyd D. "Missouri and the War." *Missouri Historical Review* 13, no. 4 (July 1919): 319–360.

Shuddekopf, Otto-Ernst. *Der Erste Weltkrieg*. Gutersloh, Germany: Bertelsmann Lexikon-Verlag, 1977.

Silberreisen, Leutnant. *Schwäbische Kunde aus dem Großen Krieg*. Stuttgart, Germany: Deutschen Verlags, 1918.

Stine, Frederick A. *Samuel Woodfill, Hero*. Newport: Northern Kentucky Historical Society, 1966.

Strachan, Hew. *The First World War*, vol. 1, *To Arms*. New York: Penguin Books, 2003.

Striner, Richard. *Woodrow Wilson and World War I: A Burden Too Great to Bear*. New York: Rowman and Littlefield, 2014.

Swindler, Henry.O. "Turkey Match." *Infantry Journal* 37, no. 4 (October 1930): 343–351.

Synan, Vinson. *The Holiness-Pentecostal Tradition: Charismatic Movements in the Twentieth Century.* Grand Rapids, Mich.: Eerdmans, 1997.

Terraine, John. *To Win a War: 1918, The Year of Victory.* London: Papermac, 1978.

Thomas, Evan. "Spymaster General." *Vanity Fair* (March 2011).

Thomas, Lowell. *Woodfill of the Regulars.* Garden City, N.Y.: Doubleday, 1929.

Thomas, Nigel. *The German Army in World War I,* vols. 1–3. Oxford, UK: Osprey, 2003.

Thompson, Leroy. *The Colt 1911 Pistol.* Long Island City, N.Y.: Osprey, 2011.

Trask, David. *The AEF and Coalition War Making 1917–1918.* Lawrence: Univ. Press of Kansas, 1993.

Turlock, Alice. *In the Hands of Providence.* Chapel Hill: Univ. of North Carolina Press, 1992.

U.S. Army. *Army Leadership.* Field Manual 6-22. Washington, D.C.: Department of the Army, October 2006.

———. *Intelligence Analysis.* Field Manual 34-3. Washington, D.C.: Headquarters, Department of the Army, 1990.

———. *Intelligence Preparation of the Battlefield.* Field Manual 34–130. Washington, D.C.: U.S. Army, July 1994.

———. *Military Leadership.* Field Manual 22-100. Washington, D.C.: Department of the Army, July 1990

U.S. Congress. Senate. Committee on Military Affairs. *Alvin C. York.* Report No 120, 75th Congress, 1st session. Washington, D.C.: Government Printing Office, 1937.

———. *Medal of Honor Recipients, 1863–1978.* 96th Cong., 1st sess. Washington, D.C.: Government Printing Office, 1979.

Walker, William. *Betrayal at Little Gibraltar.* New York: Schreibner, 2016.

Walter, John. *Allied Small Arms of World War One.* Sevenoaks, Kent, UK: Crowood Press, 2000.

———. *Military Handguns of the Two World Wars.* London: Greenhill Books, 2003.

———. *Military Rifles of the Two World Wars.* London: Greenhill Books, 2003.

Washington, George. "Farewell Address." Senate Document number 106-21, page 25. Washington, D.C.: Government Printing Office, 2000.

Werner, Bret. *Uniforms, Equipment and Weapons of the American Expeditionary Forces in World War I.* Atglen, Pa.: Schiffer Military History Books, 2006.

"Where Are the Heroes of the Great War?" *Literary Digest* 66, no. 11 (11 September 1920), 49.

Yockelson, Mitch. *Forty-Seven Days: How Pershing's Warriors Came of Age to Defeat the German Army.* New York: Nal Caliber, 2016.

Young, Kenneth Ray. *The General's General: The Life and Times of Arthur MacArthur.* Boulder, Colo.: Westview Press, 1994.

Zabecki, David. "America's Top World War I Ace." *Military History* (August–September 2009).

———. *Chief of Staff*, vol. 1. Annapolis, Md.: Naval Institute Press, 2008.

———. "Finding the Lost Battalion." *Military History* (2012): 15.

———. *Steel Wind.* London: Praeger, 1998.

Index

Page numbers in italics refer to illustrations or material in captions.

Military Units

First Army (France), 29

First Army (GB), 3, 29, 89, 93

First Army (Germany), 12, 271

First Army (USA): 35th Division collapse and, 131; area of operations, 163; British military assistance to, 33; degraded condition of, 251; Field Order No. 25 for, 96–97; French Fourth Army border with, 273; French Fourth Army coordination with, 279–82, *280*; French military assistance to, 33–34, *34*; German Argonne defenses and, 173–74; GHQ error and, 278–79; as inexperienced army, 35–36; Kriemhilde Line attacks of, 241; Liggett as commander of, 8, *98*, 195, 249, 251, 254, 276, 297; Meuse Valley advances of, 309; Montfaucon, 137; November Offensive attacks, 286, 297, 299; November Offensive preparations of, 271, 276–79, 279 map 18.2; Pershing as commander of, 195, 249; Sedan, 312; St. Mihiel Offensive (Sept. 12–15, 1918), 33–36

1st Battalion, 120th Württemberg Regiment (Germany), 101, 210–12

1st Battalion, 308th Infantry Regiment (USA), 178, 182–85

I Corps (USA), 242; AEF 1st Division movement through sector of, 329; Argonne attack of, 208; Dickman as commander of, 298, 311; divisions comprising, *98*, 227–28; frontal attacks by, 195, 199; German counterattacks, 295; Liggett as commander of, 97, *98*, 189, 195; November Offensive attacks, 297–98, 299, 309, 311; in November Offensive plans, 278–79, 286; Pershing and leadership of, 177; reassignment of, to French Second Army, 176; reserve divisions of, 201, 208; Sedan liberation and, 312, 313. *See also* 1st Infantry Division (USA); 28th Infantry Division (USA); 35th Infantry Division (USA); 77th Infantry Division (USA); 82nd Infantry Division (USA); *specific division*

1st Dismounted Cavalry (France), 87

1st Guards Infantry Division (Germany), 207

1st Guards Regiment (Germany), 60

415

General Subjects

American Expeditionary Forces (*cont.*)

to, 3, 27, 33–34, *34*, 49, 106, 271; German intelligence on, 57–58; HQs of, 329–30; as independent army, 30–31, 109; intelligence section of, 78; logistical problems, 151, 252; in Meuse-Argonne strategic plan, 2–3, 4, 29–30, 47; Pershing as commander of, 2–3, 23, 195; in Pershing Meuse-Argonne plan, 49–51; planning/coordination improvements of, 244–45; post-armistice training of, 339; Regular Army soldiers in, 235, 250, 375n10 (Ch. 11); retraining of, 276–77; return to US, 339; St. Mihiel Offensive (Sept. 12–15, 1918), 32, 33–40; as unprepared for war, 4, 35–36, 52, 109, 143–44, 166, 347–50; weaponry of choice, 87. *See also* Kriemhilde Stellung (Siegfried Line)—
AEF REDUCTION OF
—MEUSE-ARGONNE ATTACK OF (Sept. 26, 1918): air support, 60–62, 69–70; artillery support, 59–60, *61*, 366n1; Cheppy, 71–77; French support during, 59–62, 86–88; German defenses, 60–64, 87–90; heroic acts during, 67, 72–73, 74–76, 82–85, *83*, 350–51, 369n72; infantry advance, 60; Montfaucon, 77–79; situation, 63 map 7.1, 70 map 7.2; tank advance, 64–65, *65*, 66–67; Varennes, 64–69, *66*; Vauquois, 69–71, 122, *123*, 128
—NOVEMBER OFFENSIVE (Nov.

1–11, 1918): AEF preparations, 276–80, *281*; air support, 299, 304; artillery barrages, 284–86; commencement of, 271, 284; concept of operations, 271, 278–79, *279* map 18.2; French Fourth Army coordination with, 279–82; German armistice terms discussions during, 283; German defense preparations, 271–75, *274* map 18.1; German defenses, 288–89, 295–97; German intelligence preceding, 283, 289; German withdrawal, 297, 298–99, 300–304; heroic acts during, 288–89, 291–94, *292* map 19.2, 300–304; political factors affecting, 275–76; tank support, 289–90, *291*

Angelo, Joseph T., 72–73

Antietam, Battle of (1862), 259

antitank weaponry, 68

Antonson, Chris, 75

Apremont (France), 76, 87, 95–96, 107–11, *110*, 122, 178, 210

Argonne Forest (France): AEF advances in, 98–101, 102–3, 107–11, 203–4; AEF progress halted in, 78, 108, 111–12, 162–66, 172; Apremont, 107–11, *110*; eastern slopes of, AEF attack planning for, 207–9, *209* map 13.1; French advances west of, 227–28; German casualties in, 223, 276; German counterattacks in, 108, 109–11; German defenses in, 8–9, 42–47, *54*, 54–58, *64*, 100, 103–4, 106, 107, 129–30, 134, 162–63, 168, 173–74, 178–80, *179*, 188, 194–95, 206–7, 359–60n12; German rail

ordered by, 167; Groener as
replacement for, 322, 324;
Meuse-Argonne defense
preparations of, 93, 160,
166–67, 227, 250; military
background of, 92; resignation
from OHL, 276; Spring
Offensive campaign of (1918),
7, 8, 14; on US involvement in
WWI, 7, 10; Wilson and, 275
Lukert, Edward, *326*, 326–28
Lusitania, SS, 20
Luther, Martin, 285
Lynch, Andrew, *110*, 110–11, 112

MacArthur, Arthur, 229
MacArthur, Douglas, 35, *36*, 171,
226; Cote de Chatillon, 230–34,
233 map 14.2; medals awarded
to, 229; military background
of, 229–30; Sedan, 316–17;
US 1st Division detention
myth, 316–17; as US 42nd
Division chief of staff, 229; as
US 42nd Division temporary
commander, 309–11; as US
84th Brigade commander, 230
machine guns, 37–38, 44, 89
Mackin, Elton, 284, 287, 294–95, 331
Macomb, Montgomery M., 143
Mainz (Germany), 48
Maistre, Paul Andre, 279–82, *280*,
320
Malancourt (France), 78
Mallon, George H., 82–83, *83*, 85,
350–51
Malone, Paul, 244, 326–27
Manassas, Battle of (1861), 277
Mann, William A., 229
Marie Antoinette (Queen of
France), 65–66, *66*
Marne, Battle of the (1918), 26, 87,
144

Marshall, George C., 50, 278,
311–12, 318, 320, 329–30, 346,
388n14
Marshall Plan, 346–47
Marwere, Hans Heinrich, 152–53,
153, *154*
Marwitz, Elisabeth von der,
283–84
Marwitz, Georg von der: on AEF
progress, 295–96; as Army
Group Gallwitz temporary
commander, 283; on Austro-
Hungarian force withdrawal,
275; daughter's death
and, 283–84; on death and
dishonor, 271; as German Fifth
Army commander, 53, *272*,
273; Meuse Valley withdrawal
ordered by, 298, 304;
November Offensive defense
preparations of, 278, 295–96
mascots, *158*, 158–59, 289–90, *291*
Mastriano, Douglas, 342, *343*,
346–47
Mastriano, Josiah, 342, *343*, *344*
Mastriano, Rebecca, 342, *343*, *344*
Mayer, Leutnant, 334–35
McDowell, Irvin, 277
McLain, Charles L., 111, 112
McMahon, John, 244
McMurtry, George, 182, 183–84,
198, 202
Meagher, Thomas Francis, 259
Medals of Honor, 75–76, 200, 202,
229, 289, *308*, 309, 350, 369n72,
380n11
Merrill, John, 98
Metz (France), 32, 91, 249, 273
Meuse-Argonne American
Cemetery, 343, 344–45
Meuse-Argonne campaign (1918):
AEF advantages in, 52–53;
AEF artillery